Review of Suicidology, 2000

Edited by
Ronald W. Maris, PhD
Silvia Sara Canetto, PhD
John L. McIntosh, PhD
Morton M. Silverman, MD

AN OFFICIAL PUBLICATION
OF THE AMERICAN ASSOCIATION OF SUICIDOLOGY

The Guilford Press
New York   London

© 2000 The Guilford Press
A Division of Guilford Publications, Inc.
72 Spring Street, New York, NY 10012
www.guilford.com

Printed in the United States of America

This book is printed on acid-free paper.

Last digit is print number: 9 8 7 6 5 4 3 2 1

ISBN 1-57230-503-7
ISSN 1092-2199

About the Editors

Ronald W. Maris, PhD, is Director of the Center for the Study of Suicide and Professor at the University of South Carolina. Previously, he was an Associate Professor in the Department of Psychiatry at Johns Hopkins School of Medicine and an Assistant Professor at Dartmouth College. Dr. Maris is a past president of the American Association of Suicidology and Editor Emeritus of its journal, *Suicide and Life-Threatening Behavior.* Author or editor of 19 books on suicide, Dr. Maris's most recent publication is the *Comprehensive Textbook of Suicidology* (with Morton M. Silverman and Alan L. Berman).

Silvia Sara Canetto, PhD, is Associate Professor in the Department of Psychology at Colorado State University. She is a recipient of the American Association of Suicidology's Edwin Shneidman Award, a member of the International Academy for Suicide Research, and a fellow of the Division of the Psychology of Women of the American Psychological Association. Currently on the editorial boards of several suicide journals, she has also served as Director for the Research Division of the American Association of Suicidology, as well as on committees on assisted suicide, euthanasia, and end-of-life decisions of the American Association of Suicidology, the International Association for Suicide Prevention, and the American Psychological Association. Author of over 50 articles and chapters, primarily on gender and suicidal behaviors, she is coeditor (with David Lester) of *Women and Suicidal Behavior* and (with Ronald W. Maris and Morton M. Silverman) of *Review of Suicidology, 1997.*

John L. McIntosh, PhD, is Professor of Psychology and Graduate Program Director of the Master of Arts in Applied Psychology Program at Indiana University South Bend, and serves on the editorial boards of several suicide journals. Dr. McIntosh is a past president and member of the Board of Directors of the American Association of Suicidology and was the 1990 recipient of the Association's Edwin Shneidman Award, as well as the 1999 recipient of the Association's Roger Tierney Award for Service. He is the author, coauthor, and coeditor of several books on suicide, including *Elder Suicide: Research, Theory and Treatment* and *Suicide and Its Aftermath: Understanding and Counseling the Survivors,* and has contributed chapters to several books and articles to numerous professional journals.

Morton M. Silverman, MD, is Associate Professor of Psychiatry and Director of the Student Counseling and Resource Service at the University of Chicago. Since 1997, he has been the Editor-in-Chief of *Suicide and Life-Threatening Behavior.* Previously, he served as the first Chief of the Center for Prevention Research at the National Institute of Mental Health and the first Associate Administrator for Prevention in the Alcohol, Drug Abuse, and Mental Health Administration. He is the author or coauthor of over 20 articles, chapters, and books addressing prevention, youth suicide, forensic suicidology, and the treatment of suicidal individuals. Along with Ronald W. Maris and Silvia Sara Canetto, he coedited *Review of Suicidology, 1997,* and is coauthor (with Ronald W. Maris and Alan L. Berman) of *Comprehensive Textbook of Suicidology.*

Contributors

Mark J. Goldblatt, MD, is Clinical Instructor in Psychiatry at Harvard Medical School and an Attending Psychiatrist at McLean Hospital, Belmont, Massachusetts. He is also a consulting editor of *Suicide and Life-Threatening Behavior,* as well as coeditor of *Essential Papers on Suicide.*

Janet A. Grossman, DNSc, is the director of a family drug court in the Juvenile Division of the Eleventh Circuit of Miami–Dade County and Adjunct Assistant Professor of Nursing at the University of Illinois at Chicago. She was the coinvestigator, with Markus J. P. Kruesi, of Community Action for Youth Survival, a youth suicide prevention project sponsored by Ronald McDonald Children's Charities, and coauthor of the CD-ROM *Team Up to Save Lives: What Your School Should Know to Prevent Suicide.* She is a recipient of the Psychiatric Nursing Clinical Practice Award from the Society for Education and Research in Psychiatric Nursing and, along with Drs. Markus J. P. Kruesi and Jay Hirsch (posthumously), the 1999 Rieger Service Program Award for Excellence from the American Academy of Child and Adolescent Psychiatry in recognition of innovative work in the prevention, diagnosis, and treatment of mental illnesses in children and adolescents.

Markus J. P. Kruesi, MD, is Professor of Psychiatry at the Institute for Juvenile Research, University of Illinois at Chicago. He was the coinvestigator, with Janet A. Grossman, of Community Action for Youth Survival and coauthor of the CD-ROM *Team Up to Save Lives: What Your School Should Know to Prevent Suicide.* Dr. Kruesi is a corecipient of the 1999 Rieger Service Program Award for Excellence from the American Academy of Child and Adolescent Psychiatry and the recipient of the Jay G. Hirsch Award for excellence in teaching from the Institute for Juvenile Research.

Marsha M. Linehan, PhD, is Professor of Psychology and of Psychiatry and Behavioral Sciences at the University of Washington, as well as Director of Behavioral Research and Therapy Clinics, a consortium of research projects developing new treatments and evaluating their efficacy for severely disordered and multidiagnostic populations. She has been on the Board of Directors of the Association for Advancement of Behavior Therapy, as well as the editorial boards of several journals. An APA fellow, she has received several awards recognizing her clinical and research contributions, including the Dublin Award for lifetime achievement in suicidal behaviors and the American Foundation of Suicide Prevention Award for distinguished research in suicide. Dr. Linehan has published numerous articles on suicidal behaviors, drug abuse, behavior therapy, and behavioral assessment and has written three books, including two treatment manuals.

John L. McIntosh (*see* About the Editors).

Jane L. Pearson, PhD, is Associate Director for Prevention Interventions in the Division of Services and Intervention Research at the National Institute of Mental Health, as well as chair of the NIMH Suicide Research Consortium. In addition to her NIMH duties, Dr. Pearson has been active in assisting the Surgeon General's office in developing his call to suicide prevention, as well as in developing research agendas for the National Institutes of Health Office of Research on Women's Health. She is an adjunct professor at Johns Hopkins University, a fellow of the American Psychological Association, and the author of a number of papers on late life anxiety, depression and suicide, caregiver burden in Alzheimer's disease, and family processes in parenting and grandparenting. She also has had a private practice in clinical psychology.

Cynthia R. Pfeffer, MD, is Professor of Psychiatry at Weill Medical College of Cornell University, and is the Director of both the Children at Risk for Suicidal Behavior Program and the Child Bereavement Program at Weill Medical College. Dr. Pfeffer is a past president of the American Association of Suicidology and recipient of numerous awards, including the Association's Edwin Shneidman Award and the Erwin Stengel Award from the International Association for Suicide

Prevention and Crisis Intervention. She has also published extensively on the topic of youth suicidal behavior, including the books *The Suicidal Child* and *Suicide Among Youth: Perspectives on Youth and Prevention*.

David P. Phillips, PhD, is Professor of Sociology at the University of California, San Diego. Dr. Phillips is a recipient of the Edwin Shneidman Award from the American Association of Suicidology and the Socio-Psychological Prize from the American Association for the Advancement of Science. The author of numerous articles on suicide and on other types of mortality, he has published in the *New England Journal of Medicine, Science, Lancet, Journal of the American Medical Association, Suicide and Life-Threatening Behavior,* and various sociological journals.

M. David Rudd, PhD, is Professor of Psychology at Baylor University. He maintains an active clinical practice and is also a diplomate in behavioral psychology of the American Board of Professional Psychology. In addition to over 60 referred articles, Dr. Rudd is coauthor of the upcoming book, *Treating Suicidal Behavior: A Time-Limited Approach*. Dr. Rudd is the recipient of numerous awards, including the Texas Psychological Association's Award for Outstanding Contribution to Science and the Edwin Shneidman Award from the American Association of Suicidology. He serves as Vice-Chair of the Texas State Board of Examiners of Psychologists, and his primary research interests include clinical suicidology and cognitive-behavior therapy.

Natalie M. Ryan, BA, was an undergraduate sociology major at the University of California, San Diego, when she cowrote Chapter 2 with David P. Phillips for this volume. She has also copublished an article with Dr. Phillips on a related topic in the *New England Journal of Medicine*. Her undergraduate studies were supported by a scholarship from the Hiram Walker Corporation. She received her BA in 1999.

Julia Shiang, EdD, PhD, is Associate Professor at the Pacific Graduate School of Psychology in Palo Alto. She is also a lecturer in the Department of Psychiatry and Behavioral Sciences at Stanford University School of Medicine and a recipient of the American Association of Suicidology's Edwin Shneidman Award. Her published articles in *Suicide and Life-Threatening Behavior, Clinical Psychology: Science and Practice,* and other psychological journals have included a focus on suicide and race ethnicity, especially among Chinese Americans.

Morton M. Silverman (*see* About the Editors).

Steven Stack, PhD, is on the faculty at Wayne State University in Detroit and was previously on the faculty of Indiana University–Indianapolis, Penn State University, and Auburn University. He received the American Association of Suicidology's Edwin Shneidman Award in 1985 and has served as Secretary of the Association's Board of Directors. He has published extensively in professional journals and book chapters, primarily on suicide.

Ira M. Wasserman, PhD, is Professor at Eastern Michigan University and a member of the Michigan Sociological Association and the Midwest Sociological Association. Dr. Wasserman has published and done work in the areas of suicide, aging, consumer affairs, social movements, and collective violence, and has recently published a short article on retirement and the age of retirement. He is currently revising a book entitled *Lynching and the Media.*

Marjorie E. Weishaar, PhD, is a psychologist in private practice and Clinical Associate Professor of Psychiatry and Human Behavior at Brown University School of Medicine. Dr. Weishaar trained with Aaron T. Beck, the founder of cognitive therapy, and has made presentations on cognitive therapy for suicidal behavior in the United States and abroad. She is also author of *Aaron T. Beck* and coauthor (with Jeffrey Young and Janet M. Klosko) of the upcoming book *Schema-Focused Therapy,* and has written several chapters on cognitive therapy.

James L. Werth, Jr., PhD, is the American Psychological Association's AIDS Policy Congressional Fellow and is working in the office of Oregon Senator Ron Wyden. Dr. Werth has been active for over 10 years in providing direct services to persons infected with, and affected by, HIV disease. For the past nine years, he has been examining end-of-life issues. He has written one book and edited another on rational suicide and has over 30 professional publications on HIV disease and/or the end of life.

Preface

Like its 1997 predecessor, the *Review of Suicidology, 2000* grew out of sessions at the American Association of Suicidology's (AAS) annual professional conferences. Specifically, the primary origins of this volume partially derive from papers presented at the annual preconference workshop entitled "Suicide Update, 1997," on April 23, in Memphis (directed by Drs. R. W. Maris, S. S. Canetto, and M. M. Silverman). Chapters based on five papers from those presented in 1997 are included in this volume (those by Drs. M. E. Weishaar, M. J. Goldblatt and M. M. Silverman, J. A. Grossman and M. J. P. Kruesi, J. Shiang, and J. L. Werth, Jr.). Following the 1997 annual conference, the AAS Board of Directors decided to change the timing of the update session. That is, rather than continuing the longstanding practice of a preconference workshop, the update would instead take place during the time of the regular conference. Further, the update would form the foundation for a restructuring of the annual conference, wherein a Scientific Day would be designated that would have the Suicide Update papers as its core. Thus, on April 17, 1998, in Bethesda, Maryland, the first AAS Scientific Day took place (directed by Dr. J. L. McIntosh). Following a plenary keynote address by a Centers for Disease Control and Prevention official, the plenary session concluded with the first update paper by Dr. Marsha M. Linehan (see Chapter 4, this volume). Thereafter, throughout the day, update papers were presented along with concurrent other sessions, concluding with a plenary poster session. Among the papers presented at that first Scientific Day are those by Drs. C. R. Pfeffer and J. L. Pearson appearing in this volume (as well as two others not appearing here and the annual Gralnick Award paper on schizophrenia and suicide that is published in AAS's professional journal, *Suicide and Life-Threatening Behavior*). As stated in the *Review of Suicidology, 1997* volume, these update papers form a natural foundation for a regular review of suicidology, similar to the annual review volumes published in several other fields. Rather than appearing annually, however, the suicidology review volumes are planned to appear on essentially a biennial schedule.

The papers in the conference Suicide Update sessions are intended to meet the needs of the individual with no background in suicidology, as well as those of the advanced suicidologist. To meet these needs, the updates and the *Review of Suicidology* volumes provide basic information on important topics in the field of suicidology as well as present state-of-the-art ideas and knowledge, particularly in the practice and scientific investigation of suicidology.

Each volume of the *Review of Suicidology*, like the annual conference updates, will provide information on topics both distinct and recurring. For instance, in the *Review of Suicidology, 1997,* the topics of gender, schizophrenia, serotonin chemistry, and hotlines were unique to the volume. The present volume of the *Review* includes considerations of the scientific basis of clinical practice in suicidology, childhood, older adults, and assisted dying that were not in the 1997 volume. Both volumes, however, include the topics of adolescence, antidepressants/medications, social factors/social research findings, as well as the suicidal mind/cognitive factors in suicide. Thus, each volume of the *Review* complements the other, while uniquely conveying basic and detailed information about various dimensions of suicidology.

The topics presented at the 1999 conference update sessions included therapy, physician-assisted suicide, and research findings on adolescence. Although quite preliminary, the next *Review* is expected to include consideration of homicide–suicides and survivors of suicide. In the updates as well as the *Review*, our primary goal is to provide the highest-quality current information on suicidology as conveyed by high-caliber suicidologists. However, the small number of papers presented at the annual updates, as well as the inability of all update presenters to provide manuscripts, make it necessary to invite papers for the *Review* volume that were not presented as part of the update. Such was the case for the chapters included here by Drs. J. L. McIntosh, D. P. Phillips and N. M. Ryan, M. D. Rudd (originally planned to be presented as part of the 1999 conference update), and I. M. Wasserman and S. Stack.

Following are highlights of each chapter in the *Review of Suicidology, 2000.*

CHAPTER 1. McINTOSH: EPIDEMIOLOGY OF ADOLESCENT SUICIDE IN THE UNITED STATES

Increases in adolescent and young adult suicide have received much attention. Statistical and research data are needed to convey the levels, trends, and demographic risk factors associated with fatal and nonfatal suicidal behaviors among the young. Current official statistics reveal the importance of suicide as a cause of death among the young as compared to other age groups and the nation as a whole. The loss associated with the premature deaths of adolescents and young adults is large. Although present rates of suicide among adolescents are markedly higher than those observed in the 1950s, trends over time reveal relative stability since the late 1970s. This latter finding, however, is primarily associated with the young adult group 20–24 years of age. Adolescents between the ages of 15 and 19 have shown continued increases through the mid-1990s. Young men are at particular risk for fatal outcomes of their suicidal acts. Although young whites display slightly higher rates, marked recent increases among young black males have been observed. Despite increased levels of suicide, the most common suicidal behaviors in adolescence are nonfatal, including suicide attempts and suicidal ideation. Particularly high levels of nonfatal suicidal behaviors are observed among young women. A final, often neglected aspect of adolescent suicide involves survivors of suicide associated with the deaths of these young people. As with nonfatal suicidal behaviors, further epidemiological findings are needed regarding survivors of youth suicides. Epidemiological information represents one component necessary to design and implement measures for intervention and prevention of adolescent suicidal behaviors.

CHAPTER 2. PHILLIPS AND RYAN: AN ABRUPT SHIFT IN U.S. SUICIDE LEVELS AROUND THE MONTH BOUNDARY

Although it is well known that suicide often varies by day of the week, data are studied here to determine whether there are fluctuations associated with date of the month. Of particular interest here are patterns around the end/beginning of the calendar month (i.e., month boundary). Death certificate data were studied for the United States for the years 1973 to 1988. Each death was coded regarding the number of days it occurred from the end of the month. Evidence for month boundary patterns were observed. Specifically, suicides were lowest at the end of the month and are higher during the first 2 weeks of the next month. This pattern is shown among both men and women and for all age groups, though the peak at the beginning of the month is most pronounced in the youngest age groups. The first week pattern is also observed for virtually all methods of suicide. Several possible explanations are considered for this effect, but it is concluded that the explanation is unclear.

CHAPTER 3. RUDD: INTEGRATING SCIENCE INTO THE PRACTICE OF CLINICAL SUICIDOLOGY

Empirically based knowledge that forms the foundation for the treatment of suicidality is actually quite limited. Many questions may be posed regarding the efficacy and methods of treatment. However, few of these questions can be answered based on current research investigations of treatment, and those which can are only answered tentatively. A tremendous need exists for growth in the science of clinical suicidology. The available literature, reviewed in detail, includes fewer than two dozen studies that approach sound research criteria for randomness or control. Among this limited number of investigations are studies of both intervention and treatment. Most of these studies involve other research limitations, often regarding such issues as the exclusion of the most suicidal individuals from the investigation, imprecise definition of the suicidal behaviors studied or other aspects of the study, and the lack of standardized outcome measures. The limited studies generally support the use of intensive follow-up treatment for those at high risk for suicidal behavior, the use of cognitive-behavioral therapy for intervention, and the appropriateness of outpatient treatment for the highly suicidal in some circumstances. A particularly important step in improving the scientific basis of clinical suicidology is the adoption of a standard nomenclature. As a starting point, one such nomenclature system is presented (as developed by O'Carroll et al., 1996), along with a set of four categories of questions that might guide future clinical research in suicidology.

CHAPTER 4. LINEHAN: BEHAVIORAL TREATMENTS OF SUICIDAL BEHAVIORS

In a review preceding Rudd's (Chapter 3, above), investigations that have included randomized clinical trials of psychosocial and behavioral interventions for treatment of suicidal behaviors were scrutinized. Twenty studies were found that randomly assigned individuals to conditions (i.e., experimental treatment groups, treatment-as-usual groups, control groups). Four of the studies showed a significant effect for psychosocial interventions and another for pharmacotherapy. Prominent among the findings was that the psychosocial interventions were most effective with those at high risk for suicidal behaviors. It was concluded, however, that despite the above results, it is unclear how we might lower suicide deaths among suicidal individuals. More is known with regard to nonfatal suicidal behaviors, where focused behavioral interventions appear to hold promise in reducing suicide attempts and other nonfatal suicidal behaviors. Little research has been conducted to determine the efficacy of treatment for suicidal behaviors and their reduction. The obvious need for research on these issues demands attention and support.

CHAPTER 5. WEISHAAR: COGNITIVE RISK FACTORS IN SUICIDE

Cognitive factors in suicide have been clearly implicated by therapy research. These factors may operate independently in leading to suicide and may be both acute and chronic risk factors for the development of suicidal behaviors. Prominent among these are such cognitive risk factors as hopelessness, helplessness, errors in logic, as well as cognitive biases and rigidity. Aaron T. Beck and associates have conducted many of the studies of these and other cognitive factors and have developed assessment scales associated with them. The cognitive factors of hopelessness, self-concept, cognitive distortions and dysfunctional assumptions, attributional style, problem-solving deficits, suicide as a "desirable" solution, and reasons for living are each considered individually, and the research literature is reviewed with respect to suicidal behaviors. These factors are considered within a model of stress vulnerability in which possession of the cognitive risk factor represents a vulnerability to suicide that may become apparent under stressful conditions. The presentation of these cognitive risk factors and their subsequent identification may lead to cognitive interventions that reduce suicide risk. These interventions operate to reduce cognitions associated with risk for suicide while aiding in the development of adaptive cognitive patterns.

CHAPTER 6. GOLDBLATT AND SILVERMAN: PSYCHOPHARMACOLOGICAL TREATMENT OF SUICIDAL PATIENTS

Clinical research has shown that there is a close association between mental disorders and suicidal behaviors. Neurobiological research has shown that patients who have attempted suicide have alterations in their central nervous system metabolism of certain neurotransmitters. Medications have been shown to be effective and efficacious in the treatment of many psychiatric disorders. Hence there exists a role for the judicious use of medication to treat the underlying psychiatric disorders highly associated with suicidal behaviors, as well as to ameliorate or prevent the onset of suicidal behaviors in those individuals suffering from psychiatric disorders such as depression, delusional depression, schizophrenia, panic disorder/anxiety, alcohol abuse, cocaine abuse, bipolar disorder, and borderline personality disorder. The decision to use medication for individuals at risk for suicide is based on an analysis of clinical indications and contraindications. The management and monitoring of medications in suicidal patients requires a high degree of doctor–patient cooperation, collaboration, and communication. This chapter reviews some of the current medications for the treatment of major psychiatric disorders associated with suicidal behaviors.

CHAPTER 7. PFEFFER: SUICIDAL BEHAVIOR IN PREPUBERTAL CHILDREN

Despite earlier perceptions and beliefs that children do not engage in suicidal behaviors, evidence has shown that children perform fatal and nonfatal suicidal acts. Although the rate of fatal behavior is quite low, this includes prepubertal children aged 6 to 12 years. A body of research evidence has accumulated over the past three decades. This evidence has outlined the high risk for suicidal behavior among psychiatrically hospitalized children as compared to psychiatric outpatient and community children. It has also highlighted the importance of depressive disorders and symptoms as well as personality disorders in suicidal tendencies among prepubertal children. Follow-up studies of clinical populations of suicidal prepubertal children have found that prepubertal suicidal behavior predicts adolescent attempts. Investigations of other samples of children reveal the important role of family problems and histories of suicidal behavior and other psychopathology among suicidal prepubertal children. Neurobiological studies have implicated serotonin as an aspect of suicidal behavior among prepubertal children as well. It is recommended that treatment of suicidal prepubertal children involve a combination of individual and family therapies. The research literature on prepubertal children, however, remains small, and the need for additional empirical investigation is vital.

CHAPTER 8. GROSSMAN AND KRUESI: INNOVATIVE APPROACHES TO YOUTH SUICIDE PREVENTION

Suicidal behavior is a major mental health issue among youth. This chapter outlines and details a number of approaches that have been developed in an attempt to lessen suicidal behaviors among young people. These approaches include traditional mental health interventions of inpatient and outpatient treatment, public health approaches by governmental and other groups, means restriction efforts, grassroots approaches that focus on advocacy and raising public awareness of the issue, the training of gatekeepers to identify at-risk youth and refer them for intervention, as well as school-based efforts for prevention. Other strategies have targeted assessment efforts and instrument improvement; the entire range of treatment methods, such as family, psychopharmacological, cognitive-behavioral, and group therapies; and standards of care for youth suicide treatment. A final area of concern in youth suicide involves issues arising in the aftermath of the suicide. These aspects include concerns regarding imitation, contagion, and clusters of deaths following in the aftermath of youth suicide; issues surrounding appropriate media coverage of youth suicide cases; and the possibility of increased risk among the surviving young people who comprise the friends and peers of the suicide victim.

CHAPTER 9. PEARSON: SUICIDAL BEHAVIOR IN LATER LIFE

Fatal suicidal behaviors peak in late life and are particularly high among white men in old age. Despite this long-known fact, research on late-life suicide remains limited. Among other correlates of high risk for suicide among the elderly are living alone, the presence of firearms in the home, and unmarried status. A few psychological autopsy studies of older adults have been conducted, though proper control procedures have not yet been applied. Present findings, however, reveal higher levels of physical illness and depression without substance abuse problems among late-life suicides compared to younger individuals. First episodes of depression were most common, with resulting positive implications for treatment. Dementing disorders, though common in old age, generally have not been found to be associated with high suicide risk. Some findings relate personality traits and dispositions in older adult samples. Studies of brain tissue at postmortem examination have provided suggestive results overall with respect to fatal suicidal behavior, but too few studies exist at this time from which conclusions might be drawn with respect to the aged. Research has revealed lower levels of attempted suicides in late life. A small body of studies of older adults who have attempted suicide have been conducted, although some follow-up evidence exists that risk for attempted suicide among depressed elders may be higher among those with a past history of attempts and familial interpersonal strain. Other studies of older adults who have been psychiatrically hospitalized for making attempts have underscored the high risk factors of social isolation, unmarried status, depression, somatization, and hopelessness. Too few studies of suicidal ideation in late life have been conducted to provide generalizations at this time. Another set of suicide-related behaviors that have received some research attention among the old are indirect self-destructive or life-threatening behaviors. Research including adequate controls is needed for the entire range of fatal and nonfatal suicidal behaviors in late life as well as indirect forms of suicide-related behaviors. Studies have frequently shown that elders who commit suicide have recently seen a primary care physician. This fact provides excellent opportunities for the recognition of older adults at risk for suicide and for intervention.

CHAPTER 10. SHIANG: CONSIDERING CULTURAL BELIEFS AND BEHAVIORS IN THE STUDY OF SUICIDE

Following the presentation of a case example, data for suicides in San Francisco from 1987 through 1996 are presented. This racially/ethnically diverse city showed men's and women's rates highest among Caucasians (i.e., European Americans), with data presented for African Americans, Native Americans, Hispanics, and Asians as well. The number of suicides by age group was proportionately higher at varying life periods for the different racial/ethnic groups, with some (e.g., Hispanics, African Americans) showing highest numbers in young life stages while older age groups with higher numbers for others (e.g., Caucasians, Asians). Men contributed higher proportions of suicides in all racial/ethnic groups, although the ratio of men to women varied from 1.6:1 to as high as 5.5:1. All groups used firearms to effect their suicides in similar proportions (i.e., approximately 20–30% of their suicides). It is contended that culture is always an aspect of therapy for suicide. That is, each person carries the cultural background, which in turn affects the likelihood of suicidal behavior and the process of therapy in which he or she enters (by influencing the beliefs and behaviors of the individuals of the culture). Cultures vary in a number of ways and dimensions, including emphases on independence as opposed to collectivism (where the good of the group is emphasized over that of the individual) that affect suicidal behavior and the effectiveness of therapy approaches. To be most effective, diagnoses and therapy must progress based at least partly on the belief system of the individual and the manner in which the individual's culture affects behavior displayed. For instance, some cultures closely link body and mind in such a manner that physically based rather than psychologically based symptoms are more likely and thus differential diagnoses result. These issues may also influence the way in which family members respond to the affected individual. It is concluded that both individual and contextual influences must be understood to best study and prevent suicide.

CHAPTER 11. WASSERMAN AND STACK: THE RELATIONSHIP BETWEEN OCCUPATION AND SUICIDE AMONG AFRICAN AMERICAN MALES

Little research has been conducted to determine the relationship between occupational status and suicide among African Americans. Although epidemiological data for the United States reveal that blacks display suicide rates that are approximately 50% of those for whites, findings from the present study reveal a higher suicide rate among higher-occupational-status blacks than whites. The current data were derived from mortality records in Ohio for the years 1989–1991. Applying more sophisticated regression analyses comparing all natural deaths to suicides for occupational status and race (i.e., black vs. white) provided evidence for no differences between blacks and whites of high-status occupations (when the data are controlled for age, marital status, and education). However, significantly higher suicide rates were found for low-status-occupation whites compared with low-status-occupation blacks (with the same factors controlled). Possible explanations for the present findings as well as limitations of the data employed are noted. Further research is needed to determine suicide risk associated with occupational status, but among the issues to be studied are possible changes in risk associated with increased economic positions in society among blacks.

CHAPTER 12. WERTH: RECENT DEVELOPMENTS IN THE DEBATE OVER PHYSICIAN-ASSISTED DEATH

In recent years increased public, legal, legislative, and professional attention has focused on issues arising at the end of life. Among these issues is physician-assisted death. This chapter outlines the various legal and legislative acts that have taken place in the past 5 years surrounding physician-assisted death. These events include specifics of the Oregon Death with Dignity Act and its history, as well as legislative acts in other states. Particularly noted are legislative events in Michigan surrounding the actions of Dr. Jack Kevorkian and the more than 100 people whose deaths he has assisted. Court cases in several states are also discussed along with the activity of several professional organizations and their public stances surrounding end-of-life issues and physician-assisted death. The chapter concludes with some possible common ground for those favoring and those opposing physician-assisted death, including the reduction of suffering and the occurrence of irrational acts of suicide. Possible future implications are advanced with respect to the role of therapists in end-of-life circumstances. The need for additional study and debate of these issues is also suggested.

It is the hope of the editors that this second volume of the *Review of Suicidology* will advance knowledge and the exchange of ideas regarding the important and emerging issues of suicidology. It is particularly hoped that these chapters will encourage and foster the conducting of wide-ranging research investigations that include sound research principles (see, e.g., Smith & Maris, 1986). The most consistent conclusion drawn by the authors of the *Review of Suicidology* volumes for 1997 and 2000 is the tremendous need for expanded and solid scientific evidence on all issues related to suicidal behaviors. Only from an evidence-based foundation can we hope to understand more fully and intervene more effectively with those who display fatal and nonfatal suicidal behaviors.

RONALD W. MARIS, PhD
SILVIA SARA CANETTO, PhD
JOHN L. McINTOSH, PhD
MORTON M. SILVERMAN, MD

REFERENCES

O'Carroll, P. W., Berman, A. L., Maris, R. W., Moscicki, E. K., Tanney, B. L., & Silverman, M. M. (1996). Beyond the tower of Babel: A nomenclature for suicidology. *Suicide and Life-Threatening Behavior, 26,* 237–252.

Smith, K., & Maris, R. (1986). Suggested recommendations for the study of suicide and other life-threatening behaviors. *Suicide and Life-Threatening Behavior, 16,* 67–69.

Contents

I. BASIC RESEARCH AND ISSUES IN SUICIDOLOGY

1. Epidemiology of Adolescent Suicide
   in the United States 3
   John L. McIntosh, PhD

2. An Abrupt Shift in U.S. Suicide Levels Around
   the Month Boundary 34
   David P. Phillips, PhD, and Natalie M. Ryan, BA

II. ISSUES IN THE TREATMENT OF SUICIDAL INDIVIDUALS AND POPULATIONS

3. Integrating Science into the Practice
   of Clinical Suicidology: A Review of the
   Psychotherapy Literature and a Research
   Agenda for the Future 47
   M. David Rudd, PhD

4. Behavioral Treatments of Suicidal Behaviors:
   Definitional Obfuscation and Treatment Outcomes 84
   Marsha M. Linehan, PhD

5. Cognitive Risk Factors in Suicide 112
   Marjorie E. Weishaar, PhD

6. Psychopharmacological Treatment
   of Suicidal Patients 140
   Mark J. Goldblatt, MD, and Morton M. Silverman, MD

III. HIGH-RISK GROUPS AND FACTORS

7. Suicidal Behavior in Prepubertal Children:
   From the 1980s to the New Millennium   159
   Cynthia R. Pfeffer, MD

8. Innovative Approaches to Youth Suicide Prevention:
   An Update of Issues and Research Findings   170
   Janet A. Grossman, DNSc, and Markus J. P. Kruesi, MD

9. Suicidal Behavior in Later Life: Research Update
   Jane L. Pearson, PhD   202

10. Considering Cultural Beliefs and Behaviors in the
    Study of Suicide   226
    Julia Shiang, EdD, PhD

11. The Relationship between Occupation and Suicide
    among African American Males: Ohio, 1989–1991   242
    Ira M. Wasserman, PhD, and Steven Stack, PhD

IV. ETHICAL ISSUES IN SUICIDOLOGY

12. Recent Developments in the Debate
    over Physician-Assisted Death   255
    James L. Werth, Jr., PhD

Index   277

PART ONE

BASIC RESEARCH AND ISSUES IN SUICIDOLOGY

Epidemiology of Adolescent Suicide in the United States

John L. McIntosh, PhD

I n recent years the public's attention has been focused on the phenomenon of adolescent suicidal behavior. In many cases, statements about youth suicidal behavior are made that cannot be supported by existing official statistics or research results. This chapter presents data-based information from current official statistics regarding the levels, trends, and high-risk groups and factors of adolescent suicide in the United States. Included among these figures are statistical data for the age subgroupings that comprise the youth population. In addition, epidemiological and research data for the spectrum of suicidal behaviors among adolescents are briefly reviewed, including nonfatal suicidal acts, suicidal ideation, and issues of survivors of suicide (see also Pfeffer, Chapter 7, this volume, for clinical issues in child and adolescent suicide).

SUICIDE (FATAL SUICIDAL BEHAVIOR)

Deaths by suicide in the United States are compiled by the National Center for Health Statistics (NCHS) Mortality Branch from data sub-

mitted by individual states. State figures are derived from death certificates submitted by coroners and medical examiners in each jurisdiction
across the country. The NCHS ultimately publishes these data in annual
volumes of *Vital Statistics of the United States* as the official statistics for the
nation. Although they have been criticized as biased in nature (see, e.g.,
Atkinson, 1978, Chap. 3), official statistics are the only available national data and there is evidence that they are not systematically biased (see,
e.g., Sainsbury & Jenkins, 1982). It has been argued that although official figures may underestimate the actual incidence of suicides, they
represent the minimum number that occur (Allen, 1984). A detailed and
practical discussion of official statistics and their sources may be found
in McIntosh (in press). The most recent data year for which final official
statistics are available from NCHS is 1996 (Peters, Kochaneck, & Murphy, 1998; some detailed tables may be downloaded from the NCHS
website), and that year will be the primary set of data provided here,
along with archival figures.

Number of Suicides

One set of information about the levels and trends in youth suicide may
be obtained by considering the number of suicide deaths that occur annually. In recent years, there have been approximately 31,000 annual
deaths for which the death certificate indicated suicide as the primary
cause. In most years, among these 31,000 individuals each year who kill
themselves in the United States, approximately 5,000 are between the
ages of 15 and 24 years at the time of their deaths. More specifically, in
1996 there were 30,903 U.S. suicides and 4,358 by those aged 15–24
years. The majority of the literature on youth suicide has focused on the
age grouping 15 to 24 years. One reason for this choice is that available
published statistics are often first and most easily available by 10-year
age groupings (i.e., 5–14, 15–24, 25–34, etc., to 85 and above). This age
grouping is not specifically the one that is often meant by the term "adolescent." However, to remain consistent with the existing literature, data
are presented throughout this chapter for the 15–24 age group, but figures for the other U.S. youth below the age of 25 are also presented to
provide the most useful portrayal of the levels and trends in young suicides (for detailed earlier data, see Holinger, Offer, Barter, & Bell, 1994).
In this regard, there were 2,541 suicides in the 20–24 age grouping and
1,817 among those aged 15–19. There were another 298 suicides for

U.S. youth between 10 and 14 years of age (with 4 suicide deaths by children aged 5–9 years).

In an attempt to make these data more meaningful, consider that these figures would imply that, on average, there is a suicide in the United States every 17 minutes and a self-inflicted death between the ages of 15 and 24 years every 2 hours and 1 minute (i.e., 121 minutes; see Table 1.1 for figures for other young age groupings). If the suicides for those aged 10–14 were included, the pace would be one young American (10–24 years of age) every 1 hour and 53 minutes. From another perspective, of the 84 suicides daily in the United States, 12 are aged 15–24 years and another from ages 10–14 (some 6 adolescents 10–19 years of age per day kill themselves; see Table 1.1).

Cause of Death

One of the ways in which the importance of suicide as a mental health problem among youth can be seen is when it is viewed in the context of all other causes of death for these age groups. Suicide ranks ninth among the leading causes of death in the United States as a whole. As Table 1.2 reveals, the primary killers in the population as a whole are heart disease, cancer (malignant neoplasms), and stroke (cerebrovascular diseases), in that order. These three causes combined represent more

TABLE 1.1. Number and Timing of Youth Suicides in the United States, 1996

Group	Total number	One suicide every	One suicide every	Number per day
Nation	30,903	17.1 min	0.29 hr	84.4
5-yr age groupings				
5–9	4	91.5 days	2196 hr	0.01
10–14	298	1786.6 min	29 hr 29 min	0.8
15–19	1,817	290.0 min	4 hr 50 min	5.0
20–24	2,541	207.4 min	3 hr 27 min	6.9
Other age groupings				
5–14	303	1739.4 min	28 hr 59 min	0.8
10–19	2,115	249.2 min	4 hr 9 min	5.8
15–24	4,358	120.9 min	2 hr 1 min	11.9
10–24	4,656	113.2 min	1 hr 53 min	12.7

Note. 1996 was a leap year (i.e., 366 days).

TABLE 1.2. Top Five Ranking Causes of Death among U.S. Youth by Age, 1996

Age group	10–14 yr	15–19 yr	20–24 yr	15–24 yr	Nation
Total deaths	4,550	14,663	17,780	32,443	2,314,690
Total rate	24.0	78.6	101.3	89.6	872.5
Rank					
1	Accidents 1,845 9.7	Accidents 6,756 36.2	Accidents 7,053 40.2	Accidents 13,809 38.1	Diseases of heart 733,361 276.4
2	Malignant neoplasms 505 2.7	Homicide 2,924 15.7	Homicide 3,624 20.6	Homicide 6,548 18.1	Malignant neoplasms 539,533 203.4
3	Homicide 335 1.8	Suicide 1,817 9.7	Suicide 2,541 14.5	Suicide 4,358 12.0	Cerebrovascular diseases 159,942 60.3
4	Suicide 298 1.6	Malignant neoplasms 685 3.7	Malignant neoplasms 947 5.4	Malignant neoplasms 1,632 4.5	Chronic obstructive pulmonary diseases 106,027 40.0
5	Congenital anomalies 216 1.2	Diseases of heart 407 2.2	Diseases of heart 562 3.2	Diseases of heart 969 2.7	Accidents 94,948 35.8
9 (for national information purposes only)	—	—	—	—	Suicide 11.6 30,903

Note. Data sources: Peters et al. (1998); personal communication of unpublished tables provided by Sherry Murphy, National Center for Health Statistics Mortality Branch (November 1998); unpublished tables available for downloading from the NCHS website (unpublished tables gm291_1 and gm291a_1). All rates are per 100,000 population.

than 1.4 million deaths, or 62% of the total. The high number of deaths by these causes among the elderly 65 and older primarily account for the ranking of these causes. Among elderly adults these three causes account for 1.1 million, or 66%, of their deaths. Except among those 10–14 years of age, among whom extremely small numbers of death occur, none of these three causes rank in the top three causes of death among the young age groups under consideration here (see McIntosh, 1993b, 1999a).

Whereas causes of death predominantly characterized as "disease based" prevail in middle age and older adulthood, youth die almost exclusively from their own carelessness and actions or those of others (causes that are sometimes referred to collectively as "violent deaths"). For all young people, however, suicide ranks high. In fact, the ranking is considerably higher than for the nation as a whole (ninth) and older age groups, such as older adults (for whom suicide ranks 14th). By comparison, among both 15- to 19-year-olds and 20- to 24-year-olds, suicide is the third leading cause of death, ranking behind only accidents and homicides. For the young aged 5–14 years these three violent causes of death (i.e., accidents, suicide, and homicide) combine to account for more than half of their deaths (51.0%). By adolescence and young adulthood (15–24 years of age) this proportion increases to 3 of every 4 deaths (76.2%). A related subissue in recent years is the fact that many of these deaths are firearm related. Firearm deaths accounted for 27.0% of all deaths for those aged 15–24 years in 1996 (Peters et al., 1998; see also O'Donnell, 1995). Of these firearm deaths, suicides are 2,724 of 8,766 among those aged 15–24 (and 162 of 605 among youth from 5 to 14 years of age).

Although suicide represents an important component of deaths in adolescence when combined with other violent modes of death, the contribution of suicide alone to youth deaths is significant as well. For instance, in 1996 the proportion of all deaths that were suicides in the United States was only 1.3%. Among young people aged 15–24, however, suicide deaths represented 13.4% of all deaths. Similarly, for the population 10–19 years of age, suicide accounted for 11.0% of deaths (6.5%, 12.4%, and 14.3% for those aged 10–14, 15–19, and 20–24, respectively). Suicide and other violent deaths are the primary causes of death in adolescence and young adulthood, and they contribute substantially larger proportions to the deaths among these groups than for the same causes in the population as a whole or older age groups.

Years of Potential Life Lost

A different indicator of the importance of suicide deaths by young people involves a relatively new statistic called years of potential life lost (YPLL). As one reflection of the cost to society and its members, other than the loss of the individuals as reflected in the number of deaths above, this statistic attempts to portray the number of years of life that would have remained for the individual had he or she not died but instead lived to at least age 65 (YPLL-65). Conceptually, the YPLL statistic represents one dimension of the contributions lost to society over those years due to these premature deaths. The statistic is calculated by subtracting the age of the individual at death from 65 to produce the number of years lost. The resulting estimate of this concept (using the precise formula for calculation with aggregate data suggested by the Centers for Disease Control, 1990) suggests that society loses a substantial number of years annually to the deaths that occur by suicide. In fact, because this statistic emphasizes losses among young individuals, it shows that the overwhelming losses are derived from the deaths by suicide of our youth. The suicide deaths in 1996 resulted in nearly 200,000 YPLL lost as a result of suicides by those aged 15–24 years. Another almost 17,000 YPLL result from the small number of deaths among those aged 5–14 (see Figure 1.1). When viewed as part of the entire set of losses, the number of years lost to suicide approximate 700,000 years annually (686,072 total in 1996) and the proportion among those that derive from deaths under the age of 25 represents approximately one-third of

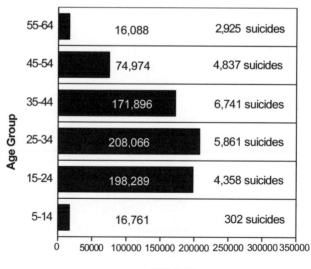

FIGURE 1.1. Years of potential life lost before age 65 (YPLL-65) by age group resulting from suicide deaths: United States, 1996.

the total. For suicides among those aged 10–19 in 1996, YPLL-65 were 106,808 years.

Suicide Rates: Levels

Although the number of suicides provides an indication of the scope of the problem of youth suicide in the United States, the best indicator of a group's risk of suicide is given by its suicide rate. The rate of suicide takes into account the number of individuals in the population who contribute to the suicides. This is a particularly important issue. For instance, the number of suicides among those 15–24 years of age was 859 in 1956, compared to 4,358 in 1996. To determine the actual increase in suicide, however, it is crucial to know among how many young people these suicides took place. There were 21.3 million youth aged 15–24 in 1956, compared to 36.2 million in 1996. Dividing the number of suicides by the population for the same year (and multiplying by a constant of 100,000) provides the suicide rate for each time period under consideration (all rates conveyed here are per 100,000 population). Therefore, although the number of suicides increased 407% from 1956 to 1996, when we take the much larger current population into account, the rate increased 200% (from 4.0 to 12.0). Using rates permits direct comparison of levels over time to determine trends and relative risk among and between groups. This is not possible by the comparison of numbers alone. An even better demonstration of the importance of using rates rather than numbers is apparent when racial differences in suicide are compared, as will be done later. Compared to the number of suicides by white youth, the very small number among black youth, for instance, would lead to the erroneous conclusion that suicide is an unimportant cause of death among these racial/ethnic minority youth. Rates, however, reveal the slightly lower but relatively comparable suicide risk for young people in both white and nonwhite racial groupings (see the presentation of racial differences below).

The more than 4,300 suicides among young Americans 15–24 years of age during 1996 produce a suicide rate of 12.0 per 100,000 compared to a similar national rate of 11.6. This rate can be interpreted to mean that if a representative group of 100,000 young people between the ages of 15 and 24 were followed from January 1 through December 31 of 1996, 12 of them could be expected to have committed suicide during the year. Trends in youth rates will be discussed at length later, but one interpretation of these rates would be that suicide is no more of a problem among the young than for the nation as a whole. While utilization of rates alone produces that conclusion, the numbers, cause of death, and YPLL statistics above provide strong arguments to extend the determination of risk beyond solely rates. In addition, trends in youth suicide rates will also argue for the importance of youth suicide as an important mental health problem.

Suicide Rates by Age

Although suicide rates by age peak in the older adult age groupings (Peters et al., 1998), increases in rates among age groups under age 45 (discussed in detail below) and declines among groups above age 45 have produced a different pattern of suicide over time, as is apparent in Figure 1.2. As can be seen in that figure, which compares data for 1956 to data for 1996, the clearly increasing rates associated with increasing age of the 1950s has become a pattern that may be described as nearly bimodal. That is, rates peak in young adulthood, decline somewhat or remain stable in the middle years, and increase again to a second, higher

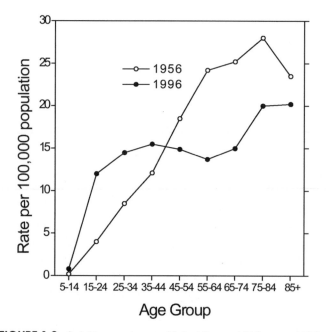

FIGURE 1.2. Suicide rates by age: United States, 1956 versus 1996.

peak in old age. Therefore, suicide risk is high among both the young and the old, although the higher peak is in late life (McIntosh, Santos, Hubbard, & Overholser, 1994). Within the youth life period, suicide rates steadily increase with age (see Figure 1.3).

Suicide Rates by Sex and Race

Similar to the nation as a whole (Canetto & Lester, 1995), one of the most important variables associated with suicide among young people is sex. As elsewhere in the life span, rates among men substantially exceed those of women. For youth aged 15–24 years, men had a 1996 rate of 20 per 100,000 population compared to 3.6 for women of the same age (see also Table 1.3), for a 5:1 male:female ratio. These gender differences are true among all young age groupings. Even among the youngest age groups (5–9 or 10–14 years), where rates are extremely low, rates of males exceed those of females.

Similar to sex differences and suicide, racial levels of suicide among the young largely mirror those for all age groups combined and across the life span. That is, white rates of suicide exceed those of nonwhites as a whole. Specifically, the suicide rate of whites 15–24 years of age in

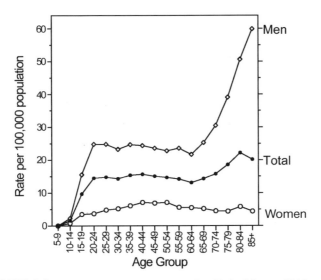

FIGURE 1.3. Suicide rates by age and gender: United States, 1996.

TABLE 1.3. U.S. Suicide Rates and the Number of Suicides by Age, Gender, and Race among the Young, 1996

Group	National total			White			All nonwhite			Black		
	T	M	W	T	M	W	T	M	W	T	M	W
Suicide rates												
Nation	11.6	19.3	4.4	12.7	20.9	4.8	6.7[b]	11.3[b]	2.5[b]	6.5[b]	11.4[b]	2.0[b]
5–9 yr[a]	0.02	0.03	0.01	0.03	0.04	0.01	b	b	b	b	b	b
10–14 yr[a]	1.6	2.3	0.8	1.6	2.3	0.9	1.4	2.2	0.6	1.2	1.9	0.6
15–19 yr	9.7	15.6	3.5	10.3	16.3	3.8	7.7	12.7	2.6	6.7	11.5	1.8
20–24 yr	14.5	24.8	3.7	15.1	25.7	3.8	11.9	20.8	3.1	12.7	22.8	2.7
5–14 yr[a]	0.8	1.1	0.4	0.8	1.2	0.4	0.7	1.1	0.3	0.6	0.9	0.3
10–19 yr	5.6	8.9	2.2	5.9	9.3	2.3	4.5	7.4	1.6	4.0	6.7	1.2
15–24 yr	12.0	20.0	3.6	12.6	20.9	3.8	9.8	16.6	2.8	9.5	16.7	2.3
10–24 yr	8.4	13.9	2.6	8.8	14.5	2.8	6.9	11.6	2.1	6.7	11.6	1.7
Number of suicides												
Nation	30,903	24,998	5,905	27,856	22,547	5,309	3,047	2,451	596	2,164	1,820	344
5–9 yr	4	3	1	4	3	1	0	0	0	0	0	0
10–14 yr	298	222	76	244	179	65	54	43	11	36	28	8
15–19 yr	1,817	1,496	321	1,522	1,249	273	295	247	48	195	169	26
20–24 yr	2,541	2,228	313	2,117	1,860	257	424	368	56	328	292	36
5–14 yr	302	225	77	248	182	66	54	43	11	36	28	8
10–19 yr	2,115	1,718	397	1,766	1,428	338	349	290	59	231	197	34
15–24 yr	4,358	3,724	634	3,639	3,109	530	719	615	104	523	461	62
10–24 yr	4,656	3,946	710	3,883	3,288	595	773	658	115	559	489	70

Note. Data sources: Peters et al. (1998); personal communication of unpublished tables provided by Sherry Murphy, National Center for Health Statistics Mortality Branch (November 1998); unpublished tables available for downloading from the NCHS website for both suicide figures and population estimates. All rates are per 100,000 population: T, both genders combined; M, men; W, women.
[a]Some or all rates in this category are calculated based on fewer than 20 deaths. Such rates do not meet standards of reliability or precision as utilized by the NCHS in calculations. Such rates are provided here for completeness but are to be viewed cautiously.
[b]No suicides occurred in this group for 1996.

1996 was 12.6 compared to 9.8 among nonwhites of the same ages. Rates for nonwhites largely reflect that for blacks among the young and at all ages (for suicide patterns by age among other racial and ethnic groups, see McIntosh et al., 1994, pp. 16–18). Young blacks exhibited a rate of 9.5 in 1996.

Perhaps the most meaningful indication of suicide risk as evidenced by suicide rates may be seen by combining the factors of sex and race. A comparison of these rates show the clearly primary importance of sex followed by race. That is, regardless of race, men display higher rates than all women's groups. Within the sex groupings, the higher rates among whites compared to nonwhites and blacks in particular are apparent. As displayed in Table 1.3, white men (rate = 20.9) have the highest rates for the 15–24 age grouping, followed by nonwhite men (16.6), with white women (3.8) and nonwhite women (2.8) substantially lower. When suicide rates by age among the young are compared for gender–race groupings, both sex and racial differences remain at all ages and rates increase as each older age grouping under age 25 is compared (see Figure 1.4 and Table 1.3).

Suicide Rates: Trends

The most widely publicized aspect of youth suicide has been the significant increase in rates over time (see, e.g., Holinger & Offer, 1982; Maris,

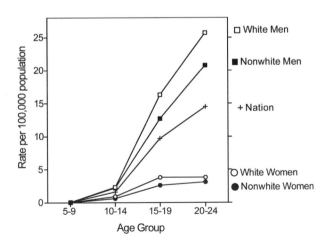

FIGURE 1.4. Suicide rates by age among young age groups by race and gender: United States, 1996.

1985). Although the tremendous publicity and attention to this issue has exaggerated perceptions of the overall risk of youth suicide compared to other groups (see, e.g., McIntosh, Hubbard, & Santos, 1985), this increase in rates has indeed been substantial. The group most often mentioned here is 15–24 years of age (see Figure 1.5). Comparing any recent year with any year in the 1950s (the period during which the rate increases began and at which youth suicide was at its lowest in U.S. history), the increase in rates has been approximately 200%. In fact, an example already noted showed that the 1956 rate for the 15–24 age group was 4.0 per 100,000 population whereas in 1996 it was 12.0. This represented an increase of exactly 200%.

Although the long-term trends in youth suicide can clearly be described as increasing, a comparison of only the beginning and present levels ignores an important fact in the characterization of these trends. More specifically, while suicide rates increased almost every year from the mid-1950s through the early 1970s, rates have not continued to increase in the more than two decades since (see Figure 1.5). Suicide rates for the 15–24 age group peaked at its second highest level ever in 1977 at 13.6 per 100,000 population. From that peak, however, subsequent rate trends are more accurately described as stable, with some rate fluctuations apparent, including some declines such as during the most re-

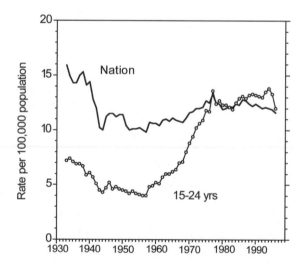

FIGURE 1.5. Suicide rates for the nations and 15- to 24-year-olds: United States, 1933–1996.

cent few data years. In 1994 the rate was slightly higher than that for 1977 at 13.8, the highest level ever for this age group. Since 1977, rates for the 15–24 age grouping have ranged from as high as 13.8 in 1994 and 13.5 in 1993 to as low as 11.8 in 1983 and 12.0 in 1996. The average rates for the 1980s and the 1990–1996 period were 12.5 and 13.1, respectively. The number of suicides actually declined for this age group over the time from 1977 to the present. The number of suicides exceeded 5,000 until 1982 and largely declined thereafter to its lowest level in 1996 at 4,358 suicides. The drop from 5,565 suicides in 1977 to 4,358 in 1996 represents a decline of 1,207 deaths, or more than 21% (and a rate decline of almost 12%).

Thus, while long-term trends are clearly toward increases for the young (as represented by 15- to 24-year-olds), recent trends have been largely unchanged for more than two decades. It must not be overlooked, however, that these rates, though largely stable from the early 1970s, remain at levels considerably higher than those observed among the young in earlier times. Current rates are similar to that for the nation as a whole (all ages combined), representing a major change from the same comparison in decades prior to the 1970s.

Other important aspects of the trends in youth suicide have also been largely unknown because almost exclusive emphasis and data portrayed have been those for the 15–24 age group. When each individual age grouping of young people are examined separately rather than in aggregate, distinct group trends are revealed. As can be seen in Figure 1.6, the long-term increases and subsequent stability that characterized rates for the 15–24 age group were produced by the same trends among the 20–24 age group. However, both 15- to 19-year-olds and 10- to 14-year-olds have actually displayed consistent increases virtually throughout the time period of the 1950s to the mid-1990s. Comparing rates for the two end points of 1956 and 1996 for these two groups reveals large increases. That is, the rate for the 10–14 age group for 1956 was 0.4 compared to a 1996 rate of 1.6. For those aged 15–19, the comparable rates were 2.3 and 9.7, respectively. The percent rate increases were 300% for the 10–14 age group and 322% for 15- to 19-year-olds.

Similar to the situation for individual young age groups, sex differences in trends of suicide rates for individual youth age groupings have also remained mostly ignored. Figure 1.7 shows that increases in youth suicide over time have largely been produced by men's rate trends.

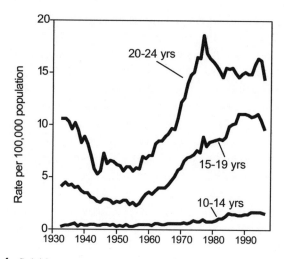

FIGURE 1.6. Suicide rates among young 5-year age groups: United States, 1933–1996.

Women's rates are lower than men's for each comparable age grouping and time period. In addition, as for the age groups overall, men 15–19 and 10–14 have shown consistent increases, with men 20–24 showing the peak and stability pattern noted already. Young women, on the other hand, have displayed only slight increases over the same four-decade time period. In fact, rates for young women aged 20–24 years peaked in

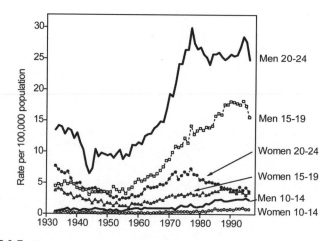

FIGURE 1.7. Suicide rates among young 5-year age groups by gender: United States, 1933–1996.

the mid-1970s and have actually declined steadily thereafter, to levels similar to that for young women aged 15–19.

A final trend in youth suicide that has received some recent attention (e.g., by Gibbs, 1997; Shaffer, Gould, & Hicks, 1994) has taken place among young black men in particular. As seen in Figure 1.8, while all rates for young men have increased noticeably from 1960, recent increases in suicide rates among young black men have been larger than those among comparably aged white men. This has lessened the racial differences among young men, producing the most comparable rates by race of any age comparisons across the life span. Black (and nonwhite as a whole) rates of suicide peak in young adulthood before the age of 30, whereas white rates continue to increase to their highest levels in late life (particularly among men; see McIntosh et al., 1994).

Other Demographic Factors and Suicide

Two other demographic issues that have been associated with differences in suicide risk are the methods employed in suicide and the geographic distribution of suicide rates. As for the nation as a whole and nearly all demographic groups (see, e.g., McIntosh, 1992a), young men and women at all ages use firearms most often in their suicides (see Table 1.4). In general, 6 of every 10 suicides among adolescents of all

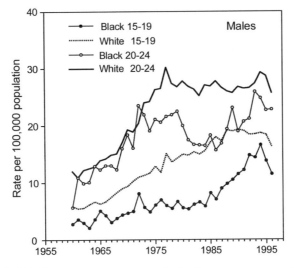

FIGURE 1.8. Suicide rates among young males by 5-year age groups and race: black versus white, 1960–1996.

TABLE 1.4. Methods of Suicide among Youth in the United States by Age and Gender, 1996

	10–14		15–19		20–24		10–19		15–24		Total	
	No.	%	No.	%	No.	%	No.	%	No.	%	No.	%
Total												
All suicides	298	100.0	1,817	100.0	2,541	100.0	2,115	100.0	4,358	100.0	30,903	100.0
Firearms	161	54.0	1,149	63.2	1,578	62.1	1,310	61.9	2,727	62.6	18,182	58.8
Hanging (HSS)	121	40.6	434	23.9	550	21.6	555	26.2	984	22.6	5,330	17.2
S&L poison	8	2.7	74	4.1	135	5.3	82	3.9	209	4.8	3,073	9.9
All other	8	2.7	101	5.6	173	6.8	109	5.2	274	6.3	2,311	7.5
Drowning	2	0.7	13	0.7	24	0.9	15	0.7	37	0.8	361	1.2
Cutting and piercing	1	0.3	10	0.6	10	0.4	11	0.5	20	0.5	435	1.4
Jumping (heights)	2	0.7	25	1.4	59	2.3	27	1.3	84	1.9	645	2.1
Gas poison	0	—	59	3.2	105	4.1	59	2.8	164	3.8	2,007	6.5
Men												
All suicides	222	100.0	1,496	100.0	2,228	100.0	1,718	100.0	3,724	100.0	24,998	100.0
Firearms	128	57.7	994	66.4	1,433	64.3	1,122	65.3	2,427	65.2	15,821	63.3
Hanging (HSS)	90	40.5	340	22.7	488	21.9	430	25.0	828	22.2	4,350	17.4
S&L poison	1	0.5	35	2.3	74	3.3	36	2.1	109	2.9	1,564	6.3

	No.	%	No.	%	No.	%	No.	%	No.	%	No.	%
All other	3	1.4	76	5.1	144	6.5	79	4.6	220	5.9	1,668	6.7
Drowning	1	0.5	13	0.9	21	0.9	14	0.8	34	0.9	237	0.9
Cutting and piercing	1	0.5	9	0.6	10	0.4	10	0.6	19	0.5	354	1.4
Jumping (heights)	1	0.5	15	1.0	45	2.0	16	0.9	60	1.6	450	1.8
Gas poison	0	—	51	3.4	89	4.0	51	3.0	140	3.8	1,595	6.4
					Women							
All suicides	76	100.0	321	100.0	313	100.0	397	100.0	634	100.0	5,905	100.0
Firearms	33	43.4	155	48.3	145	46.3	188	47.4	300	47.3	2,361	40.0
Hanging (HSS)	31	40.8	94	29.3	62	19.8	125	31.5	156	24.6	980	16.6
S&L poison	7	9.2	39	12.1	61	19.5	46	11.6	100	15.8	1,509	25.6
All other	5	6.6	25	7.8	29	9.3	30	7.6	54	8.5	643	10.9
Drowning	1	1.3	0	—	3	1.0	1	0.3	3	0.5	124	2.1
Cutting and piercing	0	—	1	0.3	0	—	1	0.3	1	0.2	81	1.4
Jumping (heights)	1	1.3	10	3.1	14	4.5	11	2.8	24	3.8	195	3.3
Gas poison	0	—	8	2.5	16	5.1	8	2.0	24	3.8	412	7.0

Note. Data source: Personal communication of unpublished tables, Sherry Murphy, National Center for Health Statistics Mortality Branch (November 1998). "S&L poison" refers to solid or liquid substances; "No." refers to the number of suicides; "HSS" refers to hanging, strangulation, and suffocation. All percentages ("%") refer to the percentage of the total number of suicides for the group.

19

ages are by firearms, and this method represents at least half of all suicides for young men and nearly half for young women. As for methods, the geographic distribution of youth suicide is the same as for the entire country and for most other groups (McIntosh, Eikens, & Ramos, 1998; Seiden, 1984); that is, suicide among adolescents and young adults is clearly highest in the Mountain states of the United States, with the Middle Atlantic states generally lowest (see Figure 1.9 for the 10–19 age group).

Explanations of Youth Suicide

An in-depth presentation of reasons for youth suicide and its changes over time are beyond the scope of this chapter. Motivations for youth suicide have been discussed at length elsewhere (see, e.g., King, 1997; Seiden, 1969). Briefly, the major motivation mentioned for youth suicide typically involves some problems in interpersonal relations, most often with parents, peers, or boyfriends/girlfriends. Other factors include school and general pressures to succeed, the lack of effective methods for coping with stress, the lack of experience with failure where one might develop such coping mechanisms, physical changes associated with puberty, feelings of loneliness and isolation, problems associated with identity crises, and various psychopathologies.

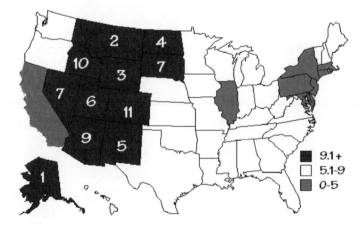

FIGURE 1.9 Geographic distribution of suicide rates for 10- to 19-year-olds: United States, 1993–1995 average rates.

Explanations for Youth Suicide Trends

Before moving to other forms of suicidal behavior among adolescents, a consideration of explanations that have been advanced to explain the serious increases in youth suicide deserve attention. It should be noted that the factors that have contributed to increases in youth suicide from the 1950s to the late-1970s–mid-1990s period are difficult to ascertain and many of those below involve correlational relationships that cannot be interpreted as necessarily causal in nature. Some of the explanations most commonly cited (for a brief review see Maris, 1985) are the following: (1) the increased competition for jobs and almost everything else in life associated with the large number in the presently young cohorts (i.e., the "baby boomers"); (2) increased use of drugs and alcohol; (3) breakdowns in the family evidenced by increased divorce rates, providing fewer people to turn to in times of crisis; (4) lessened involvement in organized religion by the young, which also lessens the resources during crisis periods; and (5) increased stresses inherent in modern industrialized society, with its rapid changes and the need to adapt.

Glaring by its omission in the above discussion is any explanation specific to the prominent sex differences in adolescent suicide mortality. The overall sex difference, noted above and elsewhere (e.g., Canetto, 1997), is presented in descriptions of existing data, but little focus on the difference has appeared beyond explanations that might explain the gender gap (e.g., method differences, reporting issues; see Canetto & Sakinofsky, 1998). In addition, and most germane to this discussion, authors (e.g., Canetto, 1997) note the sex differences in the trends of suicide rates among youth, but no differential explanation is provided for the divergent patterns. It is obvious and overdue that possible explanations for the recent stability in suicide among young women's suicide are needed and should be tested employing available data (this would include issues of cohort following immediately below). One such explanation can be extrapolated from Canetto and Sakinofsky's (1998) suggestion that changes in socialization and resulting "cultural scripts" for men and women may explain changes over time in suicidal behavior. These processes obviously affect children and adolescents but may also affect these behaviors across adulthood periods.

The first of these points is important in its own right, particularly in the context of an epidemiological consideration of adolescent suicide. Easterlin's (1980) *Birth and Fortune* suggested that when birth co-horts are large, so also will be the competition and stress for that cohort relative to other, smaller cohorts. One indicator of this stress would be suicide rates (as well as all violent deaths). This hypothesis of relative cohort size has received considerable attention and has been applied to the study of suicide in the form of cohort analyses in many countries (e.g., Asgard, Nordstrom, & Raback, 1987; La Vecchia, Bollini, Imazio, & Decarli, 1986; Moens, van Oortmarssen, Honggokoesoemo, & van de Voorde, 1987; Murphy, Lindesay, & Grundy, 1986; Reed, Camus, & Last, 1985; Wasserman, 1987). Most of these studies supported Easter-lin's (1980) premise and observed high suicide rates among large birth cohorts.

Similarly, employing official data, Holinger (1987) also documented strong correlations between population changes and violent deaths (ac-cidents, homicides, suicides, and their aggregation) in the United States. Once again, these data are consistent with what has been called the Easterlin hypothesis. Holinger (1987) found this hypothesis had strong predictive potential for the changes from 1933 to 1982 for young adult populations. This relationship was particularly true for the period be-tween the 1950s and the 1970s, when violent deaths increased dramati-cally among the young. This distressing pattern of increases in violent deaths coincided with the movement of the large "baby boom" cohort through the target ages of 15–24 years. Compared to earlier birth co-horts or generations (see, e.g., McIntosh, 1994), the "boomers" exhibit-ed high relative risk of suicide through their teens and into their 20s and 30s and now into their 40s and 50s. This has led to sometimes conflict-ing speculation regarding future trends in suicide rates as the current younger cohorts age. Based on Easterlin's hypothesis, some authors (e.g., Blazer, Bacher, & Manton, 1986; Manton, Blazer, & Woodbury, 1987; Pollinger-Haas & Hendin, 1983) have predicted that suicide rates, which are highest in late life, will be markedly *higher* than at present when the high-risk baby boomer cohort reaches older adulthood in the next cen-tury. On the other hand, predictions of *lower* rates among future elders have also been advanced (Holinger et al., 1994; McIntosh, 1992b; see also McIntosh et al., 1994). With respect to future rates of youth suicide, however, Holinger et al. (1994) predicted declines in suicide rates for 15- to 24-year-olds through the 1990s based on the relatively smaller co-horts reaching the 15–24 age grouping during that time and those who will do so in the near future.

ATTEMPTED SUICIDE (PARASUICIDE, OR NONFATAL SUICIDAL BEHAVIOR)

Although adolescent suicide is a significant problem, representing an increasingly important and substantial cause of death in this age group, the most common and characteristic form of suicidal behavior among adolescents is attempted suicide. Unlike the circumstances with suicide, where official figures are derived from death certificates, no official statistics are collected for nonfatal suicidal acts. Another pattern that is unlike that for deaths by suicide is apparent for the risk of attempted suicide by age. That is, while suicide rates reach their peak in late life, attempted suicide peaks earlier in life (before age 45) and declines significantly with advancing age (e.g., Moscicki et al., 1989; Weissman, 1974; Wexler, Weissman, & Kasl, 1978).

Number of Attempted Suicides

Although there are no official figures, estimates of the number of attempted suicides have been derived from individual studies and generalized to the population as a whole. Often this derivation involves an estimated ratio of attempted suicides to completed suicides. These estimates have varied based on the particular sample studied and with the passage of time. Earlier estimates of the ratio for the population as a whole were most often somewhere between 8 and 20 attempts for every completion (i.e., a ratio of 8:1 to 20:1; Shneidman, 1969; Wolff, 1970). Based on a more recent federally funded investigation, using a large random sample (aged 18 and above) and sound research methodology (Moscicki et al., 1989), an annual attempted suicide rate of 300 per 100,000 was found (0.3%). When compared to the national rate of suicide of approximately 12 per 100,000, this produces a ratio of 25 attempts for every death by suicide. On the other hand, Moscicki and colleagues' results suggested that 3% of the entire sample (aged 18 and above) had attempted suicide at some time in their lives (a level 10 times higher than the annual proportion noted above). Other studies have observed this lifetime occurrence of suicide attempts to be as high as 8–13% among high school students (see King, 1997; Smith & Crawford, 1986). This would imply that between 1 in every 12 to 1 in every 8 young people aged 15–19 years have a history of attempted suicide.

Although Moscicki et al. (1989) found significantly higher rates of attempted suicide among those aged 18–24 in their sample (the youngest age group of their study), the resulting rate and ratio of attempts to deaths by suicide are considerably lower than those resulting from other studies. In fact, the ratios of attempts to completions among the young (the ages which defined this group have varied across studies) have increased over time. Researchers have variously reported ratios of attempts to completions in their samples of 100:1 (Jacobziner, 1965), 200:1 (McIntire & Angle, 1981), 300:1 (Curran, 1987), and even as high as 350:1 (B. D. Garfinkel, cited in Berman & Jobes, 1991, p. 28). Moscicki and colleagues' (1989) lifetime rate for those aged 18–24 years was slightly but significantly higher than for their sample as a whole, at 3,400 attempts per 100,000 (3.4%). The rate for adolescents would be expected to be higher than that for these young adults, based on existing evidence (see King, 1997). Comparisons of figures from various sources are, as here, often difficult to make because researchers provide their data in different ways. Thus, inconsistencies among studies and the precise numerical relationship of attempted to completed suicides must still be further investigated, particularly among traditionally aged adolescents (under age 18). However, the elevated risk of youth for attempted suicide compared to adult groups is apparent from all available results.

Efforts to precisely determine the annual number of attempted suicides by young people are difficult as a result of the unclear estimates of attempts. However, based on the annual number of suicides among young people from 10 to 24 years of age (from 4,500 to 5,000 annually) and the estimated ratios of attempts to completions from 100:1 to as high as 300:1, the number of attempted suicides among adolescents and young adults could range between nearly half a million to one and a half million annually. From a lifetime perspective, Smith and Crawford (1986) extrapolated from their study results and review of the literature to place the estimate of young people of high school age who had ever attempted suicide between 1.5 and 2.4 million. It is certainly apparent that these figures offer at best a gross, imprecise estimate of such attempts among adolescents and other young people. It is clear that the methodological problems in these investigations may contribute to their diverse results. Prominent among these problems are the reliance on self-report of attempts as well as the likelihood that most attempts are of low lethality and never result in medical or other attention. Smith and Crawford (1986, p. 314) offered the general caution that these various ratios of attempts to completions in the young are often cited "without appreciation of the fact that, as Dorpat and Ripley (1967) have noted, these estimates were derived from special subpopulations of attempters, usually from attempters who have been admitted to hospitals." On the other hand, existing estimates identify attempted suicide as an important problem.

Demographic Factors and Attempted Suicide

Although the same reservations regarding the quality and interpretation of available figures for attempted suicide apply here as well, clear consensus exists regarding demographic groups at highest risk for attempted suicide. At all ages, including among adolescents, women have been observed to display considerably higher levels of suicide attempts than men (for a detailed consideration of explanations, see Canetto, 1997; Canetto & Sakinofsky, 1998). The suicide literature has long maintained that women attempt suicide three times more often than do men (e.g., Wekstein, 1979). Among Moscicki and colleagues' (1989) sample, for instance, the lifetime occurrence of suicide attempts were seen for 4.2% of women compared to 1.5% of men. Smith and Crawford (1986) found a ratio of high school women who had atttempted suicide that exceeded 5:1 compared to high school men in the sample. The Centers for Disease Control (1991) found among high school students that 10.3% of women and 6.2% of men reported at least one suicide attempt in the past year. King (1997) provided an interesting perspective for these latter figures. These figures "suggest that in a typical high school classroom, it is probable that one boy and two girls have made a suicide attempt during the past year" (p. 66).

Another demographic factor that shows different patterns for attempted than for completed suicide involves the method utilized. Unlike fatal acts, attempted suicides most often employ drugs and medications (self-poisoning). In fact, poisoning accounts for as many as 90% of attempts in some samples. Among other methods, self-cutting usually ranks after poisoning and is most often characteristic of younger individuals. Certainly method lethality as well as the time involved before the method produces death (and therefore availability for discovery and rescue) are important issues in these differences (Hawton & Catalan, 1982; King, 1997; Kreitman, 1977; McIntosh, 1992a). In this context, it is important to realize that culture/nationality differences often exist in the specific methods employed in nonfatal (and fatal) suicidal behaviors.

Regardless of the precise number of suicide attempts, the clinical and research suicidology literatures have observed that attempters are at significantly higher risk than the population as a whole to make future attempts and to eventually commit suicide. Investigations have observed that approximately 15% (about 1 in 6) of nonfatal suicide attempters eventually die by suicide (see, e.g., Maris, 1992). By comparison, suicide in the United States accounts for about 1.5% of all deaths in the population as a whole. The implication of these statistical facts is that young people who have attempted suicide are at higher risk than young people who have not, and they carry this higher risk with them as adults.

SUICIDAL IDEATION

Similar to the results with respect to attempts, the empirical literature for suicidal ideation has also yielded a range of estimates for suicidal ideation among adolescents and the young. One of the reasons for the wide range of estimates relates to the different wording of the questions asked to assess suicidal ideation or different criteria to categorize various suicidal behaviors. For instance, Moscicki et al. (1989) found that 12% (i.e., 1 in 8) of those 18–24 years of age in their sample reported feeling so low that they had thought of committing suicide. Smith and Crawford's (1986) study of Kansas high school students found that 37.4% reported never having thought about suicide or making any suicidal actions. However, a like proportion, 37.4%, reported that they had considered suicide but never developed a plan or made an attempt. Another 14.7% of these high schoolers said that they had been serious enough in their thoughts to have formulated a plan for suicide although they had never made any attempt. Finally, 10.5% of their entire sample had actually made one or more attempts. If these latter three categories are combined to represent all those who had suicidal ideation (assuming that those who made attempts had also had thoughts of suicide), then 62.6% were ideators (i.e., more than 1 of every 2). It seems unlikely that the slightly older age of the Moscicki et al. (1989) sample alone explains the discrepancy of these two investigations' estimates of suicidal ideation. Once again, although the precise number or proportion of young people who have thoughts of suicide either overall or in the past year, for example, is uncertain, they represent large enough numbers of adolescents and youth to warrant serious attention and prevention measures.

As with fatal and other nonfatal suicidal behaviors, sex differences are prominent in suicidal ideation among adolescents. As King (1997) notes, adolescent "girls are one and a half to two times more likely to report suicidal ideation" (p. 63) than are adolescent boys. Also, similar to other suicidal behaviors, there are a number of explanations for sex differences in suicidal ideation, with socialization and cultural expectations prominent among them (e.g., Canetto & Sakinofsky, 1998). In addition to sex differences, racial/ethnic differences in ideation have also been noted (e.g., Moscicki et al., 1989).

SURVIVORS OF ADOLESCENT SUICIDE

Much of the discussion here has presented data as aggregate numbers of deaths and other actions. However, a discussion of the extent to which suicide is a problem among adolescents would be incomplete without realizing the obvious fact that these nearly 5,000 young people who kill themselves annually are more than merely statistics. Each of them was someone's son, daughter, sibling, cousin, grandchild, classmate, student, or best friend (or someone in another significant relationship). This group of family members and various significant others who have lost a loved one to suicide are called suicide survivors (see Dunne, McIntosh, & Dunne-Maxim, 1987). They are the bereaved of suicide. Evidence suggests that the bereavement processes of these grieving individuals are affected by the mode of the death, particularly when the death was by suicide (for research considerations and reviews, see McIntosh, 1987a, 1987b, 1993a, 1999b).

Although no systematic epidemiological investigation has been conducted to provide definitive numbers of survivors of suicide in the population, Shneidman (1969) suggested that each suicide produced at least six survivors. If we accept this figure (see, e.g., Interaction: Survivors of suicide, 1996) as an average, it is likely that it is conservative when the suicide is by an adolescent. Such an assumption is logical due to the residence of adolescents in the homes of parents, often with siblings, and their usual involvement in school settings. There are larger numbers of people involved in the lives of young people than in those of many other life periods, and therefore the suicide of an adolescent will probably have an impact on more people than the average. However, if we assume that the 6:1 ratio is useful as an index, then there would be at least 30,000 survivors produced by each year's adolescent suicides. The cumulative number of survivors would become substantial over time.

The literature on survivors of suicide has grown considerably since the 1970s (e.g., McIntosh, 1985/86, 1996). Suicide survivorship is an issue of what has been called "postvention," the need to intervene to assist those affected following a suicidal action. If this term is indeed applied to a broader array of populations after suicidal behaviors beyond simply deaths by suicide, then there are at least two additional groups that have rarely been addressed in the clinical or research literatures. As already noted, the number of attempts among adolescents is believed to be large, but scant attention has been directed toward those adolescents who make nonfatal suicide attempts and the impact this behavior has on them and their lives in either the long or short term. Follow-up studies often focus on whether these individuals later attempted suicide again or killed themselves, but most often the emphasis of these investigations has not determined the psychosocial effects of the attempt itself. Similarly, almost no information is available as to the impact which nonfatal suicide attempts have on the family members and other loved ones of the adolescent. A complete picture of suicide in adolescence cannot be compiled without inclusion of these various groups who must live their lives following the death of or suicidal attempt of their adolescent loved one.

CONCLUSION

Several conclusions emerge from available official statistics and results from research studies of adolescents and young adults. Youth are not the highest risk group for death by suicide, but when compared to youth four decades earlier, the current risk of suicide among young people is markedly higher. In addition, suicide is a considerably more prominent cause of death among the young and accounts for a markedly higher proportion of adolescent deaths than for the nation as a whole or other age groups. Although levels of attempted suicide and suicidal ideation are more uncertain, the existing estimates show that nonfatal suicidal behaviors (attempts and ideation) are common in adolescence and that the prevalence of both are among the highest across the life span. Adolescence represents the most common life period for attempted suicide and suicidal ideation. Sex differences represent a particularly prominent aspect of suicidal behaviors at all ages. Fatal suicidal behaviors are most common among adolescent and young men, whereas nonfatal suicidal behaviors are higher among young women. A neglected though important aspect of adolescent suicidal behavior involves assessing the aftermath of each type of behavior on the surviving family members and other loved ones. Knowledge of adolescent suicide would benefit from additional well-designed epidemiological research efforts. Accurate epidemiological information is one foundation for understanding adolescent suicidal behavior and designing prevention and intervention measures to lessen risk of suicidal behaviors (see Grossman & Kruesi, Chapter 8, this volume, for prevention approaches for youth suicide).

ACKNOWLEDGMENTS

Some data reported here were provided by Sherry Murphy of the National Center for Health Statistics Mortality Branch. This chapter is based on an updated version of a presentation made at a national telecourse on the suicidal adolescent sponsored by the American Association of Suicidology and the United States Bureau of Naval Personnel from Bethesda, Maryland, April 15, 1998.

REFERENCES

Allen, N. (1984). Suicide statistics. In C. L. Hatton & S. M. Valente (Eds.), *Suicide: Assessment and intervention* (2nd ed., pp. 17–31). Norwalk, CT: Appleton-Century-Crofts.

Asgard, U., Nordstrom, P., & Raback, G. (1987). Birth cohort analysis of changing suicide risk by sex and age in Sweden 1952 to 1981. *Acta Psychiatrica Scandinavica, 76,* 456–463.

Atkinson, J. M. (1978). *Discovering suicide: Studies in the social disorganization of sudden death.* Pittsburgh, PA: University of Pittsburgh Press.

Berman, A. L., & Jobes, D. A. (1991). *Adolescent sucide: Assessment and intervention.* Washington, DC: American Psychological Association.

Blazer, D. G., Bacher, J. R., & Manton, K. G. (1986). Suicide in late life: Review and commentary. *Journal of the American Geriatrics Society, 34,* 519–525.

Canetto, S. S. (1997). Meanings of gender and suicidal behavior during adolescence. *Suicide and Life-Threatening Behavior, 27*, 339–351.

Canetto, S. S., & Lester, D. (Eds.). (1995). *Women and suicidal behavior.* New York: Springer.

Canetto, S. S., & Sakinofsky, I. (1998). The gender paradox in suicide. *Suicide and Life-Threatening Behavior, 28*, 1–23.

Centers for Disease Control. (1990). Years of potential life lost before ages 65 and 85—United States, 1987 and 1988. *Morbidity and Mortality Weekly Report, 39*, 20–22.

Centers for Disease Control. (1991). Attempted suicide among high school students—United States, 1990. *Morbidity and Mortality Weekly Report, 40*, 633–635.

Curran, D. K. (1987). *Adolescent suicidal behavior.* New York: Hemisphere.

Dorpat, T. L., & Ripley, H. S. (1967). The relationship between attempted and committed suicide. *Comprehensive Psychiatry, 8*, 74–79.

Dunne, E. J., McIntosh, J. L., & Dunne-Maxim, K. (Eds.). (1987). *Suicide and its aftermath: Understanding and counseling the survivors.* New York: Norton.

Easterlin, R. A. (1980). *Birth and fortune: The impact of numbers on personal welfare.* New York: Basic Books.

Gibbs, J. T. (1997). African-American suicide: A cultural paradox. *Suicide and Life-Threatening Behavior, 27*, 68–79.

Hawton, K., & Catalan, J. (1982). *Attempted suicide: A practical guide to its nature and management.* New York: Oxford University Press.

Holinger, P. C. (1987). *Violent deaths in the United States: An epidemiologic study of suicide, homicide, and accidents.* New York: Guilford Press.

Holinger, P. C., & Offer, D. (1982). Prediction of adolescent suicide: A population model. *American Journal of Psychiatry, 139*, 302–307.

Holinger, P. C., Offer, D., Barter, J. T., & Bell, C. C. (1994). *Suicide and homicide among adolescents.* New York: Guilford Press.

Interaction: Survivors of suicide. (1996, Fall). *Newslink* (quarterly publication of the American Association of Suicidology), *22*(3), 3, 15.

Jacobziner, H. (1965). Attempted suicide in adolescence. *Journal of the American Medical Association, 10*, 22–36.

King, C. A. (1997). Suicidal behavior in adolescence. In R. W. Maris, M. M. Silverman, & S. S. Canetto (Eds.), *Review of suicidology, 1997* (pp. 61–95). New York: Guilford Press.

Kreitman, N. (1977). *Parasuicide.* New York: Wiley.

La Vecchia, C., Bollini, P., Imazio, C., & Decarli, A. (1986). Age, period of death and birth cohort effects on suicide mortality in Italy, 1955–1979. *Acta Psychiatrica Scandinavica, 74*, 137–143.

Manton, K. G., Blazer, D. G., & Woodbury, M. A. (1987). Suicide in middle age and later life: Sex and race specific life tables and cohort analyses. *Journal of Gerontology, 42*, 219–227.

Maris, R. W. (1985). The adolescent suicide problem. *Suicide and Life-Threatening Behavior, 15*, 91–109.

Maris, R. W. (1992). Overview of the study of suicide assessment and prediction. In R. W. Maris, A. L. Berman, J. T. Maltsberger, & R. I. Yufit (Eds.), *Assessment and prediction of suicide* (pp. 3–22). New York: Guilford Press.

McIntire, M. S., & Angle, C. R. (1981). The taxonomy of suicide and self-poisoning: A pediatric perspective. In C. F. Wells & I. R. Stuart (Eds.), *Self-destructive behavior in children and adolescents* (pp. 224–249). New York: Van Nostrand Reinhold.

McIntosh, J. L. (1985/86). Survivors of suicide: A comprehensive bibliography. *Omega, 16,* 355–370.

McIntosh, J. L. (1987a). Research, therapy, and education needs. In E. J. Dunne, J. L. McIntosh, & K. Dunne-Maxim (Eds.), *Suicide and its aftermath: Understanding and counseling the survivors* (pp. 263–277). New York: Norton.

McIntosh, J. L. (1987b). Survivors family relationships: Literature review. In E. J. Dunne, J. L. McIntosh, & K. Dunne-Maxim (Eds.), *Suicide and its aftermath: Understanding and counseling the survivors* (pp. 73–84). New York: Norton.

McIntosh, J. L. (1992a). Methods of suicide. In R. W. Maris, A. L. Berman, J. T. Maltsberger, & R. I. Yufit (Eds.), *Assessment and prediction of suicide* (pp. 381–397). New York: Guilford Press.

McIntosh, J. L. (1992b). Older adults: The next suicide epidemic? *Suicide and Life-Threatening Behavior, 22,* 322–332.

McIntosh, J. L. (1993a). Control group studies of suicide survivors: A review and critique. *Suicide and Life-Threatening Behavior, 23,*146–161.

McIntosh, J. L. (1993b). Risk to life through the adult years. In R. Kastenbaum (Ed.), *Encyclopedia of adult development* (pp. 414–421). Phoenix, AZ: Oryx Press.

McIntosh, J. L. (1994). Generational analyses of suicide: Baby boomers and 13ers. *Suicide and Life-Threatening Behavior, 24,* 334–342.

McIntosh, J. L. (1996). Survivors of suicide: A comprehensive bibliography update, 1986–1995. *Omega: Journal of Death and Dying, 33,* 147–175.

McIntosh, J. L. (1999a). Death and dying across the lifespan. In T. L. Whitman, T. V. Merluzzi, & R. D. White (Eds.), *Life-span perspectives on health and illness* (pp. 249–274). Mahwah, NJ: Erlbaum.

McIntosh, J. L. (1999b). Research on survivors of suicide. In M. Stimming & M. Stimming (Eds.), *Before their time: Adult children's experiences with parental suicide* (pp. 157–180). Philadelphia: Temple University Press.

McIntosh, J. L. (in press). Quantitative methods in suicide research: Issues associated with official statistics. *Archives of Suicide Research* [to appear in a special issue on quantitative vs. qualitative methods in suicidology].

McIntosh, J. L., Eikens, M., & Ramos, M. (1998, April). *40 years of state suicide patterns by age and sex.* Paper presented at the annual meeting of the American Association of Suicidology, Bethesda, MD.

McIntosh, J. L., Hubbard, R. W., & Santos, J. F. (1985). Suicide facts and myths: A study of prevalence. *Death Studies, 9,* 267–281.

McIntosh, J. L., Santos, J. F., Hubbard, R. W., & Overholser, J. C. (1994). *Elder suicide: Research, theory, and treatment.* Washington, DC: American Psychological Association.

Moens, G. F. G., van Oortmarssen, G., Honggokoesoemo, S., & van de Voorde,

H. (1987). Birth cohort analysis of suicide mortality in Belgium 1954–1981 by a graphic and a quantitative method. *Acta Psychiatrica Scandinavica, 76,* 450–455.

Moscicki, E. K., O'Carroll, P. W., Rae, D. S., Roy, A. G., Locke, B. Z., & Regier, D. A. (1989). Suicidal ideation and attempts: The Epidemiologic Catchment Area Study. In M. L. Rosenberg & K. Baer (Eds.), *Report of the Secretary's Task Force on Youth Suicide. Volume 4: Strategies for the prevention of youth suicide* (pp. 4-115–4-128). (DHHS Publication No. ADM 89-1624). Washington, DC: U.S. Government Printing Office.

Murphy, E., Lindesay, J., & Grundy, E. (1986). 60 years of suicide in England and Wales: A cohort study. *Archives of General Psychiatry, 43,* 969–976.

National Center for Health Statistics. (Annual vols.). *Vital Statistics of the United States,* Pts. I & II (for 1937–1949 data); Vol. II (for 1950–1959 data); Volume II—Mortality, Pts. A & B (for 1960–1993 data currently). Washington, DC: U.S. Government Printing Office.

National Center for Health Statistics. (1999, January). *Mortality tables* (with downloadable files) [unpublished tables available for download at website]. URL for the site: http://www.cdc.gov/nchswww/datawh/statab/unpubd/mortabs.htm#general

O'Donnell, C. R. (1995). Firearm deaths among children and youth. *American Psychologist, 50,* 771–776.

Peters, K. D., Kochanek, K. D., & Murphy, S. L. (1998). Deaths: Final data for 1996. *National Vital Statistics Reports, 47*(Whole No. 9). (DHHS Publication No. PHS 99-1120).

Pollinger-Haas, A., & Hendin, H. (1983). Suicide among older people: Projections for the future. *Suicide and Life-Threatening Behavior, 13,* 147–154.

Reed, J., Camus, J., & Last, J. M. (1985). Suicide in Canada: Birth-cohort analysis. *Canadian Journal of Public Health, 76,* 43–47.

Sainsbury, P., & Jenkins, J. S. (1982). The accuracy of officially reported suicide statistics for purposes of epidemiological research. *Journal of Epidemiology and Community Health, 36,* 43–48.

Seiden, R. H. (1969). Suicide among youth: A review of the literature, 1900–1967. *Bulletin of Suicidology* (Suppl.), Public Health Service Publication No. 1971.

Seiden, R. H. (1984). Death in the West: A regional analysis of the youthful suicide rate. *Western Journal of Medicine, 140,* 969–973.

Shaffer, D., Gould, M., & Hicks, R. C. (1994). Worsening suicide rate in black teenagers. *American Journal of Psychiatry, 151,* 1810–1812.

Shneidman, E. S. (1969). Prologue: Fifty-eight years. In E. S. Shneidman (Ed.), *On the nature of suicide* (pp. 1–30). San Francisco: Jossey-Bass.

Smith, K., & Crawford, S. (1986). Suicidal behavior among "normal" high school students. *Suicide and Life-Threatening Behavior, 16,* 313–325.

Wasserman, I. M. (1987). Cohort, age, and period effects in the analysis of U.S. suicide patterns: 1933–1978. *Suicide and Life-Threatening Behavior, 17,* 179–193.

Weissman, M. M. (1974). The epidemiology of suicide attempts: 1960 to 1971. *Archives of General Psychiatry, 30,* 737–746.

Wekstein, L. (1979). *Handbook of suicidology: Principles, problems, and practice.* New York: Brunner/Mazel.

Wexler, L., Weissman, M. M., & Kasl, S. V. (1978). Suicide attempts, 1970–1975: Updating a United States study and comparisons with international trends. *British Journal of Psychiatry, 132,* 180–185.

Wolff, K. (1970). Observations on depression and suicide in the geriatric patient. In K. Wolff (Ed.), *Patterns of self-destruction: Depression and suicide* (pp. 33–42). Springfield, IL: Thomas.

CHAPTER TWO

An Abrupt Shift in U.S. Suicide Levels Around the Month Boundary

David P. Phillips, PhD
Natalie M. Ryan, BA

Increasingly, suicide is regarded in terms of biochemistry and genetics. However, various lines of evidence suggest that suicidal processes will never be fully explainable in purely biological terms. For example, suicide levels fluctuate by day of the week, being highest on Monday (MacMahon, 1983; Maldonado & Kraus, 1991). Because the week is a purely cultural invention, uncorrelated with biological processes, our understanding of day-of-the-week fluctuations in suicide must necessarily involve nonbiological processes.

An additional, less-often studied cultural cycle is date of the month. Like the week, the month is an arbitrary social construct, uncorrelated with natural cycles (e.g., lunar or seasonal). Examining U.S. suicides, 1972–1978, MacMahon (1983) was the first to conduct a large-scale investigation of suicide levels by date of the month. She found a small suicide peak on the first and a larger peak on the fifth of the month, and a general decline to the 29th. Because of the data she studied, MacMahon was unable to provide separate examination of males, females, or various age groups. Subdividing the study group by age and sex, Lester and Frank (1987) examined a smaller U.S. sample (for 1980 only). Based on their analysis, they concluded that the beginning-of-the-month peak in suicides appears only for persons 35 and over. According to Lester and Frank, only males produced this peak. Unfortunately, these authors did not study suicides throughout the month—they examined the suicide level for 3 days near the beginning of the month and 3 days near the end. In a larger and more sophisticated analysis, which examined U.S. suicides for 1973–1985, McCleary, Chew, Hellsten, and Flynn-Bransford (1991) concluded that the beginning-of-the-month peak was evident only for persons 60 and over. In contrast to Lester and Frank (1987), McCleary et al. (1991) also found a small female effect (for ages 60–70). Both MacMahon (1983) and McCleary et al. (1991) were unable to provide a precise description of suicide levels at the end of the month; for example, they treated deaths on the 28th as having the same meaning, regardless of the month under study. Thus, persons dying on February 28 (the last day of the month) were treated as equivalent to persons dying on January 28 (the fourth-to-last day of the month). This procedure blurs any pattern in mortality fluctuations at the end of the month.

METHODS

We studied computerized copies of all U.S. death certificates (U.S. Department of Health and Human Services, National Center for Health Statistics, 1973–1988a) classified as suicides, from 1973 (the first year providing exact date of death for all certificates) to 1988 (the last year for which exact date of death was provided). Persons committing suicide were coded according to the number of days they died from the month boundary. For example, persons dying on the last day of the month were coded in category "–1," persons dying on the penultimate day of the month were coded "–2," persons dying one day before that were coded "–3," and so on. In consequence of this coding procedure some persons dying on the 30th are coded "–1" (if they died in a month with 30 days) while others are coded "–2" (if they died in a month with 31 days). Similarly, a death on the 28th might be coded "–1," "–2," "–3," or "–4," depending on whether the death occurred in a month with 28, 29, 30, or 31 days, respectively. In contrast to the coding procedures used in earlier research, which did not make these distinctions (MacMahon, 1983; Mc-

Cleary et al., 1991), the current procedure permits precise description of mortality patterns at the boundary between one month and the next.

For each month boundary between 1973 and 1988, we analyzed mortality for a 28-day period, extending from 14 days before to 14 days after the month boundary. In all, we examined 411,853 U.S. suicides.

Conventional formulas for the calculation of standard error and significance levels were taken from the Technical Appendix of *Vital Statistics of the United States* (U.S. Department of Health and Human Services, National Center for Health Statistics, 1973–1988c), which also justifies the use of these formulas for significance testing when dealing with complete counts.

RESULTS

Figure 2.1 indicates the number of suicides before and after the month boundary. The level of suicides declines quite smoothly towards an absolute low at the end of the month. Then the trend reverses abruptly and the number of suicides increases, by more than 7 standard errors, to a relative high on the first of the next month. In general, the suicide level is below normal for the last week of the month and above normal for the first 2 weeks of the following month.

The elevated level in the second week, which was not noted by earlier investigators, is particularly apparent for some age groups. Figure 2.2 displays the ratio of the daily number of suicides in week 1 to the daily number of suicides in week –1 (top panel) and the ratio of daily suicides in week 2 to daily suicides in week –1 (bottom panel). If the suicide level did not change across the month boundary, these two ratios would equal 1.00. In fact, there is a consistent tendency for the suicide level to increase from the end of one month to the beginning of the next, for each age group ($p = (1/2)^{16} = .00002$ for each panel). The beginning-of-month peak is very large for the youngest age group, then decreases in size until about age 50. After this age, the peak increases smoothly to age 75–79, and then declines. For young age groups, the peak in suicides occurs mainly in the first week of the month; for older ages, the peak is stronger in the second week.

For some methods of suicide, like firearms, death typically follows soon after the suicidal act. For other suicide methods, like poison, there is a longer lag between the suicidal act and death. The "spreading" of the

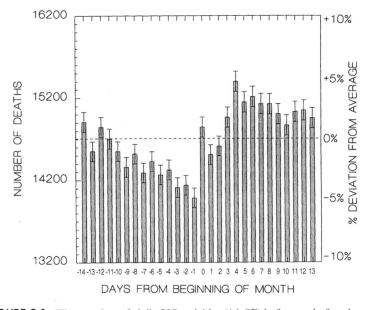

FIGURE 2.1. The number of daily U.S. suicides (±1 SE) before and after the month boundary, 1973–1988. "Day 0" indicates the first day of the month, and "day –1" indicates the last day of the preceding month. The study spans the 16 years for which an exact date of death was available from computerized data. The error bars are calculated from a Poisson approximation (U.S. Department of Health and Human Services, National Center for Health Statistics, 1973–1988c). The horizontal dashed line indicates the distribution of deaths that would be expected if mortality did not fluctuate around the month boundary. In all, 411,853 suicides were studied.

suicide peak over the first and second weeks does not occur because rapid-acting suicide methods produce a first-week peak whereas slow-acting suicide methods produce a second-week peak. For example, Figure 2.3 indicates that suicides with rapid-acting firearms display both a first-week and second-week peak, with the second-week peak being stronger. Figure 2.3 also indicates that all major methods of suicide display a drop in deaths in the last week of the month and a peak in deaths in the second week of the following month. The first-week peak is nearly as consistent across methods of suicide, being absent only for suicides by jumping.

In contrast to claims in some earlier research (Lester & Frank, 1987; McCleary et al., 1991), the month boundary (MB) effect exists for both males and females (see Figure 2.4). The MB effect for males is consistently evident for every age group; for females the effect is present for

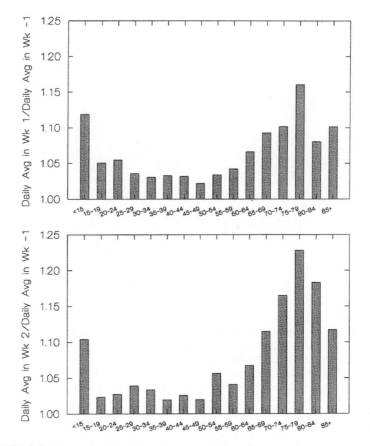

FIGURE 2.2. The ratio of suicides in the beginning of the month to suicides in the last week of the preceding month, by age. The top panel displays the ratio of the daily number of suicides in week 1 to the daily number of suicides in week −1; the bottom panel displays the equivalent information for week 2 versus week −1. For week 1, each age group (except for 45–49) displays a statistically significant MB effect at the .05 level, one-tailed test. For week 2, each age group (except for 15–19 and 35–49) displays a statistically significant MB effect at the .05 level, one-tailed test.

all ages except 35–49. Outside of this age group, there is no consistent tendency for the MB effect to be larger for males than for females.

DISCUSSION

The suicide level declines markedly to the end of the month and then increases abruptly to a peak at the beginning of the month and for the

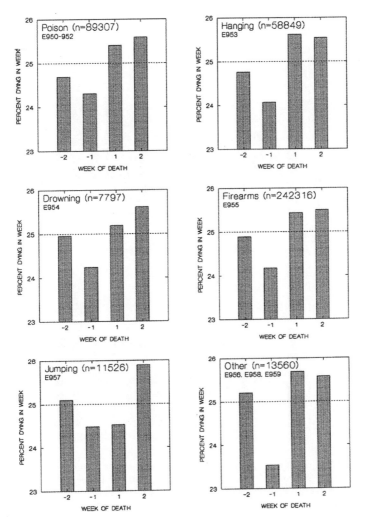

FIGURE 2.3. Percent of suicides occurring in each week around the month boundary, for six major methods of suicide. The dotted line indicates the level of suicides expected if mortality did not fluctuate around the month boundary. The International Classification of Disease (ICD) Codes (U.S. Department of Health and Human Services, National Center for Health Statistics, 1973–1988b) for the suicides in the residual category in the bottom right cell are E956 (suicide by cutting and piercing instruments), E958 (suicide by other and unspecified means), and E959 (late effects of self-inflicted injury). The ICD Codes for the other cells in this figure are E950–952 (poison), E953 (hanging), E954 (drowning), E955 (firearms), and E957 (jumping).

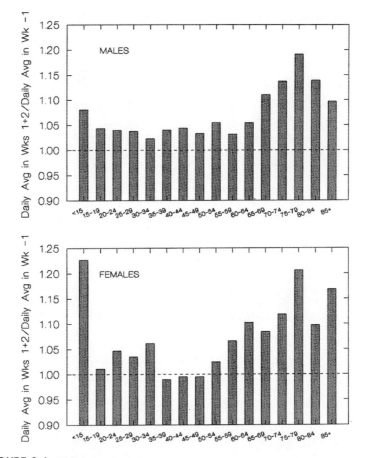

FIGURE 2.4. The ratio of suicides in the beginning of the month to suicides in the last week of the preceding month, by age and sex. The top panel displays the ratio of the daily number of male suicides in weeks 1 + 2 to the daily number of suicides in week −1 (for the 3-week period studied, $n = 234,020$); the bottom panel displays the equivalent information for females (for the 3-week period studied, $n = 75,247$). The dotted line indicates the level of suicides expected if mortality did not fluctuate around the month boundary.

next 2 weeks thereafter. In contrast to reports in earlier research, the MB effect for suicides exists for both males and females, and appears across the life span. The generality of the MB effect may not have been evident in earlier studies because these investigations (1) employed smaller samples and (2) used analytic techniques that did not give a precise picture of mortality at the end of the month.

Alternative Explanations for the Findings

Misclassification of Death Dates

Occasionally, suicides are discovered some time after death; in some of these cases the coroner may tend to record the death dates as occurring on the first of the month. Two pieces of evidence undermine the "misclassification" explanation. First, if the death date is unknown, it can be so indicated on the certificate, and often is. Second, the "misclassification" explanation cannot account for the fact that suicide mortality is elevated not only on the first day of the month but throughout the first 2 weeks.

Population Growth

The U.S. population has recently increased by about 1% annually (U.S. Department of Commerce, 1998, Table 2), implying that the number of suicides should increase with each succeeding week. However, if our findings resulted from population growth alone, that growth would have to occur by 5% per week (the size of the MB effect), rather than by 1% per year. In addition, Figure 2.1 shows mortality decreasing at the end of the month, which cannot be explained by the "population growth" hypothesis.

Changes in the Quality of Medical Care

Perhaps new medical personnel hired at the beginning of the month are less effective than are putatively more experienced personnel working at the end of the month. This hypothesis can be assessed by examination of a minor category of suicide, "Late Effects of Self-Inflicted Injury" (where the death follows many days after the suicidal act). Only this minor category fails to display the MB effect (the average number of daily suicides in the first 2 weeks of the month, 3.93, is actually less than the average number of daily suicides in the last week of the month, 5.57). This suggests that the MB effect does not result because medical personnel are less effective at the beginning of the month and more effective at the end of the month; if the "medical care" hypothesis were correct, then all forms of suicide, including those from "delayed effects," would display the MB effect.

Holding on to Life

Perhaps some persons "hold on" to life for a few days so that their families can receive one last salary or welfare or Social Security check. Putative "holding on" processes of this sort (Phillips & King, 1988; Phillips & Smith, 1990; Phillips, Van Voorhees, & Ruth, 1992) might provide a partial explanation for some findings but cannot plausibly account for the very large MB effect for young children, who are unlikely to be receiving a salary or Social Security or welfare checks (directed to them, personally, rather than their parents). For suicides younger than 15, the MB effect is 1.12 for the first week ($z = 2.12$, $p < .025$, one-tailed test). In contrast, older teens, aged 15–19, who are more likely to be heads of families and to receive salaries, produce a smaller MB effect of 1.05 ($z = 2.79$, $p < .025$, one-tailed test). It is worth noting that the first-week MB effect for persons under 15 is larger than that for any other age group in Figure 2.2 except for those who are 75–79.

Broken Promises

These findings are inconsistent with the "holding on" hypothesis unless one posits that the very young are "holding on" for something other than monthly funds. Gabennesch (1988) has proposed an explanation that might be appropriate here: He speculates that persons regard the start of the month as a "new beginning" and kill themselves when their nascent hopes are unrealized.

This explanation, though intriguing, is difficult to test because it sometimes depends on vague concepts and consequently tends to generate ambiguous predictions. For example, Gabennesch (1988) claims that his "new beginnings" hypothesis is supported by the fact that suicides are most common in the spring, which Gabennesch feels is the beginning of the year. If suicides had been most common in January or February, this could also be interpreted as support for Gabennesch's theory, because these months could also be considered as the beginning of the year. Similarly a rise in suicides in July and August would also be consistent with Gabennesch's theory, because July 1 is the beginning of the fiscal year. Finally, a rise in suicides in September could also be considered as support for Gabennesch's theory, because September is the beginning of the school year. In short, no matter when suicides increased during the year, one could claim this as support for Gabennesch's theory.

Several considerations tend to undermine the "broken promises" explanation of the MB effect. Without a great deal of additional post hoc theorizing, it is unclear how the "new beginnings" explanation can account for the following findings:

1. Why do suicides sometimes peak in the second week of the month, rather than in the first week as posited by Gabennesch (see Figures 2.2, 2.3, and 2.4)?
2. Why does the peak tend to occur in the first week for the young and in the second week for the old (see Figures 2.2 and 2.4)?
3. Why is there no peak for females aged 35–49 when males produce an MB effect for this age group (see Figure 2.4)?
4. Why does the MB effect generally increase with age, while being large also for persons under 15 (see Figures 2.2 and 2.4)?

Perhaps the most difficult findings to account for are those reported elsewhere by Phillips, Christenfeld, and Ryan (1999). These authors showed that the MB effect is not restricted to suicides, as was previously supposed, but actually appears for nearly all major causes of death. For some of these causes, the MB effect is even stronger than it is for suicides. It is hard to understand how the "broken promises" explanation can account for all these phenomena.

At present, it seems safest to conclude that the MB effect is real, robust, and sometimes large—but it is not yet explained. Epidemiological research of the sort reported here is well suited for establishing the existence of previously unknown phenomena but not for providing a detailed picture of the processes producing those phenomena. Future nonepidemiological research will probably be needed. Instead of examining a large number of cases on each of which one has a small amount of data, it will be necessary to study a small sample of people on each of whom one has a large amount of data. The best chance for elucidating the MB effect will probably arise from a combination of initial large-scale studies and subsequent small-scale investigations.

ACKNOWLEDGMENT

Writing of this chapter was supported by grants to David P. Phillips from the Marian E. Smith Foundation.

REFERENCES

Gabennesch, H. (1988). When promises fail: A theory of temporal fluctuations in suicide. *Social Forces, 67,* 129–145.

Lester, D., & Frank, M. L. (1987). Beware the nones of March: Suicide at the beginning of the month. *Psychological Reports, 61,* 938.

MacMahon, K. (1983). Short-term temporal cycles in the frequency of suicide, United States, 1972–1978. *American Journal of Epidemiology, 117,* 744–750.

Maldonado, G., & Kraus, J. F. (1991). Variation in suicide occurrence by time of day, day of the week, month, and lunar phase. *Suicide and Life-Threatening Behavior, 21,* 174–187.

McCleary, R., Chew, K. S. Y., Hellsten, J. J., & Flynn-Bransford, M. (1991). Age- and sex-specific cycles in United States suicides, 1973 to 1985. *American Journal of Public Health, 81,* 1494–1497.

Phillips, D. P., Christenfeld, N., & Ryan, N. M. (1999). An increase in the number of deaths in the United States in the first week of the month: An association with substance abuse and other causes of death. *New England Journal of Medicine, 341,* 93–98.

Phillips, D. P., & King, E. W. (1988). Death takes a holiday: Mortality surrounding major social occasions. *Lancet, ii,* 728–732.

Phillips, D. P., & Smith, D. G. (1990). Postponement of death until symbolically meaningful occasions. *Journal of the American Medical Association, 263,* 1947–1951.

Phillips, D. P., Van Voorhees, C. A., & Ruth, T. E. (1992). The birthday: Lifeline or deadline? *Psychosomatic Medicine, 54,* 532–542.

U.S. Department of Commerce. (1998). *Statistical abstract of the United States 1997.* Washington, DC: U.S. Government Printing Office.

U.S. Department of Health and Human Services, National Center for Health Statistics. (1973–1988a). *Mortality detail file, 1973–1988* [Electronic data file]. Hyattsville, MD: Author.

U.S. Department of Health and Human Services, National Center for Health Statistics. (1973–1988b). *Vital statistics of the United States* (Vol. II, Pt. A, sect. I). Hyattsville, MD: Author.

U.S. Department of Health and Human Services, National Center for Health Statistics. (1973–1988c). *Vital statistics of the United States* (Vol. II, Pt. A, sect. VII). Hyattsville, MD: Author.

PART TWO

ISSUES IN THE TREATMENT OF SUICIDAL INDIVIDUALS AND POPULATIONS

Integrating Science into the Practice of Clinical Suicidology

A Review of the Psychotherapy Literature and a Research Agenda for the Future

M. David Rudd, PhD

ESTABLISHING AN EMPIRICAL FOUNDATION FOR PRACTICE: WHAT DO WE REALLY KNOW ABOUT TREATING SUICIDALITY?

What do we really know about treating suicidality? In order to answer this question with some degree of accuracy we need to rely on scientific data, regardless of the depth or breadth of the available literature. Otherwise, we are left to conclusions based on theoretical speculation and supposition, two demons that have plagued those practicing psychotherapy. More than ever before, clinicians are being asked to do more with less and treat complex disorders in time-limited fashion. Under such conditions, an empirical foundation to practice is essential for safe, effective, and appropriate treatment, something particularly true for those presenting with suicidality.

In reviewing the literature addressing the psychotherapeutic treatment of suicidality, a number of important questions surface. Among them are the following:

- What treatments have demonstrated effectiveness for treating suicidality?
- Within identified treatments, are there *core interventions* associated with positive outcome?
- Are there identified treatments that clearly should *not* be used as a result of consistently poor outcome data?
- Can high-risk suicidal patients be treated safely *and* effectively on an outpatient basis?
- Are there prohibitive features of particular treatments such as exorbitant costs, duration, frequency, intensity, risks, or side effects?
- Are there differential dropout rates for specific treatment approaches that need to be considered?
- Does treatment setting influence outcome?
- Does treatment *delay* (i.e., the period of time from suicidal crisis to the onset of treatment) predict treatment outcome?
- Is treatment duration associated with outcome; that is, are short-term treatments more or less effective than longer ones?
- Do particular subgroups (e.g., multiple attempters or those with comorbid problems across both axis I and axis II) require specific treatment approaches?
- Does treatment effect endure, that is, what are the observed relapse rates?
- Are there identified approaches specifically targeting those who relapse?
- Does diagnostic comorbidity affect treatment selection, prognosis, or outcome (i.e., treatment matching)?
- How should treatment response or outcome be conceptualized?
- How can treatment compliance be maximized?
- How can treatment fidelity be maintained across clinicians for specific treatment approaches?

As will become evident in the following review, we can answer only a few of the most fundamental questions raised regarding the treatment of suicidality. And, at that, the answers are very much tentative. They do, nonetheless, provide an empirically derived set of conclusions on which to build. Additional answers are dependent on continued growth in the science of clinical suicidology, collegial debate and discussion, and the creative evolution of psychotherapy research. As is the case with most areas of scientific investigation, a substantial portion of the problem is simply knowing what questions to ask.

THE AVAILABLE LITERATURE:
A LIMITED DATABASE

Although a large number of studies exist in the suicidality literature, many incorporating case examples, theoretical articles, and studies without comparison or control groups, this review includes only those that are randomized or controlled in some fashion. This is consistent with the original goal of integrating existing science into suicidality practice as well as articulating and acknowledging current limitations in the *state of the science*. By doing so, we can articulate an empirically grounded approach to practice, appropriately acknowledge significant and surprising limitations in this area of scientific study, and identify a host of questions that are left unanswered.

A review of the literature (utilizing the *PsycINFO* and *MEDLINE* databases) yielded a total of 23 randomized or controlled studies targeting suicidality (see Appendix 3.1 for a detailed summary of all studies). None are specific to adolescents, although a few include older adolescents (i.e., ages 17–19) and young adults. This total incorporates both *intervention* and *treatment* studies. Those classified as *intervention* studies (i.e., $n = 6$) included investigations that were specifically described as not providing any identifiable form of psychotherapy as the study condition. These studies essentially made procedural changes in both the provision of and ease of access to traditional psychotherapeutic services, exploring any subsequent reduction in suicide attempts. All were careful to note that the study condition was not psychotherapeutic treatment, although several faced considerable confounds that are summarized below and in Appendix 3.1. Among the studies reviewed, interventions varied but included the following: (1) supportive case management by volunteer workers (Termansen & Bywater, 1975); (2) simple follow-up letters and phone calls to those refusing treatment (Motto, 1976); (3) incorporation of home visits and more intensive tracking (Litman &

Wold, 1975; van Heeringen et al., 1995); (4) brief medical hospitalization with no psychiatric care (Waterhouse & Platt, 1990); and (5) improved ease of access to 24-hour emergency services (Morgan, Jones, & Owen, 1993).

Of the 23 studies identified, three explored pharmacological treatment of suicidality and were excluded from the review, given that the focus is on psychotherapeutic treatment (Hirsch, Walsh, & Draper, 1983; D. B. Montgomery, Roy, & S. A. Montgomery, 1981; S. A. Montgomery & D. B. Montgomery, 1982). Note that the three pharmacological studies were all completed more than two decades ago, prior to some of the recent advances in the use of medications for diagnosed psychiatric disorders, particularly selective serotonin reuptake inhibitors (SSRIs), all with limited efficacy. This highlights a common problem in the scientific study of suicidality: those evidencing some form of suicidality are ordinarily excluded from clinical trials (both medication and psychotherapy) due to their high-risk nature. After excluding the three medication studies, I was left with a total of 20 controlled or randomized studies targeting the treatment of suicidality. This is consistent with a recent review of outcome studies offered by Linehan (1997; reprinted as Chapter 4 in this volume). The total includes 3 studies not previously reviewed (i.e., Lerner & Clum, 1990; Rudd et al., 1996; Joiner, Rudd, & Rajab, 1998). As noted above, this total includes 6 studies that were simple *intervention* studies not purporting to address more complex treatment issues. This leaves a total of only 14 treatment studies for critical review, a truly surprising finding for any area of science, not to mention one as fraught with controversy and importance as suicidality.

A CRITICAL REVIEW OF INTERVENTION STUDIES: DO SIMPLE PROCEDURAL CHANGES MAKE A DIFFERENCE?

Of the intervention studies reviewed, three had positive findings, but each has identifiable limitations, some of which are considerable. Termansen and Bywater (1975) found that what essentially was described as *intensive case management* by volunteer workers reduced subsequent suicide attempts during the 3-month follow-up period, relative to those receiving no follow-up care. As these authors noted, "the role [of the volunteers] was not therapeutic in the conventional psychiatric sense; rather it was the role of the helper expressing concern for the person in his total environmental situation" (p. 29). The study included four conditions, with each varying as to the nature of initial assessment and follow-up monitoring. The first group was assessed in the emergency room after a suicide attempt. They also received follow-up intervention by a mental health worker for a total of 3 months. The second group was also assessed in the emergency room after a suicide attempt but did not receive intensive intervention. They were, however, provided follow-up at a crisis center as needed. The third and fourth groups received no follow-up care of any type and served as controls, with the third receiving initial intervention in the emergency room and the fourth no initial intervention.

The findings are compromised by the fact that the intervention was poorly defined in both content and application. What actually was done is highly questionable. Further, the experimental and comparison groups were not comparable at intake, a confound that renders interpretation of results questionable if not impossible. Also, the follow-up period was inordinately brief, rendering the results of limited practical value. Finally, standardized outcome measures were not used, there was a relatively high attrition rate (37%), suicide intent was not assessed at intake and prior to randomization, and no exclusion criteria were stated. In light of the brief follow-up period noted and the considerable methodological problems cited, the findings reported by Termansen and Bywater (1975) have questionable utility and practical application.

Similar to the goal of Termansen and Bywater (1975), van Heerigan et al. (1995) explored the use of home visits by a community nurse in enhancing treatment compliance and reducing subsequent attempts in comparison to *usual outpatient care* (i.e., without home visits targeting treatment compliance). The intervention was fairly simple in nature and described as the following: "during the home visits reasons for noncompliance were assessed, needs for treatment evaluated and identified needs matched with the supply of outpatient treatment" (p. 964). Findings revealed better treatment compliance among those in the experimental group and, although not significant, at 1 year after the initial attempt a favorable trend ($p = .056$) was noted in the reduction of subsequent attempts. Although the attrition rate was 24%, the study was relatively well designed for its stated purpose, posing no severe methodological problems that would undermine the fundamental conclusions noted. The study did, however, exclude the highest-risk cases, limiting the utility of the findings. Additionally, the *mechanism of action* for the home visits was not interpretable. The actual nature of the intervention during the home visits was not directed by a standard protocol, nor were intervention process variables and related data collected. As a result, we are left to conclude that home visits improved compliance, but we can only speculate as to how or why.

In another relatively well-designed study, Morgan, Jones, and Owen (1993) found that improved ease of access to 24-hour emergency services over the period of a year following a first attempt significantly reduced subsequent attempts among those in the experimental group relative to those receiving *management as usual after an attempt* (i.e., ranging from inpatient psychiatric admission to referral back to the primary care physician). In somewhat elegant fashion, improved ease of access was accomplished simply by giving the patient a green card with emergency numbers and encouragement to seek services early in a crisis by going to either the emergency room, calling by telephone, or seeking emergency admission. The authors hoped to target the specific problem of low treatment compliance among first-time attempters. Interestingly and paradoxically, they also found that this simple procedural change significantly reduced service demand in the experimental group. Perhaps the primary limitation of the study was the fact that it targeted first-time attempters, excluding the highest-risk group, that is, those making multiple attempts and experiencing chronic suicidality.

Among negative intervention findings, Motto (1976) found that simple follow-up letters and phone calls to those refusing treatment after presenting in crisis did not reduce suicide rates over a 4-year follow-up period, although a favorable trend was observed. This finding is not particularly surprising. Actually, what is surprising is that an encouraging trend was noted after 4 years, with fewer suicides among those receiving the simple follow-up contacts. Litman and Wold (1975) found that telephone calls, home visits, and *befriending contacts* (i.e., what was termed "continuing relationship maintenance") by crisis volunteers did not reduce the frequency of suicide attempts in the experimental group over a period of 24 months, despite an improvement in *quality of life*. Litman and Wold (1975) were careful to note that "the service was not considered therapy" (p. 531). Although negative, the findings reported by Litman and Wold are compromised by considerable methodological problems and, as a result, are questionable if not simply uninterpretable. Among the problems are the following: (1) a poorly defined intervention in type, duration, content, frequency, and monitoring; (2) acknowledgment of considerable overlap between the experimental and control conditions approaching equivalence and nullifying the results; (3) integration of "individual and group meetings" (p. 531) in the intervention group raising questions about the actual provision of *therapy*; (4) failure to define and implement uniform inclusion criteria for *high-risk*; (5) no stated exclusion criteria; and (6) lack of standardized outcome measures.

As with the above, the negative findings reported by Waterhouse and Platt (1990) are also questionable. The stated purpose of the study was to evaluate the utility of simple and brief medical hospitalization (i.e., with no psychiatric care of any type provided) by nonpsychiatric staff at reducing subsequent attempts over the next 4 months. The control group was simply discharged to their homes. The average duration of the hospitalization for those in the experimental group was less than a day (i.e., 17 hours), and so it is not surprising that no subsequent differences were observed in attempts between groups. The two groups were essentially comparable. Additionally, the study targeted only those identified as low risk (i.e., "further suicidal risk was assessed as low," p. 237), raising questions as to the actual utility of the finding for clinical practice.

As is evident from the above discussion, the intervention studies available allow for only a few tentative conclusions regarding interventions involved in the psychotherapeutic treatment and clinical management of suicidal patients. Clearly there is a considerable gap in the literature when it comes to what interventions are helpful with those at highest risk, that is, chronic multiple attempters. Among the conclusions with empirical support are the following:

1. Intensive follow-up, case management, telephone contacts, or home visits may improve treatment compliance over the short term for lower-risk cases.
2. Improved ease of access (i.e., a clearly stated *crisis plan*) to emergency services can potentially reduce subsequent attempts and service demand by first-time suicide attempters.

A CRITICAL REVIEW OF TREATMENT STUDIES: AN EMERGING TREND FOR COGNITIVE-BEHAVIORAL THERAPY

The treatment studies ($n = 14$) available addressing suicidality can be divided into two broad categories: those providing short-term treatment (i.e., less than 6 months, $n = 12$), and those providing longer-term therapy (i.e., 6 months or greater, $n = 2$). Of the total, the results have been decidedly mixed, with eight rendering positive results about the efficacy of the treatment and six rendering negative results. However, among those with positive findings, the results are fairly consistent. Among the short-term studies, the majority ($n = 8$) offered some variant of a cognitive-behavioral therapy (CBT), each integrating a problem-solving component in some form or fashion as a *core intervention*. This is not particularly surprising given that CBT is perhaps the approach most amenable to a brief format. The duration of treatment varied across the CBT studies but ranged from a low of only 10 days (Liberman & Eckman, 1981) to a high of 3 months (Gibbons, Butler, Urwin, & Gibbons, 1978). Note that two of the studies actually used the same sample (Rudd et al., 1996; Joiner et al., 1998), resulting in a total of seven unique study samples on which to base conclusions about the efficacy of time-limited CBT (i.e., with a problem-solving *core component*) for suicidality.

Of the remaining four studies that fall within the brief treatment category, three explored the utility of what can be best described as an *additive component* to treatment as usual, that is, intensive follow-up care of some type, rather than the specific treatment modality (Chowdhury, Hicks, & Kreitman, 1973; Hawton et al., 1981; Welu, 1977). These studies cannot be classified as intervention studies, however, given the impossibility of differentiating the intervention from the actual treatment since the two were inextricably intertwined. One explored the impact of improved *continuity of care* on subsequent suicide attempts (Moeller, 1989).

Of those studies addressing what was essentially an additive component to short-term treatment, that is, more intensive follow-up, results were fairly negative. Both studies targeting intensive short-term follow-up utilizing a combination of home visits, telephone contact, and more frequent and flexible routine treatment appointments found no appreciable impact on subsequent attempts over periods ranging from 6 to 12 months (Gibbons et al., 1978; Hawton et al., 1981). Hawton et al. (1981), not surprisingly, found that home visits did improve treatment compliance, in contrast to those receiving weekly outpatient care. Improved compliance did not, however, translate to a reduction in subsequent attempts over the 12-month follow-up period (i.e., 10% with subsequent attempts for those receiving home visits vs. 15% for traditional outpatients). Similarly, Chowdhury et al. (1973) found that home visits, more frequent outpatient appointments, and improved access to emer-

gency services did not reduce subsequent attempts among multiple attempters in contrast to treatment as usual. Those receiving the experimental intervention did, however, report an improved psychiatric and
social status. Not surprisingly, Moeller (1989) found that efforts to improve the continuity of care by ensuring the same clinician before and
after hospitalization had no appreciable impact on suicide attempts during the year-long follow-up period.

In contrast to the above, Welu (1977) found, in a well-designed
study, that more intensive follow-up using home visits, telephone contact, and more frequent routine treatment appointments (i.e., utilizing a
broad range of therapeutic approaches) did in fact reduce subsequent
attempts in the experimental group over the 4-month follow-up period.
The results are limited, however, by the very brief nature of follow-up
monitoring. Interestingly, of the three studies addressing more intensive
follow-up as an additive component to treatment as usual, the two with
negative results purposefully excluded high-risk patients (i.e., as defined
by factors such as a history of multiple attempts, active psychiatric treatment or diagnosis, or comorbid problems). The one study that included,
and actually targeted high-risk cases was that of Welu (1977). The pattern of results might well suggest that more intensive outpatient treatment, irrespective of approach, is most appropriate and effective for
those identified as high risk, as indicated by psychiatric diagnosis, a history of multiple attempts, or comorbidity.

Of the long-term treatment studies, one evaluated the efficacy of
dialectical behavior therapy (DBT; Linehan, Armstrong, Suarez, Allmon, & Heard, 1991) and the other appraised the role of more intensive
long-term follow-up care cutting across multiple therapeutic approaches
rather than a specific therapy model (Allard, Marshall, & Plante, 1992).
In summary, out of the total of 14 studies addressing treatment outcome, only 8 actually evaluated the efficacy of a specific therapy.

As mentioned above, for the studies evaluating the efficacy of brief
cognitive-behavioral approaches, integrating a *core* problem-solving
component, results were fairly uniform, with six of eight rendering positive findings. Although differences were not found with respect to suicide attempts, results indicated reductions in suicidal ideation (Liberman & Eckman, 1981; Salkovkis, Atha, & Storer, 1990; Joiner et al.,
1998) and related symptomatology, such as depression (Lerner & Clum,
1990; Liberman & Eckman, 1981; Salkovkis et al., 1990), hopelessness
(Lerner & Clum, 1990; Patsiokas & Clum, 1985), and loneliness (Lerner

& Clum, 1990) over follow-up periods ranging from 3 months to 1 year. Interestingly, several of these studies specifically targeted the highest-risk cases, that is, multiple attempters (i.e., Joiner et al., 1998; Liberman & Eckman, 1981; Rudd et al., 1996; Salkovkis, Atha, & Storer, 1990). Additionally, the study by Salkovkis et al. (1990) found a reduction in attempts at 6 months, but the findings were not maintained over the full year of follow-up.

The two studies rendering negative findings found no reductions in suicide attempts during 9- to 12-month follow-up periods (Gibbons et al., 1978; Hawton et al., 1987). As with a number of the other studies, both excluded those at highest risk for subsequent attempts. Additional problems for both studies, which raise questions about the findings, included poorly defined treatments that did not appear to be applied in a uniform manner. Actually, in Hawton and colleagues' (1987) study, less than 50% of the experimental group actually completed treatment, but nonetheless subsequent comparisons included *nonattenders* and *dropouts*, seriously confounding the results. Those that did not successfully complete the treatment would more than likely appear comparable to the controls, rendering interpretation of the results problematic, if not impossible.

In terms of long-term treatment, the results were mixed. Linehan et al. (1991) demonstrated efficacy of DBT in reducing subsequent attempts and hospital days, and improving treatment compliance over a 1-year follow-up period. No differences were found between DBT and treatment as usual, however, with respect to depression, hopelessness, suicidal ideation, or reasons for living. Her results, along with those of Rudd et al. (1996), suggest that outpatient treatment of high-risk suicidal patients is not only safe but can be effective when acute hospitalization is available. In contrast, Allard et al. (1992) did not find a reduction in subsequent attempts at 24 months, but they utilized a mixture of therapeutic approaches, leaving some questions as to the nature of the specific treatment provided as well as methodological concerns about uniformity of application. Essentially, there were questions as to whether all subjects received a uniform intervention and treatment that could be reasonably evaluated, rendering interpretation of findings questionable.

As with the intervention studies reviewed, available results allow only a few conclusions. They are, nonetheless, important and provide an emerging scientific foundation to the treatment of suicidality. The following conclusions have adequate support in the existing literature:

1. Intensive follow-up treatment following an attempt is most appropriate and effective for those identified as high risk, as indicated by multiple attempts, psychiatric history, and diagnostic comorbidity.

2. Short-term CBT, integrating problem solving as a *core intervention*, is effective at reducing suicidal ideation, depression, and hopelessness over periods of up to 1 year. Such brief approaches do not appear effective at reducing attempts over much longer time frames.

3. Reducing suicide attempts requires longer-term treatment and treatment modalities targeting specific skill deficits, such as emotion regulation, poor distress tolerance (i.e., impulsivity), anger management, and interpersonal assertiveness, as well as other enduring problems such as interpersonal relationships and self-image disturbance (i.e., personality disorders).

4. High-risk suicidal patients can be safely and effectively treated on an outpatient basis if acute hospitalization is available and accessible.

UNANSWERED QUESTIONS: RECOGNIZING THE LIMITATIONS OF SCIENCE

Appendix 3.2 summarizes available findings across the three categories referenced earlier: intervention studies, short-term treatment, and long-term treatment. As provided in that appendix, two of the studies were uninterpretable due to serious methodological flaws. Another four studies rendered questionable findings secondary to methodological problems. Of the 20 original studies, 14 provided interpretable results, using sound designs. As indicated, those findings are relatively limited in terms of implications for day-to-day treatment and ongoing clinical management of suicidality.

As stated earlier in this chapter, we can answer only a few of the most fundamental questions raised about the treatment of suicidality. There appears to be an emerging trend for the efficacy of CBT, both over the short and the long term. It appears that CBT, integrating problem solving as a core intervention, is effective at reducing suicidal ideation and related symptoms over the short-term. Reducing attempts appears to require longer-term and more intensive treatment, with a specific focus on skill deficits and related personality dysfunction. Clearly, the most difficult scientific work is ahead of us. Of the questions posed earlier, all are yet to be answered in any definitive manner.

A RESEARCH AGENDA FOR THE FUTURE:
THINKING ABOUT BOTH ENDS OF THE EQUATION

An essential first step in the application of science to the practice of clinical suicidology is the use of a standard nomenclature. Interestingly, however, the issue of conceptualizing treatment outcome and response is seldom discussed with equal fervor. In short, both are critical to a sound research framework. It is vital that we communicate clearly about what we define as *suicidal* and how we identify a *suicide attempt*. That is, the inclusion criteria for the study must be uniformly and operationally defined. Similarly, it is important that we conceptualize treatment response and outcome with equal rigor. More often than not, we fall short with the latter. One of the primary difficulties is that suicidality by definition, at least in its most acute and extreme form, is a time-limited phenomenon. Clearly, some individuals are chronically suicidal. Even those manifesting chronic suicidality, however, are only at *extreme* risk for limited periods of time. This is generally consistent with what Litman (1990) has termed the "suicide zone." As a result of the time-limited nature of suicidality, symptom remission following acute episodes is to be expected. In short, the majority of suicidal patients will *recover*, that is, if we use markers of symptom severity as the outcome measure. This is consistent with what Rudd et al. (1996) described as a possible *ceiling effect* at intake with most acutely suicidal individuals, noting that the normal course is symptomatic recovery. A conceptual scheme that adjusts for this problem is offered below, taking into account both direct and indirect markers of suicidality.

USE OF A STANDARD NOMENCLATURE:
A CRITICAL STARTING POINT

The importance of a standard nomenclature cannot be overstated. The advantages of a standard nomenclature in clinical practice are numerous. Among them are the following: (1) improved clarity, precision, and consistency of a single clinician's practice of risk assessment, management, and treatment both over time for an individual patient and across suicidal patients; (2) improved clarity, precision, and consistency of communication(s) between clinicians regarding issues of risk assessment, ongoing management, and treatment (e.g., in cases where consultations, transfer to another provider, or hospitalization is indicated or necessitated); (3) improved clarity in documentation of suicide risk assessment, clinical decision making, related management decisions, and ongoing treatment; (4) elimination of inaccurate and potentially pejorative terminology (e.g., suicide gesture) from our clinical lexicon; (5) improved communication (and rapport) between the clinician and patient; and (6) elimination of the goal of prediction by recognizing the importance and complexity of implicit and explicit suicide intent in determining ultimate clinical outcome.

O'Carroll et al. (1996) recently proposed a standard nomenclature, offering descriptive terminology that falls into two broad categories: *instrumental behavior* (i.e., zero intent to die with other motivation such as help seeking, punishing others, or attention seeking) and *suicidal acts* (i.e., intent to die). Those definitions that will most frequently be employed in day-to-day clinical practice and related research include the following (O'Carroll et al., 1996, pp. 246–247):

- *Suicide.* Death from injury, poisoning, or suffocation where there is evidence (either implicit or explicit) that the injury was self-inflicted and that the decedent intended to kill himself or herself. *Note:* The term "completed suicide" is often used interchangeably with the term "suicide" (thus making the expression completed suicide unnecessary; for a critique of this term see Canetto, 1997).
- *Suicide attempt with injuries.* An action resulting in nonfatal injury, poisoning, or suffocation where there is evidence (either implicit or explicit) that the injury was self-inflicted and that the person intended at some level to kill him- or herself.
- *Suicide attempt without injuries.* A potentially self-injurious behavior with a nonfatal outcome for which there is evidence (either implicit or explicit) that the person intended at some level to kill him- or herself.
- *Instrumental suicide-related behavior.* Potentially self-injurious behavior for which there is evidence (either implicit or explicit) that the person did not intend to kill him- or herself (i.e., zero intent to die) and wished to use the appearance of intending to kill him- or herself in order to attain some other end (e.g., to seek help, to punish others, or to receive attention). Instrumental suicide-related behavior can occur with injuries, without injuries, or with fatal outcome (i.e., accidental death).
- *Suicide threat.* Any interpersonal action (verbal or nonverbal, stop-

ping short of a directly self-harmful act) that a reasonable person would interpret as communicating or suggesting that a suicidal act or other suicide-related behavior might occur in the near future.

• *Suicidal ideation.* Any self-reported thoughts of engaging in suicide-related behavior.

As discussed above, the use of a standard nomenclature has a number of identifiable advantages for the practicing clinician. Perhaps most important, though, is that the terminology offered is descriptive and observational in nature. The proposed nomenclature is dependent upon three essential elements of suicide-related behavior (e.g., Maris, Berman, Maltsberger, & Yufit, 1992): (1) outcome (i.e., injury, no injury, or death); (2) evidence of self-infliction; and (3) evidence of intent to die by suicide (i.e., both implicit and explicit intent). The recognition of the importance of these elements and their integration into the terminology provides the practicing clinician an opportunity to more clearly document the critical role played by intent. In particular, it serves to acknowledge the variable nature of intent over time, the difficulty of accurately assessing intent under certain conditions (e.g., a purposefully misleading and treatment-resistant patient), and the resultant dilemma and fallacy of reliably predicting a patient's behavior.

Intent is a subjective, personal motivation that is communicated in both implicit and explicit ways. Certainly, patients can tell us what their intent is if we ask them about it during the interview (i.e., explicit or subjective intent). There are, however, other means of assessing intent (i.e., implicit or objective intent) based on behavioral markers. Beck and Lester (1976) originally provided objective and subjective markers of intent, consistent with the conceptualization and nomenclature provided by O'Carroll et al. (1996). Objective markers include characteristics such as timing of the attempt, isolation, precautions taken against discovery, acting to get help, final acts in preparation of death, leaving a suicide note, lethality of method, degree of premeditation and planning, and prior suicide attempts (Beck & Lester, 1976). Subjective markers include not only the expressed purpose of the behavior (i.e., stated intent) but also prior communications, expectations of fatality and expressed understanding of the lethality of the behavior, attitude toward dying, beliefs about the probability of rescue, and reaction to surviving the attempt.

A standard nomenclature serves not only to improve clinical practice but also applicable research efforts (see also Smith & Maris, 1986). More specifically, a standard nomenclature ensures some degree of comparison across studies. In other words, when someone describes a participant as having made a *suicide attempt with injuries*, we can be quite certain about the specific inclusion criteria. If we improve our ability to compare samples across studies with some degree of certainty, then we also need the ability to compare *markers of treatment response* or outcome.

CONCEPTUALIZING TREATMENT OUTCOME AND DEFINING TREATMENT SUCCESS

Treatment outcome for suicidality can be conceptualized in many ways. It is important, however, for a conceptual scheme to represent the complexity inherent to suicidality. Consistent with the definitions offered above, suicide and suicide-related behaviors are just that, behaviors. Accordingly, the only *direct* marker of suicidality is, by definition, a behavioral outcome. In accordance with the framework provided by O'Carroll et al. (1996), this includes suicide attempts and instrumental behaviors. As illustrated in Figure 3.1, both can be further categorized as *with* or *without* injuries.

Consistent with the conceptual and organizational framework provided by Rudd (1998), indirect markers encompass associated symptoms, identified skill deficits, and maladaptive personality traits. For the most part, indirect markers tap into the individual's level of day-to-day functioning, emphasizing those variables with consistent empirical support in the existing literature. Clearly, and in accordance with the available literature, there are strong relationships between many of the direct and indirect markers referenced (e.g., see Rudd & Joiner, 1998, for a review). Associated symptoms include a broad range of those with a proven association to suicidality, including depression, anxiety, hopelessness, suicidal ideation, guilt, panic, shame, anhedonia, attention–concentration impairment, helplessness, and substance abuse. Skill deficits include problem solving, emotion regulation, distress tolerance, anger management, and interpersonal skills (e.g., assertiveness or communicativeness). Maladaptive personality traits are essentially self-explanatory and consistent with the criteria provided in the *Diagnostic and Statistical Manual of Mental Disorders*, 4th ed. (DSM-IV; American Psychiatric Association, 1994).

The importance of a clear conceptual scheme for monitoring treatment outcome cannot be overstated. I have provided what I hope is a simple and straightforward conceptual model to accomplish this goal. One of the primary benefits of such a broad conceptual framework is in the implicit recognition that suicidality is a complex phenomenon. Without a framework that represents this complexity, we lose some of the explanatory power. In all likelihood, indirect markers will evidence change before direct ones. Furthermore, it is expected that symptom measures will almost universally evidence significant change, given what was previously identified as a *ceiling effect* with this population at intake. If lasting change is to occur, then we would expect change in the individual's symptom presentation, identified skills, and ultimately personality traits and extreme behaviors such as suicide attempts or instrumental behaviors. In short, treatment success may not always mean that fewer attempts are made, at least over the short term. As was reviewed previously, few studies found short-term gains when

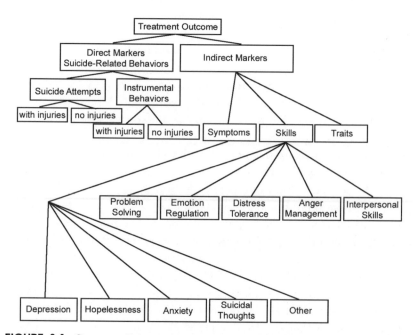

FIGURE 3.1. Conceptualizing treatment outcome. The "Other" category includes guilt, panic, shame, anger, anhedonia, attention–concentration impairment, helplessness, substance abuse, and a sense of immediacy and urgency.

the outcome measure was actual attempts. If an effect was noted, it was not lasting. This may actually be more a problem of conceptualizing outcome, rather than a shortcoming of the treatment approach. More likely than not, behavioral or direct markers of suicidality are long-term outcome goals. Short-term gains are likely to be indirect, such as with symptom remission and improved skills. A reduction in subsequent attempts will probably parallel lasting changes in prominent maladaptive personality traits.

A related concept is defining treatment *success*. How do we identify those that have been successful in treatment? That is, how do we categorize them for comparisons, more refined analysis, and studies exploring treatment response? Do we use direct markers and only consider those that make no additional attempts or engage in no instrumental behavior during the follow-up period? Do we consider those that experience symptom remission to have been successful, particularly given the very nature of suicidal crises and the expectation that symptoms will eventually subside or improve to some degree? Consistent with the above discussion, I recommend the following categorization:

1. *Direct treatment success*—characterized by a significant reduction in subsequent attempts and instrumental behaviors.
2. *Indirect treatment success*—characterized by a significant change in symptom measures, skills, and maladaptive personality traits. Outcome in this category can be analyzed in traditional fashion, identifying treatment responders and exploring clinically significant change (e.g., Borkovec & Costello, 1993; Kendall & Grove, 1988). What is important to note, however, is that these markers are considered *indirect* effects.

Treatment success can be further classified as short term or enduring, with enduring gains lasting for more than a 12-month period. To date, only a few studies have explored enduring treatment effect (e.g., Linehan et al., 1991; Rudd et al., 1996).

ESTABLISHING A RESEARCH AGENDA: FOUR TYPES OF QUESTIONS

The questions raised at the beginning of this chapter can be divided into four broad categories. First are questions that address the overall efficacy and effectiveness of actual treatment approaches. Simply put, *what works* with suicidal patients? This is a relatively straightforward and simple question but one that we have yet to successfully answer. At best, we have a few treatment approaches that are promising but none that meet the rigorous standards necessary to be deemed an *empirically validated treatment*. Second are questions that address the characteristic features of a treatment that make it successful. In other words, what are the *active* components of an identified treatment (i.e., component analysis) or *why does it work?* Third are questions that target how treatment success and outcome are actually defined, that is, *how do we know it works?* The fourth and final type of question addresses the complex issue of treatment matching: *what works best for whom?* The simple truth is that we have yet to answer any of these questions in any definitive manner. We have a limited amount of data at present, some of which lends itself to interpretation but none to particularly defensible conclusions. Now that we know the questions, the real work and challenge of answering them lie ahead.

ACKNOWLEDGMENT

Portions of this chapter are reprinted from Rudd, Joiner, Jones, and King (1999). Copyright 1999 by the American Psychological Association. Reprinted by permission.

REFERENCES

Allard, R., Marshall, M., & Plante, M. (1992). Intensive follow-up does not decrease the risk of repeat suicide attempts. *Suicide and Life-Threatening Behavior, 22*, 303–314.

American Psychiatric Association. (1994). *Diagnostic and statistical manual of mental disorders* (4th ed). Washington, DC: Author.

Beck, A., & Lester, D. (1976). Components of suicide intent in attempted and completed suicide. *Journal of Psychology, 92*, 35–38.

Borkovec, T., & Costello, E. (1993). Efficacy of applied relaxation and cognitive-behavioral therapy in the treatment of generalized anxiety. *Journal of Consulting and Clinical Psychology, 61*, 611–619.

Canetto, S. S. (1997). Gender and suicidal behavior: Theories and evidence. In R. W. Maris, M. M. Silverman, & S. S. Canetto (Eds.), *Review of suicidology, 1997* (pp. 138–167). New York: Guilford Press.

Chowdhury, N., Hicks, R., & Kreitman, N. (1973). Evaluation of an after-care service for parasuicide (attempted suicide patients). *Social Psychiatry, 8,* 67–81.

Gibbons, J., Butler, J., Urwin, P., & Gibbons, J. (1978). Evaluation of a social work service for self-poisoning patients. *British Journal of Psychiatry, 133,* 111–118.

Hawton, K., Bancroft, J., Catalan, J., Kingston, B., Stedeford, A., & Welch, N. (1981). Domiciliary and outpatient treatment of self-poisoning patients by medical and non-medical staff. *Psychological Medicine, 11,* 169–177.

Hawton, K., McKeown, S., Day, A., Martin, P., O'Connor, M., & Yule, J. (1987). Evaluation of outpatient counseling compared with general practitioner care following overdoses. *Psychological Medicine, 17,* 751–761.

Hirsch, S., Walsh, C., & Draper, R. (1983). The concept and efficacy of the treatment of parasuicide. *British Journal of Clinical Psychopharmacology, 15,* 189S–194S.

Joiner, T., Rudd, M. D., & Rajab, M. (1998). *An intriguing interaction between comorbid diagnostic status and treatment type in predicting treatment response among suicidal young adults.* Manuscript submitted for publication.

Kendall, P., & Grove, W. (1988). Normative comparisons in therapy outcome. *Journal of Behavioral Assessment, 10,* 147–158.

Lerner, M., & Clum, G. (1990). Treatment of suicide ideators: a problem-solving approach. *Behavior Therapy, 21,* 403–411.

Liberman, R., & Eckmen, T. (1981). Behavior therapy vs. insight-oriented therapy for repeated suicide attempters. *Archives of General Psychiatry, 38,* 1126–1130.

Linehan, M. M. (1997). Behavioral treatments of suicidal behaviors. In D. M. Stoff & J. J. Mann (Eds.), *The neurobiology of suicide* (pp. 302–328). New York: Annals of the New York Academy of Sciences.

Linehan, M. M., Armstrong, H. E., Suarez, A., Allmon, D., & Heard, H. L. (1991). Cognitive-behavioral treatment of chronically parasuicidal borderline patients. *Archives of General Psychiatry, 48,* 1060–1064.

Litman, R. (1990). Suicides: What do they have in mind? In D. Jacobs & H. Brown (Eds.), *Suicide: Understanding and responding* (pp. 143–156). Madison, CT: International Universities Press.

Litman, R., & Wold, C. (1975). Beyond crisis intervention. In E. Shneidman (Ed.), *Suicidology: Contemporary developments* (pp. 528–546). New York: Grune & Stratton.

Maris, R. W., Berman, A. L., & Maltsberger, J. T. (1992). Summary and conclusions: What have we learned about suicide assessment and prediction? In R. W. Maris, A. L. Berman, J. T. Maltsberger, & R. I. Yufit (Eds.), *Assessment and prediction of suicide* (pp. 640–672). New York: Guilford Press.

Moeller, H. (1989). Efficacy of different strategies of aftercare for patients who have attempted suicide. *Journal of the Royal Society of Medicine, 82,* 643–647.

Montgomery, D. B., Roy, D., & Montgomery, S. A. (1981). Mianserin in the prophylaxis of suicidal behavior: A double-blind placebo-controlled trial. In J. P. Soubrier & J. Vedrinne (Eds.), *Depression and suicide: Proceedings of the 11th International Congress of Suicide Prevention, Paris* (pp. 786–790). Fairview Park, NY: Pergamon Press.

Montgomery, S. A., & Montgomery, D. B. (1982). Pharmacological prevention of suicidal behavior. *Journal of Affective Disorders, 4*, 291–298.

Morgan, H., Jones, E., & Owen, J. (1993). Secondary prevention of non-fatal deliberate self-harm: The green card study. *British Journal of Psychiatry, 163*, 111–112.

Motto, J. (1976). Suicide prevention for high-risk persons who refuse treatment. *Suicide and Life-Threatening Behavior, 6*, 223–230.

O'Carroll, P., Berman, A., Maris, R., Moscicki, E., Tanney, B., & Silverman, M. (1996). Beyond the tower of Babel: A nomenclature for suicidology. *Suicide and Life-Threatening Behavior, 26*, 237–252.

Patsiokas, A., & Clum, G. (1985). Effects of psychotherapeutic strategies in the treatment of suicide attempters. *Psychotherapy, 22*, 281–290.

Rudd, M. D. (1998). An integrative conceptual and organizational framework for treating suicidal behavior. *Psychotherapy, 35*, 346–360.

Rudd, M. D., & Joiner, T. (1998). The assessment, management, and treatment of suicidality: Towards clinically informed and balanced standards of care. *Clinical Psychology: Science and Practice, 5*, 135–150.

Rudd, M. D., Joiner, T., Jones, D. A., & King, C. A. (1999). The outpatient treatment of suicidality: An integration of science and recognition of its limitations. *Professional Psychology: Research and Practice, 30*(5), 437–446.

Rudd, M. D., Rajab, H., Orman, D., Stulman, D., Joiner, T., & Dixon, W. (1996). Effectiveness of an outpatient problem-solving intervention targeting suicidal young adults: Preliminary results. *Journal of Consulting and Clinical Psychology, 64*, 179–190.

Salkovskis, P., Atha, C., & Storer, D. (1990). Cognitive-behavioural problem solving in the treatment of patients who repeatedly attempt suicide: A controlled trial. *British Journal of Psychiatry, 157*, 871–876.

Smith, K., & Maris, R. (1986). Suggested recommendations for the study of suicide and other life-threatening behaviors. *Suicide and Life-Threatening Behavior, 16*, 67–69.

Termansen, P., & Bywater, C. (1975). S.A.F.E.R.: A follow-up service for attempted suicide in Vancouver. *Canadian Psychiatric Association Journal, 20*, 29–34.

van Heeringen, C., Jannes, S., Buylaert, W., Henderick, H., De Bacquer, D., & Van Remoortel, J. (1995). The management of non-compliance with referral to outpatient after-care among attempted suicide patients: A controlled intervention study. *Psychological Medicine, 25*, 963–970.

Waterhouse, J., & Platt, S. (1990). General hospital admission in the management of parasuicide: A randomised controlled trial. *British Journal of Psychiatry, 156*, 236–242.

Welu, T. (1977). A follow-up program for suicide attempters: Evaluation of effectiveness. *Suicide and Life-Threatening Behavior, 7*, 17–30.

APPENDIX 3.1. Description of Psychotherapeutic Treatment and Intervention Studies Targeting Suicidal Behavior

Author(s)	Design	Inclusion/exclusion criteria	Total N (E/C)[a]	Treatment or intervention study[b]: E and C conditions	Treatment or intervention duration	Outcome measures	Follow-up period	Attrition[c]	Results[d]
Chowdhury, Hicks, & Kreitman (1973)	Controlled but not randomized, alternate group (2) assignment including treatment and control.	Included suicide attempters, but excluded those at *high risk* (not clearly *defined*) for future attempts. However, the low-risk nature of the sample is confirmed by the fact that approximately 40% of both the treatment and control groups did not receive a formal psychiatric diagnosis.	155 (71/84)	*Treatment study* (outpatient, individual). The primary goal was to see if more intensive aftercare services (i.e., in addition to normal treatment) for those hospitalized following an attempt would reduce subsequent attempts. An *extension* of routine outpatient services was offered as the experimental condition. E = extension of regular aftercare services including domiciliary (i.e., home) visits and 24-hour emergency service in addition to more frequent outpatient care. Actual content of aftercare treatment was not provided. C = conventional outpatient care, without specific information as to content.	Inpatient treatment duration was not stated; 6-month duration for *aftercare* program. The frequency of visits was not stated for either E or C groups.	Frequency of subsequent attempts, subjective ratings on a *suicidal behavior risk rating scale*, and subjective ratings of *psychiatric* and *social status*. The instruments were not described in any detail, and psychometric properties were not provided. However, it appeared that the ratings were simply subjective in nature.	6 months.	Not provided	Q Results were comparable between E and C conditions on subsequent suicide attempts. The E group had greater improvement relative to C group in *social status* at 6 months. *Psychiatric status* was comparable between the 2 groups. Results are Q due to the following: (1) confound created by excluding *high-risk* cases; (2) lack of a *defined* treatment (i.e., content, frequency) or intervention provided in either group; (3) failure to assess intent in standardized manner to select subjects (i.e., subjectively excluding *high-risk* cases); and (4) lack of psychometrically sound outcome measures. *Conclusions:* No definitive conclusions can be offered.

(continued)

APPENDIX 3.1. (*continued*)

Author(s)	Design	Inclusion/exclusion criteria	Total N (E/C)[a]	Treatment or intervention study[b]: E and C conditions	Treatment or intervention duration	Outcome measures	Follow-up period	Attrition[c]	Results[d]
Termansen & Bywater (1975)	Controlled but not randomized; alternate group (4) assignment including: initial assessment with follow-up *type a*, initial assessment with follow-up *type b*, and assessment with no follow-up and no assessment with follow-up only.	Included suicide attempters presenting to emergency room; no exclusion criteria were stated.	202 (57/57/50/ 38)	*Intervention study* (outpatient, individual). The primary goal of the study was to evaluate if more intensive supportive intervention following an attempt would reduce subsequent attempts. Two types of outpatient intervention were offered, along with 2 control conditions. E1 = assessment in emergency room by mental health worker, follow-up for 3 months by the same worker. E2 = assessment in emergency room by mental health worker, follow-up for 3 months by different *crisis volunteer*. C1 = assessment in emergency room with no follow-up. C2 = follow-up assessment only.	The intervention was described as *not therapeutic* rather *supportive* in nature. Follow-up was poorly defined and variable in frequency and type. It varied from face to face to telephone contact. Minimum contact was defined as daily to every 2 weeks. The duration of follow-up was for a period of 3 months.	Frequency of subsequent attempts and ratings of anxiety, depression, alcohol abuse, among other variables with an instrument that was not described in any detail. Psychometric properties were not provided. The ratings appeared to be simply subjective in nature, made by the *mental health worker*.	3 months	37% (74/202) Rates for each group were: 21% 42% 36% 53%	Q E1 was found to have fewer suicide attempts at follow-up in comparison to C1. Results are seriously confounded and Q due to the following: (1) lack of equivalence between the groups at intake; (2) poorly defined intervention in type (i.e., content) and frequency; (3) failure to assess intent in standardized manner for subject selection; and (4) lack of psychometrically sound outcome measures. *Conclusions:* No definitive conclusions can be offered.

Study	Design	Sample	N	Intervention	Follow-up	Outcome measure	Duration	Attrition	
Motto (1976)	Controlled but not randomized. Self-selected groups.	Self-selected groups, those accepting treatment following psychiatric admission for depression or *suicidal state* and those refusing treatment. Of those refusing treatment, only those accepting *contact* were followed.	3,006 E = 401 C1 = 452 C2 = 1,993 Attrited = 160	*Intervention study* (outpatient, individual). The primary goal was to evaluate if follow-up letters and phone calls to those refusing treatment following a *depressive or suicidal state* would reduce subsequent suicide rates. E = follow-up letters or phone calls. C1 = regular follow-up treatment. C2 = no contact of any type.	5 years; 24 total contacts.	Completed suicide.	5 years.	Not provided.	**I** Results were comparable between E, C1, and C2, although a trend was noted with E having the lowest percentage of suicides after 4 years. For intervention purposes, results are I. *Conclusions:* Follow-up contact can potentially have preventive value.
Litman & Wold (1975)	Random assignment to groups T and C.	*High-risk* callers to a suicide prevention center were assigned to 2 groups. The inclusion criteria were not specifically stated, nor were any exclusion criteria summarized.	400 (200/200)	*Intervention study* (outpatient, individual, potentially some group). The primary goal was to evaluate if intensive supportive intervention would reduce subsequent suicide attempts. The intervention was described as *continuing relationship maintenance*, and it was specifically stated that it *was not considered therapy* (p. 531). E = combination of telephone calls, home visits, and *befriending* contacts. Also individual and group *meetings*.	*Average* of 18 months. Specifics, including range, frequency, and type of intervention were not provided.	Frequency of suicide attempts, completed suicides, frequency of suicide ideation. Various subjective quality of life measures were also used. Psychometric properties of the instruments were not provided.	2 years.	32% (129/400) Not provided for E and C groups separately.	**Q** Results were comparable between E and C groups. E evidenced an improved *quality of life* in contrast to C subjects. Interpretation of the results are limited due to the following: (1) poorly defined intervention both in type and frequency; (2) apparent comparability of intervention provided the 2 groups; (3) failure to define high risk in a standardized way; (4) lack of psychometrically sound outcome measures; and (5) no stated exclusion criteria.

(continued)

APPENDIX 3.1. (continued)

Author(s)	Design	Inclusion/exclusion criteria	Total *N* (E/C)[a]	Treatment or intervention study[b]: E and C conditions	Treatment or intervention duration	Outcome measures	Follow-up period	Attrition[c]	Results[d]
Litman & Wold (1975) (*cont.*)				C = treatment as usual when the person phoned the crisis center, but individual and group follow-up was acknowledged for up to 70% of this group. Although the E intervention was not *considered therapy*, it was described in traditional therapeutic terminology.					*Conclusions:* Intensive follow-up contact can potentially improve overall quality of life.
Welu (1977)	Random assignment to groups.	Suicide attempters were assigned to 2 groups (i.e., intent was addressed, with the author noting a *full gamut of seriousness*). Exclusion criteria were as follows: (1) under age 16; (2) students in college or university housing; (3) individuals living in a care-giving institution (e.g., state hospital); and (4) those institutionalized at the time of the attempt.	120 (63/57)	*Treatment study* (outpatient, individual). The primary goal was to evaluate the effectiveness of a more intensive outpatient treatment program at reducing subsequent suicide attempts. E = special outreach program incorporating home visits and telephone contacts on a weekly or biweekly basis along with traditional psychotherapeutic techniques and approaches. C = treatment as usual including inpatient and outpatient care.	4 months	Frequency of subsequent suicide attempts, excessive use of alcohol, drug use, or *purposive accidents*.	4 months.	Not provided.	E group had significantly fewer attempts at 4-months in comparison to C subjects. E group also had reduced alcohol abuse in comparison to C participants. *Conclusions:* Results are I and provide evidence that an intensive treatment program (with an *outreach* component) for suicide attempters reduces subsequent attempts and alcohol abuse during a brief follow-up period. I

Study	Design	N (E/C)	Sample	Treatment	Length	Measures	Assessment	Attrition	Results	Rating
Gibbons, Butler, Urwin, & Gibbons (1978)	Random assignment to groups.	400 (200/200)	Suicide attempters (i.e., included only attempts by overdose) were assigned to 2 groups. Exclusion criteria were as follows: (1) under age 17; (2) formal *psychiatric illness*; (3) at *high risk* for suicide; and (4) currently in *another treatment*.	*Treatment study* (outpatient, individual). The primary goal was to evaluate the effectiveness of an outpatient treatment at reducing subsequent suicide attempts. E = *task-centered* social work (i.e., crisis intervention for a total of 3 months with a social worker). The E condition was described as *systematic, explicitly time limited, immediately available, and offered in the patient's home* (p. 113). C = *routine* follow-up service including referral back to a general practitioner, psychiatric referral, and *other referral*.	3 months	Frequency of subsequent suicide attempts. Also assessed *changes in depressive mood* (Beck Depression Inventory), *social problems, and satisfaction*.	4 and 12 months	Half (200) were randomly selected for follow-up. Of this, 159 (79%) were assessed. E = 81% C = 78%	E and C groups were comparable with respect to subsequent attempts (at 12 months) and depression (at 4 months). E subjects reported fewer *social problems* at 12 months compared to C. Although the results are I, they are seriously compromised by the exclusion of psychiatric and *high-risk* patients. The resultant sample represents relatively *low-risk* patients with limited *personal and social pathology* (p. 116). Implications for treatment of suicidality are therefore limited. *Conclusions:* Intensive, time-limited follow-up was not effective at reducing attempts among lower-risk patients, although it can lead to fewer social problems.	I
Liberman & Eckman (1981)	Random assignment to groups.	24 (12/12)	Suicide attempters (i.e., multiple attempters) referred to a 10-day inpatient program. Exclusion criteria included the following: (1) psychosis; (2) organic brain syndrome; and (3) alcohol or drug dependence.	*Treatment study* (10-day inpatient program, mixed individual and group). The primary goal was to evaluate the efficacy of brief behavioral therapy in reducing subsequent suicidality.	10 days as inpatient with continuing outpatient aftercare.	Frequency of subsequent suicide attempts, Zung Self-Rating Depression Scale, Beck Depression Inventory (BDI), Fear Survey	Comprehensive assessment at 9 months, with follow-up interview at 24 months to assess	No attrition during follow-up.	E group showed less frequent suicidal thoughts than did C subjects at 9 months. E and C groups were comparable with respect to suicide attempts. E group evidence more comprehensive improvement with respect	I

(continued)

APPENDIX 3.1. (continued)

Author(s)	Design	Inclusion/exclusion criteria	Total N (E/C)[a]	Treatment or intervention study[b]: E and C conditions	Treatment or intervention duration	Outcome measures	Follow-up period	Attrition[c]	Results[d]
Liberman & Eckman (1981) (cont.)				E = behavioral therapy (i.e., social skills training, anxiety management, family negotiation and contingency contracting). C = insight-oriented therapy (i.e., individual therapy, psychodrama, group therapy, and family therapy).		Schedule (FSS), Reinforcement Survey Schedule (RSS), Assertiveness Questionnaire (AQ), and Minnesota Multiphasic Personality Inventory (MMPI)	suicidal ideation and attempts only.		to symptomatology (i.e., BDI, Zung, MMPI, AQ, FSS, RSS) at 9 months in contrast to C subjects. Results are I, but potentially compromised by questions raised about *treatment overlap* and *contamination* (p. 1129). Also, the small sample size limits the impact of the findings. *Conclusions:* Time-limited, intensive behavior therapy was effective at reducing suicidal ideation and related symptomatology over a 9-month follow-up period.
Hawton et al. (1981)	Random assignment to groups.	Suicide attempters by overdose only. Exclusion criteria included the following: (1) under 16 years old; (2) in active psychiatric treatment; (3) living outside of the study area; (4) requiring alcohol or drug treatment; (5) requiring inpatient or	96 (28/28/ 20/20)	*Treatment study* (outpatient, individual). The primary goal was to evaluate the efficacy of a home-based brief problem-oriented treatment at reducing subsequent attempts, varying both setting (domiciliary, i.e., home, and outpatient) and providers (medical vs. nonmedical).	Variable but less than 3 months. For the first 2 months, frequency of visits was not controlled; during the last month, a maximum of 2 sessions was permitted.	Frequency of subsequent attempts, mood (i.e., Lorr & McNair Mood Scale), suicidal ideation, social adjustment (i.e., Social Adjustment Scale), and *target problems*.	12 months	85% (82/96) Not provided for each group separately.	Q No differences were observed between E1, E2, C1, and C2. Results are highly questionable and have limited value for treatment in light of the following: (1) exclusion of psychiatric patients; (2) exclusion of high-risk suicidal patients; (3) poorly defined treatment (i.e., in content); (4) considerable

Study	Assignment	Sample (N)	Treatment	Follow-up	Attrition	Outcome measures	Results
		day treatment; (6) serious suicide risk; (7) *not suitable for random assignment* (e.g., not having a fixed address); and (8) refusal of treatment.	Treatment was provided in a *domiciliary* facility and an outpatient setting. A brief problem-oriented approach was used, and setting and provider were controlled. The treatment approach was the same in all groups. E1 = nonmedical staff in domiciliary setting. E2 = nonmedical staff in outpatient setting. C1 = medical staff in domiciliary setting. C2 = medical staff in outpatient setting.			The psychometric properties of the instruments were not provided.	variability in application of treatment (e.g., frequency of sessions, inclusion of family members or friends in treatment); (5) variable treatment completion rates; (6) inclusion of only those making overdose attempt; and (7) use of questionable outcome instruments. *Conclusions:* Home visits were of limited value in reducing subsequent attempts and ideation for lower-risk suicidal patients in comparison to traditional outpatient care.
Patsiokas & Clum (1985)	Random assignment to groups.	Hospitalized suicide attempters. Exclusion criteria included the following: (1) those with psychosis; (2) alcohol dependence; and (3) drug abuse. 15 (5/5/5)	*Treatment study* (inpatient, individual). The primary goal was to evaluate the efficacy of a brief problem-solving therapy at reducing suicidality. Treatment was inpatient for all three groups and was conducted as individual therapy sessions. E1 = cognitive restructuring. E2 = problem-solving group. C = nondirective control group. A total of 3 weeks, incorporating 10 hour-long sessions.	End of treatment, 3 weeks.	No attrition.	Suicidal ideation (frequency and severity as measured by the Beck Scale for Suicidal Ideation), hopelessness (Beck Hopelessness Scale), and problem-solving (Means-Ends Problem-Solving and Alternate Uses Test).	I Both E1 and E2 conditions and the C group were comparable on measures of suicidal ideation, suicidal intention, and impersonal problem-solving. E2 evidenced improved problem-solving skills relative to E1 and C. Additionally, E2 was less hopeless (but comparable to E1) than those in the C group. Findings are limited due to the lack of follow-up monitoring and small sample size. *Conclusions:* Brief problem-solving therapy can reduce acute suicidality and improve problem-solving over an acute time frame.

(continued)

73

APPENDIX 3.1. (continued)

Author(s)	Design	Total N (E/C)[a]	Inclusion/exclusion criteria	Treatment or intervention study[b]: E and C conditions	Treatment or intervention duration	Outcome measures	Follow-up period	Attrition[c]	Results[d]
Hawton et al. (1987)	Random assignment to groups.	80 (41/39)	Included suicide attempters by overdose only. Additional inclusion criteria were as follows: (1) older than 16 years of age; (2) living within a reasonable distance of the hospital; (3) considered *suitable* for outpatient *counseling;* (4) not in need of formal psychiatric care (i.e., inpatient or day treatment); (5) not currently in treatment; (6) willing to accept treatment. Exclusion criteria were as follows: (1) would not accept help; (2) no indicated need for additional care (e.g., resolution of crisis during hospital stay); (3) currently in other psychiatric treatment; (4) requiring drug or alcohol treatment; and (5) relocation out of the study area.	*Treatment study* (outpatient, individual). The primary goal was to evaluate the efficacy of a brief problem-oriented therapy at reducing subsequent attempts. E = described as a *brief problem-oriented counseling.* Conjoint marital therapy was included when possible. Frequency and duration of treatment were variable, with range and averages not provided. C = general practitioner (GP) care. GP was provided with *recommendations and advice.* The GP potentially referred patients for additional treatment.	Variable, not clearly stated but apparently 2 month duration.	Subsequent suicide attempts, intent (Beck Suicidal Intent Scale, depression (Beck Depression Inventory), social adjustment (Social Adjustment Scale), general health (General Health Questionnaire), and *target problems* (subjective). Psychometric properties of instruments were not provided.	9 months	19% (65/80) For each group rates were: E = 27% C = 10%	UI E and C groups were comparable across all measures. Results are UI and seriously compromised by the fact that only 49% of the E group actually completed treatment and analyses included those that were termed *dropouts* and *nonattenders.* Additional problems included the following: (1) poorly defined treatment; (2) question of comparable treatment and considerable overlap across E and C groups; (3) considerable variability in application of treatment (e.g., frequency of sessions, inclusion of family members in treatment); (4) variable treatment completion rates; (5) inclusion of only those making overdose attempts; and (6) and exclusion of those with psychiatric diagnoses and potentially higher suicide risk. *Conclusions:* None noted given the problems referenced above with the E group.

Moeller (1989)	Random assignment to groups.	Included suicide attempters by overdose only. Exclusion criteria were not stated.	141 (68/73)	*Treatment study* (outpatient therapy following inpatient hospitalization, individual). The primary goal was to evaluate whether continuity of care in brief treatment following hospitalization reduced subsequent attempts and suicidality. E = short-term outpatient therapy by same doctor as during inpatient stay. C = treatment as usual with addition of motivational interviewing.	12 sessions completed within 3 months of discharge.	Frequency of subsequent attempts, treatment compliance.	12 months	4% (5/141) E = 3% C = 4%	E and C groups were comparable with respect to frequency of suicide attempts during follow-up. E did evidence better treatment compliance than C. *Conclusions:* Improved continuity of care did not reduce subsequent attempts during a 12-month follow-up period but did improve treatment compliance with brief treatment.	I
Salkovkis, Atha, & Storer (1990)	Random assignment to groups[a]	Suicide attempters (i.e., multiple attempters) were included. Additional inclusion/exclusion criteria were as follows: (1) between ages 16 and 65; (2) living in geographic region and *in a fixed abode*; (3) *not judged to require immediate psychiatric treatment or would not benefit from the range of treatment options normally available* (p. 871); (4) no psychosis; and (5) no serious organic illness.	20 (12/8)	*Treatment study* (outpatient, individual). The primary goal was to evaluate the efficacy of brief cognitive-behavioral therapy at reducing subsequent attempts and suicidality. Treatment followed a brief inpatient stay. E = cognitive-behavioral problem-solving therapy with home visits. The treatment was not specifically defined.	5 sessions completed over a total of 1 month.	Frequency of subsequent attempts, suicidal ideation (Beck Scale for Suicidal Ideation), depression (Beck Depression Inventory), mood (Profile of Mood States), hopelessness (Beck Hopelessness	12 months	No attrition.	E group evidenced reduced suicidal ideation, depression, hopelessness, and identifiable problems in comparison to C group at 1 year. E group also evidenced fewer attempts at 6 months in comparison to C. Results are limited by a potential confound of a selection bias, essentially consistent with a *chronic group not in acute crisis,* depending on the initial screening and the fact that those requiring *immediate*	I

(continued)

APPENDIX 3.1. (*continued*)

Author(s)	Design	Inclusion/exclusion criteria	Total N (E/C)[a]	Treatment or intervention study[b]: E and C conditions	Treatment or intervention duration	Outcome measures	Follow-up period	Attrition[c]	Results[d]
Salkovskis, Atha, & Storer (1990) (*cont.*)				C = treatment as usual in the outpatient setting.		Scale), and problem solving (Personal Questionnaire Rapid Scaling Technique).			treatment were excluded. Also, the small sample is a problem for generalizing findings. Some concern was raised about *pretreatment* differences between groups. *Conclusions:* Time-limited cognitive behavioral therapy was effective at reducing suicidal ideation and related symptoms among multiple attempters over a 12-month follow-up period relative to treatment as usual. Also, subsequent attempts were reduced for a limited time, that is, 6 months.
Lerner & Clum (1990)	Controlled but not randomized, sequential assignment to groups.	Inclusion criteria were: (1) those experiencing *clinically significant* suicidal ideation and (2) ages 18–24. Exclusion criteria were: (1) evidence of psychosis and (2) substance abuse.	18 (9/9)	*Treatment study* (outpatient, group format). The primary goal was to evaluate the efficacy of brief problem-solving therapy at reducing suicidality. E = problem-solving therapy group C = supportive therapy group.	Both treatments included 10 sessions completed over a period of 5–7 weeks.	Suicidal ideation (Modified Scale for Suicidal Ideation), depression (Beck Depression Inventory), hopelessness (Beck Hopelessness Scale), loneliness (UCLA Loneliness	3 months	Not provided, but appeared to be 17% (15/18) from degrees of freedom in analyses. Not provided	I E and C groups were comparable at treatment completion and follow-up with respect to suicidal ideation. E subjects evidenced less depression and hopelessness in comparison to C at follow-up. Small sample size and clinical composition limit interpretation.

							Follow-up	Attrition	
						Scale, and problem solving (Modified Means-Ends Problem Solving).			*Conclusions:* Brief problem-solving group therapy more effectively reduced depression and hopelessness at 3-month follow-up than supportive group therapy among a small sample of ideators.
									for E and C groups.
Waterhouse & Platt (1990)	Random assignment to groups.	Included suicide attempters by overdose (those that were *assessed as having no immediate medical or psychiatric treatment needs,* p. 237). Exclusion criteria were as follows: (1) suicide attempts by method other than overdose; (2) under age 16; (3) no *fixed abode*; (4) living outside of geographic area; (5) current psychiatric inpatients or other treatment needs; (6) *self-discharges from hospital*; and (7) direct referrals to medical wards.	77 (38/39)	*Intervention study* (outpatient and inpatient, individual). The primary goal was to assess the effectiveness of hospitalization by nonpsychiatric physicians on medical wards for suicide attempters as compared to discharge home. E = hospital admission on medical ward with no psychiatric care provided. C = discharged to home by general physician evaluating them after attempt.	E group was hospitalized for an average of 17 hours with only four participants staying longer than 12 hours. They received *no treatment or counselling* (p. 237). No treatment provided after discharge for C group. The two groups differed only on admission status.	Frequency of subsequent attempts, psychological symptoms (Psychiatric Status Schedule), hopelessness (Beck Hopelessness Scale), and social functioning (Social Behavior Assessment Schedule).	4 months	52% (40/77) E = 47% C = 59%	UI E and C groups were comparable on all measures. **Results** are essentially UI given the following: (1) identified goal of the study (i.e., no treatment provided during hospital stay or discharge home) is unusual; (2) excluded high-risk patients; (3) the average hospital stay was less than one day so the two conditions were essentially identical; and (4) unusually high attrition rates at 4 months. *Conclusions:* None noted given the above problems.

(continued)

Author(s)	Design	Inclusion/exclusion criteria	Total N (E/C)[a]	Treatment or intervention study[b]: E and C conditions	Treatment or intervention duration	Outcome measures	Follow-up period	Attrition[c]	Results[d]
Linehan, Armstrong, Suarez, Allmon, & Heard (1991)	Random assignment to groups.	Inclusion criteria were as follows: (1) met diagnostic criteria for borderline personality disorder; (2) 2 suicide attempts in last 5 years (i.e., multiple attempters), with one during last 2 months; (3) between ages of 18 and 45; and (4) agreed to *study conditions*. Exclusion criterion was a diagnosis of schizophrenia, bipolar disorder, substance dependence, or mental retardation.	44 (22/22)	*Treatment study* (outpatient, concomitant individual and group). The primary goal was to evaluate the efficacy of dialectical behavior therapy (DBT) at reducing subsequent suicide attempts and suicidality. E = DBT. C = treatment as usual, individual therapy.	12 months	Frequency of subsequent attempts, maintenance of therapy, inpatient treatment, depression (Beck Depression Inventory), hopelessness (Beck Hopelessness Scale), suicidal ideation (Scale for Suicide Ideators), and reasons for living (Reasons for Living Inventory).	12 months	No attrition.	I E group had fewer suicide attempts, better maintenance of treatment, and fewer inpatient days in comparison to C subjects. E and C were comparable with respect to depression, hopelessness, suicidal ideation, and reasons for living. Results are compromised by small sample and restriction to patients with borderline personality disorder. *Conclusions:* Severe multiple attempters were safely and effectively treated on a long-term outpatient basis, with reductions in attempts, better treatment compliance, and fewer inpatient days.
Allard, Marshall, & Plante (1992)	Random assignment to groups.	Inclusion criteria were as follows: (1) having been seen in the Emergency Room following a suicide attempt; (2) residing within the catchment area of the hospital; and	150 (76/74)	*Treatment study* (outpatient, individual). The primary goal was to evaluate the efficacy of more intensive *psychosocial* treatment following an attempt at reducing subsequent attempts.	12 months.	Frequency of subsequent attempts.	24 months.	16% (24/150) E = 17% C = 15%	I E and C groups were comparable with respect to suicide attempts during follow-up. The primary limitation of the study is the acknowledged variability of the treatment plan implemented.

Study	Assignment	Sample	N	Method	Follow-up	Measures	Attrition	Results
		(3) speaking French or English. Exclusion criteria were as follows: (1) not having a fixed address; (2) already in separate treatment; (3) presence of a physical handicap preventing attendance; (4) incapacity to give informed consent; (5) sociopathy, with physical threat to hospital personnel; and (6) the attempt dating back more than 1 week.		E = intensive outpatient treatment, with more frequent visits, at least one home visit, reminders by telephone and letters if appointments were missed, and referral for ongoing treatment after the year-long study period was completed. C = treatment as usual.	12 months.		No attrition.	Essentially, E participants did not receive comparable treatment. *Conclusions:* More intensive psychosocial treatment (i.e., utilizing a nonspecific theoretical approach) following an attempt did not reduce subsequent attempts over a 24-month follow-up period.
Morgan, Jones, & Owen (1993)	Random assignment to groups.	Included first-time suicide attempters. Exclusion criteria were not stated, aside from multiple attempters.	212 (101/111)	*Intervention study* (outpatient, individual). The primary goal was to evaluate whether improved ease of access to emergency services would reduce subsequent attempts. E = were provided a *green card* which detailed the availability of emergency services when needed. C = *management as usual* after the attempt.	12 months.	Frequency of subsequent attempts.		1 E group had significantly fewer attempts during follow-up period in comparison to C subjects. They also made fewer demands on psychiatric services. *Conclusions:* Improved ease of access to emergency services reduced subsequent attempts for first-time attempters over a period of 1 year.

(continued)

79

APPENDIX 3.1. (continued)

Author(s)	Design	Inclusion/exclusion criteria	Total N (E/C)[a]	Treatment or intervention study[b]: E and C conditions	Treatment or intervention duration	Outcome measures	Follow-up period	Attrition[c]	Results[d]
van Heeringen et al. (1995)	Random assignment to groups.	Inclusion criteria were as follows: (1) suicide attempters referred from an Emergency Department; (2) age 15 or older; and (3) living in the catchment area of the hospital. Exclusion criterion was need for inpatient treatment.	516 (218/218)	*Intervention study* (outpatient, individual). The primary goals was to evaluate the efficacy of home visits by a community nurse in improving treatment compliance and reducing subsequent suicide attempts. E = home visit by community nurse who explored reasons for noncompliance, treatment needs. C = usual outpatient care following attempt.	2 weeks.	Frequency of subsequent attempts, treatment compliance.	12 months.	24% (125/516)	I E subjects were significantly more compliant with treatment than C group. E = C with respect to frequency of attempts at 1 year, although a favorable trend was apparent for the E subjects. *Conclusions:* Treatment compliance was improved over a 12-month period for suicide attempters by use of home visits within 2 weeks of the original presentation to the Emergency Room.
Rudd et al. (1996)	Random assignment to groups.	Inclusion criteria were as follows: (1) suicide attempt precipitating referral; (2) mood disorder with concurrent suicidal ideation; and (3) episodic alcohol abuse with concurrent ideation. Exclusion criteria were as follows: (1) substance	302 (181/121)	*Treatment study* (outpatient, group). The primary goal was to evaluate the efficacy of a brief outpatient group treatment at reducing subsequent suicidality in comparison to treatment as usual. E = outpatient group treatment (problem-solving oriented). C = treatment as usual.	2 weeks.	Frequency of sub-sequent attempts, suicidal ideation (Modified Scale for Suicidal Ideation, Suicide Probability Scale), depression (Beck Depression Inventory), hopeless-	12 months.	73% (193/264)	I E and C groups were comparable on all measures. E group was more effective at retaining *high-risk* subjects than was C group. Findings are compromised by the nature of the sample (military and young age) and the extremely high attrition rate.

Study	(exclusion criteria)		Measures	Conclusions
Joiner, Rudd, & Rajab (1998)	Same as above.	dependence or chronic abuse requiring separate treatment; (2) psychosis or diagnosed thought disorder; and (3) severe personality disorder in which group treatment was unmanageable.	ness (Beck Hopelessness Scale), life stress (Life Experiences Survey), problem-solving (Problem-Solving Inventory), and personality traits (Millon Clinical Multiaxial Inventory).	*Conclusions:* High-risk suicidal patients were as safely and effectively treated on an intensive outpatient basis as were those given treatment as usual. Problem-solving therapy may be more effective at retaining those at highest risk.
	Same as above.	Same as above.	Same as above.	I E subjects with comorbid depression and anxiety diagnoses evidenced greater reductions in suicidal ideation in comparison to similar C subjects at the 12-month follow-up point. *Conclusions:* The *highest-risk* suicidal patients (i.e., those with comorbidity) were more effectively treated with problem-solving therapy than with treatment as usual.

Note. Studies are listed in chronological order.

[a]E, experimental conditions; C, control conditions.

[b]Inpatient/outpatient, individual/group. Intervention studies have had two identifiable goals: (1) improve treatment compliance; and (2) facilitate access to crisis intervention, supportive, and/or treatment services.

[c]Attrition for the entire sample at the last identifiable follow-up point, expressed as the overall attrition percentage, along with the actual N/total sample size. Attrition for each group is also provided, if available.

[d]I, interpretable; Q, questionable; UI, uninterpretable.

[e]Not considered *therapy or treatment*, described as intervention.

[f]Not considered *therapy or treatment*, described as intervention, although clearly it is described in a fashion consistent with psychotherapy, as well as incorporating individual and group sessions.

[g]Patients were randomly assigned only after it was determined that *treatment would not normally be offered*, potentially consistent with a low-risk group.

APPENDIX 3.2. Summary of Current Findings in the Treatment of Suicidality

Study type	Results[a]	Findings[b]	General implications for treatment/intervention
Intervention studies			
Termansen & Bywater (1975)	Q	+	No definitive conclusions can be offered secondary to methodological problems.
Motto (1976)	I	+	Follow-up can potentially have preventive value over the long term.
Litman & Wold (1975)	Q	−	No definitive conclusions can be offered secondary to methodological problems.
Waterhouse & Platt (1990)	UI	−	Results were uninterpretable due to methodological problems.
Morgan, Jones, & Owen (1993)	I	+	Improved ease of access to emergency services can reduce subsequent attempts for first-time attempters over a period of 1 year.
van Heeringen et al. (1995)	I	−	Home visits can improve treatment compliance following an attempt.
Treatment studies: Short-term			
Chowdhury, Hicks, & Kreitman (1973)	Q	−	No definitive conclusions can be offered secondary to methodological problems.
Welu (1977)	I	+	Intensive time-limited treatment can reduce attempts over brief periods.
Gibbons, Butler, Urwin, & Gibbons (1978)	I	−	Intensive time-limited follow-up can lead to fewer social problems and improved social functioning.
Liberman & Eckman (1981)	I	+	Time-limited behavior therapy can reduce suicidal ideation and related symptoms over enduring periods but is effective at reducing attempts for only brief periods of time.
Hawton et al. (1981)	Q	−	No definitive conclusions can be offered secondary to methodological problems.
Patsiokas & Clum (1985)	I	+	Brief problem-solving therapy can reduce acute suicidality and improve problem-solving skills.

APPENDIX 3.2. (*continued*)

Study type	Results[a]	Findings[b]	General implications for treatment/intervention
Treatment studies: Short-term (*cont.*)			
Hawton et al. (1987)	UI	–	Results are uninterpretable.
Moeller (1989)	I	–	Improved continuity of care from inpatient to outpatient treatment does not reduce suicidality.
Salkovkis, Atha, & Storer (1990)	I	+	Time-limited cognitive-behavioral therapy is effective at reducing suicidal ideation and related symptoms over relatively long periods of time, but attempts are reduced for only brief periods.
Lerner & Clum (1990)	I	+	Brief problem-solving group therapy can reduce suicidal ideation, depression, and hopelessness for brief periods.
Rudd et al. (1996)	I	+	High-risk suicidal patients can be treated safely and effectively with intensive brief outpatient problem-solving therapy.
Joiner, Rudd, & Rajab (1998)	I	+	The highest-risk patients (i.e., comorbid suicidal patients) are more effectively treated with brief problem-solving therapy than with treatment as usual.
Treatment studies: Long-term			
Linehan, Armstrong, Suarez, Allmon, & Heard (1991)	I	+	Severe multiple attempters can be effectively treated in long-term outpatient care, with reductions in suicide attempts, improved treatment compliance, and reduced hospitalization.
Allard, Marshall, & Plante (1992)	I	–	Nonspecific intensive follow-up is not effective at reducing attempts over the long term.

[a]Q, questionable; UI, uninterpretable; I, interpretable.
[b]+, positive findings, –, negative findings.

CHAPTER FOUR

Behavioral Treatments of Suicidal Behaviors
Definitional Obfuscation and Treatment Outcomes

Marsha M. Linehan, PhD

Intentional nonfatal self-injury (otherwise known as parasuicide) includes both suicide attempts and acts without suicide intent and is estimated at about 300 persons per 100,000 population per year for all types of parasuicide (for reviews of prevalence estimates, see Favazza, 1987, and Walsh & Rosen, 1988). In Europe the estimated rate for medically treated parasuicides is 139 per 100,000 for males and 189 for females (Platt et al., 1992). The likelihood of encountering parasuicidal behavior during the course of mental health treatment is especially high when one is treating severely dysfunctional patients. Diagnosis of a DSM axis I disorder is associated with increased risk of both suicide and parasuicide. Although other disorders are associated with suicidal behavior, the most pervasive association is that between suicidal behavior (suicide ideation, suicide attempts, and suicide) and major depression. For example, major depression puts one at increased risk for suicide (for a review, see Tanney, 1992), attempted suicide (Lewinsohn, Rohde, & Seeley, 1994, 1996), and nonsuicidal self-mutilation (Dulit, Fyer, Leon,

Brodsky, & Frances, 1994). Among individuals meeting criteria for any personality disorder, parasuicidal behavior with and without suicidal intent is most prevalent among those meeting criteria for borderline personality disorder (BPD) (Gunderson, 1984; Schaffer, Carroll, & Abramowitz, 1982; Simeon et al., 1992; Zanarini, Gunderson, Frankenburg, & Chauncey, 1990). As many as 69–75% of those with BPD have a history of parasuicide (Clarkin, Widiger, Frances, Hurt, & Gilmore, 1983; Cowdry, Pickar, & Davies, 1985), approximately 1 out of 10 patients with BPD eventually kill themselves (Kroll, Carey, & Sines, 1985; Paris, Brown, & Nowlis, 1987; Stone, 1989), and as many as one-third of patients who meet all eight DSM-III criteria for BPD commit suicide (Stone, 1989). Among patients meeting criteria for BPD, major depression increases the risk of serious suicide attempts (Fyer, Frances, Sullivan, Hurt, & Clarkin), although increased risk of completed suicide has not been demonstrated (Kjelsberg, Eikeseth, & Dahl, 1991; Kullgren, 1988; Paris, Nowlis, & Brown, 1989).

This chapter begins with an overview of the definitional difficulties in this field and then proceeds to an overview of treatment issues and a comprehensive review of treatment studies aiming to reduce suicidal behavior among suicidal individuals. That is, the focus is on tertiary care rather than programs aimed at preventing the emergence of suicide in the first place. To be included in the review, the treatment under investigation had to target suicidal behavior directly and be designed specifically to reduce suicide. The treatment study had to select subjects because they were suicidal and report outcomes on suicide ideation, parasuicidal acts, including suicide attempts and/or suicide. There are a huge number of uncontrolled studies of treatments for suicidal individuals, from case studies to large sample longitudinal follow-up studies. They are not included inasmuch as designs without a comparison condition offer little information about the efficacy of a treatment. I could find no well-controlled single-subject experimental designs.

Studies without random assignment to condition, or a close approximation to randomization, are also not included. Without random assignment, any findings are essentially correlational. To determine whether any treatment gains are due to the experimental treatment, an experimental design is required. In addition, without randomization, extraneous factors, such as subject, therapist, or program characteristics, simply cannot be ruled out as important influences on outcome. Twenty studies are discussed. Eighteen studies randomly assigned subjects to the experimental and control condition; the other two assigned subjects in an alternating sequential fashion. Although in neither of the latter two studies did the authors suggest that the first subject was assigned randomly, they are very close to a randomized design. Studies were located by searching *Psychological Abstracts, MEDLINE,* and the archives of the Suicide Information and Education Centre located in Calgary, Alberta, Canada. All published studies meeting the above inclusion criteria were selected for review. Unpublished dissertation research was not included, although there were several listed in *Psychological Abstracts.*

DEFINITIONAL OBFUSCATION

One problem in research on nonfatal self-injury is the confusion resulting from the numerous terms used to refer to this behavior and the failure to define the terms precisely, if at all. Some investigators label all intentional self-injurious behavior not resulting in death as "suicide attempts." At times the use of the term "suicide attempt" is not even associated with intent to die. For example, Velamoor and Cernovsky (1992) report that of 96 individuals admitted to a general hospital for a suicide attempt (their term) by means of self-poisoning, 17.7% carried out their attempt with the intent not to die. Others (e.g., Brent, 1987; and Lewinsohn et al., 1996) report that among adolescent suicide attempters (defined by Lewinsohn and colleagues as "self-inflicted behaviors intended to result in death," p. 26), approximately one-fourth report no intent to die and only about a third of those seen in an emergency room state that they had wanted to die (Brent, 1987, referenced in Lewinsohn et al., 1996). It is difficult to know what is meant by a suicide attempt with no intent to die. Such terminology mislabels the large number of people that injure themselves without intending to die (cf. Linehan, 1986).

When referring specifically to intentional self-injurious behavior without accompanying intent to die, ambiguous terminology is more the rule than the exception. In the absence of a generally accepted term, investigators often label the behavior under study by its form or method (e.g., self-mutilation, overdosing, self-poisoning) or simply by the general terms "self-injury" or "self-harm." Although these terms do not explicitly state that the behavioral act and resulting bodily injury or harm are intentional, the context generally implies an assumption that the behavior and outcome consequences are not accidental. In clinical environments, unfortunately, the term "self-harm" is also frequently used to refer to any behavior pattern that results in psychological or physical harm to the individual, including driving fast and staying in abusive relationships. This further obscures the meaning of the term.

As can be seen in Tables 4.1–4.4 (see pp. 95–103), efforts to actually measure suicide intent are more the exception than the rule in research on nonfatal suicide attempts. Instead, investigators often use the topography (i.e., overt form of behavior or self-injury method) and circumstances (e.g., alone or with others) to infer psychological intent, with little or no effort to actually measure intent to die (i.e., suicide intent) in a systematic and reliable manner. Thus, for example, clinicians or researchers may assume that all self-mutilation is intended solely to mutilate (and often manipulate others) rather than cause death. Or they may assume that all overdoses taken in the near vicinity of another individual are suicide "gestures" (i.e., behaviors where the intent is to gesture or communicate with others rather than to die). Other investigators infer intent based on the medical (e.g., medical treatment and/or physical condition) and social (e.g., reinforcing interpersonal reactions, avoidance of situations) consequences of the behavior, as if intended outcomes and actual outcomes of behavior are so strongly associated that independent assessment of intent is unnecessary—an unwarranted assumption.

Given the difficulties in the field arriving at a consensus on how to measure or infer intent to die during deliberate self-injurious acts, Kreitman (1977) coined the term "parasuicide" to refer to all nonfatal self-injurious behavior with clear intent to cause bodily harm or death (i.e., both the behavioral act and the injurious outcomes are not accidental) that results in actual tissue damage, illness, or risk of death or serious injury. In the ongoing multinational WHO/Euro parasuicide epidemiological monitoring studies, parasuicide is defined as "an act with nonfatal outcome, in which an individual deliberately initiates a non-habitual behaviour that, without intervention from others, will cause self-harm, or deliberately ingests a substance in excess of the prescribed or generally recognized therapeutic dosage, and which is aimed at realizing changes which the subject desired via the actual or expected physical consequences" (Platt et al., 1992, p. 99).

Platt et al. (1992) go on to say, "It should be noted that the apparent purpose of motivation underlying the act was not taken into account when making the [parasuicide] diagnosis" (p. 99). Parasuicide, then, is a heterogeneous category that includes self-injurious behavior with intent to die (a suicide attempt) as well as behavior without intent to die (e.g., putting out a cigarette on one's arm with no thought of dying). Although it represents an inaccurate reading of the actual definition as proposed by Kreitman (1977) and used by major researchers in the field, many clinicians in the United States (e.g., Lewinsohn et al., 1996, and Sederer, 1994) understand the term parasuicide as limited to intentional self-injury that is not a suicide attempt. This is probably because there is no agreed-upon term for nonsuicidal but otherwise intentional self-injury to parallel the terms "suicide attempt" or "ambivalent suicide attempt." Unfortunately, the misuse of the term in this manner simply confounds the interpretability of research on suicidal behavior. Definitional ambiguity and vagueness in a field of study, especially when it is as rampant as in the area of suicidal behavior, has at least two major negative consequences. First, heterogeneous definitional practices make it almost impossible to compare findings across studies of parasuicidal individuals. This is of course made much worse by the fact that so few investigators actually define their terms operationally. Second, the tendency to use terms that implicitly (at least) imply intent to die (e.g., suicide attempt) or absence of intent to die (e.g., deliberate self-injury), in the absence of any reliable or valid assessment of actual intent, confounds intent and action and can lead investigators to falsely classify behavior as not suicidal when it is and as suicidal when it is not. A field of inquiry simply cannot grow without clear and precise definitions of the variables one is investigating.

When behavioral and outcome intent can be reliably assessed, they can be useful as a means of discriminating the class of behaviors that are suicide attempts (i.e., deliberate self-injury with moderate-to-high intent to die) from the class of acts with either no or very low intent to die (see Linehan, 1986, for a review of this point). The absence of reliable and valid measurement of behavioral intent can lead to research findings that are unnecessarily confounded by high heterogeneity of the subject pool and difficult to interpret. The importance of measuring intent, independent of medical seriousness, is suggested by data collected as part of the multinational WHO/Euro parasuicide studies. Verbal reports (either spontaneously or following questioning) of an intent to die following a parasuicide episode predicted suicide but not repetition of parasuicide during the next 12 months, even when medical seriousness of the parasuicide and a report of psychiatric problems were controlled (Hjelmeland, 1996). Similar results were found by Lönnqvist and Ostamo (1991; also Ostamo et al., 1991) when analyzing the number of suicides following a first suicide attempt within at a 5-year follow-up point.

Behavioral intent, however, can be quite difficult to measure. For example, during a specific intentional self-injurious act a substantial minority of individuals may be thinking about suicide (and even wanting to suicide) while simultaneously expecting not to die (Gardner & Gardner, 1975; Pattison & Kahan, 1983). As noted above, individuals may come to the emergency room for a purported suicide attempt and then say that they had no actual intent to die. In a study in our clinic with suicidal women meeting criteria for BPD, all endorsed intent for multiple outcomes even when "to die" was the primary intended outcome (Brown & Linehan, 1996). The good news is that we have found that, when interviewers are well trained and use a structured interview format, they can be quite reliable judges of suicide intent. In data analyses of the Parasuicide History Interview, intraclass interrater reliabilities in estimating suicidal intent have typically been over .80 (Linehan, Heard, Wagner, & Brown, 1997).

An additional source of obfuscation is the repetitive nature of parasuicide in some individuals. In the general population sample investigated by the WHO/Euro studies, 1-year parasuicide repetition rates varied from a low of 1.03 to 1.30 within a 1-year time frame. Repetition rates can be considerably higher in some diagnostic groups, such as patients with BPD (Linehan, Armstrong, Suarez, Allmon, & Heard, 1991). Among individuals who repeat parasuicide, there may be considerable cooccurrence of different types of parasuicidal behaviors within a single individual over time. That is, although actions can be labeled, individuals often cannot be. In a sample of women meeting criteria for BPD with chronic parasuicidal behavior or current drug abuse and entering treatment in our research clinic, 71% had both cut and burned themselves and had parasuicided using another method at least once in the past year (none had only cut or burned themselves), and almost 80% reported both in their lifetime (Brown & Linehan, 1996). In a sample of 10 women with suicide attempts severe enough to require inpatient medical treatment, 9 also had one or more nonmedically serious parasuicidal acts (Linehan et al., 1997). In a sample of (nonsuicidal) self-mutilating adolescents, 31% had made a serious suicide attempt close to the time of self-mutilation (Walsh, 1987).

TREATMENT DEVELOPMENT AND EVALUATION: IMPEDIMENTS TO RESEARCH

In almost all treatment studies addressing mental disorders of any kind, potential subjects who are judged at high risk for suicide are rejected at screening or are dropped from ongoing treatments. Exclusion is generally based on the belief that randomization of highly suicidal individuals to treatment condition is unethical, or—at a minimum—too risky. This belief, in turn, is based on an assumption that we actually know that some interventions, or the prevailing standards of care, are better than other interventions for this population. The problem here is very much like the problems that have arisen because of the exclusion of pregnant women from clinical trials of almost all drugs. The exclusion has led to a paucity of information about how to treat pregnant women and is a policy now under fire from many quarters. Similarly, the exclusion of highly suicidal individuals from most controlled clinical trials of pharmacotherapy and behavioral interventions has led to a lack of information about how to treat individuals at high risk for suicide and/or parasuicide.

There are clearly a lot of reasons for the paucity of research on suicide. The first is the traditional faith in standards of care independent of hard experimental data demonstrating effectiveness. Although it is easy to experiment with standards of care in the abstract, it is considerably more difficult in the individual case. In contrast to other life-and-death disorders such as cancer, treatment researchers, funding agencies, and universities appear unwilling to take the chance that a patient might die by suicide. Part of this is due to a legal system that holds individual practitioners, including those practicing within a research context, to the prevailing community standards of care. That much of the time those standards are based on dogma rather than on empirical evidence may not sway the average jury. In a sense, we in the clinical field have been too successful in getting the public at large, including the legal system, to believe that our collective clinical judgment is, in fact, the best basis for decision making even when the data on clinical judgment suggest that it is an extremely fallible basis for clinical predictions.

A different impediment is the difficulty in getting research funding for treatment studies that do not address a specific mental health diagnosis. The belief in the United States, in particular, that suicidal behavior is a symptom of some other disorder is so strong that studies of suicidal behavior independent of a related mental disorder are hard to fund, hard to mount, and hard to publish. The exception here is suicide primary prevention efforts where there have been a number of requests for research proposals issued by the National Institute of Mental Health over the years. This volume promises to begin to turn this state of affairs around by focusing on suicidal behavior as a behavior that may be associated with, but not caused by, other mental health disorders.

REDUCING SUICIDAL BEHAVIORS: WHAT SHOULD TREATMENT TARGET?

All treatment interventions attempt to change or ameliorate the factors that are presumed to underlie or control the problem behaviors or symptoms of the patient. How that is done, however, varies widely across treatments. There are two basic strategies for treating suicidal behaviors in clinical populations. The first strategy assumes that suicidal behaviors are a symptom of some other underlying mental disorder. Treatment time and focus are allocated to treating the mental disorders presumably related to suicidal behavior in the belief that their cure will lead to reductions in suicidal behaviors. Except to maintain life, no special modifications are made in the treatment of the underlying disorder. Reductions in suicidal behaviors are an indirect benefit of therapy. This approach is the model underlying most psychodynamic and biological approaches to treatment. The second strategy is to target the reduction of suicidal behaviors directly. Reduction of suicidal behaviors is an explicit treatment goal and target of intervention. In behavioral approaches, the therapy session agenda engages the patient in a discussion of current and immediately past suicidal behaviors, including suicide ideation, threats, and communications, as well as parasuicide episodes, and explicit connections are made to presumed underlying or controlling factors. In biological approaches, the selection of medications is based on remediating biological patterns believed to be specific to suicidal behavior. This approach assumes that suicide ideation, suicide risk, and parasuicidal acts can be reduced independently of other disorders and is the approach favored by crisis intervention and behavior therapists. The belief that there are specific biological parameters associated with suicidal behavior is the basis for this book. The promise is that once these are discovered, it will be possible to develop specific antisuicide drugs. Suicidal behaviors are also targeted directly by almost everyone during emergencies, that is, when suicide or parasuicidal behavior is imminent.

TREATING SUICIDAL BEHAVIORS INDIRECTLY BY TREATING ASSOCIATED DISORDERS

Unfortunately, data are very sparse regarding which treatments (if any) for primary mental disorders actually reduce the risk for suicide and parasuicide. The exclusion of highly suicidal individuals notwithstanding, investigators frequently include measures of suicidal behaviors in their outcome battery. Because studies consistently find that affective disorders are the most common diagnoses related to suicide, most attention has been given to the effect of treating depression on subsequent suicidal behaviors, the assumption being that effective treatment of depression will reduce the incidence of suicide. Although this assumption makes intuitive sense, there are actually no empirical data from controlled trials to back up the assumption. Pharmacotherapy regimes that are more effective than placebo for reducing depression may or may not be more effective in reducing suicide ideation (e.g., Beasley et al., 1992; and Smith & Glaudin, 1992). To date, there are no data that antidepressants reduce the incidence of either parasuicide or suicide. Buchholtz-Hansen, Wang, and Kragh-Sorensen (1993) followed 219 depressed inpatients who had previously been participants in psycho-pharmacological multicenter trials. Not only were suicide rates higher than expected at follow-up, but there was no association between response to the antidepressant treatment in the trial and the suicide risk during the first 3 years of observation. Meta-analyses of clinical trial data in studies of fluoxetine and tricyclic antidepressants in the treatment of depressed individuals show no significant reductions in suicidal acts as a result of taking such antidepressants (Beasley et al., 1992). The reason these studies failed to demonstrate an effect on suicidal acts may be because of the very low base rate of suicidal acts in studies where actively suicidal individuals were not enrolled. Looking at the relationship of reducing depression to reducing suicidal behavior from the reverse direction, Linehan et al. (1991) showed that a cognitive-behavioral therapy that resulted in a significant reduction in parasuicide repeat rates compared to treatment as usual did so despite being no more effective in reducing depression or hopelessness than the control condition. (Depression and hopelessness improved in both treatments.) A similar finding was reported by Sakinofsky, Robin, Brown, Cumming, & James (1990), who found that improvement in depression, hostility, locus of control, powerlessness, self-esteem, sensitivity to criticism, and social adjustment, measured following a parasuicide episode, was not related to reduced risk for repeated parasuicide over the next 3 months.

TREATING SUICIDAL BEHAVIORS DIRECTLY

Despite the frequency of suicide and parasuicide (including suicide attempts) among those with mental disorders, especially those in treatment, and the high therapist stress and legal liability associated with such behaviors, there is remarkably little research on whether therapeutic interventions aimed directly at reducing suicide risk and parasuicidal behaviors are effective in achieving these aims. There are many books, articles, professional workshops, and legal precedents dictating treatment of suicidal behaviors, but very few of the recommended or required interventions have been subjected to controlled clinical trials. Thus, although there are standards of care for intervening with individuals at high risk for suicidal acts, there are little or no empirical data confirming that these standards of care are effective in preventing suicide or reducing the frequency or medical severity of parasuicidal acts.

Although hopelessness, depression, and other problems in living may be vulnerability factors for suicidal behavior in some individuals, it is obvious that they are neither sufficient nor always necessary for suicidal behavior to occur. Suicide and parasuicide are not inevitable responses to severe depression and hopelessness. Thus, it may be that treatments will be more efficient, and possibly more effective, if they target first the suicidal individual's response to events causing suicide (including depression) rather than the events or psychopathology itself. In surveying the literature on direct treatments of suicidal behavior, I have been able to locate 20 controlled clinical trials where subjects were selected for study due to suicidality (18 following a parasuicide episode, 2 following assessment of high risk for suicide). Characteristics of these studies are outlined in Tables 4.1–4.4.

As can be seen in those tables, inclusion criteria, treatment setting, and length and extensiveness of the interventions examined are highly variable. For example, two interventions involved no in-person contact, relying on letters or phone calls only (Litman & Wold, 1976; Motto, 1976), whereas two other studies were conducted wholly within psychiatric inpatient settings (Liberman & Eckman, 1981; Patsiokas & Clum, 1985). Of the studies examining the effectiveness of counseling or psychotherapy, the briefest treatment was 8 days (Liberman & Eckman, 1981) and the longest was 1 year (Linehan et al., 1991). There are 13 studies examining outpatient psychosocial interventions, 2 studies examining inpatient psychosocial interventions, 3 pharmacotherapy studies, and 2 studies with nonhospitalized high-risk individuals that did not involve in-person contact.

Eight of the studies examined whether or not some type of additional or more intensive clinical outreach, such as brief admission to an inpatient unit (Waterhouse & Platt, 1990), home visits (Chowdhury, Hicks, & Kreitman, 1973; Hawton et al., 1981; van Heeringen et al., 1995; Welu, 1977), letters and/or phone calls (Litman & Wold, 1976; Motto, 1976) or a simple card with an emergency phone number (Morgan, Jones, & Owen, 1993), added on to treatment as usual would decrease the probability of subsequent parasuicide and suicide. In these studies, the actual content of the outreach interventions was not always described; the experimental factor was the increase in outreach to the suicidal person. Two of the studies (van Heeringen et al., 1995; Welu, 1977) showed a significant reduction in parasuicide by follow-up, and a third (Morgan et al., 1993) found a significant reduction in parasuicide acts and suicide threats combined. Five studies (Allard, Marshall, & Plante, 1992; Hawton et al., 1987; Linehan et al., 1991; Salkovskis, Atha, & Storer, 1990; Welu, 1977) examined the effectiveness of some sort of focused outpatient psychotherapy or counseling offered by mental health professionals compared to referral to outpatient psychotherapy or to one's primary care physician (where follow-through on the referral often did not occur). Three of the six studies found lower rates of parasuicide among those receiving the experimental treatments (Linehan et al., 1991; Salkovskis et al., 1990; Welu, 1977). One study looked at who offered treatment and found no differences between continuing outpatient care with the treating inpatient psychiatrist versus outpatient referral to a suicide prevention center (Moeller, 1989). Three pharma-

TABLE 4.1. Outpatient Treatment Studies with Suicidal Patients: Controlled Randomized Trials Targeting Reductions in Parasuicide and Suicide in Chronological Order

Author	Sample	Interventions	Time Treat	Time Assess	Pretreatment analyses	Results
Chowdhury et al. (1973)[a]	Patients with multiple parasuicides admitted to poison center for parasuicide[b] (high suicide risk excluded)	1. (E[c]) Regular frequent appointments, home visits, 24-hr emergency phone, home visits and drop-in service (n = 71). 2. (C[d]) TAU[e]: referral to outpatient clinic (n = 84).	6 mo	6 mo	E = C baseline measures.	E = C: parasuicide [17/71 (24%) vs. 19/84 (23%)].
Termansen & Bywater (1975)[a]	Patients admitted to emergency room (ER) for attempted suicide[f] (high suicide risk included).	1. (E$_1$) In-person follow-up (daily tapering to biweekly, up to 19 visits) by mental health worker (n = 57). 2. (E$_2$) Phone contact follow-up (daily tapering to biweekly by crisis center volunteers (n = 57). 3. (C) No follow-up (n = 50).	3 mo	3 mo	Significant pretreatment differences across measures of psychopathology	E$_1$ = E$_2$: parasuicide [1/45 (2.2%) vs. 2/33 (6.5%)]. E$_2$ = C: parasuicide [2/33 (6.5%) vs. 7/32 (21.9%)]; z^g = 1.85. E$_1$ < C: parasuicide; z = 2.79. E$_1$ > (E$_2$ = C): treatment compliance.
Welu (1977)	Patients > 6 yr old admitted to ER for suicide attempt[h] (excluded: living in institutional setting, high suicide risk included).	1. (E) TAU, home visits, and weekly contact by mental health worker (CPN[i], SW[j], counselors) monitoring or providing psychotherapy; crisis intervention, and/or family therapy as needed (n = 62). 2. (C) TAU: Referral to outpatient, or inpatient followed by outpatient referral (n = 57).	4 mo	4 mo	Not reported.	E < C: parasuicide [3/62 (4.8%) vs. 9/57 (15.8%)]; z = 1.98. E > C: treatment compliance.

(continued)

TABLE 4.1. (continued)

Author	Sample	Interventions	Time Treat	Time Assess	Pretreatment analyses	Results
Gibbons, Butler, Urwin, & Gibbons (1978)	Patients >17 yr old admitted to ER for deliberate self-poisoning[k] (excluded: in treatment, needing immediate psychiatric treatment; high suicide risk excluded).	1. (E) Immediate time-limited, task-centered casework by SWs in home ($n = 200$). 2. (C) TAU: Referral to treatment ($n = 200$).	3 mo	1 yr	E = C baseline measures.	E = C: parasuicide [29/200 (14.5%) vs. 27/200 (13.5%)]; $z = -.29$ (not significant). E > C: treatment completers.
Hawton et al. (1981)	Patients > 17 yr old admitted to ER for deliberate self-poisoning[l] (excluded: in treatment, needing psychiatric inpatient, substance abuse, or day treatment, no fixed abode; high suicide risk excluded).	1. (E) As needed (mean = 4.3 visits) problem-oriented counseling in home, and phone consultation by MD[m], CPN, SW ($n = 48$). 2. (C) Problem-oriented counseling (mean = 4.95 visits) in clinic ($n = 48$).	3 mo	1 yr	E = C all but one baseline measure.	E > C: treatment completion
Hawton et al. (1987)	Patients >16 yr old admitted to hospital for deliberate self-poisoning,[n] suitable for outpatient counseling (excluded: in-treatment needing psychiatric inpatient, substance abuse, or day treatment; high suicide risk excluded).	1. (E) Brief, problem-oriented counseling in clinic ($n = 41$). 2. (C) Referral and advice given to general practitioner ($n = 39$).	2 mo	2,4,6 mo	E = C parasuicide (10% vs. 15%). E = C baseline measures.	E = C: suicide [1/41 (2.4%) vs. 0]. E = C: parasuicide [3/41 (7.3%) vs. 6/39 (15.4%)]. E = C: treatment compliance.

Study	Sample	Treatment conditions				Baseline	Results
Moeller (1989)	Patients admitted to hospital for attempted suicide,[a] by self-poisoning (excluded: 50% of self-poisoners deemed unsuitable for brief outpatient psychotherapy; high suicide risk excluded).	1. (E) Inpatient crisis intervention and short-term outpatient psychotherapy with MD in charge of patient in hospital ($n = 68$). 2. (C) Inpatient crisis intervention with additional motivational interviewing and contacts, and referral to suicide prevention services ($n = 73$).	3 mo	1 yr	E = C baseline measures.	E = C: suicide [3/66 (4.6%) vs. 2/70 (2.9%)]. E = C: parasuicide [9/66 (13.6%) vs. 3/70(4.3%)]; $z = 1.92$ (against prediction). E = C: suicide and suicide attempts; $z = 1.95$ (against prediction). E > C: treatment compliance.
Waterhouse & Platt (1990)	Patients >16 yr old admitted to casualty department for parasuicide by self-poisoning[b] (excluded: needing immediate medical or psychiatric treatment, no fixed abode, current inpatient; high suicide risk excluded).	1. (E) Hospital admission, TAU at discharge ($n = 38$). 2. (C) TAU: referral to general practitioner ($n = 39$).	1 wk	4 mo	E = C all but one baseline measure; E > C: age.	E = C: parasuicide at 1 week [2/38 (5.3%) vs. 2/39 (5.1%)]. E = C: parasuicide at 1 wk–4 mo [1/38 (2.6%) vs. 2/39 (5.1%)].
Salkovskis et al. (1990)	Multiple high-risk suicide attempters[g] 16–65 yr old admitted to ER for anti-depressant overdose (excluded: needing immediate psychiatric treatment, psychotic or organic illness, no fixed abode; high suicide risk included).	1. (E) TAU and brief (5 sessions) problem-oriented counseling by CPN ($n = 12$). 2. (C) TAU: referral to general practitioner ($n = 8$).	1 mo	1 yr	E = C all but one baseline measure; E > C: males.	E < C: parasuicide at 6 mo [0 vs. 3/8 (37.5%)]; $z = 2.3$. E = C: (cumulative) parasuicide at 18 mo [3/12; (25%) vs. 4/8 (50%)].

(continued)

97

TABLE 4.1. (continued)

Author	Sample	Interventions	Time		Pretreatment analyses	Results
			Treat	Assess		
Allard et al. (1992)	Suicide attempters[t] admitted to ER (excluded: no fixed abode, currently in primary care, sociopathy, parasuicide > 1 week previous excluded) (high suicide risk included).	1. (E) Weekly (mean = 12 visits) therapy (supportive or psychoanalytic, or behavioral, psychosocial), tapering to monthly meetings with psychiatrist, and home visit (n = 76). 2. (C) TAU: referral to treatment (mean = 1.5 visits; n = 74).	1 yr	2 yr	E = C baseline measures.	E = C: suicide attempts [22/63 (34.9%) vs. 19/63 (30.2%)]. E = C: suicide [3/63 (4.8%) vs. 1/66 (1.6%)].
Linehan et al. (1991, 1993)	Patients with multiple parasuicides[s] (1 in last 8 weeks) with borderline personality disorder (excluded: males, schizophrenics, bipolar disorder, primary substance abuse; high suicide risk included).	1. (E) Dialectical behavior therapy (weekly individual therapy, group skills training, as needed phone calls) mainly by PSY[t] (n = 24). 2 (C) TAU: referral to outpatient treatment (n = 23).	1 yr	2 yr	E = C baseline measures.	E = C: suicide [1/22 (4.6%) vs. 0] at 2 yr E < C: parasuicide at 1 yr [13/22 (59.1%) vs. 21/22 (95.5%)]; $z = 2.88$. E < C: suicide and parasuicide at 1 yr [14/22 (63.6%) vs. 21/22 (95.5%)]; $z = 2.62$. E < C: parasuicide at 1–2 yr [5/19; (26.3%) vs. 12/20 (60%)]; $z = 2.12$. E > C: treatment compliance.

Study	Population	Conditions			Baseline	Results
Morgan et al. (1993)	All patients admitted to a general hospital for nonfatal deliberate self-harm[a] with no history of prior parasuicidal behavior (high suicide risk included).	1. (E) TAU and a card offering rapid, easy access (drop-in and on-demand hospitalization if no parasuicide during the episode) to on-call psychiatrists; encouragement to use such services ($n = 101$). 2. (C) TAU: referral to primary healthcare team or to inpatient unit ($n = 111$).	1 yr	1 yr	E = C baseline measures.	E = C: parasuicide [5/101 (4.9%) vs. 12/111 (10.81%)]; $z = 1.57$. E < C: parasuiciders and serious threateners [5/101 (4.95%) vs. 15/111 (13.51%)]; $z = 2.13$.
van Heeringen et al. (1995)	Consecutively referred to the ER for parasuicide[b] and 15 yr or over, who did not need inpatient medical treatment other than intensive care unit (high suicide risk included).	1. (E) TAU and home visits (up to 3) to treatment noncompliers by a CPN to discuss noncompliance with treatment recommendations ($n = 258$). 2. (C) TAU: referral to treatment ($n = 258$).	2–4 wks	1 yr	E = C baseline measures.	E < C: parasuicide [15/196 (7.7%) vs. 27/195 (13.9%)]; $z = 1.98$. E = C: suicide [6/196 (3.1%) vs. 7/195 (3.6%)]. E < C: parasuicide and suicide [21/196 (10.7) vs. 34/195 (17.4)]; $z = 1.98$. E > C: treatment compliance.

[a]Each of these two studies are sequential alternate rather than random assignment to condition.

[b]"Any deliberate act of self-poisoning or self-injury which resulted in the patient being referred to hospital" (p. 70); clinical assessment; no reliability; no mention of blind assessment.

[c]E, experimental treatment.

[d]C, control condition.

[e]TAU, treatment as usual in clinical community where research occurs.

(continued)

TABLE 4.1. (continued)

[f]"Any act of self-injury, regardless of its seriousness, which was motivated by self-destructive tendencies" (p. 29); clinical assessment; no reliability; no mention of blind assessment.

[g]All z scores are based on a binomial test calculated by the author and are included when the value is ≥ 1.57, which is $p = .05$ value for a one-tail test.

[h]"Any nonfatal act of self-damage inflicted with self-destructive intention, however vague and ambiguous" (p. 19); clinical assessment; no reliability; no mention of blind assessment.

[i]CPN, community psychiatric nurse.

[j]SW, social worker.

[k]"Deliberate taking of a pharmacologically active substance in more than the prescribed dose or the usual consumption which resulted in the patient being admitted to a hospital unit" (p. 112); clinical assessment and medical records; no reliability; blind assessment.

[l]"Intentional self-administration of more than the prescribed or recommended dose of any drugs whether or not there was evidence that the act was intended to cause self-harm" (p. 172); alcohol intoxication alone not included; clinical assessment; no reliability; no mention of blind assessment.

[m]MD, psychiatrist.

[n]No definition of overdose given; interviews with patients, their general practitioners, and by monitoring service of hospital; interviewers blind to treatment.

[o]Suicide attempt not defined; assessment not described.

[p]"A non-fatal act in which an individual deliberately ingests a substance in excess of any prescribed or generally recognised therapeutic dosage" (p. 237); clinical interviews; no reliability; assessors not blind.

[q]Suicide attempt not defined; structured clinical interviews; no reliability; no mention of blind assessment.

[r]"Any life-threatening behavior, with a real or professed intention of causing one's own death, not resulting in death" (pp. 306–307); clinical interview by researcher or therapist; no reliability; assessment not blind.

[s]"Any intentional, acute self-injurious behavior with or without suicidal intent, including both suicide attempts and self-mutilative behaviors" (p. 1060); Parasuicide History Interview; reliability given; blind assessment.

[t]PSY, psychologist.

[u]Self-harm not defined; clinical assessment; review of medical records; no reliability; no mention of blind assessment.

[v]"The deliberate ingestion of more than the prescribed amount of medical substances, or ingestion of substances never intended for human consumption irrespective of whether harm was intended"; "any intentional self-inflicted injury, irrespective of the apparent purpose of the act" (p. 964); no reliability; no mention of blind assessment.

TABLE 4.2. Treatment Studies with Suicidal Patients: Controlled Randomized Trials Targeting Reductions in Parasuicide and Suicide—Inpatient Treatment of Patients Following a Parasuicide Episode[a]

Author	Sample	Interventions	Time Treat	Time Assess	Pretreatment analyses	Results
Liberman & Eckman (1981)	Multiple suicide attempters[b] admitted to psychiatric inpatient unit for suicide attempt (excluded: psychotic, organic brain syndrome, currently addicted to substances; high suicide risk included).	1. (E) Behavior therapy by PSY($n = 12$). 2. (C) Insight-oriented therapy by PSY($n = 12$).	8 days	2 yr	E = C baseline measures.	E = C: parasuicide [2/12 (16.7%) vs. 3/12 (25%)].
Patsiokas & Clum (1985)	Patients admitted to psychiatric inpatient unit for suicide attempts[c] (excluded: psychotic or substance abuse; high suicide risk included)	1. (E) Cognitive therapy ($n = 5$). 2 (E) Skills training in problem solving ($n = 5$). 3. (C) Nondirective, reflective psychotherapy ($n = 5$).	3 wk	3 wk	E = C baseline measures.	$E_1 = E_2 = C$: suicide ideation and intent.

[a]See footnotes on Table 4.1 for explanation of symbols.
[b]No definition of suicide attempt given; structured interviews; no reliability; no mention of blind assessment.
[c]No definition of suicide attempt given.

TABLE 4.3. Treatment Studies with Suicidal Patients: Controlled Randomized Trials Targeting Reductions in Parasuicide and Suicide—Pharmacotherapy Trials Following a Parasuicide Episode[a]

Author	Sample	Interventions	Time Treat	Time Assess	Pretreatment analyses	Results
Montgomery, Roy, & Montgomery (1981)	Patients admitted to hospital after ≥ third suicide attempt[b]; personality disorder (mainly BPD, histrionic (without schizophrenia or depression).	1. (E) Mianserin, 30 mg (n = 17). 2 (C) Placebo (n = 21).	6 mo	6 mo	E = C on gender, age, personality disorder diagnosis (34% dropout rate).	E = C: repeated self-harm[c] [8/17 (47%) vs. 12/21 (57%)].
Montgomery et al. (1979) referred to in Montgomery & Montgomery (1982)	Patients admitted to hospital after ≥ third suicidal act[d]; personality disorder (mainly BPD, histrionic (without schizophrenia or depression).	1. (E) Flupenthixol, 20 mg im/4 wk (n = 14). 2. (C) Placebo (n = 16).	6 mo	6 mo	Not reported.	E < C: suicide attempts [3/14 (21%) vs. 12/16 (75%)].
Draper & Hirsch reported in Hirsch, Walsh & Draper (1983)	Patients admitted to hospital following parasuicide[e] not already in treatment, consenting to treatment, and sufficiently high on a general health questionnaire to need psychiatric treatment (schizophrenia and depression not excluded).	1. (E) Mianserin, 60 mg (n = 38). 2. (E) Nomifensine, 150 mg (n = 38). 3. (C) Placebo (n = 38).	6 wk	12 wk	$E_1 = E_2 = C$ on Ham-D	$E_1 = E_2 = C$ (21% vs. 13% vs. 13%).

[a]See footnotes to Table 4.1 for explanation of symbols.
[b]No definition of suicide attempt given.
[c]No definition of self-harm given.
[d]No definition of suicidal act given, but from context appears to refer to suicide attempts or any parasuicide.
[e]No definition of parasuicide given.

TABLE 4.4. Treatment Studies with Suicidal Patients: Controlled Randomized Trials Targeting Reductions in Parasuicide and Suicide—Psychosocial Treatments Following Determination of High Risk for Suicide[a]

Author	Sample	Interventions	Time — Treat	Time — Assess	Pretreatment analyses	Results
Motto (1976)	High suicide risk[b]; psychiatric inpatients refusing further treatment.	1. (E) Intermittent, nondemanding letters expressing concern (n = 401). 2. (C) No follow-up (n = 452).	4 yr	4 yr	Not reported.	E = C: suicide [12/230 (5.2%) vs. 20/242 (8.3%)].
Litman & Wold (1976)	High suicide risk[c]; persons calling crisis phone line	1. (E) TAU and weekly "befriending" phone calls by crisis center volunteers to the subject (n = 200). 2. (C) TAU: Telephone crisis intervention when subject called (n = 200).	18 mo	18 mo	Not reported.	E = C: suicide [7/200 (3.5%) vs. 2/200 (1%)]. E = C: suicide risk.

[a]See footnotes to Table 4.1 for explanation of symbols.
[b]High suicide risk not defined.
[c]High suicide risk determined by consensus of research psychologist and experienced paraprofessionals based on scores on unspecified suicide risk measures.

cotherapy studies examined the efficacy of antidepressants (Draper & Hirsch referenced in Hirsch, Walsh & Draper, 1983, and Montgomery et al., 1979) or neuroleptics (Montgomery et al., 1979). Antidepressants were not effective, but results in the neuroleptic study showed an astounding decrease in parasuicidal acts. In the two inpatient treatments, neither found an added benefit in subsequent suicide and parasuicide rates by adding an experimental treatment to the usual inpatient treatment regime.

What are we to make of these findings? Five psychosocial treatment regimes (Linehan et al., 1991; Salkovskis et al., 1990; Termansen & Bywater, 1975; van Heeringen et al., 1995; Welu, 1977), and one pharmacotherapy regime (Montgomery et al., 1979) showed significant reductions in subsequent parasuicidal acts, and the simple act of making nondemanding phone calls and sending a letter produced a trend towards lower suicide rates over time (Motto, 1976). The quality of the studies and focus of the treatments, however, were extremely variable. Unknown or large pretreatment differences between conditions make results of both Termansen and Bywater (1975) and Welu (1977) hard to interpret. The failure to publish in a refereed journal and the subsequent absence of a published replication study in 19 years makes one wonder about the generalizability of the neuroleptic effectiveness reported by Montgomery et al. (1979). Results in the Motto (1976) study did not reach significance, and the study has not been replicated. We are left with three reasonably well-designed studies showing psychosocial interventions that appear effective in reducing the risk of subsequent parasuicidal behavior. Each study employed a very specific behavior and problem-solving focus. Both the Salkovskis et al. (1990) and van Heeringen et al. (1995) studies were very brief interventions aimed at acutely suicidal individuals who did not need immediate treatment for mental disorders. The Linehan et al. (1991) study was a 1-year intervention aimed at chronically suicidal, high-risk, difficult-to-treat individuals meeting criteria for BPD, and having multiple behavioral dysfunctions and significant mental disorders. At the 18-month posttreatment point, Salkovskis et al. (1990) found a parasuicide repeat rate of 25% among those receiving behavior therapy versus 50% receiving treatment as usual, a difference that was not statistically significant. Although this difference could certainly have been due to chance, the small sample size ($n = 20$) suggests that the study may have had inadequate power. During the 1 year after treatment ended, the parasuicide patients receiving the home visits in van Heeringen and colleagues' (1995) intervention and the patients receiving Linehan and associates' (1990) dialectical behavior therapy (DBT) had fewer parasuicide episodes than did patients receiving treatment as usual.

Who is included and who is excluded from the clinical trials is an extremely important factor in understanding the results of these treatment studies. Nine studies (45%) excluded subjects needing immediate psychiatric treatment, or at high risk for suicide (Chowdhury et al., 1973; Gibbons et al., 1978; Hawton et al., 1981, 1987; Moeller, 1989; Waterhouse & Platt, 1990), or who had characteristics known to increase suicide risk (Montgomery et al., 1981; Montgomery et al., 1979; Morgan et al., 1993). The remaining 11 (55%) focused on patients at high risk for suicide or parasuicide (Allard et al., 1992; Liberman & Eckman, 1981; Linehan et al., 1991; Litman & Wold, 1976; Morgan et al., 1993; Motto, 1976; Patsiokas & Clum, 1985; Salkovskis et al., 1990; Termansen & Bywater, 1975; van Heeringen et al., 1995; Welu, 1977). If we look at just the 13 outpatient studies, the effectiveness of the experimental condition compared to the control condition can be predicted almost perfectly by whether individuals at high risk of suicide are included or excluded from the trial. In each of the six studies that excluded individuals at high risk for suicide, no significant differences were found between the experimental treatments and treatment as usual. On the other hand, six of the seven outpatient studies that included individuals at high risk for suicide did show a significant beneficial effect of the experimental treatment under study. The exception is the study by Allard et al. (1992), where there appeared to be no attempt to control the type of behavioral intervention. This finding suggests that individuals who parasuicide but do not have current serious mental disorders or high suicide risk may benefit from very minimal interventions. This suggests that a policy of hospitalizing individuals based simply on an acute episode of parasuicide is not warranted. Intensive or special outpatient treatments, however, are likely to be effective when the individual is seriously disordered or at high risk for further suicidal behavior.

CONCLUSION

The most important conclusion that can be drawn from this review of treatment studies is that we do not appear to know how to reduce the incidence of death by suicide among individuals going for help with suicidal behavior or disorders associated with suicidal behavior. The closest anyone has come to reducing suicide rates was Motto (1976), who found a trend toward reduced suicide rates by the very simple procedure of sending nondemanding letters and making brief phone calls to high-risk individuals refusing further treatment. Indirect treatment of suicidal behavior by treating depression has failed to demonstrate effectiveness in reducing suicide or suicide attempts, although this may be a consequence of inadequate power in studies. Inadequate statistical power, however, remains a hypothesis rather than a fact until it is tested.

We know more about how to reduce the incidence of suicide attempts and other parasuicidal acts. When high-risk parasuicidal individuals are not excluded from the population being treated, focused, behavioral interventions appear promising. The above studies by Linehan, Salkovskis, and van Heeringen and their colleagues are well designed and very promising. They are the strongest evidence we have that outpatient behavioral interventions are effective with highly suicidal patients. It is remarkable, however, that the treatment that is the standard of care in many locations, namely, inpatient psychiatric hospitalization, has never been shown effective, not in one single study that I could locate.

The most compelling conclusion that can be drawn from this review is that the treatment of those individuals exhibiting suicidal behavior appears to be an exceptionally low priority within the clinical research community. Not only were they excluded in 45% of the studies aimed directly at treating suicidal behavior, they were also excluded from 15 of the 17(88%) pharmacotherapy trials examining fluoxetine as a treatment for depression reviewed by Beasley et al. (1992). The exclusion of suicidal individuals from most research studies has all but ensured that we do not know how to treat these individuals. Until they are included in clinical trials and until treatment researchers focus directly on developing treatments for these individuals, progress will be limited and suicide rates undoubtedly will remain high.

What directions do we need for the future? Two avenues would improve the state of our science. First, it is paramount that we begin to include individuals at high risk for suicide in clinical trials. We need first a review of clinical inclusion, exclusion, and treatment termination guidelines that have been employed in randomized clinical trials to date. The obvious ethical concerns, especially of placebo medication conditions, must be surmounted. This could perhaps be done by developing a standardized, across-study, crisis intervention protocol for use with patients who are or who become suicidal during treatment trials. This protocol could incorporate the key behavioral interventions that have so far been found effective with this population (e.g., specific focus on the suicidal behavior). The use of neuroleptics with personality-disordered, suicidal individuals needs to be thoroughly tested to understand and possibly replicate the findings of Montgomery, Montgomery, and their colleagues. Second, we simply must increase the interest of well-trained clinical scientists in the field of suicide and increase the number of young investigators interested, willing, and trained to develop treatments explicitly targeting suicidal behaviors. The absence of treatment development and randomized, controlled trials, especially given the seriousness of the problem, is remarkable. Part of this problem is due to the overreliance on standards of care, expert opinion, open clinical trials, and anecdotal case reports as guides to what is effective and ethical treatment. Longitudinal designs and open clinical trials can tell us what is safe to examine further. Nonrandomized trials can tell us what is promising enough to study further. Neither, however, can tell us what treatments are actually effective in reducing suicidal behavior. Another impediment to research is the fear of litigation following the suicide of a research subject who is not getting either the standard of care or the experimental treatment. A concerted effort to get consumer groups involved in developing research guidelines may be a useful first step. A public and professional educational program to inform human-subject review committees, professionals, and the public that we have very little evidence about what is effective in reducing suicidal behaviors and virtually no evidence that the standard treatments work is necessary to increase public support for this type of research.

ACKNOWLEDGMENTS

Writing of this chapter was partially supported by Grant No. MH34486 from the National Institute of Mental Health. This chapter originally appeared in *The Neurobiology of Suicide* (pp. 302–328), edited by D. M. Stoff and J. J. Mann. New York: Annals of the New York Academy of Sciences, 1997. Copyright 1997 by the New York Academy of Sciences. Reprinted by permission.

REFERENCES

Allard, R., Marshall, M., & Plante, M. C. (1992). Intensive follow-up does not decrease the risk of repeat suicide attempts. *Suicide and Life-Threatening Behavior, 22*(3), 303–314.

Beasley, C. M., Dornseif, B. E., Bosomworth, J. C., Sayler, M. E., et al. (1992). Fluoxetine and suicide: A meta-analysis of controlled trials of treatment for depression. *International Journal of Clinical Psychopharmacology, 6*, 35–57.

Brent, D. A. (1987). Correlates of the medical lethality of suicide attempts in children and adolescents. *Journal of the American Academy of Child and Adolescent Psychiatry, 26*, 87–91.

Brown, M., & Linehan, M. M. (1996). *The relationship of negative emotions and parasuicidal behavior in borderline personality disorder.* Poster presented at an Association for the Advancement of Behavior Therapy meeting, New York.

Buchholtz-Hansen, P. E., Wang, A. G., & Kragh-Sorensen, P. (1993). Mortality in major affective disorder: Relationship to subtype of depression. *Acta Psychiatrica Scandinavica 87*, 329–335.

Chowdhury, N., Hicks, R. C., & Kreitman, N. (1973). Evaluation of an aftercare service for parasuicide (attempted suicide) patients. *Social Psychiatry, 8*, 67–81.

Clarkin, J. F., Widiger, T. A., Frances, A. J., Hurt, F. W., & Gilmore, M. (1983). Prototypic typology and the borderline personality disorder. *Journal of Abnormal Psychiatry, 92*(3), 263–275.

Cowdry, R. W., Pickar, D., & Davies, R. (1985). Symptoms and EEG findings in the borderline syndrome. *International Journal of Psychiatry in Medicine, 15*, 201–211.

Dulit, R. A., Fyer, M. R., Leon, A. C., Brodsky, B. F., & Frances, A. J. (1994). Clinical correlates of self-mutilation in borderline personality disorder. *American Journal of Psychiatry, 151*, 1305–1311.

Favazza, A. R. (1987). *Bodies under siege: Self-mutilation in culture and psychiatry.* Baltimore: Johns Hopkins University Press.

Fyer, M. R., Frances, A. J., Sullivan, T., Hurt, S. W., & Clarkin, J. (1988). Suicide attempts in patients with borderline personality disorder. *American Journal of Psychiatry, 145*, 737–739.

Gardner, A. R., & Gardner, A. J. (1975). Self-mutilation, obssessionality and narcissism. *British Journal of Psychiatry, 127*, 127–132.

Gibbons, J. S., Butler, J., Urwin, P., & Gibbons, J. L. (1978). Evaluation of a social work service for self-poisoning patients. *British Journal of Psychiatry, 133*, 111–118.

Gunderson, J. G. (1984). *Borderline personality disorder.* Washington, DC: American Psychiatric Press.

Hawton, K., Bancroft, J., Catalan, J., et al. (1981). Domiciliary and out-patient treatment of self-poisoning patients by medical and non-medical staff. *Psychological Medicine, 11*, 169–177.

Hawton, K., McKeown, S., Day, A., et al. (1987). Evaluation of out-patient counseling compared with general practitioner care following overdoses. *Psychological Medicine, 17*, 751–761.

Hirsch, S. R., Walsh, C., & Draper, R. (1983). The concept and efficacy of the treatment of parasuicide. *British Journal of Clinical Pharmacology, 15*, 189S–194S.

Hjelmeland, H. (1996). Verbally expressed intentions of parasuicide: II. Predictions of fatal and nonfatal repetition. *Crisis, 17*, 10–14.

Kjelsberg, E., Eikeseth, P. H., & Dahl, A. A. (1991). Suicide in borderline patients: Predictive factors. *Acta Psychiatrica Scandinavica 84,* 283–287.

Kreitman, N. (1977). *Parasuicide.* London: Wiley.

Kroll, J. L., Carey, K. S., & Sines, L. K. (1985). Twenty-year follow-up of borderline personality disorder: A pilot study. In C. Stragass (Ed.), *IVth world congress of biological psychiatry.* New York: Elsevier.

Kullgren, G. (1988). Factors associated with completed suicide in borderline personality disorder. *Journal of Nervous and Mental Disease, 176,* 40–44.

Lewinsohn, P. M., Rohde, P., & Seeley, J. R. (1994). Psychosocial risk factors for future adolescent suicide attempts. *Journal of Consulting and Clinical Psychology, 62,* 297–305.

Lewinsohn, P. M., Rohde, P., & Seeley, J. R. (1996). Adolescent suicidal ideation and attempts: Prevalence, risk factors, and clinical implications. *Clinical Psychology Science and Practice, 3,* 25–46.

Liberman, R. P., & Eckman, T. (1981). Behavior therapy vs. insight-oriented therapy for repeated suicide attempters. *Archives of General Psychiatry, 38,* 1126–1130.

Linehan, M. M. (1986). Suicidal people: One population or two? In J. J. Mann & M. Stanley (Eds.), *Psychobiology of suicidal behavior* (pp. 16–33). New York: Annals of the New York Academy of Sciences (No. 487).

Linehan, M. M., Armstrong, H. E., Suarez, A., Allmon, D., & Heard, H. L. (1991). Cognitive-behavioral treatment of chronically parasuicidal borderline patients. *Archives of General Psychiatry, 48,* 1060–1064.

Linehan, M. M., Heard, H. L., & Armstrong, H. E. (1993). Naturalistic follow-up of a behavioral treatment for chronically parasuicidal borderline patients. *Archives of General Psychiatry, 50,* 971–974.

Linehan, M. M., Heard, H. L., Wagner, A. W., & Brown, M. (1997). *Parasuicide history interview: Development of validity and reliability.* Available at the Department of Psychology, University of Washington, Seattle.

Litman, R. E., & Wold, C. I. (1976). Beyond crisis intervention. In E. S. Shneidman (Ed.), *Suicidology: Contemporary developments* (pp. 528–546). New York: Grune & Stratton.

Lönnqvist, J., & Ostamo, A. (1991). Suicide following the first suicide attempt: A five-year follow-up using a survival analysis. *Psychiatria Fennica, 22,* 171–179.

Moeller, H. J. (1989). Efficacy of different strategies of aftercare for patients who have attempted suicide. *Journal of the Royal Society of Medicine, 82,* 643–647.

Montgomery, D. B., Roy, D., & Montgomery, S. A. (1981). Mianserin in the prophylaxis of suicidal behaviour: A double-blind placebo-controlled trial. In J. P. Soubrier & J. Vedrinne (Eds.), *Depression and suicide: Proceedings of the 11th International Congress for Suicide Prevention, Paris* (pp. 786–790). Fairview Park, NY: Pergamon Press.

Montgomery, S. A., Montgomery, D. B., Rani, S. J., Roy, D., Shaw, P. H., & McAuley, R. (1979). Maintenance therapy in repeat suicidal behaviour: A placebo-controlled trial. *Proceedings of the 10th International Congress for Suicide Prevention and Crisis Intervention, Ottawa, Canada* (pp. 227–229).

Montgomery, S. A., & Montgomery, D. B. (1982). Pharmacological prevention of suicidal behaviour. *Journal of Affective Disorders, 4,* 291–298.

Morgan, H. G., Jones, E. M., & Owen, J. H. (1993). Secondary prevention of nonfatal deliberate self-harm: The green card study. *British Journal of Psychiatry, 163,* 111–112.

Motto, J. A. (1976). Suicide prevention for high-risk persons who refuse treatment. *Suicide and Life-Threatening Behavior 6*(4), 223–230.

Ostamo, A., Lönnqvist, J., Heinonen, S., Leppavuori, A., et al. (1991). Epidemiology of parasuicides in Finland. *Psychiatria Fennica, 22,* 181–189.

Paris, J., Brown, R., & Nowlis, D. (1987). Long-term follow-up of borderline patients in a general hospital. *Comprehensive Psychiatry, 28*(6), 530–535.

Paris, J., Nowlis, D., & Brown, R. (1989). Predictors of suicide in borderline personality disorder. *Canadian Journal of Psychiatry, 34,* 8–9.

Patsiokas, A., & Clum, G. A. (1985). Effects of psychotherapeutic strategies in the treatment of suicide attempters. *Psychotherapy, 22,* 281–290.

Pattison, E. M., & Kahan, J. (1983). The deliberate self-harm syndrome. *American Journal of Psychiatry, 140,* 867–872.

Platt, S., Bille-Brahe, U., Kerkhof, A., Schmidtke, A., Bjerke, T., Crepet, P., De Leo, D., Haring, C., Lönnqvist, J., Michel, K., Philippe, A., Pommereau, X., Querejeta, I., Salander-Renberg, E., Temesvary, B., Wasserman, D., & Faria, J. (1992). Parasuicide in Europe: The WHO/Euro multicentre study on parasuicide: I. Introduction and preliminary analysis for 1989. *Acta Psychiatrica Scandinavica 85,* 97–104.

Sakinofsky, I., Robin, R. S., Brown, Y., Cumming, C., & James, P. (1990). Problem resolution and repetition of parasuicide: A prospective study. *British Journal of Psychiatry, 156,* 395–399.

Salkovskis, P. M., Atha, C., & Storer, D. (1990). Cognitive-behavioral problem solving in the treatment of patients who repeatedly attempt suicide: A controlled trial. *British Journal of Psychiatry, 157,* 871–876.

Schaffer, C. B., Carroll, J., & Abramowitz, S. I. (1982). Self-mutilation and the borderline personality. *Journal of Nervous and Mental Disease, 170,* 468–473.

Sederer, L. I. (1994). Managing suicidal inpatients. In A. A. Leenaars, J. T. Maltsberger, & R. A. Neimeyer (Eds.), *Treatment of suicidal people* (pp. 167–176). Washington, DC: Taylor & Francis.

Simeon, D., Stanley, B., Frances, A., Mann, J. J., Winchel, R., & Stanley, M. (1992). Self-mutilation in personality disorders: Psychological and biological correlates. *American Journal of Psychiatry, 149,* 221–317.

Smith, W. T., & Glaudin, V. (1992). A placebo-controlled trial of paroxetine in the treatment of major depression. *Journal of Clinical Psychiatry, 53,* 36–39.

Stone, M. H. (1989). The course of borderline personality disorder. In A. Tasman, R. E. Hales, & A. J. Frances (Eds.), *Review of psychiatry* (Vol. 8, pp. 103–122). Washington, DC: American Psychiatric Press.

Tanney, B. L. (1992). Mental disorders, psychiatric patients, and suicide. In R. W. Maris, A. L. Berman, & J. T. Maltsberger (Eds.), *Assessment and prediction of suicide* (pp. 277–320). New York: Guilford Press.

Termansen, P. E., & Bywater, C. (1975). S.A.F.E.R.: A follow-up service for attempted suicide in Vancouver. *Canadian Psychiatric Association Journal, 20,* 29–34.

van Heeringen, C., Jannes, S., Buylaert, W., Henderick, H., De Bacquer, D., & Van Remoortel, J. (1995). The management of non-compliance with referral to out-patient after-care among attempted suicide patients: A controlled intervention study. *Psychological Medicine, 25,* 963–970.

Velamoor, V. R., & Cernovsky, Z. Z. (1992). Suicide with the motive "to die" or "not to die" and its socioanamnestic correlates. *Social Behavior and Personality, 20,* 193–198.

Walsh, B. W. (1987). *Adolescent self-mutilation: An empirical study.* Unpublished doctoral dissertation, Boston College Graduate School of Social Work.

Walsh, B. W., & Rosen, P. M. (1988). *Self-mutilation: Theory, research, and treatment.* New York: Guilford Press.

Waterhouse, J., & Platt, S. (1990). General hospital admission in the management of parasuicide: A randomized controlled trial. *British Journal of Psychiatry, 156,* 236–242.

Welu, T. C. (1977). A follow-up program for suicide attempters: Evaluation of effectiveness. *Suicide and Life-Threatening Behavior, 7*(1), 17–30.

Zanarini, M. C., Gunderson, J. G., Frankenburg, F. R., & Chauncey, D. L. (1990). Discriminating borderline personality disorder from other axis II disorders. *American Journal of Psychiatry, 147,* 161–167.

CHAPTER FIVE

Cognitive Risk Factors in Suicide

Marjorie E. Weishaar, PhD

C ognitive therapy research, most notably the work of Aaron T. Beck and his associates, has contributed considerably to our understanding of the clinical risk factors in suicide. Beck's suicide research was a natural outgrowth of his research on unipolar depression and, thus, benefited from his use of clinical samples and the conceptual model generated from his findings on depression.

The model posits that during psychological distress a person's thinking becomes more rigid and biased, judgments become absolute, and the individual's core beliefs about the self, one's personal world, and the future become fixed. Errors in logic, called cognitive distortions, negatively skew perceptions and inferences, and lead to faulty conclusions.

The notion of a cognitive vulnerability to depression rests on the schema concept. Schemas are cognitive structures that hold core beliefs. These beliefs are usually out of a person's awareness until triggered by a life event, at which time they emerge accompanied by strong emotion. In depression, these core beliefs and assumptions reflect themes of loss, deprivation, defeat, and worthlessness. Beck's definition of the cognitive triad—the negative view of the self as a failure, the world as harsh and overwhelming, and the future as hopeless—encapsulates the themes apparent in depressogenic beliefs. Thus, in depression, these beliefs are negative, maladaptive, and idiosyncratic, as are those accompanying personality disorders.

For many, cognitive flexibility returns and negative thinking decreases as depression remits. For others, negative beliefs and assumptions, particularly those established early in life, persist and lead to more chronic depressions and, in some cases, incipient suicidality.

In order to investigate risk factors in suicide, cognitive therapy research used the classification of suicidal behaviors developed by the National Institute of Mental Health (NIMH) task force on suicide prevention (Beck et al., 1973). Cognitive therapy research developed scales to assess suicide ideation and intent and conducted prospective studies with clinical samples. The finding that hopelessness is a key psychological variable in suicide paved the way for the identification of additional cognitive variables and the construction of models to describe and explain the paths to suicide.

ASSESSMENT SCALES

As part of the task force of the National Institute of Mental Health Center for Studies of Suicide Prevention, Beck helped to establish a tripartite classification system to describe suicidal behaviors: suicide ideation, suicide attempt, and completed suicide (Beck et al., 1973). These categories are further subdivided by suicide intent, lethality of attempt, and method of suicide or attempt. Such distinctions aid in investigating differences among groups and reinforce the finding that intent cannot always be inferred by the lethality of an attempt. While some (Goldney, 1981) have found an association between intent and the lethality of an attempt, Beck, Beck, and Kovacs (1975) found that intent and lethality are positively correlated only when the person has an accurate conception of the lethality of his or her chosen method of suicide.

In addition, cognitive therapy research has yielded assessment scales to investigate the nature of suicide. These scales were originally intended for prospective studies but have clinical utility as well. Beck's use of prospective studies was a major contribution to suicide research, for their longitudinal dimension allowed for the identification of risk factors not due to chance or hindsight bias. The cognitive therapy scales developed are the Beck Depression Inventory (BDI; Beck & Steer, 1987), the Dysfunctional Attitude Scale (DAS; Weissman & Beck, 1978), the Scale for Suicide Ideation (SSI; Beck, Kovacs, & Weissman, 1979), the Suicide Intent Scale (SIS; Beck, Schuyler, & Herman, 1974), the Beck Hopelessness Scale (BHS; Beck, Weissman, Lester, & Trexler, 1974), and the Beck Self-Concept Test (BST; Beck, Steer, Epstein, & Brown, 1990). These scales have been used to identify cognitive risk factors in suicide. Thus, in addition to demographic, proximate, and clinical risk factors, we may consider cognitive precursors to suicide as well.

Beck Depression Inventory

The BDI (Beck & Steer, 1987) is a 21-item, self-report questionnaire that asks respondents to rate, on a 4-point scale, their depressive symptoms over the past week. Among the symptoms assessed are vegetative signs of depression as well as feelings of failure, guilt, and pessimism, and suicidal wishes. Beck and Steer (1987) present the psychometric properties of the BDI.

The BDI has been found to correlate with suicide intent when a broad, heterogeneous sample, such as a general clinic population, is studied. When a homogeneous group, specifically a highly depressed population of suicide ideators, is studied, the BHS (Beck, Weissman, et al., 1974) and the BST (Beck, Steer, et al., 1990) are better indicators of intent.

Dysfunctional Attitude Scale

The DAS (Weissman & Beck, 1978) is a 100-item scale designed to measure the assumptions and beliefs underlying clinical depression. In addition to identifying beliefs that might interact with life stress to produce clinical symptoms (Beck & Weishaar, 1989), the total score is presumed to reflect the overall severity of negative dysfunctional attitudes. The DAS was originally developed to measure specific beliefs and assumptions but has been used as a general measure of cognitive vulnerability to depression (Shaw & Segal, 1988). Dysfunctional attitudes have been correlated with suicidal ideation in a number of studies (Bonner & Rich, 1987, 1988a; Ellis & Ratliff, 1986; Ranieri et al., 1987).

Scale for Suicide Ideation

The SSI (Beck, Kovacs, & Weissman, 1979; Beck & Steer, 1991) assesses the degree to which someone is presently thinking of suicide. The SSI is a 19-item scale administered in a structured clinical interview, with ratings made on a 3-point scale. It evaluates the intensity of specific attitudes, plans, and behaviors concerning suicide such as the frequency and duration of suicidal thoughts, subjective feelings of control, the relative strengths of the wish to live and the wish to die, deterrents, and the availability of method. Studies of the reliability and validity of the SSI support its usefulness (Beck, Kovacs, & Weissman, 1979). A self-report version of the SSI has been developed (Beck, Steer, & Ranieri, 1988), as has a modified version (Miller, Norman, Bishop, & Dow, 1986).

Suicide Intent Scale

The SIS is a 15-item questionnaire administered in a clinical interview to individuals who have attempted suicide. It assesses the severity of the individual's psychological intent to die at the time of the attempt by investigating relevant aspects of the attempter's behavior before, during, and after the attempt. Items include the degree of isolation and likelihood of being discovered, final acts, conception of lethality and medical rescuability, attitudes toward living and dying, and purpose of the attempt.

The SIS has been consistently validated as a measure of the seriousness of intent to die (Beck, Kovacs, & Weissman, 1975; Beck & Lester, 1976; Beck, Morris, & Beck, 1974; Beck, Schuyler, & Herman, 1974; Minkoff, Bergman, Beck, & Beck, 1973; Silver, Bohnert, Beck, & Marcus, 1971). The Precautions subscale of the SIS was found to be the only predictor, compared to the BDI and the BHS, of eventual suicide among alcoholics (Beck, Steer, & Trexler, 1989; Beck & Steer, 1989). Alcoholic suicide attempters who eventually killed themselves took more precautions against discovery at the time of their index attempt than did those who did not die.

Beck Hopelessness Scale

The BHS (Beck, Weissman, et al., 1974) is a 20-item, true–false, self-report questionnaire. It assesses the level of pessimism or negative view of the future held by the respondent. The psychometric properties of the BHS are presented by Beck, Kovacs, and Weissman (1975). A version of the BHS has been developed for use with children (Hopelessness Scale for Children; Kazdin, Rodgers, & Colbus, 1986). In additon, a rating scale based on clinical interview, the Clinician's Hopelessness Scale (CHS), has been developed (Beck, Weissman, et al., 1974). It appears comparable to the BHS in terms of sensitivity but lower in specificity for both inpatient and outpatient samples (Beck, Brown, & Steer, 1989). The BHS itself has a high false positive rate (Beck, Brown, Berchick, Stewart, & Steer, 1990), which is reduced by adding the BST to the research protocol. For clinical use, the BHS is the most sensitive indicator of suicide risk; in research, the combination is recommended.

Beck Self-Concept Test

The BST (Beck, Steer, et al., 1990) asks respondents to rate themselves, using a 5-point scale, on each of 25 personal characteristics. A total score reflects overall self-concept. The BST has been found to be of greater specificity than the BHS, but also to decrease the number of true positives.

A number of researchers have identified cognitive characteristics of suicidal individuals beyond Beck's establishment of hopelessness and low self-concept as risk factors. These cognitive differences between suicidal and nonsuicidal people persist even with degree of pathology or level of depression controlled. The cognitive factors in suicide that have been examined are hopelessness, low self-concept, cognitive rigidity, dysfunctional assumptions, attributional style, poor interpersonal problem-solving skills, the view of suicide as a "desirable" solution, and deficient reasons for living. Some of these factors have stronger support than others and thus make varying contributions to models of suicidality.

HOPELESSNESS

Hopelessness, or a negative view of the future, is the cognitive feature most consistently related to suicide ideation, intent, and completion in adult (Beck, Brown, et al., 1990; Beck, Steer, Kovacs, & Garrison, 1985; Fawcett et al., 1987; Goldney, 1981; Wetzel, 1976) and child (Asarnow & Guthrie, 1989; Carlson & Cantwell, 1982; Kazdin, French, Unis, Esveldt-Dawson, & Sherrick, 1983) clinical populations. In terms of *suicide ideation,* Beck, Kovacs, and Weissman (1975) found hopelessness to be a better indicator of current suicide ideation among suicide attempters than depression. Also, Nekanda-Trepka, Bishop, and Blackburn (1983) found an association between hopelessness and increased suicidal wishes among psychiatric outpatients.

Hopelessness has been found to be more strongly related to *suicide intent* than is depression per se among clinical samples of suicide ideators (Beck, Kovacs, & Weissman, 1975; Bedrosian & Beck, 1979; Wetzel, Margulies, Davis, & Karam, 1980) and suicide attempters (Dyer & Kreitman, 1984; Goldney, 1981; Wetzel, 1976). In a study of depressed and nondepressed (schizophrenic) patients, those who had high levels of hopelessness, even in the absense of depression, had high levels of suicide intent (Minkoff et al., 1973). Beck, Kovacs, and Weissman (1975) report that hopelessness mediates the relationship between depression and suicidal intent among suicide attempters.

Among drug abusers, hopelessness has been found more strongly associated with suicide intent than has depression (Emery, Steer, & Beck, 1981) or drug use per se (Weissman, Beck, & Kovacs, 1979). However, the role of hopelessness in the relationship between alcoholism and suicide attempts is less clear. Although it was thought to play a mediating role (Beck, Weissman, & Kovacs, 1976), it has not been found predictive of eventual suicide in alcoholic suicide attempters (Beck, Steer, & Trexler, 1989). In this sample, only the Precautions subscale of the SIS, compared to the BDI and the BHS, predicted suicide over a 5- to 10-year period.

Prospective studies have found hopelessness to be predictive of eventual suicide in adults (Beck et al., 1985; Beck, Brown, et al., 1990; Drake & Cotton, 1986; Fawcett et al., 1987). Fawcett et al. (1987) identified hopelessness, loss of pleasure or interest, and mood fluctuations as variables discriminating those who committed suicide from those who didn't. Longitudinal studies by Beck and his associates found that a score of 9 or more on the BHS predicted suicide over a 10-year period for both patients hospitalized with suicide ideation (Beck et al., 1985; Beck, Brown, & Steer, 1989) and psychiatric outpatients (Beck, Brown, et al., 1990). In the sample of outpatients, the BHS yielded a high percentage of false positives (59%), so hopelessness is more accurately conceptualized as a risk factor than as a predictor of suicide. Nevertheless, in clinical decision making, such overinclusiveness is preferable to missing some true positives.

Hopelessness may be conceptualized as a relatively stable schema incorporating negative expectations. During psychiatric distress, such as a depressive episode, hopelessness increases, posing an acute risk to suicide. For most, hopelessness decreases as the depression remits. Yet, high hopelessness in one episode is predictive of high hopelessness in subsequent episodes (Beck, 1988; Beck, Brown, et al., 1990). For other individuals, hopelessness is more chronic and suicide becomes a more constant threat (Beck, 1987). Thus, hopelessness can be conceived as both an acute and chronic risk factor in suicide.

Among adolescents and in nonclinical samples, the relationship of hopelessness to suicide ideation and intent is less clear. While a number of researchers have found that hopelessness increases with severity of suicidal ideation in child and adolescent psychiatric patients (Asarnow & Guthrie, 1989; Brent, Kolko, Goldstein, Allan, & Brown, 1989; Carlson & Cantwell, 1982; Kazdin et al., 1983; Rich, Kirkpatrick-Smith, Bonner, & Jans, 1992; Spirito, Williams, Stark, & Hart, 1988), others have found that this relationship drops to a nonsignificant level when depression is partialed out (Asarnow, Carlson, & Guthrie, 1987).

Gender differences may be important in adolescents, for Cole (1989) found that, after controlling for depression, hopelessness had a modest correlation with suicidal behavior for girls but not for boys.

In contrast, Rotheram-Borus and Trautman (1988, p. 703) argue that "hopelessness is not a meaningful predictor of suicide intent for girls and young women." They found that, among minority adolescent girls, hopelessness did not differentiate suicide attempters from psychiatrically disturbed nonattempters. In this study, although depression and hopelessness were highly correlated, neither predicted suicide intent. Similar findings were achieved by Dyer and Kreitman (1984) among females 15 to 34 years old.

So different are the findings on adolescents that most youthful suicide attempters do not even have high intent (Brent, 1987; Hawton, Osborn, O'Grady, & Cole, 1982). When suicide intent is present, however, it is an indication of the need for hospitalization (Brent & Kolko, 1990).

Results are similarly equivocal in nonclinical samples. Cole (1989) and Rudd (1990) both found depression to be more related to suicide ideation and self-reported behavior than was hopelessness in adolescent groups. Rich et al. (1992) found that both depression and hopelessness, along with substance abuse and few reasons for living, were predictive of suicidal ideation in high school students.

In a college sample of suicide ideators, Clum and his associates (Clum, Patsiokas, & Luscomb, 1979; Schotte & Clum, 1982) found that depression was the best predictor of suicide intent at low levels of suicide ideation. Hopelessness was the best predictor of suicide intent at high levels of suicide ideation. So, the relationship between hopelessness and intent in nonclinical, adolescent samples may be different at differing levels of suicide ideation.

SELF-CONCEPT

Self-concept has been identified in adults as an indicator of suicide risk independent of hopelessness (Beck, Steer, et al., 1990; Beck & Stewart, 1989; Wetzel & Reich, 1989). Among children as well, negative expectations of oneself as well as negative views of the future are related to depression and to suicide intent (Kazdin et al., 1983). In terms of the cognitive model of depression, negative self-concept or low self-esteem represents one component of the cognitive triad: the negative view of the self. Hopelessness, the negative view of the future, is another component of the triad.

COGNITIVE DISTORTIONS AND DYSFUNCTIONAL ASSUMPTIONS

Cognitive Distortions

Some evidence indicates that particular cognitive distortions are associated with suicidal ideation. For example, Prezant and Neimeyer (1988) found, among moderately depressed persons, that once the level of depression was controlled for, selective abstraction and overgeneralization emerged as predictors of suicide ideation. Selective abstraction is a perceptual error by which an individual attends to only a portion of relevant information. Overgeneralization is an error of inference in which a person abstracts a general rule from a single event and applies it to both related and unrelated events. Prezant and Neimeyer conclude that the combination of cognitive distortions and depressive symptomotology is a superior predictor of suicidality over self-reported level of depression alone.

Cognitive Rigidity

In addition to selective abstraction and overgeneralization, the cognitive distortion of dichotomous or all-or-nothing thinking has been found characteristic of suicidal persons (Neuringer, 1961, 1967, 1968;

Neuringer & Lettieri, 1971). Dichotomous thinking is viewed as a form of cognitive rigidity and has been incorporated into that category in more recent research on problem solving. It is discussed below.

Dysfunctional Assumptions

Some studies have endeavored to ascertain whether particular dysfunctional assumptions lead to suicidal thinking. Ellis and Ratliff (1986) compared suicide attempters to equally depressed nonsuicidal patients using a battery of cognitive measures. They found that the suicidal patients scored higher than the nonsuicidal patients in terms of irrational beliefs, hopelessness, and depressogenic attitudes. Bonner and Rich (1987) found dysfunctional assumptions to play an important role in predicting suicide ideation in college students. Lastly, Ranieri et al. (1987) found overall severity of dysfunctional assumptions to be positively correlated with suicidal ideation in psychiatric inpatients, even after hopelessness and depression were controlled for. In addition, perfectionistic attitudes toward the self and sensitivity to social criticism accounted for independent variance in suicide ideation.

Additional work by Beck, Steer, and Brown (1993) with psychiatric outpatients attempted to determine whether specific sets of dysfunctional attitudes distinguished suicide ideators from nonideators and whether certain dysfunctional attitudes were asssociated with the severity of suicidal ideation. In this sample, the overall severity of dysfunctional attitudes as well as four sets of specific attitudes—feeling vulnerable to becoming depressed, accepting other people's expectations, feeling that it is important to impress others, and being sensitive to the opinions of others—were positively associated with being a suicide ideator. However, these attitudes did not discriminate ideators from nonideators when age, sex, a clinical diagnosis of a primary mood or panic disorder, comorbidity, presence of a personality disorder, history of past suicide attempt, BDI score, BHS score, and BST score were controlled for. History of past suicide attempt and hopelessness were the two most important variables for identifying suicide ideators. Hopelessness superimposed on dysfunctional attitudes may increase one's wish to die.

In addition to the work of Ranieri et al. (1987), Hewitt, Flett, and Turnbull-Donovan (1992) found a type of perfectionism associated with suicidal threat or impulses, as measured by the Minnesota Multiphasic Personality Inventory (MMPI). The authors examined three types of perfectionism—expectations of self (self-oriented), expectations of others (other-oriented), and expectations that others hold for the person (socially prescribed perfectionism)—and their possible relationships to suicide ideation in psychiatric inpatients. Only socially prescribed perfectionism predicted variance in suicide ideation scores that was not accounted for by depression or hopelessness. This finding indicates that the tendency to perceive others as holding unrealistic expectations for oneself is associated with suicide ideation. This may relate to the third aspect of Beck's cognitive triad: that the world holds exorbitant demands for the individual.

ATTRIBUTIONAL STYLE

Attributional style has been investigated in suicide research because of its demonstrated relationship to depression (Abramson, Metalsky, & Alloy, 1989). According to the model, depressed individuals are more likely than nondepressed persons to attribute causality of negative events to internal, stable, and global factors. Positive events would be attributued to external, unstable, and specific causes. There is evidence that life events precipitate many suicide attempts, particularly among adolescents (Spirito, Overholser, & Stark, 1989), alcoholics (Heikkinen, Aro, & Lönnqvist, 1993), and those with personality disorders (Lester, Beck, & Steer, 1989). Thus, the study of attributional style may illuminate the manner in which suicidal persons evaluate events.

The findings on the role of attributional style in suicide are mixed. Rotheram-Borus, Trautman, Dopkins, and Shrout (1990) found, in a study of suicide-attempting and non-suicide-attempting female minority adolescents, that the adolescent suicide attempters did not fit the pattern observed in depressed adults. Rather, the adolescent attempters perceived positive events as due to one's own intiative, stable across time, and global. Adolescent attempters reported significantly fewer dysfunctional attributions in positive situations than did the psychiatrically disturbed nonattempters.

Spirito, Overholser, and Hart (1991) also compared adolescent suicide attempters with a sample of psychiatrically hospitalized adolescents. Differences in attributional style by diagnostic groups were not found. However, adolescent patients on welfare were more likely than those not on welfare to attribute negative events to global causes and positive events to specific causes. The authors conclude that the consistent lack of relationships between attributional style and suicide attempts indicates that a specific attributional style does not exist among adolescent attempters.

Results more consistent with the pattern in depressed adults were obtained by Priester and Clum (1992), who studied the relationship of attributional style to depression, hopelessness, and suicide ideation in college students. A failing grade on an exam was the negative event imposed on students who had pre- and postexam measures taken on all three criteria. It was found that the negative–stable attributional style was related to all criteria: A tendency to attribute exam failue to stable causes was associated with higher levels of depression, hopelessness, and suicidal ideation. Those who attributed positive events (i.e., good grades) to internal causes were less likely to feel depressed, hopeless, or suicidal. It was the interaction between a poor exam score and the negative–stable attributional style that was key. Poor performance alone did not relate to suicidal ideation.

PROBLEM-SOLVING DEFICITS

Much of the recent research on cognitive risk factors in suicide has focused on the poor problem-solving skills of suicide ideators and attempters. Problem-solving deficits have been found to be characteristic of suicidal children (Asarnow et al., 1987; Orbach, Rosenheim, & Hary, 1987), adolescents (Curry, Miller, Waugh, & Anderson, 1992; Levenson & Neuringer, 1971; Rotheram-Borus et al., 1990), and adults (Linehan, Camper, Chiles, Strosahl, & Shearin, 1987; Schotte & Clum, 1987), and these difficulties become more profound as problems increase in interpersonal content (McLeavey, Daly, Murray, O'Riodan, & Taylor, 1987).

Suicidal children, adolescents, and adults have limited abilities to find solutions to impersonal tasks, for they have difficulty producing new ideas, identifying solutions (Orbach et al., 1987; Patsiokas, Clum, & Luscomb, 1979), and deliberating alternatives (Cohen-Sandler & Berman, 1982; Levenson, 1974). Suicidal adolescents were found to persist with ineffective solutions even when a more effective strategy was offered to them (Levenson & Neuringer, 1971). Such stereotyped responsivity and cognitive rigidity help explain how repeated suicide attempts get established as a behavioral outcome.

Interpersonal problem solving has greater clinical relevance to the study of suicide for several reasons. First, suicide attempters report greater difficulty with interpersonal problems than do suicide ideators, nonsuicidal psychiatric patients, and general population controls (Linehan, Chiles, Egan, Devine, & Laffaw, 1986). Second, there is evidence that suicide ideators (Mraz & Runco, 1994) and attempters (Rotheram-Borus et al., 1990) perceive more numerous problems but generate fewer solutions than do patient and nonpatient controls. Third, suicide attempters, compared to nonsuicidal patients and normal controls, are less likely to engage in interpersonal problem solving when it is called for. In one of the few studies of the coping strategies of suicidal children, Asarnow et al. (1987) found them less likely than nonsuicidal children to use instrumental problem solving in the face of stressful life events.

Lack of active problem solving has also been noted in adult suicide attempters as compared to suicide ideators and nonsuicidal medical patients (Linehan et al., 1987). The suicide attempters waited for problems to resolve or found someone else to solve the problems. This finding, however, is contradicted by the findings of Orbach, Bar-Joseph, and Dror (1990), who compared the problem-solving styles of adult suicide ideators, suicide attempters, and nonsuicidal psychiatric patients. Both the suicide attempters and the nonsuicidal patients generated more active solutions than did the suicide ideators. The clinical implication is that active problem solving needs to be channeled in a positive direction.

Avoidance, or lack of engagement in problem solving, has also been noted in adolescent suicide attempters. Rotheram-Borus et al. (1990) found that suicide-attempting female minority adolescents were more likely to use wishful thinking under stress than were normal controls. Spirito et al. (1989) found that suicidal adolescents used social withdrawal more frequently than did psychiatric and normal controls. It appears that, like the control groups, the suicidal adolescents used a variety of coping strategies, but at some point they gave up and withdrew from others.

The above studies of "coping style" address whether or not suicidal individuals attempt to solve problems, not how well they do. Some people cope by avoiding their problems; others cope by trying to solve them. Schotte and Clum (1987) argue that, among other deficits, suicidal patients lack an appropriate orientation toward problem solving. They have trouble engaging in problem solving and have difficulty accepting problems as a normal part of life.

Coping style has been systematically investigated by Josepho and Plutchik (1994). They define it as "the methods people use to handle particular classes of emotional conflicts" (p. 50). They compared the coping styles of hospitalized suicide attempters with those of nonsuicidal patients. Suppression, the avoidance of the person or problem that one believes created the situation, had the strongest positive relationship to suicidality. It amplifies suicide risk. Conversely, replacement, the effort to improve stressful situations or limitations in oneself, had the strongest negative association with suicide risk. Increased use of suppression and decreased use of replacement were asssociated with increased risk of suicidal behavior.

Once suicidal individuals engage in interpersonal problem solving, the same deficits accompanying impersonal problem solving emerge but are magnified (McLeavey et al., 1987). McLeavey et al. (1987) found that, compared to nonsuicidal psychiatric patients and nonpatient controls, suicide attempters were less able to orient themselves to a goal and conceptualize a means of moving toward it. They were less able to generate alternatives, anticipate consequences of various solutions, and deal with actual problems in their own lives.

Schotte and Clum (1987) similarly found that hospitalized suicide ideators were able to generate fewer than half as many potential solutions to interpersonal problems selected from their own lives as were depressed control subjects. In addition, suicide ideators tended to focus on the potential negative consequences of implementing any solutions. This "yes, but . . ." reaction to potential solutions may be an important characteristic of suicidal thinking (Priester & Clum, 1993b).

Orbach et al. (1990) compared the problem-solving styles of adult suicide ideators, suicide attempters, and nonsuicidal psychiatric patients. The solutions offered by the suicidal patients to interpersonal dilemmas showed less versatility, less relevance, more avoidance, more negative affect, and less reference to the future than did the solutions of nonsuicidal patients. Orbach and his associates (1987) similarly found that suicidal children were less able than medically ill and normal children to generate alternatives to life-and-death dilemmas in stories. Moreover, they were the only group to show an interaction between such cognitive rigidity and an attraction to death.

The research literature on problem solving has recently encompassed the notion of *perceived*, rather than actual, problem-solving ability (Bonner & Rich, 1988b; Dixon, Heppner, & Anderson, 1991; Rudd, Rajab, & Dahm, 1994). Bonner and Rich (1988b) and Dixon et al. (1991) found that both life stress and self-appraised problem-solving skills predicted hopelessness and suicide ideation in college students. However,

Priester and Clum (1993a) found that college students who rated their problem solving lower at time 1 were more vulnerable to the stress of a low grade and showed higher levels of depression and hopelessness, but *not* suicidal ideation, at time 2 than students with higher self-appraisal. Rudd et al. (1994) also found problem-solving appraisal more predictive of hopelessness than suicide ideation in a clinical sample.

Problem-solving self-appraisal is more a measure of self-efficacy than of problem-solving ability (Bonner & Rich, 1988b). Indeed, a person's confidence in his or her ability to solve problems may be quite different from actual performance, particularly among depressed persons. The construct needs to be clarified: Is it a measure of self-efficacy or of outcome expectations? In addition, it is not clear whether problem-solving ability, self-appraisal, or some combination is most important in predicting hopelessness. It could also be argued that hopelessness causes low problem-solving appraisal (Bonner & Rich, 1988b). Thus, the theoretical and clinical significances of the observed relationship among problem-solving skills, problem-solving appraisal, and hopelessness need to be established.

SUICIDE AS A "DESIRABLE" SOLUTION

In *Cognitive Therapy of Depression* (Beck, Rush, Shaw, & Emery, 1979), the authors observe that suicidal individuals have a unique cognitive deficit in solving interpersonal problems: When their usual strategies fail, they become paralyzed and view suicide as a way out. Beck and colleagues describe the attraction to suicide in these cases as an "opiate."

Suicidal persons may have difficulty tolerating the anxiety of problem solving. Suicidal children, for example, have been found less able than nonsuicidal children to generate self-comforting statements in the face of stressful life events (Asarnow et al., 1987).

Linehan et al. (1987) report that the level of expectancy that suicide can solve one's problems predicts higher suicide intent. In addition, Strosahl, Chiles, and Linehan (1992) found, among parasuicides with high intent to die, a positive relationship between survival/coping beliefs and suicide intent. As intent increases, the person becomes more focused on the problem-solving effects of suicide.

Orbach et al. (1987) found evidence of the view of suicide as a desirable solution among children. In comparing suicidal children, medically ill children, and normal children, they found that the interaction between the inability to generate solutions to life-and-death dilemmas in stories and an attraction to death was unique to suicidal children. There was no such interaction for either the chronically ill or normal children, who may not have been adept at problem solving but weren't attracted to suicide.

Thus, suicide may appear as a solution when a person is unable to shift to a new strategy, is incapable of tolerating the anxiety of problem solving, or has faulty assumptions about suicide's effectiveness to solve problems.

REASONS FOR LIVING

In contrast to hopelessness is the notion of adaptive beliefs or positive expectations that may serve to keep people alive or buffer them from life events. The role of positive attitudes in preventing suicide has been explored by a number of researchers, most notably Linehan and her colleagues (Linehan, Goodstein, Nielson, & Chiles, 1983; Strosahl et al., 1992; Strosahl, Linehan, & Chiles, 1983). They take the point of view that suicidal people lack positive expectations rather than, or in addition to, having negative ones. The Reasons for Living Inventory (RFLI; Linehan et al., 1983) was devised to assess the influence of adaptive or coping beliefs on suicidal behavior. Additionally, BHS is a global measure of pessimism; it is not suicide specific. The RFLI, in contrast, identifies suicide-specific beliefs. As one becomes increasingly suicidal, cognitions may shift from generalized hopelessness to appraisals of suicide as a solution. For these reasons, the RFLI has been used to study suicidal cognitions. Indeed, a study of inpatients and normal controls found RFLI scores to be inversely related to suicide ideation and previous suicide attempts (Linehan et al., 1983). Suicidal individuals were significantly less likely to endorse reasons to live. Recent life stress and pathology in general did not identify those who had few reasons to live.

Six sets of reasons for living distinguished nonsuicidal individuals from suicidal ones: (1) Survival and Coping Beliefs, (2) Responsibility to Family, (3) Child-Centered Concerns, (4) Fear of Suicide, (5) Fear of Social Disapproval, and (6) Moral Objections to Suicide. Survival and Coping Beliefs include such items as "I have future plans I am looking forward to carrying out" and "I believe I can learn to adjust or cope with my problems." Linehan et al. (1983) describe this set of beliefs as combining beliefs that are the converse of some beliefs on the BHS with those of self-efficacy and those supporting the value of life. Survival and Coping Beliefs is the subset of the RFLI that has received the most attention, as will be discussed below.

Using a sample of college students, Westefeld, Cardin, and Deaton (1992) developed the College Student Reasons for Living Inventory (CSRFLI). Factor analysis yielded six factors, five of which are the same identified by Linehan et al. (1983) with the addition of "and Friends" to the factor Responsibility to Family. Among college students, Child-Centered Concerns were, understandably, not present. Instead, the factor College and Future-Related Concerns was unique to this group.

Research has investigated the role of coping beliefs in suicidal ideation, intent, and behavior. Specifically, attention has been devoted to establishing whether the BHS and the RFLI measure different constructs (Dyck, 1991; Strosahl et al., 1983) and how hopelessness and reasons for living differentially influence suicidal ideation and behavior at various levels of intent (Strosahl et al., 1992) and in different populations (Cole, 1989; Connell & Meyer, 1991; Rich et al., 1992). In several studies, Linehan and her associates (Linehan et al., 1983; Strosahl et al., 1983, 1992) established the Survival and Coping Beliefs subscale of the RFLI as a useful predictor of suicide intent. Strosahl et al. (1983) demonstrated that Survival and Coping Beliefs could discriminate among levels of suicide intent even among patients with significant levels of hopelessness. A further study of hospitalized parasuicides (Strosahl et al., 1992) identified Survival and Coping Beliefs, hopelessness, and depression as the most important predictors of suicide intent. Survival and Coping Beliefs emerged as the single best predictor of suicide intent for parasuicides. Hopelessness achieved a significant predictor effect only when analyzed apart from Survival and Coping Beliefs, but even then not among repeat parasuicides.

The findings on both repeat parasuicides and a subsample of high-intent parasuicides in this study support the idea that suicide as a solution becomes fixed in a self-limiting response repertoire. Lester, Beck, and Narrett (1978) found that suicide intent increases with successive attempts, and among these high-intent parasuicidal patients there was a positive association between Survival and Coping Beliefs and intent. Theoretically, this could reflect the focus on suicide as a solution, however maladaptive. It could also indicate that as one becomes more suicidal, cognitions shift from general hopelessness to suicide-specific beliefs. Moreover, the presence of a set of suicidal expectancies may establish a "readiness to respond" (Strosahl et al., 1992, p. 371) to negative life events, making what appears to be impulsive acts actually based in a highly specific belief system.

Social Desirability, Hopelessness, and Coping

One of the debates to emerge from the identification of cognitive risk factors in suicide revolves around the concept of social desirability or the tendency to attribute socially desirable qualities to oneself and reject socially undesirable values.

Linehan and her associates (Linehan & Nielson, 1981, 1983; Strosahl, Linehan, & Chiles, 1984) found that the BHS negatively correlated with the Edwards Social Desirability Scale (ESD; Edwards, 1970) and therefore questioned the predictive validity of the BHS. It was argued that people might not fully divulge the extent of their hopelessness, suicidal ideation, and past suicidal behavior and thus bias results.

In fact, social desirability was found to play a greater role in the responses of the general population than among psychiatric patients (Strosahl et al., 1984). Cole (1988), in a study of college students, also found that social desirability influenced the relationship between hopelessness and parasuicide only among those who were not seeking psychological treatment. For students seeking treatment, hopelessness was related to parasuicide even controlling for depression and social desirability. Cole's study concluded that both the nature of the sample and the manner in which social desirability is operationalized affect the results.

In studies of nonclinical groups, social desirability has come to be defined as a reflection of good social and psychological adjustment (Strosahl et al., 1984; Connell & Meyer, 1991). This has led to some confusion over what the construct measures: Is it an attempt to portray oneself in the most favorable light, or is it a self-report measure of general capability? While the theoretical meaning of social desirability remains unclear, the clinical implication is that one should interpret self-reports of hopelessness with the possibility of social desirability in mind.

Finally, Holden, Mendonca, and Serin (1989) examined the relationships among suicide, hopelessness, and a two-factor model of social desirability. One factor of social desirability contained items reflecting focused and realistic thinking, social integration, self-confidence, and hardiness. The other factor contained items relating to considerateness, social sensitivity, and tolerance. The authors define hopelessness as pessimistic cognitions about the future and negative social desirability as a low sense of self-efficacy and coping. In two studies of clinical and non-clinical groups, Holden et al. (1989) found that both hopelessness and a component of social desirability representing a general sense of capability are important for the prediction of suicidal behavior. There is an interaction in which this general sense of capability moderates the relationship between hopelessness and suicidality. Lack of self-efficacy and pessimistic expectations are both associated with suicide, but self-capability reduces the link between hopelessness and suicide. Thus, it is argued that different sets of cognitions are relevant for understanding suicide.

MODELS OF SUICIDAL BEHAVIOR

Models that integrate cognitive risk factors for suicide have been proposed and tested in various samples. These models are based primarily on the stress–vulnerability format in which life stressors imposed on a set of cognitive risk factors result in suicidal behavior. Thus, the risk factors pose a vulnerability to suicide that becomes apparent under adverse conditions.

Bonner and Rich constructed (Bonner & Rich, 1987) and tested (Rich & Bonner, 1987) a model based on a college student sample in which cognitive distortions, social–emotional alienation, and deficient reasons for living predispose an individual to suicide ideation. Once suicide ideation is elicited, the person is at risk for increased alienation, depression, and stress. At this point, hopelessness can develop, which can lead to overt suicidal behavior. A linear combination of social–emotional alienation, cognitive distortions, deficient adaptive resources, hopelessness, and life stress was found to account for both past suicidal behavior (Bonner & Rich, 1987) and current suicidal ideation (Rich & Bonner, 1987). A further test of the interaction of the variables (Bonner & Rich, 1988a) concluded that any or all of the factors may increase the risk for suicide ideation; they are independent risk factors.

Clum and his colleagues (Clum et al., 1979; Schotte & Clum, 1982) developed models that focus on the relationship between problem-solving deficits and hopelessness. They proposed that the combination of life stress and poor problem-solving ability leads to hopelessness, which in turn discourages the person from trying to solve problems (Clum et al., 1979). A test of this model with suicidal patients, however, found no relationship between hopelessness and levels of interpersonal problem-solving skill (Schotte & Clum, 1987). This finding supports the hypothesis that they are independent risk factors in suicide.

The relationships among problem-solving skills, depression, and suicide have been examined in longitudinal work. Schotte, Cools, and Payvar (1990) followed the course of hospitalized suicide ideators and found that problem-solving ability was not a trait, but fluctuated with levels of depression, state anxiety, hopelessness, and suicide intent. This suggests that problem-solving deficits are concomitant to, rather than the cause of, depression, hopelessness, and suicide intent.

Schotte et al. (1990) called into question the notion that problem-solving deficits are antecedents of depression, hopelessness, and suicidal behavior. So, Priester and Clum (1993b) assessed the role of problem-solving deficits prior to a stressor in the eventual development of these criteria. The results generally support the hypothesis that problem-solving deficits alone and in interaction with levels of stress predict depression, hopelessness, and suicide ideation, but not all aspects of problem solving were important in predicting all criteria. The pattern of predictive relationships was most similar for hopelessness and suicide ideation but different for symptoms of depression. Specifically, individuals who could think of only negative consequences for their identified solutions became hopeless and suicidal when stressed by a life event. This attitude of rejecting solutions prevents them from implementing solutions. It was not, however, related to depression. Subjects who became depressed and hopeless were those less able to generate relevant solutions to problems.

There are several implications of these findings: (1) the finding that different problem-solving variables were predicitve of hopelessness, suicide ideation, and depression suggests that it is important to measure all aspects of problem solving, for specific deficits may lead to specific dysfunctions; (2) the finding that, if profound enough, problem-solving deficits alone can lead to suicide ideation suggests that they are more trait-like than state-like for this sample; and (3) the tendency to focus on negative consequences was associated with both hopelessness and suicide ideation. This same variable did not covary with mood in the Schotte et al. (1990) study. So, it may be a good measure of enduring problem-solving deficits.

Beck's research (Beck, 1987; Lester et al., 1989) on suicide ideation and repeat attempters also provides information on the state- or trait-like aspects of problem-solving deficits. The suicide ideators in this study were depressed patients hospitalized for suicide ideation. When depressed, they were also hopeless and had negative self-concepts and problem-solving deficits. These features resolved when the depression remitted. For them, problem-solving deficits were state dependent.

In contrast, the suicide attempters were characterized by personality disorders, alcoholism, and antisocial behavior. Their hopelessness and low self-concepts were chronic and reinforced by society. This group displayed cognitive rigidity, impulsivity, and poor problem-solving deficits that persisted between suicidal episodes (Lester et al., 1989) and were trait-like. At the time of suicidal crises, both groups had low self-concepts, elevated levels of hopelessness, and poor interpersonal problem-solving skills, but from different "causes."

CLINICAL PRESENTATION OF SUICIDAL CLIENTS

The cognitive factors investigated help form a clinical picture of suicidal clients. Persons at high risk for suicide display high levels of hopelessness with each depressive episode or, especially in the case of clients with personality disorders, whenever a life event precipitates an interpersonal crisis. Selective abstraction would allow the individual to see only part of the picture, overgeneralization would lead to faulty and broad conclusions, and dichotomous thinking would lead to extreme emotions and behavior. Incidentally, one can easily imagine the influence alcohol would have on this cognitive processing. Such cognitive distortions serve to maintain the person's depressogenic or dysfunctional assumptions by screening out other, relevant information. The inability to generate alternative perspectives or solutions to problems leads the client to a mental impasse. Suicide, particularly if it has been previously attempted, appears as a way out of this gridlock and becomes a stereotyped response. Suicide ideation that is frequent or continuous, over which the individual feels little control, and which provides some solace is indication of high risk.

In assessing for suicide risk, it is necessary to ascertain how the client has previously responded to stressful life events. What types of self-control strategies or coping skills has the client employed? These might include distraction from persistent suicide ideation, disputing suicidal ideas, utilizing social supports, engaging in alternative behaviors, and taking a problem-solving stance. Someone at risk of suicide might feel incapable of or hostile toward problem solving and avoid it altogether. Instead, the client might demonstate an attraction to death as a way of solving problems.

Finally, the cognitive rigidity apparent in suicidal clients may be accompanied by difficulty tolerating the process of problem solving. Certainly, a challenge to the therapist is to engage the patient in this process and create some disequilibrium in a fixed set of beliefs while encouraging and teaching the patient to withhold judgment until an alternative solution can safely be chosen.

CONCLUSION

Cognitive characteristics of suicidal individuals may be conceptualized as both acute and chronic risk factors in the development of suicidal behavior. There is strong support for the independent roles of hopelessness, problem-solving deficits, and few reasons for living in the paths to suicide. The relationships among these cognitive features may vary by level of suicide ideation and intent, with other factors, such as stressful life events, posing a more proximate risk.

Identification of cognitive factors in suicide can lead to therapeutic interventions to reduce suicide risk. For example, both cognitive therapy (Rush, Beck, Kovacs, Weissenburger, & Hollon, 1982) and problem-solving training (Lerner & Clum, 1990; Salkovskis, Atha, & Storer, 1990) have been found to reduce hopelessness and, in one study (Salkovskis et al., 1990), suicide ideation and short-term frequency of attempts. In addition, the importance of coping beliefs in ameliorating suicide risk has been noted. Such a finding lends further support to interventions that reduce cognitive distortions and bolster more adaptive ways of thinking. Therapeutic strategies aimed at increasing cognitive flexibility, toleration of anxiety in interpersonal conflicts, and suspension of judgment until a solution has been tested would, presumably, reduce the use of suicide as a response to seemingly intolerable situations.

ACKNOWLEDGMENT

This chapter originally appeared in *Frontiers of Cognitive Therapy* (pp. 226–249), edited by P. M. Salkovskis. New York: Guilford Press, 1996. Copyright 1996 by The Guilford Press. Reprinted by permission.

REFERENCES

Abramson, L. Y., Metalsky, G. I., & Alloy, L. B. (1989). Hopelessness depression: A theory-based subtype of depression. *Psychological Review, 96*(2), 358–372.

Asarnow, J. R., Carlson, G. A., & Guthrie, D. (1987). Coping strategies, self-perceptions, hopelessness, and perceived family environments in depressed and suicidal children. *Journal of Consulting and Clinical Psychology, 55,* 361–366.

Asarnow, J. R., & Guthrie, D. (1989). Suicidal behavior, depression, and hopelessness in child psychiatric inpatients: A replication and extension. *Journal of Clinical Child Psychology, 18,* 129–136.

Beck, A. T. (1987, November). *Cognitive approaches to hopelessness and suicide.* Paper presented at the annual meeting of the Association for Advancement of Behavior Therapy, Boston.

Beck, A. T. (1988). *Stability of hopelessness scale scores over repeated admissions.* Unpublished manuscript, Center for Cognitive Therapy, Philadelphia.

Beck, A. T., Beck, R. W., & Kovacs, M. (1975). Classification of suicidal behaviors: I. Quantifying intent and medical lethality. *American Journal of Psychiatry, 132,* 285–287.

Beck, A. T., Brown, G., Berchick, R. J., Stewart, B. L., & Steer, R. A. (1990). Relationship between hopelessness and ultimate suicide: A replication with psychiatric outpatients. *American Journal of Psychiatry, 147*(2), 190–195.

Beck, A. T., Brown, G., & Steer, R. A. (1989). Prediction of eventual suicide in psychiatric inpatients by clinical ratings of hopelessness. *Journal of Consulting and Clinical Psychology, 57*(2), 309–310.

Beck, A. T., Davis, J. H., Frederick, C. J., Perlin, S., Pokorny, A. D., Schulman, R. E., Seiden, R. H., & Wittlin, B. J. (1973) Classification and nomenclature. In H. C. P. Resnik & B. C. Hathorne (Eds.), *Suicide prevention in the seventies* (DHEW Publication No. HSM 72-9054, pp. 7–12). Washington, DC: U.S. Government Printing Office.

Beck, A. T., Kovacs, M., & Weissman, A. (1975). Hopelessness and suicidal behavior: An overview. *Journal of the American Medical Association, 234*(11), 1146–1149.

Beck, A. T., Kovacs, M., & Weissman, A. (1979). Assessment of suicidal intention: The Scale for Suicide Ideation. *Journal of Consulting and Clinical Psychology, 47*(2), 343–352.

Beck, A. T., & Lester, D. (1976). Components of suicidal intent in completed and attempted suicides. *Journal of Psychology, 92,* 35–38.

Beck, A. T., Rush, A. J., Shaw, B. F., & Emery, G. (1979). *Cognitive therapy of depression.* New York: Guilford Press.

Beck, A. T., Schuyler, D., & Herman, I. (1974). Development of suicidal intent scales. In A. T. Beck, H. C. P. Resnik, & D. Lettieri (Eds.), *The prediction of suicide* (pp. 45–56). Bowie, MD: Charles Press.

Beck, A. T., & Steer, R. A. (1987). *Manual for the revised Beck Depression Inventory.* San Antonio, TX: Psychological Corporation.

Beck, A. T., & Steer, R. A. (1989). Clinical predictors of eventual suicide: A 5-

to 10-year prospective study of suicide attempters. *Journal of Affective Disorders, 17,* 203–209.

Beck, A. T., & Steer, R. A. (1991). *Manual for the Beck Scale for Suicide Ideation.* San Antonio, TX: Psychological Corporation.

Beck, A. T., Steer, R. A., & Brown, G. (1993). Dysfunctional attitudes and suicidal ideation in psychiatric outpatients. *Suicide and Life-Threatening Behavior, 23*(1), 11–20.

Beck, A. T., Steer, R. A., Epstein, N., & Brown, G. (1990). The Beck Self-Concept Test. *Psychological Assessment: A Journal of Consulting and Clinical Psychology, 2*(2), 191–197.

Beck, A. T., Steer, R. A., Kovacs, M., & Garrison, B. (1985). Hopelessness and eventual suicide: A ten-year prospective study of patients hospitalized with suicidal ideation. *American Journal of Psychiatry, 142*(5), 559–563.

Beck, A. T., Steer, R. A., & Ranieri, W. F. (1988). Scale for Suicide Ideation: Psychometric properties of a self-report version. *Journal of Clinical Psychology, 44*(4), 499–505.

Beck, A. T., Steer, R. A., & Trexler, L. D. (1989). Alcohol abuse and eventual suicide: A five to ten year prospective study of alcohol abusing suicide attempters. *Journal of Studies on Alcohol, 50*(3), 202–209.

Beck, A. T., & Stewart, B. (1989). *The self-concept as a risk factor in patients who kill themselves.* Unpublished manuscript, Center for Cognitive Therapy, Philadelphia.

Beck, A. T., & Weishaar, M. (1989). Cognitive therapy. In A. Freeman, K. M. Simon, L. E. Beutler, & H. Arkowitz (Eds.), *Comprehensive handbook of cognitive therapy* (pp. 21–36). New York: Plenum Press.

Beck, A. T., Weissman, A., & Kovacs, M. (1976). Alcoholism, hopelessness and suicidal behavior. *Journal of Studies on Alcohol, 37*(1), 66–77.

Beck, A. T., Weissman, A., Lester, D., & Trexler, L. (1974). The measurement of pessimism: The Hopelessness Scale. *Journal of Consulting and Clinical Psychology, 42,* 861–865.

Beck, R. W., Morris, J. B., & Beck, A. T. (1974). Cross-validation of the Suicide Intent Scale. *Psychological Reports, 34,* 445–446.

Bedrosian, R. C., & Beck, A. T. (1979). Cognitive aspects of suicidal behavior. *Suicide and Life-Threatening Behavior, 9*(2), 87–96.

Bonner, R. L., & Rich, A. R. (1987). Toward a predictive model of suicidal ideation and behavior: Some preliminary data in college students. *Suicide and Life-Threatening Behavior, 17,* 50–63.

Bonner, R. L., & Rich, A. R. (1988a). A prospective investigation of suicidal ideation in college students: A test of a model. *Suicide and Life-Threatening Behavior, 18*(3), 245–258.

Bonner, R. L., & Rich, A. (1988b). Negative life stress, social problem-solving, self-appraisal, and hopelessness: Implications for suicide research. *Cognitive Therapy and Research, 12*(6), 549–556.

Brent, D. A. (1987). Correlates of medical lethality of suicide attempts in children and adolescents. *Journal of the American Academy of Child Psychiatry, 26,* 87–89.

Brent, D. A., & Kolko, D. J. (1990). The assessment and treatment of children and adolescents at risk for suicide. In S. J. Blumenthal & D. J. Kupfer (Eds.), *Suicide over the life cycle: Risk factors, assessment and treatment of suicidal patients* (pp. 253–302). Washington, DC: American Psychiatric Press.

Brent, D., Kolko, D., Goldstein, C., Allan, M., & Brown, R. (1989, October). *Cognitive distortion, familial stress, and suicidality in adolescent inpatients.* Poster presented at the annual meeting of the American Academy of Child and Adolescent Psychiatry, New York.

Carlson, G. A., & Cantwell, D. P. (1982). Suicidal behavior and depression in children and adolescents. *Journal of the American Academy of Child Psychiatry, 21,* 361–368.

Clum, G. A., Patsiokas, A. T., & Luscomb, R. L. (1979). Empirically based comprehensive treatment program for parasuicide. *Journal of Consulting and Clinical Psychology, 47,* 937–945.

Cohen-Sandler, R., & Berman, A. L. (1982). *Training suicidal children to problem-solve in nonsuicidal ways.* Paper presented at the annual meeting of the American Association of Suicidology, New York.

Cole, D. A. (1988). Hopelessness, social desirability, depression, and parasuicide in two college student samples. *Journal of Consulting and Clinical Psychology, 56*(1), 131–136.

Cole, D. A. (1989). Psychopathology of adolescent suicide: Hopelessness, coping beliefs, and depression. *Journal of Abnormal Psychology, 98*(3), 248–255.

Connell, D. K., & Meyer, R. G. (1991). The Reasons for Living Inventory and a college population: Adolescent suicidal behaviors, beliefs, and coping skills. *Journal of Clinical Psychology, 47*(4), 485–489.

Curry, J. F., Miller, Y., Waugh, S., & Anderson, W. B. (1992). Coping responses in depressed, socially maladjusted, and suicidal adolescents. *Psychological Reports, 71,* 80–82.

Dixon, W. A., Heppner, P. P., & Anderson, W. (1991). Problem-solving appraisal, stress, hopelessness, and suicide ideation in a college population. *Journal of Counseling Psychology, 38,* 51–56.

Drake, R. E., & Cotton, P. G. (1986). Depression, hopelessness, and suicide in chronic schizophrenia. *British Journal of Psychiatry, 148,* 554–559.

Dyck, M. J. (1991). Positive and negative attitudes mediating suicide ideation. *Suicide and Life-Threatening Behavior, 21*(4), 360–373.

Dyer, J. A. T., & Kreitman, N. (1984). Hopelessness, depression and suicidal intent in parasuicide. *British Journal of Psychiatry, 144,* 127–133.

Edwards, A. (1970). *The measurement of personality traits by scales and inventories.* New York: Holt, Rinehart & Winston.

Ellis, T. E., & Ratliff, K. G. (1986). Cognitive characteristics of suicidal and nonsuicidal psychiatric patients. *Cognitive Therapy and Research, 10,* 625–634.

Emery, G. D., Steer, R. A., & Beck, A. T. (1981). Depression, hopelessness and suicidal intent among heroin addicts. *International Journal of the Addictions, 16*(3), 425–429.

Fawcett, J., Schefter, W., Clark, D., Hedeker, D., Gibbons, R., & Coryell, W. (1987). Clinical predictors of suicide in patients with major affective disorder: A controlled prospective study. *American Journal of Psychiatry, 144,* 35–40.

Goldney, R. D. (1981). Attempted suicide in young women: Correlates of lethality. *British Journal of Psychiatry, 139,* 382–390.

Hawton, K., Osborn, M., O'Grady, J., & Cole, D. (1982). Classification of adolescents who take overdoses. *British Journal of Psychiatry, 140,* 124–131.

Heikkinen, M., Aro, H., & Lönnqvist, J. (1993). Life events and social support in suicide. *Suicide and Life-Threatening Behavior, 23*(4), 343–358.

Hewitt, P. L., Flett, G. L., & Turnbull-Donovan, W. (1992). Perfectionism and suicide potential. *British Journal of Clinical Psychology, 31,* 181–190.

Holden, R. R., Mendoca, J. D., & Serin, R. C. (1989). Suicide, hopelessness, and social desirability: A test of an interactive model. *Journal of Consulting and Clinical Psychology, 57*(4), 500–504.

Josepho, S. A., & Plutchik, R. (1994). Stress, coping and suicide risk in psychiatric inpatients. *Suicide and Life-Threatening Behavior, 24*(1), 48–57.

Kazdin, A. E., French, N. H., Unis, A. S., Esveldt-Dawson, K., & Sherrick, R. B. (1983). Hopelessness, depression, and suicidal intent among psychiatrically disturbed inpatient children. *Journal of Consulting and Clinical Psychology, 51,* 504–510.

Kazdin, A. E., Rodgers, A., & Colbus, D. (1986). The Hopelessness Scale for Children: Psychometric characteristics and concurrent validity. *Journal of Consulting and Clinical Psychology, 54,* 241–245.

Kovacs, M., Beck, A. T., & Weissman, A. (1975). Hopelessness: An indicator of suicidal risk. *Suicide and Life-Threatening Behavior, 5*(2), 98–103.

Lerner, M. S., & Clum, G. A. (1990). Treatment of suicide ideators: A problem-solving approach. *Behavior Therapy, 21,* 403–411.

Lester, D., Beck, A. T., & Narrett, S. (1978). Suicidal intent in successive suicidal actions. *Psychological Reports, 43,* 110.

Lester, D., Beck, A. T., & Steer, R. A. (1989). Attempted suicide in those with personality disorders. *European Archives of Psychiatry and Neurological Sciences, 239,* 109–112.

Levenson, M. (1974). Cognitive characteristics of suicide risk. In C. Neuringer (Ed.), *Psychological assessment of suicide risk* (pp. 150–163). Springfield, IL: Thomas.

Levenson, M., & Neuringer, C. (1971). Problem-solving behavior in suicidal adolescents. *Journal of Consulting and Clinical Psychology, 37,* 433–436.

Linehan, M. M., Camper, P., Chiles, J., Strosahl, K., & Shearin, E. (1987). Interpersonal problem-solving and parasuicide. *Cognitive Therapy and Research, 11,* 1–12.

Linehan, M. M., Chiles, J. A., Egan, K. J., Devine, R. H., & Laffaw, J. A. (1986). Presenting problems of parasuicides versus suicide ideators and nonsuicidal psychiatric patients. *Journal of Consulting and Clinical Psychology, 54,* 880–881.

Linehan, M. M., Goodstein, J. L., Nielson, S. L., & Chiles, J. A. (1983). Reasons for staying alive when you are thinking of killing yourself: The Reasons for Living Inventory. *Journal of Consulting and Clinical Psychology, 51,* 276–286.

Linehan, M., & Nielson, S. (1981). Assessment of suicide ideation and parasuicide: Hopelessness and social desirability. *Journal of Consulting and Clinical Psychology, 49,* 773–775.

Linehan, M., & Nielson, S. (1983). Social desirability: Its relevance to the measurement of hopelessness and suicidal behavior. *Journal of Consulting and Clinical Psychology, 51,* 141–143.

McLeavey, B. C., Daly, R. J., Murray, C. M., O'Riodan, J., & Taylor, M. (1987). Interpersonal problem-solving deficits in self-poisoning patients. *Suicide and Life-Threatening Behavior, 17,* 33–49.

Miller, I. W., Norman, W. H., Bishop, S., & Dow, M. G. (1986). The modified Scale for Suicidal Ideation: Reliability and validity. *Journal of Consulting and Clinical Psychology, 54,* 724–725.

Minkoff, K., Bergman, E., Beck, A. T., & Beck, R. (1973). Hopelessness, depression, and attempted suicide. *American Journal of Psychiatry, 130*(4), 455–459.

Mraz, W., & Runco, M. A. (1994). Suicide ideation and creative problem-solving. *Suicide and Life-Threatening Behavior, 24*(1), 38–47.

Nekanda-Trepka, C. J. S., Bishop, S., & Blackburn, I. M. (1983). Hopelessness and depression. *British Journal of Clinical Psychology, 22,* 49–60.

Neuringer, C. (1961). Dichotomous evaluations in suicidal individuals. *Journal of Consulting Psychology, 25,* 445–449.

Neuringer, C. (1967). The cognitive organization of meaning in suicidal individuals. *Journal of General Psychology, 76,* 91–100.

Neuringer, C. (1968). Divergencies between attitudes towards life and death among suicidal, psychosomatic, and normal hospitalized patients. *Journal of Consulting and Clinical Psychology, 32,* 59–63.

Neuringer, C., & Lettieri, D. J. (1971). Cognition, attitude, and affect in suicidal individuals. *Suicide and Life-Threatening Behavior, 1,* 106–124.

Orbach, I., Bar-Joseph, H., & Dror, N. (1990). Styles of problem solving in suicidal individuals. *Suicide and Life-Threatening Behavior, 20*(1), 56–64.

Orbach, I., Rosenheim, E., & Hary, E. (1987). Some aspects of cognitive functioning in suicidal children. *Journal of the American Academy of Child and Adolescent Psychiatry, 25*(2), 181–185.

Patsiokas, A. T., Clum, G. A., & Luscomb, R. L. (1979). Cognitive characteristics of suicide attempters. *Journal of Consulting and Clinical Psychology, 47,* 478–484.

Prezant, D. W., & Neimeyer, R. A. (1988). Cognitive predictors of depression and suicide ideation. *Suicide and Life-Threatening Behavior, 18*(3), 259–264.

Priester, M. J., & Clum, G. A. (1992). Attributional style as a diathesis in predicting depression, hopelessness, and suicide ideation in college students. *Journal of Psychopathology and Behavioral Assessment, 14*(2), 111–122.

Priester, M. J., & Clum, G. A. (1993a). Perceived problem-solving ability as a predictor of depression, hopelessness and suicidal ideation in a college population. *Journal of Counseling Psychology, 40*(1), 79–85.

Priester, M. J., & Clum, G. A. (1993b). The problem-solving diathesis in depression, hopelessness and suicide ideation: A longitudinal analysis. *Journal of Psychopathology and Behavioral Assessment, 15*(3), 239–254.

Ranieri, W. F., Steer, R. A., Lavrence, T. I., Rissmiller, D. J., Piper, G. E., & Beck, A. T. (1987). Relationship of depression, hopelessness, and dysfunctional attitudes to suicide ideation in psychiatric patients. *Psychological Reports, 61,* 967–975.

Rich, A. R., & Bonner, R. L. (1987). Concurrent validity of a stress vulnerability model of suicidal ideation and behavior: A follow-up study. *Suicide and Life-Threatening Behavior, 17*(4), 265–270.

Rich, A. R., Kirkpatrick-Smith, J., Bonner, R. L., & Jans, F. (1992). Gender differences in psychosocial correlates of suicidal ideation among adolescents. *Suicide and Life-Threatening Behavior, 22*(3), 364–373.

Rotheram-Borus, M. J., & Trautman, P. D. (1988). Hopelessness, depression, and suicidal intent among adolescent suicide attempters. *Journal of the American Academy of Child and Adolescent Psychiatry, 27*, 700–704.

Rotheram-Borus, M. J., Trautman, P. D., Dopkins, S. C., & Shrout, P. E. (1990). Cognitive style and pleasant activities among female adolescent suicide attempters. *Journal of Consulting and Clinical Psychology, 58*(5), 554–561.

Rudd, M. D. (1990). An integrative model of suicidal ideation. *Suicide and Life-Threatening Behavior, 20*(1), 16–30.

Rudd, M. D., Rajab, M. H., & Dahm, P. F. (1994). Problem-solving appraisal in suicide ideators and attempters. *American Journal of Orthopsychiatry, 64*(1), 136–149.

Rush, A. J., Beck, A. T., Kovacs, M., Weissenburger, J., & Hollon, S. (1982). Comparison of the differential effects of cognitive therapy and pharmacotherapy on hopelessness and self-concept. *American Journal of Psychiatry, 139*, 862–866.

Salkovskis, P. M., Atha, C., & Storer, D. (1990). Cognitive-behavioural problem solving in the treatment of patients who repeatedly attempt suicide: A controlled trial. *British Journal of Psychiatry, 157*, 871–876.

Schotte, D. E., & Clum, G. A. (1982). Suicide ideation in a college population: A test of a model. *Journal of Consulting and Clinical Psychology, 50*, 690–696.

Schotte, D. E., & Clum, G. A. (1987). Problem-solving skills in suicidal psychiatric patients. *Journal of Consulting and Clinical Psychology, 55*, 49–54.

Schotte, D. E., Cools, J., & Payvar, S. (1990). Problem solving deficits in suicidal patients: Trait vulnerability or state phenomenon? *Journal of Consulting and Clinical Psychology, 58*(5), 562–564.

Shaw, B. F., & Segal, Z. V. (1988). Introduction to cognitive theory and therapy. In A. J. Frances & R. E. Hales (Eds.), *Review of psychiatry* (Vol. 7, pp. 538–553). Washington, DC: American Psychiatric Press.

Silver, M. A., Bohnert, M., Beck, A. T., & Marcus, D. (1971). Relation of depression of attempted suicide and seriousness of intent. *Archives of General Psychiatry, 25*, 573–576.

Spirito, A., Overholser, J., & Hart, K. (1991). Cognitive characteristics of adolescent suicide attempters. *Journal of the American Academy of Child and Adolescent Psychiatry, 30*(4), 604–608.

Spirito, A., Overholser, J., & Stark, L. J. (1989). Common problems and coping strategies II: Findings with adolescent suicide attempters. *Journal of Abnormal Child Psychology, 17*(2), 213–221.

Spirito, A., Williams, C., Stark, L. J., & Hart, K. (1988). The Hopelessness Scale for Children: Psychometric properties and clinical utility with normal and emotionally disturbed adolescents. *Journal of Abnormal Child Psychology, 16*, 445–458.

Strosahl, K., Chiles, J. A., & Linehan, M. (1992). Prediction of suicide intent in hospitalized parasuicides: Reasons for living, hopelessness, and depression. *Comprehensive Psychiatry, 33*(6), 366–373.

Strosahl, K., Linehan, M., & Chiles, J. (1983, August). *Predictors of suicide intent in psychiatric patients: Reasons for living, hopelessness, and depression.* Paper presented at the annual convention of the American Psychological Association, Anaheim, CA.

Strosahl, K. D., Linehan, M. M., & Chiles, J. A. (1984). Will the real social desirability please stand up?: Hopelessness, depression, social desirability, and the prediction of suicidal behavior. *Journal of Consulting and Clinical Psychology, 52*(3), 449–457.

Weissman, A. N., & Beck, A. T. (1978, November). *Development and validation of the Dysfunctional Attitude Scale: A preliminary investigation.* Paper presented at the meeting of the Association for Advancement of Behavior Therapy, Chicago.

Weissman, A., Beck, A. T., & Kovacs, M. (1979). Drug abuse, hopelessness, and suicidal behavior. *International Journal of the Addictions, 14*, 451–464.

Westefeld, J. S., Cardin, D., & Deaton, W. L. (1992). Development of the College Student Reasons for Living Inventory. *Suicide and Life-Threatening Behavior, 22*(4), 442–452.

Wetzel, R. D. (1976). Hopelessness, depression and suicide intent. *Archives of General Psychiatry, 33*, 1069–1073.

Wetzel, R. D., Margulies, T., Davis, R., & Karam, E. (1980). Hopelessness, depression, and suicide intent. *Journal of Clinical Psychology, 41*, 159–160.

Wetzel, R. D., & Reich, T. (1989). The cognitive triad and suicide intent in depressed inpatients. *Psychological Reports, 65*, 1027–1032.

CHAPTER SIX

Psychopharmacological Treatment of Suicidal Patients

Mark J. Goldblatt, MD
Morton M. Silverman, MD

I n this chapter we focus on the psychopharmacological treatment of psychiatric disorders that are closely associated with suicidal behavior and review the pharmacological management of psychiatric disorders and behavioral dysfunctions associated with the range of suicidal behaviors most often encountered in hospital and outpatient settings.

Large-scale empirical studies of suicides emphasize the correlation between mental illness and suicide (Robins & Murphy, 1959; Dorpat & Ripley, 1960; Barraclough, Bunch, Nelson, & Sainsbury, 1974; Kuperman, Black, & Burns, 1988; Martin, Cloninger, Guze, & Clayton, 1985; Barraclough & Harris, 1994; Harris & Barraclough, 1998). Robins and Murphy (1959) reported 134 cases of completed suicide where 94% were found to have psychiatric diagnoses at the time of death. Just over 50% of these were due to primary depression, and almost 33% were associated with chronic alcoholism.

Although there are a number of mental disorders associated with suicide, depression and alcoholism generally are most closely linked to self-destructive behavior. Panic disorder/anxiety, mania, and substance abuse, in particular cocaine, are diagnoses that also correlate significantly with suicide. Suicide may be considered a lethal component of many psychiatric illnesses. In this chapter we focus on the appropriate use of medication to treat the underlying psychiatric illness and potentially alleviate the accompanying suicidal component.

TREATMENT OF SUICIDAL PATIENTS

All patients undergoing psychiatric evaluation should be assessed as to their level of psychological pain and extent of suicidal ideation, intent, and/or plans. In addition, it is essential to inquire about access to lethal means of self-harm. This assessment takes place within the context of the psychiatric interview, with the patient's psychopathology and personality structure noted, as well as any concurrent medical illness or use of medication, and available social and interpersonal support systems. This is more fully described elsewhere. (Maris, Berman, Maltsberger, & Yufit, 1992).

In general, somatic therapies should be aimed at treating symptoms of the underlying psychiatric condition. This occurs within the context of the overall therapeutic and psychoeducational approach to the illness. Medication should be delivered in the context of a positive physician–patient relationship, one that includes mutual respect and conveys a sense of hope. The clinician should not expect to dissuade patients of their hopelessness; rather, he or she must win the patient's cooperation to undergo a collaborative course of treatment. This requires a supportive approach and the building of a working alliance. The clinician's communication of the treatment plan and expectation that the patient will respond are crucial. Physicians need to acknowledge the potential for side effects of current medications, as well as the potential lethality when they are taken in overdose (Silverman, 1998). However, once treatment has begun, all efforts should be expended to ensure a full trial of medication and prevent undertreatment.

Psychopharmacological evaluation includes a careful review of previous medication trials with particular attention to specific medication type, dosage, duration of treatment, and history of compliance. Inquiry should also be made as to any history of allergies or complicating medical illnesses. Family histories of psychopathology, response to somatic therapies, and suicidal behaviors are also important to explore.

As the process of evaluation and treatment begins, a treatment alliance is formed. This is the capacity of the patient and doctor to work together to address the patient's symptoms. For those patients who remain at some risk for suicide, the physician relies on this alliance to gauge how much autonomy can be tolerated by the patient and how committed the patient is to the treatment plan (Bongar, Maris, Berman, Litman, & Silverman, 1993; Silverman, Berman, Bongar, Litman, & Maris, 1994). In this context, the physician prescribes a limited amount of medication to last until the next appointment, commensurate with the patient's ability to safely manage the total number of pills provided. The treatment alliance places responsibilities on the patient too. These include being truthful about reporting symptoms and mental state, as well as compliance with the treatment protocol. Willingness to adhere to the medication trial is a crucial aspect, as is candidness about noncompliance or increased suicidality (Goldblatt, Silverman, & Schatzberg, 1998).

The decision to begin a patient on psychotropic medication involves great consideration and thoughtfulness. The therapeutic consequences are weighed against the risk of side effects, stigma, financial burden, and legal and psychological concerns. Medications are usually only one part of the overall treatment plan and should be discussed with the patient in terms of the treatment goals and limitations of outcome. The medication should be understood relative to its potential for good and for harm for each individual. If used prudently and reasonably, pharmacological agents have an important role to play in the overall treatment of the suicidal patient, but appropriate monitoring and oversight is necessary.

Prevention of suicidal behaviors depends on the appropriate treatment of the underlying psychiatric disorders. What follows is specific consideration of somatic treatments of depression, delusional depression, bipolar affective disorder, schizophrenia, alcoholism, cocaine abuse, panic disorder/anxiety, and borderline personality disorder.

Depression

The National Institute of Mental Health (NIMH) Extramural Collaborative Study of Depression revealed that a substantial undertreatment of depressed patients was common, even in academic medical settings.

The generally low dosages of medications and the variability of treatment regimens were attributable to individual medical practitioners' decision making (Keller et al., 1986). Less than half of the medication trials that "refractory" depressed patients received were reported to be adequate in dosage or duration (Schatzberg et al., 1983).

In the past the pharmacological treatment of seriously depressed patients began with a tricyclic antidepressant (TCA). More recently, selective serotonin reuptake inhibitors (SSRIs) have become increasingly popular. More and more clinicians are using SSRIs as first line treatment for depression, given their effectiveness and low incidence of side effects (Stahl, 1997).

Fluoxetine (Prozac) is probably the best known of the new group of antidepressant drugs—the SSRIs—that selectively inhibit the reuptake of serotonin. Its side-effect profile is generally more favorable than that of TCAs; it appears to facilitate weight loss and does not potentiate seizures in humans (Stahl, 1998). Fluoxetine has a long half-life, and appears relatively safe even when taken in overdose.

Shortly after the market introduction of fluoxetine, a small number of case reports (e.g., Teicher, Glod, & Cole, 1990) noted the emergence of suicidal ideation in patients taking fluoxetine. A great deal of publicity in the media surrounded such reports, which hypothesized that fluoxetine may trigger emergent suicidal and homicidal ideation in a small proportion of patients taking this medication. Further study has clarified that there is no "increased risk of suicidal acts or emergence of substantial suicidal thoughts among depressed patients" associated with the treatment of fluoxetine (Beasley et al., 1991). The American College of Neuropsychopharmacology Task Force review of suicidal behavior and psychotropic medication concluded that

> new generation low-toxicity antidepressants, including SSRIs, may carry a lower risk for suicide than older TCAs. There is no evidence that antidepressants such as the SSRIs, for example fluoxetine, trigger emergent suicidal ideation over and above rates that may be associated with depression and other antidepressants. What is clear is that most patients receive substantial benefit from treatment with this drug and related antidepressants. (Mann, Goodwin, O'Brien, & Robinson, 1993, p. 182)

Other new agents have proven to be valuable additions to the antidepressant armamentarium. Sertraline (Zoloft), paroxetine (Paxil), bupropion (Wellbutrin), venlafaxine (Effexor), nefazodone (Serzone), citalopram (Celexa), and mirtazapine (Remeron) appear to be equally effective in the treatment of depression and usually are well tolerated with relatively few side effects.

Trazadone, a mixed serotonin reuptake and receptor blocker is another alternative for the treatment of depressed patients. An additional advantage is that it is less lethal than TCAs when taken in overdose. Clomipramine (Anafranil), a new TCA, exerts a considerable effect on blocking serotonin reuptake and thus may prove to be a useful alternative treatment for suicidal patients, but this has not been well tested.

If patients are not responding to a course of antidepressant medication, the clinician must assess whether an adequate trial has been achieved. The response to TCAs is often slower than one might wish— up to 4 weeks at therapeutic levels. Quitkin et al. (1984) concluded in their review of a series of studies on TCAs in depressed patients that relatively few patients demonstrate significant improvement after only 2 weeks of therapy and many require as long as 6 weeks to respond. SSRIs can take up to 8 or 10 weeks to achieve effectiveness. The necessary time course for treatment response remains in considerable debate. The physician should remain responsive to the clinical picture of the individual patient, as well as to the effects that the psychiatric illness may have on the potential for suicidal behaviors.

For some patients, adding lithium carbonate or liothyronine (Cytomel) to an antidepressant can facilitate a delayed clinical response. If these adjunctive therapies are not effective, the physician is faced with the option of either changing the medication within the same class of drug, moving on to another class of antidepressant, or electroconvulsive therapy (ECT; Salzman, 1999).

Another class of antidepressants are the monoamine oxidase inhibitors (MAOIs). These medications block the intraneuronal action of monoamine oxidase, the enzyme that degrades various neurotransmitters, including norepinephrine, dopamine, and serotonin. MAOIs have been reported to be particularly effective in patients with atypical or refractory depressions. Clinicians frequently worry that suicidal patients might kill themselves by ignoring their special diets or using proscribed agents. Although case studies have been reported in the literature, we have seldom seen this occur. Generally, even suicidal patients are frightened by the potential pain and sequelae of hypertensive reactions, such that this becomes an unattractive method of self-harm. Rather, MAOIs are often very effective for some suicidal depressives and should be strongly considered.

In the treatment of major depression, the newer antidepressants, including the SSRIs, appear safer than the TCAs, as they are less toxic when taken in overdose and are generally less problematic while equally effective. Depressed patients should be warned that "suicidal ideation may occasionally worsen in the course of treatment, as may overall depression and that such an event would be a reason for immediately contacting their doctor" (Mann et al., 1993).

ECT has generally been shown to be the most broadly effective treatment of depression, with response rates of approximately 80%. ECT should be considered for any seriously depressed patient who has failed to respond to other treatments, or for those patients with delusions (Tanney, 1986). In patients with compromised physical states due to anorexia, catatonia, or psychosis, and in cases of pronounced suicidal ideation/behavior, ECT should be considered early in treatment.

Delusional Depression

Suicide risk is five times higher in delusional versus nondelusional depressions. Robins (1986) reported that 19% of 134 subjects who committed suicide had also been psychotic, a finding that has been confirmed by others. Roose et al. (1983) found that delusionally depressed patients were five times more likely to commit suicide than were nondelusionally depressed patients. In our experience, these patients are among the most difficult to treat. They often hide the degree of their cognitive disturbance, become frozen or distant, and are difficult to assess for true suicidal risk. Responding to their paranoia, these patients often are afraid of their medication and may be noncompliant with treatment. Clinicians should be wary in accepting any assurances about control of suicidal behavior in a delusionally depressed patient.

These patients respond better to neuroleptic–TCA treatment or to ECT than to TCAs alone (Spiker et al., 1981; Avery & Lubrano, 1979). Responsivity of this condition to other antidepressants (e.g., SSRIs or MAOIs) or to combinations of these agents with antipsychotics has not been well studied.

Mania

Although mania is usually associated with mood elevation and euphoria, several authors have described patients with manic features including affective lability, irritability, anger, and severe dysphoria characterized by depression and anxiety (Post et al., 1989). One such patient recently reported to one of the authors that he felt "gloriously suicidal" during a manic episode.

The mainstay of treatment is lithium carbonate. Antipsychotic medications are also helpful in the acute management of this state. Second-line drugs that are frequently used are carbamazepine (Tegretol) and valproic acid (Depakene). In some cases these patients appear to have a relatively poor response to treatment with lithium carbonate, as compared with "pure" manics (Secunda et al., 1986). Post and colleagues have suggested that this group of patients may show a relatively better therapeutic response to carbamazepine (Post, Uhde, Roy-Byrne, & Joffe, 1987).

Occasionally, it is difficult to distinguish agitated depression from an irritable, dysphoric manic state. The most notable feature in the clinical treatment is that dysphoric manic patients become worse when treated with antidepressant medication.

Schizophrenia

Although schizophrenic disorders are primarily considered to involve difficulties with cognition and thinking, rather than with mood, suicide is a serious and unfortunately common complication of this disorder (Kaplan & Harrow, 1999). More than 20% of patients hospitalized for schizophrenia will attempt suicide at some time. The majority of schizophrenic suicides occur in outpatients, usually soon after discharge from hospital (Caldwell & Gottesman, 1992).

Some schizophrenic patients who commit suicide demonstrate increased agitation or psychosis. In this subgroup adequate treatment with antipsychotic medication is essential. Depression in the schizophrenic population is particularly difficult to define or study. The consensus in the literature is that suicidal schizophrenic patients are more likely to be depressed than nonsuicidal schizophrenic patients. However, it is often difficult to distinguish depression from the "negative symptoms of schizophrenia." Initially it was believed that antidepressant treatment of the symptoms resulted in an exacerbation of the schizophrenic condition. However, more recent studies have argued that some of these symptoms respond to treatment with antidepressants or alprazolam (Xanax, an antianxiety medication), and so such treatments are considered worth a trial. In severe cases, ECT and lithium carbonate can also be considered.

There have been reports of at least two patients who attempted suicide to relieve severe akathisia (Shear, Frances, & Weiden, 1983). Thus selecting the "right" drug for schizophrenic patients may be less relevant than developing effective approaches to symptom relief.

Clozapine (Clozaril) and risperdone (Risperdal) are two new additions to the treatment armamentarium for schizophrenia. They are structurally different from the more common antipsychotics. Clozapine has been shown to decrease suicidality in neuroleptic-resistant schizophrenic patients, associated with improvement in depression and hopelessness (Meltzer & Okayli, 1995). Although more studies are indicated to assess the role of clozapine and risperdone in suicidal patients, these two new drugs have already proven to be highly valued for their improved response in treatment-refractory psychosis. Other recently released antipsychotic agents include olanzapine (Zyprexa) and quetiapine (Seroquel).

Thioridazine (Mellaril) is approved by the Food and Drug Administration (FDA) for use in moderate-to-marked depression with anxiety or agitation. However, there is no evidence that any neuroleptic is generally superior to standard antidepressants for the treatment of depression. Thioridazine should probably be avoided in sexually active young males because it may produce retrograde ejaculation.

For patients who do not begin to improve on an adequate dose of an antipsychotic medication, and for those who report distressing side effects, a different class of antipsychotic drug can be tried. Pragmatically, more than 2 weeks without response in a markedly psychotic patient and 5–6 weeks in a patient with milder symptoms generally indicate the need to consider a change in medication regime.

Clozapine is an alternative treatment for patients who have failed on standard neuroleptics. Risperdone, a unique serotonergic–dopaminergic antagonist, is also an alternative for refractory as well as for newly diagnosed patients. Sometimes the addition of a different class of drug, such as lithium or a TCA, may be effective. Depot preparations (injectable forms of antipsychotic medication) ensure compliance in patients who have difficulty with daily medication regimens.

The risks of tardive dyskinesia from conventional neuroleptic medication makes the long-term use of these drugs worrisome. It is currently not possible to predict which patients will develop tardive dyskinesia. However, the best available data suggest a rate of development of dyskinesia of about 3–4% over the first 4 or 5 years of exposure. Elderly women and patients with affective disorders appear at greater risk than schizophrenic patients (Gardos & Casey, 1984).

Suicide is a considerable risk in schizophrenic patients. The illness is debilitating, and the patient is easily demoralized by the cycles of decompensation and recompensation. However, interventions aimed at reducing psychosis and alleviating distress and depressive/negative symptoms should help to decrease the likelihood of untoward outcomes.

Alcohol-Related Disorders

Alcoholism, drug abuse, and affective disorders are among the most common psychiatric illnesses. The lifetime risk for suicide is approximately 15% for patients with alcoholism, as compared to 1% in the general population. Alcohol abuse increases the risk for suicidal behavior for both alcoholic and nonalcoholic populations, being associated with 50% of all suicides and 5–27% of suicides in alcoholics (Robins et al., 1984).

Alcoholics can suffer from other psychiatric illnesses as well, and depression is particularly common (Murphy, 1992). Serotonin represents a possible link between alcoholism and depression. Sellers, Naranjo, and Peachey (1981) reported that serotonin reuptake blockers reduce alcohol consumption in heavy drinkers. Weingartner, Buchsbaum, and Linnoila (1983) reported that zimelidine (Zelmid), a relatively specific serotonin reuptake blocker, attenuates the impairing effects of ethanol on learning and memory. Thus, serotonin activity may provide a link between suicidality in alcoholic and depressed patients. Prospective studies on SSRIs as a treatment for suicidal alcoholics seem reasonable, as does this approach on a clinical basis. Eventually SSRIs may be included in an overall approach to the treatment of this debilitating disorder. However, at this point there is no substitute for treatment programs aimed at abstinence, vocational rehabilitation, and psychoeducation.

Cocaine-Related Disorders

Abuse of illicit substances is associated with an increased risk of suicidal behavior. The San Diego Suicide Study, conducted from 1981 to 1983, found that substance abuse was associated with 58% of suicides in young adults and that substance abuse was the primary diagnosis in 39% of all cases (Fowler, Rich, & Young, 1986). Of particular concern was the finding that suicide risk appears to be highly correlated with multiple drug abuse (Marzuk & Mann, 1988). Although alcohol is the most commonly found drug of abuse, it is often found in combination with other illicit drugs, including marijuana, hallucinogens, opiates, and cocaine.

The precise causative mechanisms by which psychoactive drug use promotes suicidal behavior remains unclear. Data from the NIMH Epidemiologic Catchment Area (ECA) study showed that the risk of panic attacks was greater for identified cocaine users. The estimated relative risk (odds ratio, or O.R. = 13) were greatest among cocaine users who reported no marijuana use during the follow-up interval (Anthony, Tien, & Petronis, 1989). In a related report based on the full ECA data set, Petronis, Samuels, Moscicki, and Anthony (1990) conducted multivariate conditional logistics regression analyses on data collected during a 1-2-year follow-up period to identify potential personal and behavioral risk factors for suicide attempts. They found that being a user of cocaine was associated with increased risk of making a suicide attempt (O.R. = 62), but illicit use of marijuana, sedative-hypnotics, or sympathomimetic stimulants was not. Depression was associated with increased risk of suicide attempt (O.R. = 41) as was active alcoholism (O.R. = 18).

A recent study by Marzuk et al. (1992) showed that approximately 20% of completed suicides among residents of New York City had used cocaine within days of their death. After controlling for demographic variables and ethanol use, these investigators found that individuals who committed suicide with firearms were twice as likely to have used cocaine as those who used other methods. There appears to be a relationship between cocaine use, anxiety, and panic attacks that requires further study. Clinicians should routinely inquire about all types of substance abuse and advocate interventions aimed at abstinence.

Panic Disorder

Follow-up studies of patients with panic disorder (dating back to 1982) have reported significantly increased rates of unnatural mortality, most resulting from suicide (Coryell, Noyes, & Clancy, 1982; Coryell, 1988; Allgulander & Lavori, 1991). Based on data from the ECA survey, Weissman, Klerman, Markowitz, and Ouellette (1989) reported that 20% of community members surveyed who met criteria for a diagnosis of panic disorder, reported a history of suicide attempts (the odds ratio for suicide attempts compared to other disorders was 2.62). In addition, 12% of those who experienced panic attacks but who failed to meet full criteria for a DSM-III diagnosis of panic disorder were reported to have a history of suicide attempts. A reanalysis of the data found 7% of respondents with uncomplicated panic disorder reported a history of suicide attempts (O.R. = 5.4) (Johnson, Weissman, & Klerman, 1990).

These ECA findings have been criticized from a methodological perspective (Clark & Kerkhof, 1993; Appleby, 1994), as well as from a clinical perspective, relating to the presence of comorbidity (particularly depression), which may have accounted for the high prevalence of suicidal ideation and attempts in the cohort reporting panic attacks and panic disorder (Fawcett et al., 1990; Beck, Steer, Sanderson, & Skeie, 1991). Nevertheless, other studies have found an increased rate of suicide attempts in patients with panic disorder (Lepine, Chignon, & Teherani, 1993; Korn et al., 1992).

Many clinicians now believe that panic attacks appear to be one of several contributing factors that are associated with an increased risk of suicide attempts and completions when they are associated with other psychiatric disorders, especially major affective disorder (Clark & Fawcett, 1992; Appleby, 1994). This underscores the importance of rapid, appropriate treatment for patients with panic attacks and panic disorder, especially when they occur in association with other DSM-IV axis I or II disorders.

The initial treatment of panic disorder and panic attacks is either with alprazolam or with antidepressants such as imipramine, desipramine, phenelzine, or fluoxetine. Patients with panic attacks generally require lower doses of antidepressants.

Borderline Personality Disorder

Borderline personality disorder (BPD) is characterized by the following symptoms: impulsivity; unstable and intense interpersonal relationships; inappropriate, intense anger; identity disturbance; affective instability; self-destructive acts; and a chronic sense of loneliness and emptiness. Generally, patients with BPD are not marked responders to psychopharmacological treatments; however, medication may alleviate certain key symptoms.

One report of 58 patients with BPD who were treated with mianserin or placebo noted no significant reduction in the number of suicidal acts during the 6-month treatment period (Montgomery, Roy, & Montgomery, 1981). However, in a flupenthixol versus placebo double-blind study, there was a significant reduction over placebo in the number of suicidal acts in the patients treated with flupenthixol at 4, 5, and 6 months (Montgomery et al., 1979). Although various underlying mechanisms are probably involved, flupenthixol's effect on dopamine systems may be inferred to be involved in decreasing suicidal behavior in personality disorders.

Soloff and his colleagues (1986) reported that haloperidol produced significant improvement on a broad spectrum of symptom patterns including depression, anxiety, hostility, paranoid ideation, and psychoticism in patients with BPD. In contrast, amitriptyline was found to be minimally effective, with some improvement noted in areas of depressive content. On a composite measure of overall symptom severity, haloperidol was found to be superior to both amitriptyline and placebo, with no difference noted between amitriptyline and placebo. Goldberg and colleagues (1986) also reported a therapeutic benefit from thiothixene over placebo in treating some selected symptoms of BPD. Significant drug–placebo differences were found on illusions, ideas of reference, psychoticism, obsessive–compulsive symptoms, and phobic anxiety, but not on depression. The mean daily dosage was lower than that used in outpatient schizophrenics.

Although at least two studies have indicated that phenothiazines are helpful in reducing suicidal and other symptoms in patients with BPD, there is still much debate about how and whether to use them. Gunderson (1986) has noted that neuroleptics should be reserved for patients with BPD who present with sustained and severe symptoms of the kind described above (i.e., illusions, ideas of reference, and psychoticism). For patients with BPD without these symptoms, or those in whom symptoms are either acute, reactive, or nonsevere, drugs are less likely to be useful and may present unnecessary risks of harmful side effects. This area requires further study.

Two other treatment strategies that may be helpful in patients with BPD are MAOIs and anticonvulsants. MAOIs may be most useful in treating anxiety with related depression in patients with BPD. Cowdry and Gardner (1986) noted that carbamazepine was effective in decreasing the self-destructive behavior of patients with BPD, when compared to other drug regimens. However, self-destructive behaviors in this group were by no means eliminated. Further studies on this approach appear warranted.

Recent studies about the effects of SSRIs on patients with BPD are encouraging, but more work needs to be done to clarify their potential role for these patients.

CONCLUSION

The suicidal patient represents a challenge to the practitioner (Bongar, 1991). Treatment must begin with a careful assessment of the patient's psychological condition, physical status, and suicidal potential (Bongar, Berman, Litman, & Maris, 1992). Thereafter, an organized approach to treating the underlying condition can be undertaken. This approach should include consideration of proven psychotherapeutic interventions and the prescription of appropriate medications in adequate trials— both in time and amount of drug (Maltsberger, 1994). Biological and psychopharmacological studies suggest that selective serotonin reuptake inhibitors may prove particularly helpful for alcoholic and depressed patients with suicidal behavior, and that neuroleptics have an important place in treating schizophrenic patients, some patients with BPD, and those with psychotic depression (Goldblatt & Schatzberg, 1990, 1992).

ACKNOWLEDGMENT

Portions of this chapter are adapted from Goldblatt et al. (1988). Copyright 1998 by The Guilford Press. Adapted by permission.

REFERENCES

Allgulander, C., & Lavori, P. W. (1991). Excess mortality among 3302 patients with "pure" anxiety neurosis. *Archives of General Psychiatry, 48*, 599–602.

Anthony, J. C., Tien, A. Y., & Petronis, K. R. (1989). Epidemiologic evidence on cocaine use and panic attacks. *American Journal of Epidemiology, 129*, 543–549.

Appleby, L. (1994). Panic and suicidal behavior. *British Journal of Psychiatry, 164*, 719–721.

Avery, D., & Lubrano, A. (1979). Depression treated with imipramine and ECT: The De Caroles study revisited. *American Journal of Psychiatry, 136*, 559–562.

Barraclough, B., Bunch, J., Nelson, B., & Sainsbury, P. (1974). A hundred cases of suicide: Clinical aspects. *British Journal of Psychiatry, 125*, 355–373.

Barraclough, B., & Harris, E. C. (1994). Suicide as an outcome for mental disorders. *British Journal of Psychiatry, 164*, 205–228.

Beasley, C. M., Dornseif, B. E., Bosomworth, J. C., Sayler, M. E., et al. (1991). Fluoxetine and suicide: A meta-analysis of controlled trials of treatment for depression. *British Medical Journal, 303*, 685–692.

Beck, A. T., Steer, R. A., Sanderson, W. C., & Skeie, T. M. (1991). Panic disorder and suicidal ideation and behavior: Discrepant findings in psychiatric out-patients. *American Journal of Psychiatry, 148*, 1191–1195.

Bongar, B. M. (1991). *The suicidal patient: Clinical and legal standards of care.* Washington, DC: American Psychiatric Press.

Bongar, B. M., Berman, A. L., Litman, R. E., & Maris, R. W. (1992). Outpatient standards of care in the assessment, management and treatment of suicidal persons. *Suicide and Life-Threatening Behavior, 22*, 453–478.

Bongar, B. M., Maris, R. W., Berman, A. L., Litman, R. E., & Silverman, M. M. (1993). Inpatient standards of care and the suicidal patient: Part I. General clinical formulations and legal considerations. *Suicide and Life-Threatening Behavior, 23*, 245–256.

Caldwell, C., & Gottesman, I. I. (1992). Schizophrenia—A high risk factor for suicide: Clues to risk reduction. *Suicide and Life-Threatening Behavior, 22*, 479–493.

Clark, D. C., & Fawcett, J. (1992). An empirically based model of suicide risk assessment for patients with affective disorder. In D. Jacobs (Ed.), *Suicide and clinical practice* (pp. 55–74). Washington, DC: American Psychiatric Press.

Clark, D. C., & Kerkhof, A. J. F. M. (1993). Panic disorders and suicidal behavior. *Crisis 14*, 2–5.

Coryell, W. (1988). Panic disorders and mortality. *Psychiatric Clinics of North America, 11*, 433–440.

Coryell, W., Noyes, R., & Clancy, J. (1982). Excess mortality in panic disorder: A comparison with primary unipolar depression. *Archives of General Psychiatry, 39*, 701–703.

Cowdry, R. W., & Gardner, D. C. (1986). Pharmacotherapy of borderline personality disorder. *Archives of General Psychiatry, 45*, 111–119.

Dorpat, T. L., & Ripley, H. (1960). A study of suicide in the Seattle area. *Comprehensive Psychiatry, 1*, 349–359.

Fawcett, J., Scheftner, A., Fogg, L., et al. (1990). Time-related predictors of suicide in major affective disorder. *American Journal of Psychiatry, 147*, 1189–1194.

Fowler, R. C., Rich, C. L., & Young, D. (1986). San Diego Suicide Study II. Substance abuse in young cases. *Archives of General Psychiatry, 43*, 962–965.

Gardos, G., & Casey, D. (1984). *Tardive dyskinesia and affective disorders.* Washington, DC: American Psychiatric Press.

Goldberg, S. C., Schulz, S. C., Schulz, P. M., et al. (1986). Borderline and schizotypal personality disorders treated with low-dose thiothixene vs. placebo. *Archives of General Psychiatry, 43*, 680–686.

Goldblatt, M. J., & Schatzberg, A. F. (1990). Somatic treatment of the adult suicidal patient: A brief survey. In S. J. Blumenthal & D. J. Kupfer (Eds.), *Suicide over the life cycle: Risk factors, assessment and treatment of suicidal patients* (pp. 425–440). Washington, DC: American Psychiatric Press.

Goldblatt, M. J., & Schatzberg, A. F. (1992). Medication and the suicidal patient. In D. Jacobs (Ed.), *Suicide and clinical practice* (pp. 23–41) Washington, DC: American Psychiatric Press.

Goldblatt, M. J., Silverman, M. M., & Schatzberg, A. F. (1998). Psychopharmacological treatment of suicidal inpatients. In B. Bongar, A. L. Berman, R. W. Maris, M. M. Silverman, E. A. Harris, & W. L. Packman (Eds.), *Risk management with suicidal patients* (pp. 110–129). New York: Guilford Press.

Gunderson, J. G. (1986). Pharmacotherapy for patients with borderline personality disorder. *Archives of General Psychiatry, 43*, 698–700.

Harris, E. C., & Barraclough, B. (1998). Excess mortality of mental disorders. *British Journal of Psychiatry, 173*, 11–53.

Johnson, J., Weissman, M. M., & Klerman, G. (1990). Panic disorder, comorbidity and suicide attempts. *Archives of General Psychiatry, 47*, 805–808.

Kaplan, K. J., & Harrow, M. (1999). Psychosis and functioning as risk factors for later suicidal activity among schizophrenia and schizoaffective patients: A disease-based interactive model. *Suicide and Life-Threatening Behavior, 29*(1), 10–24.

Keller, M. B., Lavori, P. W., Klerman, G. L., et al. (1986). Low levels and lack of predictors of somatotherapy received by depressed patients. *Archives of General Psychiatry, 43*, 458–466.

Korn, M. L., Kotler, M., Macho, A., et al. (1992). Suicide and violence associated with panic attacks. *Biological Psychiatry, 31*, 607–612.

Kuperman, S, Black, D. W., & Burns, T. L. (1988). Excess suicide among formerly hospitalized child psychiatry patients. *Journal of Clinical Psychiatry, 49*, 88–93.

Lepine, J. P., Chignon, J. M., & Teherani, M. (1993). Suicide attempts in patients with panic disorder. *Archives of General Psychiatry, 50*, 144–149.

Maltsberger, J. T. (1994). Calculated risk-taking in the treatment of suicidal patients: Ethical and legal problems. In A. A. Leenaars, J. T. Maltsberger, & R. A. Neimeyer (Eds.), *Treatment of suicidal people*. Washington, DC: Taylor & Francis.

Mann, J. J., Goodwin, F. K., O'Brien, C. P., & Robinson, D. S. (1993). Suicidal behavior and psychotropic medication [Accepted as a consensus statement by the American College of Neuropsychopharmacology (ACNP) Council, March 2, 1992.] *Neuropsychopharmacology, 8*, 177–183.

Maris, R. W., Berman, A. L., Maltsberger, J. T., & Yufit, R. I. (1992). *Assessment and prediction of suicide*. New York: Guilford Press.

Martin, R. L., Cloninger, C. R., Guze, S. B., & Clayton, P. J. (1985). Mortality in a follow-up of 500 psychiatric outpatients: II. Cause-specific mortality. *Archives of General Psychiatry, 42*, 58–66

Marzuk, P. M., & Mann, J. J. (1988). Suicide and substance abuse. *Psychiatric Annals, 18*, 639–645.

Marzuk, P. M., Tardiff, K., Leon, A. C., Stajic, M., Morgan, E. B., & Mann, J. J. (1992). Prevalence of cocaine use among residents of New York City who committed suicide during a one-year period. *American Journal of Psychiatry, 149*, 371–375.

Meltzer, H. Y., & Okayli, G. (1995). Reduction of suicidality during clozapine treatment of neuroleptic-resistant schizophrenia: Impact on risk-benefit assessment. *American Journal of Psychiatry, 152*, 183–190.

Montgomery, D. B., Roy, D., & Montgomery, S. A. (1981). Mianserin in the prophylaxis of suicidal behavior: A double-blind placebo-controlled trial. In J. P. Soubrier & J. Vedrinne (Eds.), *Depression and suicide: Proceedings of the 11th International Congress of Suicide Prevention, Paris* (pp. 786–790). Fairview Park, NY: Pergamon Press.

Montgomery, S. A., Montgomery, D. B., Rani, S. J., Roy, D., Shaw, P. H., & McCauley, R. (1979). Maintenance therapy in repeat suicidal behavior: A placebo-controlled trial. In *Proceedings of the 10th International Congress for Suicide Prevention and Crisis Intervention, Ottawa, Canada* (pp. 227–229).

Murphy, G. E. (1992). *Suicide in alcoholism.* New York. Oxford University Press.

Petronis, K. R., Samuels, J. F., Moscicki, E. K., & Anthony, J. C. (1990). An epidemiologic investigation of potential risk factors for suicide attempts. *Social Psychiatry and Psychiatric Epidemiology, 25,* 193–199.

Post, R. M., Rubinow, D. R., Uhde, T. W., et al. (1989). Dysphoric mania: Clinical and biological correlates. *Archives of General Psychiatry, 46,* 353–358.

Post, R. M., Uhde, W. T., Roy-Byrne, P. P., & Joffe, R. T. (1987). Correlates of antimanic response to carbamazepine. *Psychiatry Research, 21,* 71–83.

Quitkin, F. M., Rabkin, J. G., Ross, D., et al. (1984). Duration of antidepressant drug treatment: What is an adequate trial? *Archives of General Psychiatry, 41,* 238–245.

Robins, E. (1986). Psychosis and suicide. *Biological Psychiatry; 21,* 665–672.

Robins, E., & Murphy, G. E. (1959). Some clinical considerations in the prevention of suicide based on a study of 134 successful suicides. *American Journal of Public Health, 49,* 888–889.

Robins, L. N., Helzer, J. E., Weissman, M. M., et al. (1984). Lifetime prevalence of specific psychiatric disorders in three sites. *Archives of General Psychiatry, 41,* 947–958.

Roose, S. P., Glassman, A. H., Walsh, T. B., et al. (1983). Depression, delusions and suicide. *American Journal of Psychiatry, 140*(9), 1159–1162.

Salzman, C. (1999). Treatment of the suicidal patient with psychotropic drugs and ECT. In D. Jacobs (Ed.), *The Harvard Medical School guide to suicide assessment and intervention* (pp. 372–382). San Francisco: Jossey-Bass.

Schatzberg, A. F., Cole, J. O., Cohen, B. M., et al. (1983). Survey of depressed patients who have failed to respond to treatment. In J. M. Davis & J. W. Maas (Eds.), *The affective disorders.* Washington, DC: American Psychiatric Press.

Secunda, S. K., Katz, M. M., Swann, A. C., et al. (1986). *Mixed mania: Diagnosis and treatment* (pp. 79–94). Washington, DC: American Psychiatric Press.

Sellers, E. M., Naranjo, C. A., & Peachey, J. E. (1981). Drugs to decrease alcohol consumption. *New England Journal of Medicine, 305,* 1255–1262.

Shear, M., Frances, A., & Weiden, P. (1983). Suicide associated with akathisia and depot fluphenazine treatment. *Journal of Clinical Psychopharmacology, 3,* 235–236.

Silverman, M. M. (1998). Clinical psychopharmacotherapy with hospitalized patients: A forensic perspective. In B. Bongar, A. L. Berman, R. W. Maris, M. M. Silverman, E. A. Harris, & W. L. Packman (Eds.), *Risk management with suicidal patients* (pp. 130–149). New York: Guilford Press.

Silverman, M. M., Berman, A. L., Bongar, B., Litman, R. E., & Maris, R. W. (1994). Inpatient standards of care and the suicidal patient: Part II. An integration with clinical risk management. *Suicide and Life-Threatening Behavior 24,* 152–169.

Soloff, P. H., George, A., Nathan, S., et al. (1986). Progress in pharmacotherapy of borderline disorders: A double-blind study of amitriptyline, haloperidol and placebo. *Archives of General Psychiatry, 43,* 691–700.

Spiker, D. G., Hanin, I., Cofsky, J., et al. (1981). Pharmacological treatment of delusional depressives. *Psychopharmacology Bulletin, 17*, 201–202.

Stahl, S. M. (1997). *Psychopharmacology of antidepressants*. London: Marton Press.

Stahl, S. M. (1998). Selecting an antidepressant by using mechanism of action to enhance efficacy and avoid side effects. *Journal of Clinical Psychiatry, 59*(Suppl. 18), 23–29.

Tanney, B. L. (1986). Electroconvulsive therapy and suicide. In R. W. Maris (Ed.), *Biology of suicide* (pp. 116–140). New York: Guilford Press.

Teicher, M. H., Glod, C., & Cole, J. O. (1990). Emergence of intense suicidal preoccupation during fluoxetine treatment. *American Journal of Psychiatry, 147*, 207–210.

Weingartner, H., Buchsbaum, M. S., & Linnoila, M. (1983). Zimelidine effects on memory impairments produced by ethanol. *Life Sciences, 33*, 2159–2163.

Weissman, M. M., Klerman, J. L., Markowitz, J. S., & Ouellette, R. (1989). Suicidal ideation and suicide attempts in panic disorder and attacks. *New England Journal of Medicine, 321*, 1209–1214.

PART THREE

HIGH-RISK GROUPS AND FACTORS

Suicidal Behavior in Prepubertal Children

From the 1980s to the New Millennium

Cynthia R. Pfeffer, MD

A spectrum of suicidal tendencies that includes suicidal thinking, suicidal threats, suicide attempts, and suicide is observed in prepubertal children (Pfeffer, 1986). Prior to the early 1980s, the possibility that these phenomena existed in prepubertal children was not accepted because of the following:

1. Lack of systematic observations of the characteristics of suicidal tendencies in children.
2. Theoretical concepts that children are too immature to have feelings of depression and hopelessness, and to effect self-destructive methods.
3. Beliefs that children are protected from life adversities by benevolent caretakers.

In the late 1970s and early 1980s, clinical reports were published about characteristics of prepubertal children aged 6–12 years who expressed suicidal ideation and engaged in suicidal behavior and who were referred for psychiatric treatment in emergency services, outpatient clinics and psychiatric hospitals (Pfeffer, 1978, 1979, 1980, 1981a; Pfeffer, Conte, Plutchik, & Jerrett, 1979, 1980). These reports described issues important in identifying suicidal states among children, such as their verbalizations about suicidal thinking and their suicidal behavior, and indicators in play that provided clues of suicidal tendencies. One report described children and young adolescents who committed suicide (Shaffer, 1974). These reports provided the first systematic information about prevalence of suicidal phenomena among prepubertal children. They highlighted the importance of evaluating young children for suicidal risk and developing empirical research that would identify factors that elevate the likelihood of a child carrying out suicidal acts.

At approximately the same time, suicide among adolescents was highlighted in the national media principally because these events seemed to occur within specific communities and proximate in time. These suicide cluster phenomena alarmed communities and motivated intensive efforts to mount suicide prevention efforts. The proposed aims of such efforts were to decrease the escalating rate of suicide, especially among 15- 24-year-olds by (1) involving community services and agencies in developing preventive interventions, (2) promoting political action to initiate legislation to establish suicide prevention programs, and (3) stimulating national efforts to develop policy to encourage extensive research on suicidal behavior among youth.

By the mid-1980s, suicidal behavior in youth was recognized and considered a national mental health problem, especially among adolescents and young adults who were 15 to 24 years old. Prepubertal suicidal behavior was recognized as a valid phenomenon, although the rates of suicide among prepubertal children and young adolescents were the lowest of all age groups. Clinical reports were published to help clinicians and professionals in the community on topics involving "An Overview for Educators of Suicidal Behavior of Children" (Pfeffer, 1981b), "Interventions for Suicidal Children and Their Families" (Pfeffer, 1982a), "Basic Concepts in Recognizing Suicidal Children" (Pfeffer, 1982b), and "Suicidal Behavior in Normal School Children" (Pfeffer, Zuckerman, Plutchik, & Mizruchi, 1984). Estimates of prevalence rates of suicidal behavior among prepubertal children were provided as a result of empirical research (Pfeffer, Plutchik, Mizruchi, & Lipkins, 1986). Notably, rates of suicide attempts were greater among prepubertal psychiatrically hospitalized children (34.0%) than among prepubertal psychiatric outpatients (1.0%) and nonpatient prepubertal children in the community (1.0%) (Pfeffer et al., 1986). These estimated rates focused attention on the importance of identifying suicidal children and providing them with intensive psychiatric treatment.

The role of family adversity in promoting suicidal behavior among children was highlighted in reports suggestive of "The Family System of Suicidal Children" (Pfeffer, 1981c). The finding that suicidal children perceived themselves in fantasies as being expendable to their families (Sabbath, 1969) provided a conceptual approach that organized treatment to focus on improving family communication and reducing burdens on children's perceptions that they felt guilt and shame for causing family strife.

Early reports highlighted that certain psychopathologies were associated with suicidal behavior of prepubertal children. The significance of depressive symptoms and mood disorders, such as major depressive disorder, as risk factors for prepubertal suicidal behavior was replicated and validated in samples of prepubertal psychiatric patients and nonpatients (Pfeffer et al., 1982c, 1986). The presence of suicidal tendencies among psychotic children and those with serious personality disorders was described (Pfeffer, Solomon, Plutchik, Mizruchi, & Weiner, 1982). Thus, contrary to common beliefs that all children are susceptible to exhibiting suicidal behavior, these reports suggested that those who were most vulnerable were those with distinct psychopathology.

In 1989, the Secretary's Task Force on Youth Suicide, a national committee mandated by the U.S. Department of Health and Human Services (DHHS) to develop policy to reduce the national rates of youth suicidal behavior, published recommendations that oriented efforts to prevent the morbidity and mortality involved with suicidal behavior among children and adolescents (Alcohol, Drug Abuse, and Mental Health Administration, 1989). These recommendations were the precursors of more systematic efforts to research this problem and to promote effective suicide prevention efforts.

In the 1990s, a burgeoning of empirical research on childhood and adolescent suicidal behavior has provided important insights about the characteristics of suicidal behavior among children and adolescents. Techniques of interviewing prepubertal children regarding their suicidal ideation or suicidal attempts have been discussed to illustrate that young children can describe their plans, intent, and motivations to carry out suicidal behavior (Jacobsen et al., 1994). Building upon the knowledge gleaned from these clinical reports and empirical investigations, this chapter will highlight some of the key areas of study regarding pre-pubertal suicidal behavior that might be relevant for improving the clin-ical care of children at risk for such behavior as well as for developing future directions for research.

EPIDEMIOLOGY OF PREPUBERTAL SUICIDE

Suicide in 1995 among children and young adolescents aged 5–14 years was the fifth leading cause of death; it followed accidents, malignancies, homicide, and congenital anomalies (Anderson, Kochanek, & Murphy, 1997). This age group in 1995 had the lowest suicide rate. Table 7.1 in-dicates the number of suicidal deaths and rates of suicide for children and young adolescents with regard to demographic characteristics. The highest rate of suicide for this age group was among white males, for whom suicide was the third leading cause of death. Hispanics of both sexes had the next highest suicide rate. Racial differences in rates of sui-cide suggest that it is important to study the characteristics of specific racial groups regarding risk for suicide. Such studies should focus on un-derstanding sociocultural and neurobiological chararacteristics that may be associated with distinctions in gender and racial features of sui-cide.

TABLE 7.1. Child and Young Adolescent Suicide, Age Group 5–14 Years

Group	Rate	Number	Rank
All races, both sexes	0.9	337	5
All races, male	1.3	260	4
All races, female	0.4	77	>10
White, both sexes	1.0	289	5
Black, both sexes	0.5	31	10
Hispanic, both sexes	0.8	40	4
White, male	1.4	223	3
White, female	0.4	66	6
Black, male	0.8	25	8
Black, female	A	A	>10

Note. Data from Anderson, Kochanek, and Murphy (1997). A, data not listed in Anderson et al. (1997). Hispanics were not listed in that reference as regards age groups by gender. "Rank" indicates the rank order of suicide relative to other causes of death.

NATURAL HISTORY OF PREPUBERTAL
SUICIDAL BEHAVIOR

Few studies have prospectively followed prepubertal suicidal children. Such research methodology enables the identification of true risk factors, which are factors present prior to the expression of suicidal behavior. Pfeffer, Lipkins, Plutchik, and Mizruchi (1989), reporting on a 2-year follow-up of a cohort of prepubertal children in the community who were selected because they had no history of psychiatric intervention, found that the incidence of suicide attempts in the children was 1%. They also reported on a 6- to 8-year follow-up of prepubertal suicidal and nonsuicidal psychiatric patients and nonpatients (Pfeffer et al., 1991, 1993). This research indicated that a history of suicidal behavior in prepuberty predicts suicide attempts in adolescence (Pfeffer et al., 1993). Specifically, a history of a suicide attempt in prepubertal psychiatric patients imparts a 6 times greater risk of a suicide attempt in adolescence than not having a history of a suicide attempt in childhood. A history of suicidal ideation among prepubertal psychiatric patients imparts a 3.7 times greater risk of making a suicide attempt in adolescence than not having a history of suicidal ideation in childhood. Thus, suicidal ideation and suicidal acts in childhood are important risk factors for suicidal behavior in adolescence. Such research suggests a continuity in suicidal behavior from childhood to adolescence. It would be important to learn if there is a long-term continuity in childhood suicidal behavior by determining if prepubertal suicidal behavior predicts suicidal acts in late adolescence or young adulthood.

The aforementioned research also suggested that factors present in prepuberty, such as life event stress, major depressive disorder, and poor social adjustment predicted suicide attempts in adolescence (Pfeffer et al., 1993). Depressive disorders, such as major depression, in prepubertal children constitute a risk factor for subsequent episodes of major depression and other comorbid disorders, such as conduct and substance abuse disorders, and also constitute a risk factor for suicide attempts in adolescence (Kovacs, Goldston, & Gatsonis, 1993). The complexity of interactions among risk factors for prepubertal suicidal behavior is an important issue requiring systematic empirical research to test models that identify the pathways to childhood and adolescent suicidal states. For example, research on the impact of early life event adversity on the development of children may enhance our understanding of processes that promote suicidal risk as well as risk for poor social adaptation and incidence of such psychopathologies as mood disorders, substance abuse, and violence.

FAMILY PSYCHOPATHOLOGY AND PREPUBERTAL SUICIDAL BEHAVIOR

Dependency on familial social relationships is strong during the preschool and prepubertal periods of development. Despite the transitions in which the school-age child must confront new social relationships with teachers and peers, family bonds remain the foremost interpersonal context. Modifications in the intensity of family relations begins as children approach puberty when adolescent social roles emerge. Clinical reports have highlighted the importance of family problems in increasing risk for prepubertal suicidal behavior (Pfeffer, 1981c; Sabbath, 1969). Notably, prepubertal suicidal children often feel enmeshed in intense family turmoil and find it difficult to emerge from these stressful interactions (Pfeffer, 1981c, 1986). Often prepubertal suicidal children perceive that they are the cause of family problems and that they are expendable to the family; in such cases the child may feel that the family would be better off if he or she vanished (Sabbath, 1969). The prepubertal child who feels despondent, hopeless, guilty, and ashamed may think that suicide is the best means to solve the family dilemma.

Recent empirical research utilizing systematic family history methodology with relatives of prepubertal suicidal and nonsuicidal children suggested that prepubertal psychiatric patients with a history of a suicide attempt had significantly higher rates of parents or siblings who reported suicide attempts than did nonsuicidal prepubertal psychiatric patients or nonsuicidal prepubertal children living in the community (Pfeffer, Normandin, & Kakuma, 1994). Furthermore, prepubertal children who reported a suicide attempt and those who reported suicidal ideation had comparable rates of suicide attempts among first-degree relatives. These results suggest, as with results of studies of suicidal adolescents (Brent et al., 1994) and adults (Egeland & Sussex, 1985), that suicidal behavior aggregates in families. The methodology of such studies is not able to suggest underlying mechanisms, for example, whether it is genetic vulnerability or social modeling that promotes these correlations. Research that focuses on identifying genetic influences of suicidal behavior in children is needed.

Since suicidal behavior runs in families, an important issue to discern is whether children of first-degree relatives who commit suicide exhibit heightened tendencies for suicidal behavior and other psychopathologies. A recent report (Pfeffer et al., 1997) described psychosocial features of prepubertal children who experienced the recent suicidal death of a relative. It suggested that such children have an elevated prevalence of internalizing symptoms, such as depressive and anxiety symptoms, and problematic school adjustment within a year of the suicidal death of a parent or sibling. No child attempted suicide within the year after the suicide of a relative. This study, among the few to systematically study the development of young children who were bereaved by the suicidal death of a relative, highlighted the importance of evaluating young family members of individuals who are suicidal and the need to offer appropriate intervention to reduce risk for adverse outcomes. Such vulnerable populations may be an important group in which to target preventive interventions.

A constellation of psychiatric symptoms and disorders involving assaultiveness, substance abuse disorders, and antisocial personality disorder has been identified among first-degree relatives of prepubertal suicidal patients (Pfeffer et al., 1994). These findings support research suggesting that children exposed to physical or sexual abuse are at high risk for suicidal acts, regardless of gender or racial backgrounds (Dyken, Alpert, & McNamara, 1985). These results may suggest issues to pursue regarding identifying neurobiological mechanisms such as dysfunctions in serotonergic systems that have been identified among adults with impulsivity, violence, and substance abuse disorders (Coccaro et al., 1989; Mann & Stanley, 1986). These results also imply that children of parents with histories of such psychopathologies should be evaluated for suicidal tendencies and appropriate intervention provided.

NEUROBIOLOGY OF PREPUBERTAL SUICIDAL BEHAVIOR

There has been a large number of studies of variations in serotonin-related measures of adults with suicidal behavior, violent acts, impulsivity, substance abuse disorders, and antisocial personality disorder (Mann & Stanley, 1986). Recent research identified that the same genes encode proteins of neuronal and platelet serotonin transporters, thereby suggesting similarities between these proteins (Cook et al., 1994). Thus, studies of variations in platelet serotonin measures may provide an acceptable model for identifying neurobiological correlates of suicidal behavior in prepubertal children. Utilizing such methodology, Pfeffer and colleagues (1998) reported that the level of whole-blood tryptophan, a precursor of serotonin, was significantly lower in prepubertal child psychiatric inpatients with a recent history of a suicide attempt than among normal children or prepubertal psychiatric inpatients with suicidal ideation. The importance of these results is to suggest that variations in serotonin-related measures may be among the neurobiological risk factors for suicidal behavior in young children, as has been identified for samples of adults with histories of suicidal behavior, violent acts, substance abuse, or personality disorders. Additional research about the predictive validity of such variations in serotonergic measures is warranted.

TREATMENT OF PREPUBERTAL SUICIDAL BEHAVIOR

The complex individual, family, and other environmental factors identified to be associated with prepubertal suicidal behavior offer venues upon which to intervene in ameliorating risk for suicidal behavior among young children. At present, relatively little empirical research has been conducted to evaluate the efficacy of psychotherapeutic treatments for prepubertal suicidal children. Clinical experience suggests that suicidal prepubertal children require psychotherapeutic approaches that combine individual intervention with family-oriented treatment (Pfeffer, 1986).

Recent investigation discerned that selective serotonin reuptake inhibitor (SSRI) medication, such as fluoxetine, is efficacious in treating major depressive disorder in children and adolescents (Emslie et al., 1997). Whether these and other types of medications will reduce risk for suicidal behavior in prepubertal children requires additional research.

SUMMARY

This chapter provides a brief overview of clinical knowledge and research results about prepubertal suicidal behavior. It suggests that a significant amount of research has been conducted that has elucidated the multiple facets of this clinical phenomenon. It suggests that underlying neurobiological factors contribute to suicidal risk in children but that the effects of these vulnerability factors may be influenced by other environmental factors involving stress of discordant family life and other adverse life events occurring in the formative period of human development. This chapter points out the dearth of systematic treatment studies of suicidal children, which may be one of the most important issues for future investigations regarding prepubertal suicidal behavior as we enter the new millennium.

REFERENCES

Alcohol, Drug Abuse, and Mental Health Administration. (1989). *Report of the Secretary's Task Force on Youth Suicide: Vol. I. Overview and recommendations* (DHHS Publication No. ADM 89–1621). Washington, DC: Superintendent of Documents, U.S. Government Printing Office.

Anderson, R. N., Kochanek, K. D., & Murphy, S. L. (1997). Report of final mortality statistics, 1995. *Monthly Vital Statistics Report, 45*(11, Suppl. 2). Hyattsville, MD: National Center for Health Statistics.

Brent, D. A., Perper, J. A., Moritz, G., Liotus, L., Schweers, J., Balach, L., & Roth, C. (1994). Familial risk factors for adolescent suicide: A case–control study. *Acta Psychiatrica Scandanavica, 89,* 52–58.

Coccaro, E. F., Siever, L. J., Klar, H. M., Mauer, G., Cochrane, K., Cooper, T. B., Mohs, R. C., & Davis, K. L. (1989). Serotonergic studies in patients with affective and personality disorders. *Archives of General Psychiatry, 46,* 587–599.

Cook, E. H., Fletcher, K. E., Wainwright, M., Marks, N., Yan, S. Y., & Leventhal, B. (1994). Primary structure of the human platelet serotonin 5-HT–2A receptor: Identity with frontal cortex serotonin 5-HT-2A receptor. *Journal of Neurochemistry, 63,* 465–469.

Dyken, E. Y., Alpert, J. J., & McNamara, J. J. (1985). A pilot study of the effect of exposure to child abuse or neglect on adolescent suicidal behavior. *American Journal of Psychiatry, 142,* 1299–1303.

Egeland, J. A., & Sussex, J. N. (1985). Suicide and family loading for affective disorders. *Journal of the American Medical Association, 254,* 915–918.

Emslie, G., Rush, A., Weinberg, W., Kowatch, R. A., Hughes, C. W., Carmody, T., & Rintelmann, J. (1997). A double-blind, randomized placebo-controlled trial of fluoxetine in children and adolescents with depression. *Archives of General Psychiatry, 54,* 1031–1037.

Jacobsen, L. K., Rabinowitz, I., Popper, M. S., Solomon, R. J., Sokol, M. S., & Pfeffer, C. R. (1994). Interviewing prepubertal children about suicidal ideation and behavior. *Journal of the American Academy of Child and Adolescent Psychiatry, 33,* 439–452.

Kovacs, M, Goldston, D., & Gatsonis, C. (1993). Suicidal behaviors and childhood-onset depressive disorders: A longitudinal investigation. *Journal of the American Academy of Child and Adolescent Psychiatry, 32,* 8–20.

Mann, J. J., & Stanley, M. (1986). *Annals of the New York Academy of Sciences: Vol. 487. Psychobiology of suicidal behavior*. New York: New York Academy of Sciences.

Pfeffer, C. R. (1978). Psychiatric hospital treatment of latency age suicidal children. *Suicide and Life-Threatening Behavior, 8*, 150–160.

Pfeffer, C. R. (1979). Clinical observations of play of hospitalized suicidal children. *Suicidal and Life-Threatening Behavior, 9*, 235–244.

Pfeffer, C. R. (1980). Unanswered questions about childhood suicidal behavior: Perspective for the practicing physician. *Journal of Developmental and Behavioral Pediatrics, 1*, 11–14.

Pfeffer, C. R. (1981a). Suicidal behavior of children: A review with implications for research and practice. *American Journal of Psychiatry, 138*, 154–159.

Pfeffer, C. R. (1981b). An overview for educators of suicidal behavior of children. *Exceptional Children, 48*, 170–172.

Pfeffer, C. R. (1981c). The family system of suicidal children. *American Journal of Psychotherapy, 35*, 330–341.

Pfeffer, C. R. (1982a), Interventions for suicidal children and their families. *Suicide and Life-Threatening Behavior, 12*, 240–248.

Pfeffer, C. R. (1982b). Basic concepts in recognizing suicidal children. *Medicine and Hygiene, 40*, 2365–2368.

Pfeffer, C. R. (1982c). Clinical observations of suicidal behavior in a neurotic, a borderline, and a psychotic child: Common processes of symptom formation. *Child Psychiatry and Human development, 13*, 120–134.

Pfeffer, C. R. (1986). *The suicidal child*. New York: Guilford Press.

Pfeffer, C. R., Conte, H. R., Plutchik, R., & Jerrett, I. (1979). Suicidal behavior in latency age children—An empirical study. *Journal of the American Academy of Child Psychiatry, 18*, 679–692.

Pfeffer, C. R., Conte, H. R., Plutchik, R., & Jerrett, I. (1980). Suicidal behavior in latency age children—An empirical study: An outpatient population. *Journal of the American Academy of Child Psychiatry, 19*, 703–710.

Pfeffer, C. R., Klerman, G. L., Hurt, S. W., Kakuma, T., Peskin, J. R., & Siefker, C. A. (1993). Suicidal children grow up: Rates and psychosocial risk factors for suicide attempts during follow-up. *Journal of the American Academy of child and Adolescent Psychiatry, 32*, 106–113.

Pfeffer, C. R., Klerman, G. L., Hurt, S. W., Lesser, M., Peskin, J. R., & Siefker, C. A. (1991). Suicidal children grow up: Demographic and clinical risk factors for adolescent suicide attempts. *Journal of the American Academy of Child and Adolescent Psychiatry, 30*, 609–616.

Pfeffer, C. R., Lipkins, R., Plutchik, R., & Mizruchi, M. (1989). Normal children at risk for suicidal behavior: A two-year follow-up study. *Journal of the American Academy of Child and Adolescent Psychiatry, 27*, 34–41.

Pfeffer, C. R., Martins, P., Mann, J., Sunkenberg, M., Ice, A., Damore, J. P., Gallo, C., Karpenos, I., & Jiang, H. (1997). Child survivors of suicide: Psychosocial characteristics. *Journal of the American Academy of Child and Adolescent Psychiatry, 36*, 65–74.

Pfeffer, C. R., McBride, A., Anderson, G. M., Kakuma, T., Fensterheim, L., & Khait, V. (1998). Peripheral serotonin measures in prepubertal psychiatric inpatients and normal children: Associations with suicidal behavior and its risk factors. *Biological Psychiatry, 44,* 569–577.

Pfeffer, C. R., Normandin, L., & Kakuma, T. (1994). Suicidal children grow up: Suicidal behavior and psychiatric disorders among relatives. *Journal of the American Academy of Child and Adolescent Psychiatry, 33,* 1087–1097.

Pfeffer, C. R., Plutchik, R., Mizruchi, M. S., & Lipkins, R. (1986). Suicidal behavior in child psychiatric inpatients and outpatients and in nonpatients. *American Journal of Psychiatry, 143,* 733–738.

Pfeffer, C. R., Solomon, G., Plutchik, R., Mizruchi, M. S., & Weiner, A. (1982). Suicidal behavior in latency-age psychiatric inpatients: A replication and cross validation. *Journal of the American Academy of Child Psychiatry, 21,* 564–569.

Pfeffer, C. R., Zuckerman, S., Plutchik, R., & Mizruchi, M. S. (1984). Suicidal behavior in normal school children: A comparison with child psychiatric inpatients. *Journal of the American Academy of Child Psychiatry, 23,* 416–423.

Sabbath, J. C. (1969). The suicidal adolescent: The expendable child. *Journal of the American Academy of Child Psychiatry, 8,* 272–289.

Shaffer, D. (1974). Suicide in childhood and adolescence. *Journal of Child Psychology and Psychiatry, 15,* 275–291.

CHAPTER EIGHT

Innovative Approaches to Youth Suicide Prevention
An Update of Issues and Research Findings

Janet A. Grossman, DNSc
Markus J. P. Kruesi, MD

Youth suicide in America has reached epidemic proportions. In a recent comparison with 26 other Westernized countries, the United States had the highest rate of childhood suicide. Suicide is the third leading causes of death in 15- to 19-year-olds, the fourth leading cause in 10- to 14-year-olds, and the sixth leading cause in 5- to 14-year-olds (Centers for Disease Control and Prevention, 1997). Although suicide is a rare event, youth 15–19 years of age have displayed increases in suicide rates from the 1950s through the 1990s. In a 1997 national study of high school students, almost 8% reported attempting suicide in the past year (Centers for Disease Control and Prevention, 1998b).

YOUTH SUICIDE MORTALITY AND MORBIDITY

Suicide Mortality (Fatal Suicidal Behavior)

The rate of suicide for people ages 15 to 19 more than quadrupled between 1950 and 1990. The rates for people ages 20–24 were higher during this period, while the rates for most other adult age groups declined (Kachur, Potter, James, & Powell, 1995; see McIntosh, Chapter 1, this volume, for greater details). In 1996, the suicide mortality rate for youth aged 15–19 was 9.7 (per 100,000 population; McIntosh, Chapter 1, this volume). Almost 2,000 adolescents died by suicide that year in the United States alone. While the reported number has remained constant for many years, many believe the exact number is underreported and is actually much higher (Kachur et al., 1995).

Data collected over the past 40 years indicate that the rates for completed suicide among young people aged 15–19 have varied by gender and ethnicity. White males are at the greatest risk for suicide and have traditionally had the highest rates of suicide. The ratio of males to females in the 15–19 age group is approximately 4.5:1. The greatest net increase in age-specific suicide rates across all gender and age–race groups in 1980–1992 was in 10- to 14-year-old youth—an increase of 120%. Relatively speaking, however, the overall rate (and number of deaths) remains low. There has also been a significant increase in suicides of minority youths, especially black males. The suicide rates for minority youths have been steadily climbing since 1965 and have increased more rapidly since 1980. The rate for black males aged 15–19 years increased 164% between 1980 and 1992 (Centers for Disease Control and Prevention, 1995a; Shaffer, Gould, & Hicks, 1994).

Firearms and Youth Suicide

The choice of methods is a strong predictor of outcomes. Firearms are the most common method used by suicide victims of all ages and both genders. The majority of adolescents (60%–70%) in the United States who complete suicide die by the use of firearms (National Center for Health Statistics, 1996; Ryland & Kruesi, 1992). In 1996, firearms accounted for 63% of suicides among people aged 15–24 (Peters, Kochanek, & Murphy, 1998). Firearm-related suicides accounted for 81% of the increase in the overall 15- to19-year-old rate of suicide from 1980 to 1992 (Kachur, Potter, James, & Powell, 1995).

Many people, including health professionals, do not realize that firearms are the most frequent method used in youth suicide. In a 1995 survey of doctors and nurses working in emergency departments, the majority did not recognize that firearms are the most frequent method by which male and female adolescents complete suicide (Fendrich, Kruesi, Wisker, et al., 1998). *USA Today* conducted a telephone survey on October 28, 1993, and found that between 40% and 50% of households in the United States contain firearms. This figure is consistent with U.S. Department of Justice estimates that 49% of U.S. households contain firearms.

Case–Control Studies

Case–control studies have consistently found that the presence of a firearm in the house increases the risk of adolescent suicide. (Brent, Perper, & Allman, 1987; Brent et al., 1991; Brent, Perper, Moritz, Baugher, et al., 1993; Kellerman et al., 1992). The studies compared adolescents who completed suicide with those who were at similar risk but did not complete suicide. Odds ratios indicate how much the risk is increased. The risk of suicide was anywhere from two to almost five times greater when a gun was in the house. When psychiatric illness was present in an adolescent, having a gun in the house still significantly increased the odds of completed suicide (Brent et al., 1987; Brent et al., 1991). For those adolescents without a psychiatric illness who completed suicide, the presence of a firearm in the house is the only potentially modifiable risk factor that has been identified (Community Action for Youth Survival, 1997).

Suicide Morbidity (Nonfatal Suicidal Behavior)

Nonfatal suicidal behaviors have been studied through the use of clinical studies of youth attempts, surveillance of emergency department visits of adolescent suicide attempts, and surveys of youth health risk behaviors. The national Youth Risk Behavior Surveillance System established by the Centers for Disease Control and Prevention (CDC) is a study of health risk behaviors leading to mortality, morbidity, and social problems of adolescents. In 1997, high school students reported the following rates of nonfatal suicidal behavior in the past year: 20.5% had seriously considered suicide; 15.7% had made a plan to attempt suicide; 7.7% had attempted suicide; and 2.6% had injury, poisoning, or overdose resulting from the attempt that required treatment by a doctor or nurse. Compared to all other gender and ethnic groups, Hispanic females had the highest rate of attempted suicide (23.1%), a level approximately twice the national average (Centers for Disease Control and Prevention, 1998b).

The majority of youth who make attempts are not seen for medical services. Of those who are seen, however, they are most likely to receive emergency medical services (Centers for Disease Control and Prevention, 1995b; Seidel, 1991). Thus, surveillance in these services provide some data on youth attempters. Oregon is the only state with a legal requirement for hospital emergency departments to report suicide-related injuries among youth aged 17 years and younger. The state also requires referral for counseling, and maintenance of a surveillance system. The surveillance data collected during the 1988–1993 period indicated that 3,783 youth age 17 years and younger made serious suicide attempts in Oregon, including 124 who died. Youth aged 15–17 years had the highest rate of attempts, and only 10 children were less than 10 years old. The ratio of female to male attempts was 4:1. Overdose was the most common method, accounting for 75.5% of attempts (Centers for Disease Control and Prevention,1995b). In another regional emergency department surveillance in Cobb County, Georgia, youth aged 15–19 years had a higher rate of suicide-related visits as compared to any other age group (Birkhead, Galvin, Meehan, O'Carroll, & Mercy, 1993).

Youth at Risk for Suicide and Youth Exposed to Suicide

Youth suicide is a complex phenomenon, determined by multiple factors intersecting at one point in the life of an individual. Several frameworks of suicide risk are reported in the literature (e.g., Blumenthal & Kumpfer, 1990; Ryland & Kruesi, 1992; Shneidman, 1985). Moscicki (1995) provides an epidemiological framework for risk factors for both suicide morbidity and mortality. The framework includes four risk factor categories: psychiatric, biological, familial, and situational. Moscicki makes a distinction between proximal and distal risk factors. The interaction of proximal and distal risk factors occurring together are associated with the greatest risk of suicide (Hennricksson et al., 1993).

The risk factors for suicide mortality as identified from youth psychological autopsy studies are psychiatric disorders, symptoms, and circumstances including mood disorders, anxiety disorders, adjustment disorders, conduct disorders, antisocial personality, inhibited personality, learning disorders, comorbidity of psychiatric disorders, substance use and abuse, excessive anxiety, perfectionism, past suicidal ideation with a plan, past suicide attempt, previous suicidal behavior, exposure to a relative's or friend's suicide, parental or family psychopathology, parental absence or abusiveness, acute disciplinary crises or rejection, and firearm availability. Studies have consistently found that over 90% of youth who die by suicide have a psychiatric disorder, primarily depression (Brent, Perper, Goldstein et al., 1988; Brent, Perper, Moritz, Allman, Friend, et al., 1993; Martunnen, Aro, Hennricksson, & Löngvist,1991; Shaffer, Garland, Gould, Fisher, & Trautman, 1988; Shaffi, Stelz-Lenarsky, Derrick, Beckner, & Whittinghill, 1988). Similarly, depression, substance abuse, and aggressive behaviors were significantly more prevalent in suicidal youth than nonsuicidal youth (Andrews & Lewinsohn, 1992; Garrison, McKeown,Vallois, &Vinncent, 1993).

Familial risk factors include psychiatric disorders in family members, father absence, family discord, and family abuse and violence (Andrews & Lewinsohn, 1992; Brent, Perper, Moritz, Allman, Friend, et al., 1993; Centers for Disease Control and Prevention, 1995b; de Wilde, Kienhorst, Diekstra, & Wollers, 1991). As previously noted, the presence of a firearm in the home is one of the strongest situational risk factors for adolescent suicide (Brent, Perper, Goldstein, et al., 1988; Brent et al., 1991). Other situational risk factors include interpersonal conflict, loss, and external stressors (e.g., legal and disciplinary problems, incarceration). There is evidence that biological risk factors, such as epilepsy, AIDS, diabetes, and serotonergic dysfunction may also increase risk (Arango et al., 1993; Callahan, Clark, Grossman, & Donoghue, 1998).

APPROACHES TO YOUTH SUICIDE

The Mental Health Approach

Brent and colleagues' (Brent, Perper, Goldstein et al., 1988; Brent et al., 1991), psychological autopsy studies of youth have estimated that approximately one-fourth of youth under age 19 were in mental health services at the time of their death and approximately three quarters had been in mental health services at some time during their lifetme. The individuals studied were primarily Caucasian youth.

Traditional mental health services are less likely to reach minority youth. For example African American males, whose rates of youth suicide are rising rapidly, are the least likely to report depression and suicidal behavior and to seek mental health care. Community-based outreach programs may be the best way to reach these youth. The high rate of suicide risk behavior in Hispanic females underscores the need for interventions directed at this group (Centers for Disease Control and Prevention, 1995a; Grossman & Cotes, 1996; Grossman, Dontes, Kruesi, Pennington, & Fendrich, 1997). There is a high probability that Hispanic populations will enter the health care system through public sector institutions (Ruiz, 1995). Therefore, settings such as schools and dropout programs emergency services, and mental health and public health clinics should be targeted for suicide prevention among Hispanic youth. Protocols for suicide attempters should be developed and instituted for youth suicide attempters, including risk assessment, means restriction intervention, and parent psychoeducation (Department of Health and Human Services, 1992; Grossman & Cotes, 1996).

The Public Health Approach

Traditionally, the mental health approach to youth suicide has focused on the identification and treatment of those with mental disorders. Although this approach remains a cornerstone of youth suicide prevention, there has been a recognition of the variety of factors contributing to youth suicide and thus an expansion of the conceptualization to a public health approach (Centers for Disease Control and Prevention, 1992). Public health efforts have successfully reduced unintentional injuries and deaths, including programs such as the "Buckle Up" campaign for child automobile passengers (Department of Health and Human Services, 1992).

Healthy People 2000: National Health Promotion and Disease Prevention Objectives

The U.S. government's Healthy People 2000 campaign labeled prevention as the nation's number one health priority (Department of Health and Human Services, 1991). The Year 2000 National Health Objectives established by the U.S. Public Health Service provide a national strategy for improving the health of the nation in the next century. This strategy includes objectives regarding youth suicide: reducing suicide to no more than 8.2 (per 100,000 population) among young people ages 15 to 19 years; reducing by 15% the incidence of injurious suicide attempts among adolescents ages 14 to 17 years; and reducing by 20% the proportion of people who possess weapons that are inappropriately stored and therefore dangerously available (Department of Health and Human Services, 1991).

Injury Control

The CDC efforts to address violence are also underscored in the National Plan for Injury Control's suicide-specific strategies that target children and adolescents, rural settings, and firearm interventions. Recommendations of the National Plan for Injury Control include such strategies as the development, implementation, and evaluation of programs to reduce injuries related to violence (e.g., injuries from firearms), as well as enhancement of the training of professionals at all levels of prevention, acute care, and rehabilitation (Department of Health and Human Services, 1992).

Guidelines for Youth Suicide Prevention

The Centers for Disease Control and Prevention (1992) surveyed exemplary youth suicide prevention programs and developed a resource guide to describe the rationale and evidence for the effectiveness of various strategies. Eight prevention strategies were identified, along with model programs that incorporate these different strategies: school gatekeeper training, community gatekeeper training, general suicide education, screening programs, peer support programs, crisis centers, telephone hot lines, and means restriction program and intervention. These eight strategies for youth suicide prevention can be combined into two general categories: (1) identifying and referring suicidal youths to mental health resources; (2) directly addressing known or suspected risk factors for youth suicide. More recently, the CDC has called for suicide prevention programs targeted for children (under 15 years) and minority youth (Centers for Disease Control and Prevention, 1992).

The CDC also made five general recommendations for all adolescent suicide prevention programs: (1) new and current suicide prevention programs should link closely with professional mental health resources in the community; (2) programs should avoid a single prevention strategy; (3) underused strategies that are worthwhile should be incorporated into current programs; (4) suicide prevention efforts should be expanded for young adults aged 20–24; and (5) evaluation efforts should be incorporated into all new and existing suicide prevention programs.

Evaluation of Suicide Prevention

Researchers have noted that many suicide prevention programs fail to include an adequate evaluation component (Angerstein, Linfield-Spindler, & Payne, 1991; Garland & Zigler, 1993; Tierney, 1994).The CDC has called for evaluation of the effectiveness of prevention strategies in reducing morbidity and mortality using such frameworks as *behavioral prevention strategy* and *reduction/control of risk factors.* Preventive effectiveness efforts include identification of efficacious and effective strategies, determination of potential and practical consequences, determination of optimal methods for implementation, and evaluation of the impact (Teutsch, 1992). Both the CDC and the National Institutes of Health (NIH) have designated suicide as a priority area for research and have funded evaluation studies of youth suicide prevention strategies.

The Grassroots Approach

The Suicide Prevention Advocacy Network (SPAN) is a nonprofit grass-roots organization connecting survivors with leaders in science, business, government, education, and public health to produce a national force for change. Gerald and Elsie Weyrauch, who lost a daughter to suicide, started SPAN in 1996. The organization is dedicated to the creation and implementation of a national suicide prevention strategy. Through the efforts of SPAN, Senate Resolution No. 84 and House Resolution No. 212 were passed, declaring suicide a national problem and establishing prevention as a high-priority goal. A conference cosponsored by SPAN and CDC, "National Strategy for Suicide Prevention: Linking Research and Practice," was held in October 1998. As part of this conference, youth were identified as one of the target groups and a youth suicide expert prepared a review of youth suicide prevention research (Clark, 1998). Additionally, SPAN's lobbying and political efforts have led to the inclusion of suicide prevention in the U.S. Surgeon General's health agenda as well as the designation of additional federal dollars for suicide research.

Means Restriction Strategy

Background and Rationale

Drug overdoses account for the majority of suicide attempts, whereas firearms contribute to the majority of deaths in both male and female adolescents. Means restriction is a safety intervention designed to prevent suicide by reducing a person's access to lethal means of completing suicide. Disposing of medications and locking up or removing firearms from the home of a suicidal adolescent are forms of means restriction. Health professionals can take part in this process by educating parents/caretakers of at-risk adolescents about means restriction techniques to reduce the likelihood of adolescent suicide (Community Action for Youth Survival, 1997).

Limited research has been done on the effects of restricting access to lethal methods of suicide as part of suicide prevention efforts. The case for means restriction was informed by events in Great Britain in the 1960s. Prior to that time, asphyxiation by coal gas (used for cooking) had been a major method of suicide in Great Britain. However, as the country began to lower the carbon monoxide content of the coal gas supplied to homes for domestic use, there was a marked reduction in the rate of suicide due to coal gas asphyxiation, along with a decrease in the overall suicide rate. This suggested that suicidal people who were restricted from using coal gas as a means of suicide did not switch to another means of suicide (Centers for Disease Control and Prevention, 1992; Farmer, Preston, & O'Brien, 1977). A recent report also looked at the rates of suicide and homicide in the District of Columbia after passage of a 1976 law banning the purchase, sale, transfer or possession of handguns by civilians. There was an observed decrease in rates of both suicide and homicide after passage of this law (Loftin, McDowall, Wiersema, & Cottey, 1991). The fact that the detoxifying of Great Britain's coal gas supply and the ban of handguns in the District of Columbia were not initiated specifically to test means restriction as a suicide prevention intervention has no bearing on the eventual outcome of these actions. Indeed, this may provide support for the theory that means restriction will work best if undue attention is not called to the fact that it is being carried out (Community Action for Youth Survival, 1997).

Impulsiveness appears to play an important role in many attempts/completions (Shaffer et al., 1988). Additionally, in many suicidal youth, the determination to commit suicide is not steady. That is, it rises and falls. If the most lethal and/or "convenient" methods of suicide are not available to an impulsively suicidal youth, considerable effort and energy may have to be expended to arrange a suitable method of suicide, all of which may result in an attempt never being made (Centers for Disease Control and Prevention, 1992).

There are further aspects related to possible impulsive components of a suicidal act. If an adolescent experiencing a suicidal crisis is denied access to the most lethal method(s) of committing suicide, one or both of the following things may occur: (1) the adolescent will not be able to make the attempt for a period of time, after which the urge to commit suicide may pass; (2) the adolescent will turn to another, less lethal method of suicide that will decrease the chance of dying from the attempt and increase the chance for a lifesaving intervention (Centers for Disease Control and Prevention, 1992). Means restriction can decrease the number of suicide deaths even if it does not decrease the number of suicide attempts.

If a suicidal adolescent does not have access to a firearm, will he or she substitute another method to attempt suicide? Related to the example of coal gas in Great Britain, evidence suggests the answer is often no. Marzuk and his associates, in studying the rate of suicide in the five boroughs of New York City, noted that some methods of suicide are more available in one borough than another (Marzuk et al., 1992). For example, some people commit suicide in New York City by jumping into the path of subway trains, but that method is not available in Staten Island where there are no subways. The differences in overall rates of suicide between the boroughs were not accounted for by methods that are equally available in all the boroughs, such as firearms. Rather, the higher suicide rates in some boroughs were explained by the methods that were more available in those boroughs, such as jumping in front of trains. This suggests that method substitution does not happen on a large scale and supports the idea of restricting means as a method of suicide prevention. If you limit access to a commonly used method of suicide in an identified population, then you will reduce the suicidal behaviors overall, because individuals tend not to substitute means that are less available.

Adoption of Hospital Safety Practices

Health care is moving from a predominantly in-hospital focus to outpatient locations. However, concepts used in inpatient settings can be employed to help keep at-risk individuals safe. Suicide precautions used in hospitals include increasing observation of the patient and taking away means of attempting suicide. If an adolescent enters a psychiatric hospital because he or she is actively suicidal, a physician will specify an order for "suicide precautions or suicide watch." Two elements of suicide precautions employed in a hospital setting are the following:

1. *Increased observation*—patients may not be allowed to spend much time alone in their rooms or will be observed by staff more frequently than nonsuicidal patients. Literally, this translates to "keeping an eye on them."
2. *Limiting access to lethal means*—patients may have their access to sharp objects limited (e.g., silverware will be counted before and after use to prevent patients from keeping a knife for making an attempt at a later time) (Community Action for Youth Survival, 1997).

It cannot be overemphasized that the most common means of death in adolescent suicide is guns, and having a gun in the house greatly increases the risk of suicide by adolescents. Survival following a self-inflicted gunshot wound is far less likely than with most other methods.

Parents/caretakers need to be educated about limiting access to lethal means. In this regard, the *three-step means restriction intervention* was developed and tested in a 3-year adolescent youth suicide prevention program (see Table 8.1).

Unfortunately, most parents are not told that their adolescent is at risk for suicide (Wislar et al., 1998). Data derived from a telephone follow-up study of parents and other adult caretakers who accompanied an adolescent to an emergency room following a suicide attempt (McManus et al., 1997) showed that only 14% of parents were warned to take action to limit access to medications. This was true despite the fact that all of these adolescents were in the emergency room as a result of overdose attempts. Six of seven parents limited access when told to do so, but only about one in three parents had limited access to methods of their own accord. Not one of the parents in the study was instructed to limit firearm access, despite acknowledgement by 25% that there was a gun in the house (Kruesi et al., 1999).

Firearm Disposal

Disposing of firearms involves a number of practical considerations. Obviously, it is not a good idea to put a gun in the trash. The idea is to

TABLE 8.1. Three-Step Intervention for Parents/Caretakers of Suicidal Adolescents

1. *Inform the parents/caretakers that their adolescent is at risk for suicide and why you think so.* This is especially true for an adolescent who has made a previous attempt, since that puts him or her at risk for another attempt. For this intervention, talk to the parents or caretakers out of the presence of the child to avoid calling the child's attention to firearms as a means of suicide.

2. *Tell parents/caretakers that they can reduce the risk of suicide by getting guns out of the house.* The risk of suicide doubles if a gun is in the house, even if the gun is locked up. The parents/caretakers must understand the importance of removing access to a firearm. Tell them this even if they do not own a firearm.

3. *Tell parents/caretakers to dispose of or, at the very least, limit access to a firearm.* Help them to accomplish this. A number of police departments are willing to help with disposal of firearms. During the intervention, offer parents/caretakers your assistance in contacting the local police department. If they cannot or will not dispose of the gun, help figure out how they can *make sure the at-risk adolescent cannot get to the gun.*

Note. Data from Kruesi, Hirsch, and Grossman (1995).

ensure that someone at suicidal risk cannot pick up the weapon. One safe method of disposal of a firearm is to turn it in to the police for disposal. Legal considerations are central to discussion of the practicalities of voluntary surrender of firearms for disposal. Gun ownership laws differ from state to state. Residents will need to consult relevant authorities in their states. The state's attorney's office is a good place to start an inquiry for questions such as the following (Community Action for Youth Survival, 1997):

- Who owns the gun?
- What happens if someone wants to voluntarily dispose of a gun and does not have a registration?
- Can the person reacquire the gun once it has been turned in?

Youth Suicide and Firearms

The American Association of Suicidology, with funding from the Joyce Foundation, convened an expert task force and developed a Consensus Statement on Youth Suicide by Firearms (Berman et al., 1997); the following summarizes this statement:

> Given the costs to American society and families wrought by youth suicide, we believe that immediate action needs to be taken. There is

clear evidence that intervening in or preventing the immediate accessibility of a lethal effort weapon can save lives. We have identified the safe storage of guns as one preventive intervention approach that would result in a decrease in the number of youth suicides. We believe that a combination of indicated, selected and universal interventions addressing this objective can successfully lead to a reduction in youth suicides in our homes and communities. The achievement of this goal can only come through the cooperation, coordination and collaboration of concerned organizations at all levels of the community (p. 92).

The Violent Injury Prevention Center at Children's Memorial Medical Center in Chicago was represented in the expert task force (Handgun Epidemic Lowering Plan [HELP] Network, 1996). This center has been extremely active for many years in education and policy issues related to youth and firearms. Suicidologists need to be active to ensure that youth suicide is included in youth firearm prevention policy issues.

Limitation of Other Means

While it is not possible to eliminate access to every possible means of suicide, parents/caretakers can curtail access to lethal means. For example, most guns with which youth shoot themselves come from their own household. As a factor in their behavior, alcohol is often found in the bloodstream of adolescents completing suicide, and drinking may facilitate a suicide even if it is not the actual cause of death. The use, abuse, or misuse of alcohol or other legal or illegal drugs or chemicals can impair judgment, lower inhibitions, cloud consciousness, increase impulsive tendencies, and worsen depressive and morbid thoughts and intentions. While it may not be possible to limit access to alcohol from all possible sources, it is possible to limit household access. Similarly, during the height of suicidal crises, preventing the misuse of automobiles can help (Community Action for Youth Survival, 1997).

Gatekeeper Training/Health Communication Campaigns

It is estimated that one-half of premature deaths are preventable. Preventable deaths such as suicide are related to culturally sustained behavior and lifestyle factors, for example, youth risk. Although preventive behavior change is difficult to achieve and there is no single approach, health communication campaigns are one scheme to the prevention of youth suicide deaths. As an example, campaigns specific to preventable injury deaths in youth include child restraint education directed at health professionals and parents. These campaigns have contributed to decreased rates of child morbidity and mortality due to restraint injuries (Backer, Rogers, & Sopory, 1992). In this regard, the Centers for Disease Control and Prevention (1992) recommendations for youth suicide prevention include training health professionals in suicide prevention. Print and computerized media offer a way to present health information and to stimulate awareness and change behavior (Department of Health and Human Services, 1992). The American Association of Suicidology and the American Foundation for Suicide Prevention have been active for many years in using these media for communication related to youth suicide prevention. Studies of medical education have emphasized that face-to-face training has a greater impact on changing practice than print campaigns.

Several of the strategies recommended for youth suicide prevention involve health communication campaigns to encourage professionals to adopt strategies such as risk assessment, means restriction, and postvention. These are behavior prevention strategies that will predictably lead to a level of behavior change in health professionals. Prevention innovations are more difficult to disseminate rapidly, as the person must take action to prevent something in the future that may occur even if the action is taken. The impact of health campaigns can have different levels of effect including the following: (1) the audience exposure to the message; (2) audience awareness of the message; (3) the audience being informed of the message; (4) the audience being persuaded by the message; (5) audience expression of interest in changing behavior; (6) actual change in audience behavior; and (7) maintenance of audience behavior change. At higher levels, individuals will change their practice methods and adopt youth suicide prevention strategies (e.g., means restriction) to intervene with youth at risk for suicide. Adoption of innovations requires the individual or the organization to change, a prospect that can lead to fears, resistance, and other inhibitions (Backer et al., 1992). Behavioral approaches to behavior change have been used to conceptualize and develop intervention and evaluate behavior change in addictions, psychological stress, and mental disorders.

School Gatekeeper Training

Given long-term and recent upward trends in adolescent suicide, there is an urgent need for cost-effective and timely approaches to the dissemination of the latest knowledge in adolescent suicide prevention and postvention. School gatekeeper training is an example of such an approach. Youth at risk for suicide may be identified early if school and community gatekeepers are trained in youth suicide prevention. The Centers for Disease Control and Prevention (1992) has targeted school and community caregivers for training in youth suicide prevention and recommended intervention protocols for suicide attempters (see also Department of Health and Human Services, 1992).

The goal of school gatekeeper training is to train professionals to identify children at risk for suicidal behavior and to refer them to appropriates sources of help. The triage or gatekeeper function can be undertaken by anyone who has significant contact with youth in the course of professional or volunteer activities. Examples of school gatekeepers for youth include social workers, psychologists, nurses, administrators, teachers, and coaches (Centers for Disease Control and Prevention, 1992).

The rationale for gatekeeper programs is that children at risk for suicide often come in contact with gatekeepers who do not recognize the presence of depression or suicide risk. Therefore, they do not access, obtain, or arrange appropriate help for the youth. Gatekeeper programs are designed to increase a potential gatekeeper's sense of confidence and competency in helping a child at risk for suicide (Centers for Disease Control and Prevention, 1992, p. 39). School gatekeepers are particularly well positioned to identify and intervene early with at-risk/exposed youth. However, recent studies of mental health professionals have revealed that graduate training includes little suicide prevention training (Bongar, 1991).

There is no national consensus on the role of gatekeeper training in suicide prevention, little systematic gatekeeper training in youth suicide prevention, and little documentation of systematic delivery of gatekeeper training in youth suicide prevention (Centers for Disease Control and Prevention, 1992). Public health and suicidology experts have underscored the paucity of evaluation of existing school and gatekeeper training in youth suicide prevention (Centers for Disease Control and Prevention, 1992; Silverman & Maris, 1995). Given that youth suicide is a major public health problem, more systematic programs of gatekeeper training, intervention, and evaluation are needed.

Community Action for Youth Survival

Consistent with the public health recommendations, a group of investigators conducted a youth suicide prevention program and evaluation in high schools and hospital emergency departments integrating several youth suicide prevention strategies. Community Action for Youth Survival (CAYS) was developed in collaboration and with funding from Ronald McDonald House Charities (RMHC; Grossman, Kruesi, & Hirsch, 1993). These efforts incorporated three of the CDC recommended strategies: *caregiver training (recognizing the danger), means restriction (reducing the risk),* and *postvention (responding to loss).* The development of CAYS was driven in substantial measure by the CDC guidelines and recommendations for youth suicide prevention, youth psychological autopsy studies, and studies of risk factors for youth suicide. A comprehensive battery of measures was designed to assess program implementation as well as the impact of training on the behavior of school and health care professionals (Fendrich, Kruesi, & Wislar, 1998, Fendrich, Kruesi, Freeman, & Grossman 1998; Grossman et al., 1995; Grossman, Dontes, Kruesi, Pennington, & Fendrich, 1999; Grossman & Cotes, 1996; Kruesi et al., 1995, 1999; McManus et al., 1997; Wislar et al., 1998). Key findings from the evaluation suggested that CAYS prevention efforts led to gains in knowledge, sense of preparedness, and suicide prevention practice among school-based caregivers. Longitudinal follow-up telephone surveys of school gatekeepers 4–5 months after CAYS training revealed changes in gatekeepers behavior (Mackesy-Amiti, Fendrich, Libby, Goldenberg, & Grossman, 1996). They were significantly more likely to make follow-up plans for at-risk youth, educate parents about restricting access to means of suicide, and internally disseminate youth suicide training (Callentine, Vlasak, Goldenberg, & Kruesi, 1999; Kruesi et al., 1999).

In the final phase of the investigation, a national suicide prevention innovation was included. This took the form of disseminating a computer-based interactive educational CD–ROM based on the CAYS project. Whereas previous efforts to implement CDC recommendations for youth suicide prevention have been at state and local levels, this initiative targeted a national population. The CD–ROM, *Team Up to Save Lives: What Your School Can Do to Prevent Suicide,* was released in February 1997 (Community Action for Youth Survival, 1997). The program components of this project included school-based training of gatekeepers, postvention consultation services, and a means restriction program of school professionals and community service providers. The CD–ROM, like the CAYS program itself, was targeted toward school professionals and other gatekeepers who may come into contact with at-risk students. The CD–ROM was based on the CAYS program, incorporated the three aforementioned strategies of the program, and was informed by evaluation studies. The dissemination plan utilized a novel diffusion method: mailing the program to principals of 27,000 high schools and junior high schools, providing copies to school and mental health professional organizations, conducting a broad-based media campaign, offering a toll-free number for distribution to individual professionals by the McDonald's educational distribution center, and hand delivering copies to schools by individual McDonald's franchises.

Pilot Evaluation Studies of the CD–ROM Impact

Two pilot studies have attempted to assess the impact of the CD–ROM. Ronald McDonald House Charities sent a brief questionnaire to the sample of 27,000 schools approximately 6 months after the CD–ROM dissemination. The response rate was extremely low (3%) and underscored problems in dissemination (e.g., mailing the CD–ROM to the principals who frequently never passed it on to the counseling gatekeepers). In another evaluation, Mackesey-Amiti and Fendrich used a mail survey targeted at the Chicago area. Copies of the CD-ROM were disseminated to school gatekeepers who reported that they had not received it in the original dissemination. Of schools contacted, 68% completed the phone survey. Nearly all school informants reported access to the necessary technology for viewing the CD–ROM. A subgroup of respondents (30%) showed a tendency for increased endorsement of youth suicide as a public health problem and a tendency for a decreased sense of preparedness, suggesting that the CD–ROM might set the stage for additional hands-on training for school staff (Mackesey-Amiti et al., 1996).

EXPANSION OF YOUTH SUICIDE PREVENTION STRATEGIES

Berman and Jobes (1995, p. 148) recommend a second generation of youth suicide prevention strategies, with a focus on primary and secondary prevention. These strategies may take many forms, dependent upon whether the target is the individual, the social milieu, or proximal agents (see Table 8.2).

TABLE 8.2. A Conceptual Model of Prevention Strategies

Individual predisposition	Social milieu	Proximal agents
	Primary prevention	
Depression management	Dropout prevention	Gun safety training for
Anger management	Early detection/referral	parents and
Loneliness prevention	of parental pathology	pediatricians
Problem-solving training	Surrogate role models	Suicide awareness
Competency	Media guidance	among health care
enhancement		providers
Critical viewing skills		Federal firearms
Help-seeking training		prevention education
	Secondary prevention	
Triage programs	Gatekeeper training	Medication: emetics
Volunteerism	Peer counseling	Environmental safety
Outpatient treatment	Parental pathology	Decrease access to guns
	Case finding	
	Caregiver training	
	Tertiary prevention	
Psychiatric treatment	Community mental	Treatment with selective
Substance abuse	health treatment	serotonin reuptake
treatment	Juvenile justice programs	inhibitors
	Case management	Psychotherapy for
	Follow-up	depression
		Neuroleptic for
		psychosis

Note. From Berman and Jobes (1995). Copyright 1995 by the American Association of Suicidology. Reprinted by permission of The Guilford Press.

Secondary and Tertiary Prevention

Mental health and pediatric health professionals often intervene with youth at risk for suicide in mental health services, emergency medical services, medical units, schools, and substance abuse specialty programs. Given that only one-third of high school students in the national Youth Risk Behavior Surveillance survey who reported a suicide attempt in the past year ever saw a physician or nurse, nontraditional settings provide opportunities for early identification and intervention that has the potential to save lives. The following subsections provide an overview of some secondary and tertiary prevention strategies for youth.

Suicide Prediction

There is no single specific clue, risk factor, symptom, or diagnosis that can be used to predict which adolescents will attempt suicide. Likewise, no single test can predict which youths will die by suicide. Similarly, there are no reliable or valid tests that can predict suicide. Although there have been many attempts to develop tests, such as psychological inventories, depression scales, and suicide intent scales that predict suicide risk, these tools are imperfect (Leenaars & Lester, 1995). Furthermore, there are few tests or tools developed specifically for adolescents.

Assessment of Suicidality

A task force on the assessment of suicidal behavior in adolescents was organized by the National Institute of Mental Health (NIMH). This task force reviewed all the available instruments used to assess adolescent suicidality and concluded that few, if any, are useful (Garrison, Lewinsohn, Marsteller, Langhinrichsen, & Lann, 1991). Others have reached the same conclusion, but they emphasized the need to focus on the person, not the test. It was concluded that the complexity and diversity of suicidal behavior cannot be reduced to a single, definitive test (Leenaars & Lester, 1995; Maltsberger, 1986). Despite the limited predictability of suicide screening tools, these tools can be effective if they are used as one component of a comprehensive psychiatric assessment in a mental health setting.

Assessment of suicidality in youth is based on clinical interviews; history of the youth and the family; reports of parents, school caregivers, and peers; and structured tools. In addition to the standard child psychiatric evaluation, the following factors should be assessed: demographic risk factors, immediate danger, suicide ideation, suicide intent, concept and expectation of death, hopelessness, balance of wish to live and wish to die, attitudes toward suicidal ideation, sense of control, deterrents, purpose of attempt, existence and extent of a suicidal plan, problem solving-skills, coping skills, and current circumstances (Berman & Jobe, 1991; Community Action for Youth Survival, 1997; Weishaar, Chapter 5, this volume). Based on this assessment, a response to risk is developed to reflect the level of risk—from no apparent risk to low, moderate, and high risk. The risk response should include an *individualized action plan* describing actions to be followed by the youth, the parents, the physician, the school caregivers, peers, and community caregivers (Community Action for Youth Survival, 1997).

Crisis Intervention in Medical Services

In addition to the child psychiatric assessment, the evaluation should focus on thorough evaluation of suicidality. Suicidality should be confronted early in the interview to establish the seriousness and purpose of the visit. Catenaccio (1995) suggests a concrete, specific, factual, but not exhaustive approach in which the topic is revisited later in the interview.

Families of suicidal youth tend to have poor compliance with treatment recommendations. There is therefore a need for cost-effective short-term interventions focused on developing improved coping and problem-solving skills (Rotheram-Borus, Piacentini, Miller, Graae, & Castro-Blanco, 1994). Rotheram-Borus and her colleagues developed an emergency medical services program to improve outpatient treatment adherence with disadvantaged Hispanic adolescent attempters (Rotheram-Borus et al., 1996). These attempters received either a standard or specialized emergency room (ER) protocol. The specialized protocol included a structured family therapy session with a bilingual family therapist who acted as a liaison for the family with ER and outpatient staff.

Consultation–Liaison in Medical Units

Child psychiatrists are often asked to provide consultation for a youth regarding the medical consequences of an intentional or accidental overdose. The central issue involves whether this is a patient who can be sent home safely, usually with a referral to outpatient therapy or, instead, whether this is a patient for whom nothing less restrictive than placement in a secure psychiatric inpatient service for protective custody and a medication trial will be safe and appropriate. Given issues such as managed care approval for hospitalization, brief hospital admissions, and the low frequency of follow-through with outpatient referrals, brief, focused therapies are indicated (Zimmerman & Asnis, 1995).

PSYCHOTHERAPEUTIC INTERVENTION

Keeping a youth alive requires a team effort of all those involved with the youth—parents, caretakers, school caregivers, mental health professionals, and peers. The efforts of all those involved should be recognized and encouraged (Community Action for Youth Survival, 1997; Zimmerman & Asnis, 1995).

Family Intervention

Meeting with families after the suicide attempt of a youth to clarify and repair relationships can increase the likelihood of keeping that youth alive. Anger, fear, or mistrust between family members may indicate the need for individual meetings (Catenaccio, 1995). Rotheram-Borus and her colleagues have developed the Standardized Family Therapy (SNAP), a six-session structured behavioral and cognitive protocol in which positive family problem solving is learned (Rotheram-Borus et al., 1994). It has become too frequent that suicidal youth have no family and are in the child protection system. Early, frequent, and severe life disruptions distinguish suicidal adolescents from depressed adolescents (de Wilde et al., 1991). For these reasons, interventions may need to be adopted to involve alternative caretakers.

Psychopharmacological Treatment

Treatment of the suicidal youth cannot be separated from the psychopharmacological treatment of an underlying disorder (e.g., affective disorders, anxiety disorders, substance abuse disorders, and schizophrenia) and the associated supportive psychotherapy. Patients with these disorders are known to be at increased risk for suicide. Some of the factors that complicate psychopharmacological treatment of suicidal youth are delayed response time, anxiety associated with depression in many suicidal patients, the risk of using medications in an attempt, and brief hospital stays. Ongoing evaluation of dangerousness and the monitoring of medication are part of the therapeutic responsibility when dispensing medications. Psychopharmacology is a sensitive treatment area because of controversy over such issues as compliance, substance abuse, risk after response to medication, and standard of care for psychopharmacological treatment (see Goldblatt and Silverman, Chapter 6, this volume).

Psychoeducation

Suicidal youths as well as their parents and caregivers need to be educated about a number of relevant topics, including depression as chronic and recurrent illness with multiple etiologies; suicidal ideation and attempt; problem-solving alternatives; recognition of emotional states; effective communication; familial and genetic components of affective disorders and suicide; pharmacotherapy and mechanisms of action, side effects, and rationale; removal of lethal methods; myths of suicide; clinic procedures; the evaluation and treatment process; and resources for other family members in need of mental health services (Brent, Poling, et al., 1993; Zimmerman & Asnis, 1995)

Cognitive-Behavioral Therapy

Cognitive therapy derived from studies with depressed persons has been extended to therapy with suicidal persons (see Weishaar, Chapter 5, this volume, for more details). Research in the past decade, primarily by A. T. Beck and colleagues, has revealed a number of common cognitive characteristics of suicidal individuals, including dichotomous thinking, cognitive rigidity, problem-solving deficits, hopelessness, and the acceptance of suicide as a desirable solution. Cognitive techniques for the treatment of the depressed, suicidal patients include the following: (1) identification of the relationships between negative thoughts and attitudes and affective and behavioral symptoms; (2) identification of the sequences between thoughts and motivation toward suicide; (3) exploration of depressive and suicidal thoughts and the meanings assigned to events; (4) examination, reality testing, and revision of faulty cognition using logic and empirical evidence; and (5) consideration of alternative explanations for events.

Although cognitive therapy with suicidal patients is similar to standard cognitive therapy, the therapist is considerably more active and directive in cases of suicidality. The therapist and suicidal patient work to generate perspectives, interpredictions, and solutions other than suicide to presenting problems. Weishaar (Chapter 5, this volume) reports that cognitive approaches to understanding and intervening with suicidal adults have also been effective with suicidal adolescents but that the understanding and intervention with children is less well developed.

Group Psychotherapy

Group therapy is a treatment method congruent with group life as a crucial aspect of adolescent development. Group therapy can provide a safe, cohesive atmosphere; support; a sense of universalization; and a way to explore new coping and behavior patterns. The group should be presented as a way to talk with other adolescents about problems and issues rather than as a suicide prevention group. Psychotic or violence-prone (other-directed) adolescents should not be included in the group. Although this modality is widely used with adolescents, it is underutilized with suicidal adolescents, most likely due to mental health professionals' fear of contagion. This modality provides a cost-effective method congruent with decreases in mental health services. However, research is needed to assess the effectiveness of this modality (Zimmerman & LaSorsa, 1995).

STANDARD OF CARE AND SUICIDAL YOUTH

There is no universally accepted list of minimum standards for the inpatient care of suicidal patients, nor is there a uniform set of standards that provide an optimum procedure for the care of such patients. Although it is not possible to predict well who will commit suicide, clinicians can engage in reasonable and prudent risk management and intervention. Silverman and Bongar and their colleagues provide actions that must be performed to provide the minimum standards of care for the assessment, treatment, and clinical management of suicidal inpatients and outpatients (Bongar, Berman, Litman, & Maris, 1992; Bongar, Maris, Litman, & Silverman, 1993). These standards are based on case law, statutory determined professional standards, legal commentary on case law, clinical practice and the teaching of clinical management skills, and reports by forensic suicidologists of cases settled out of court. Failure to assess the possibility of suicidality (i.e., foreseeability), leads to a failure to provide appropriate treatment, environmental interventions and constraints, and restrictions to prevent suicidal behavior from being enacted. Silverman, Berman, Bongar, Litman, & Maris (1994) provide a description of duties and responsibilities between and among clinicians, hospital staff, and hospital administration. There is a need to adapt these standards to suicide prevention with youth in the context of levels of clinical services within managed care.

AFTERMATH OF YOUTH SUICIDE

Imitation, Contagion, and Clusters

One of the most severe reactions to the suicide of a peer is suicidal imitation or contagion. A cluster has been defined as "a group of suicides or suicide attempts, or both, which occur closer together in time and space than would be normally expected in a given community" (Centers for Disease Control and Prevention, 1994). Adolescents or young adults are more vulnerable to suicide imitation, particularly if they are not a close friend or acquaintance of the victim and had preexisting psychiatric vulnerabilities such as depression or suicidal behavior.

Research to support the existence of this phenomenon includes anecdotal reports of outbreaks, or clusters, of suicide and suicidal behavior; studies that have demonstrated a relationship between sensationalized media coverage of a suicide and a subsequent increased suicide rate (Phillips, & Cartensen, 1986); and statistical evidence supporting the existence of a cluster (Brent, Perper, Moritz, Allman, Friend, et al., 1993; Davidson & Gould, 1988; Gould, Wallenstein, & Kleinman, 1987).

Brent et al. (1989) studied an outbreak of suicidal behavior over an 18-day period in a high school of 1,496 students. The outbreak consisted of 2 completed suicides, 7 attempted suicides, and 23 students with suicidal ideation. The risk of imitative suicidal behavior was found to be highest in the first 3 weeks following the suicide. The researchers found that the adolescents who become suicidal following exposure had a greater incidence of current depression, history of depression, and risk for depression.

In other reported findings, Brent and his colleagues found that although many symptoms were similar in cases of depression and post-traumatic stress disorder (PTSD), a few symptoms appeared to differentiate between suicide survivors with depression as opposed to PTSD. Specifically, adolescents who developed PTSD had intrusive visual images of the event, a feeling that others could not understand the experience, obsessive alertness, exaggerated startle reactions, and avoidance of reminders of the event cluster (Brent, Perper, Moritz, Allman, Liotus, et al., 1993; Brent et al., 1995; Brent, Moritz, Bridge, Perper, & Canobbio, 1996; see Community Action for Youth Survival, 1997, for a review of bereavement and postvention with youth suicide survivors).

Responsible Media Coverage

Another aspect of the aftermath of adolescent suicide involves schools and the media. Suicidal behaviors occurring in the school community can be expected to attract media attention, and such coverage is often sensationalized, sometimes portraying suicide as glamorous. Although not conclusive, evidence suggests there is a significant association between sensationalized media coverage of suicide and imitative suicidal behavior in vulnerable peers of adolescent suicide victims.

The Centers for Disease Control and Prevention (1994) sponsored a workshop on "Suicide and the Media" in New Jersey attended by suicidologists, health officials, researchers, mental health professionals, and members of the news media. Several aspects of media coverage that increase the risk for suicide contagion were identified, including the following:

1. Presenting a simplistic explanation for the suicide.
2. Providing excessive news coverage of the suicide.
3. Providing sensationalized coverage—morbid details and dramatic photographs.
4. Reporting the method and other technical details.
5. Presenting suicide as an effective coping strategy—reporting the suicide was a means to avoid disciplinary action.
6. Glorifying or awarding celebrity status to the victim—for example, holding public memorials.
7. Focusing on the victim's positive characteristics.

Vulnerability in Youth Suicide Survivors

Brent and his colleagues have provided the only systematic longitudinal study of the psychiatric aftereffects of peer suicide for friends and acquaintances. The study followed 160 friends and acquaintances of 26 adolescent suicide victims at three intervals: approximately 7 months, 12–18 months, and 3 years following the death. The researchers found these adolescents to be at increased risk for developing pathological bereavement in comparison to unexposed peers. These severe reactions included major depression, PTSD, anxiety, and suicidal ideation involving a plan. An increase in major depression was consistently identified in the friends and acquaintances exposed to a peer's suicide. The average length of depression in adolescents who become depressed after their peer's suicide was 8 months. Brent and his colleagues reported that depressed survivors differed from their "normally" bereaved peers in their experience of a preoccupation with worthlessness, prolonged and marked impairment in functioning, and physical sluggishness (Brent, Perper, Moritz, Allman, Liotus, et al., 1993; Brent et al., 1995, 1996).

The friends and acquaintances of the victims had a higher incidence of depression during the follow-up period when compared with the unexposed youths. This higher risk emerged even after a prior history of depression and other risk factors was considered that might increase suicidal behavior, such as a family history of psychiatric disorders (Brent et al., 1989). Brent and colleagues (Brent, Perper, Moritz, Baugher, et al., 1993; Brent et al., 1994) found that friends and acquaintances of suicide victims did not have an increased risk of suicide attempts during a 3-year follow-up period. The youths confided to interviewers that the devastating effect of their friends' suicide inhibited them from engaging in suicidal behavior. This is similar to the report of a national sample by Gold and Forman (1994), who found no close friends of suicide victims among those participating in suicide clusters. Therefore, evidence suggests that those most vulnerable to contagion are not the closest friends of the deceased, but rather are peers who have psychiatric vulnerabilities (Brent, Perper, Moritz, Allman, Liotus, et al., 1993; Brent et al., 1996).

In summary, although scientific knowledge of youth suicide morbidity and mortality has increased over the past decades, there has been little impact on the overall youth rates. In fact, the rates have increased for minority youth as well as for young people aged 10–14 years. There have been few rigorously designed and evaluated youth suicide prevention efforts (Brent & Perper, 1985). In addition to such efforts, there is a need for culturally sensitive, community-based, locally adapted, and empirically based efforts to address this national tragedy. Youth suicide prevention deserves a high priority in local, state, national, and international health agendas.

ACKNOWLEDGMENT

This chapter was adapted in part from a program supported by a grant from Ronald McDonald House Charities to Drs. Grossman and Kruesi and Dr. Jay Hirsch, and was coordinated by Cathy Mazur.

REFERENCES

Andrews, J., & Lewinsohn, P. (1992). Suicidal attempts among older adolescents: Prevalence and co-occurrence with psychiatric disorders. *Journal of the American Academy of Child and Adolescent Psychiatry, 31*, 655–662.

Angerstein, G., Linfield-Spindler, S., & Payne, L. (1991). Evaluation of an urban school adolescent suicide prevention program. *School Psychology International, 12*, 25–48.

Arrango, V., Ernsberger, P., Marzuk, P., Chen, J., Tierney, H., Stanley, M. Reis, D., & Mann, J. (1990). Autoradiographic demonstration of increased serotonin 5-HT (2) and ß-adrenergic receptor binding sites in the brains of suicide victims. *Archives of General Psychiatry, 47,* 1038–1047.

Backer, T., Rogers, E., & Sopory, P. (1992). *Designing Health Communication Campaigns: What Works?* Newbury Park, CA: Sage.

Berman, A., & Jobes, D. (1991). *Adolescent suicide: Assessment and intervention.* Washington, DC: American Psychological Association.

Berman, A., & Jobes, D. (1995). Suicide prevention in adolescents (ages 12 to 18). *Suicide and Life-Threatening Behavior, 22,* 453–477.

Berman, A. et al. (1997). *Consensus statement on youth suicide by firearms.* Washington, DC: American Association of Suicidology.

Birkhead, G., Galvin, V., Meehan, P., O'Carroll, P., & Mercy, J. (1993). The emergency department in surveillance of attempted suicide: Findings and methodologic considerations. *Public Health Reports, 108,* 323–331.

Blumenthal, S. & Kupfer, D. (Eds.) (1990). *Suicide over the lifespan: Risk factors, assessment, and treatment of suicidal patients.* Washington, DC: American Psychiatric Press.

Bongar, B. (1991). *The suicidal patient: Clinical and legal standards of care.* Washington, DC: American Psychological Association.

Bongar, B., Berman, A. L., Litman, R. E., & Maris, R. W. (1992). Outpatient standards of care in the assessment, management, and treatment of sucidal persons. *Suicide and Life-Threatening Behavior, 22*(4), 453–478.

Bongar, B., Maris, R. W., Litman, R. E., & Silverman, M. M. (1993). Inpatient stadards of care and the suicidal patient: Part I. General clinical formulations and legal considerations. *Suicide and Life-Threatening Behavior, 23*(4), 245–256.

Brent, D., Kerr, M., Goldstein, C., Bozigar, J., Wartella, M., & Allan, M. (1989). An outbreak of suicide and suicidal behavior in high school. *Journal of the American Academy of Child and Adolescent Psychiatry, 6,* 918–924.

Brent, D., Moritz, G., Bridge, J., Perper, J., & Canobbio, R. (1996). Long-term impact of exposure to suicide: A three-year controlled follow-up *Journal of the American Academy of Child and Adolescent Psychiatry, 35*(5), 646–653.

Brent, D., & Perper, J. (1985). Research in adolescent suicide: Implications for training, service, delivery, and public policy. *Suicide and Life-Threatening Behavior, 25,* 222–230.

Brent, D., Perper, J., & Allman, C. (1987). Alcohol, firearms, and suicide among youth. *Journal of the American Medical Association, 257*(24), 3369–3372.

Brent, D., Perper, J., Allman, C., Moritz, G., Wartella, M., & Zelenak, J. (1991). The presence and accessibility of firearms in the homes of adolescent suicides: A case–control study. *Journal of the American Medical Association, 266* (21), 2989–2995.

Brent, D. A., Perper, J. A., Goldstein, C. E., Kolko, D. J., Allan, M. J., Allman, C., & Zelenak, J. (1988). Risk factors for adolescent suicide. *Archives of General Psychiatry, 45,* 581–588.

Brent, D., Perper, J., Moritz, G., Allman, C., Friend, C., Roth, C., Schweers, J., Balach, L., & Baugher, M. (1993). Psychiatric risk factors for adolescent suicide: A case-contol study. *Journal of the American Academy of Child and Adolescent Psychiatry, 32*(3), 521–529.

Brent, D., Perper, J., Moritz, G., Allman, C., Liotus, L., Schweers, J., Roth, C., Balach, L., & Canobbio, R. (1993). Bereavement or depression?: The loss of a friend to suicide. *Journal of the American Academy of Child and Adolescent Psychiatry, 32*(6), 1189–1197.

Brent, D., Perper, J., Moritz, G., Baugher, M., Schweers, J., & Roth, C. (1993). Firearms and adolescent suicide: A community case–control study. *American Journal of Diseases of Children, 147,* 1066–1071.

Brent, D., Perper, J., Moritz, G., Liotus, L., Richardson, D., Canobbio, R., Schweers, J., & Roth, C. (1995). Post-traumatic stress disorder in peers of adolescent suicide victims: Predisposing factors and phenomenology. *Journal of the American Academy of Child and Adolescent Psychiatry, 32*(4), 770–774.

Brent, D., Perper, J., Moritz, G., Liotus, L., Schweers, J., & Canobbio, R., (1994). Major depression or uncomplicated beravement? A follow-up study of youth exposed to suicide. *Journal of the American Academy of Child and Adolescent Psychiatry, 3*(2), 231–239.

Brent, D., Poling, K., McKain, B., & Baugher, M. (1993). A psychoeducation program for families of affectively ill children and adolescents. *Journal of the American Academy of Child and Adolescent Psychiatry, 32*(4), 770–774.

Callahan, J., Clark, D. C., Grossman, J. A., & Donoghue, E. (1998). *Prototypes of adolescent suicide.* Manuscript in review.

Callentine, V., Vlasak, S., Goldenberg, D., & Kruesi, M. J. P. (1999). Avoiding the icebergs: Preparation for crisis in school communities. Manuscript submitted for publication.

Catenaccio, R. (1995). Crisis intervention with suicidal adolescents: A view from the emergency room. In J. K. Zimmerman & G. M. Asnis (Eds.), *Treatment approaches with suicidal adolescents* (pp. 71–90). New York: Wiley.

Centers for Disease Control and Prevention. (1992). Youth suicide prevention programs: A resource guide (pp. 147–151). Atlanta, GA: National Center for Injury Prevention and Control.

Centers for Disease Control and Prevention. (1994). Programs for the prevention of suicide among adolescents and young adults and suicide contagion and the reporting of suicide: Recommendations from a national workshop. *Morbidity and Mortality Weekly Report 1994, 43* (No. RR-6).

Centers for Disease Control and Prevention. (1995a). Suicide among children, adolescents, and young adults: United States, 1980–1993. *Morbidity and Mortality Weekly Report, 44*(15), 289–290.

Centers for Disease Control and Prevention. (1995b). Fatal and non-fatal suicide attempts among adolescents: Oregon, 1988–1993. *Morbidity and Mortality Weekly Report, 44*(16), 312–323.

Centers for Disease Control and Prevention. (1997). Rates of homicide, suicide, and firearm related death among children-26 industrialized countries, *Morbidity and Mortality Weekly Report, 46*(5).

Centers for Disease Control and Prevention. (1998a). A framework for assessing the effectiveness of disease and injury prevention. *Morbidity and Mortality Weekly Report 1992, 47* (No.RR-3).

Centers for Disease Control and Prevention (1998b). CDC surveillance summaries, August 14, 1998. *Morbidity and Mortality Weekly Report, 1998, 47* (No. SS-3), 1–31.

Clark, D. (1998 October). *Youth suicide: A national strategy.* Paper presented at the National Strategy Meeting for Suicide Prevention: Linking Research and Practice, Reno, NV.

Community Action for Youth Survival (1997). *Team up to save lives: What your school should know about preventing youth suicide.* (CD ROM) Chicago: University of Illinois at Chicago and Ronald McDonald House Charities. (Distributed to 30,000 schools in the United States February 1997; available for cost of mailing, McDonald's Resource Center at 1-800-627-7646)

Davidson, L., & Gould, M. (1988). Contagion as a risk factor for youth suicide. In *Report of the Secretary's task force on youth suicide, Vol. II. Risk factors for youth suicide.* Washington, DC: U.S. Government Printing Office.

Department of Health and Human Services. (1991). *Healthy people 2000: National health promotion and disease prevention objectives.* (DHHS Publication No. 91-50212). Washington, DC: U.S. Government Printing Office.

Department of Health and Human Services. (1992). *The third national injury control conference.* (DHHS Publication No. 192-634–666). Washington, DC: U.S. Government Printing Office.

deWilde, E., Kienhorst, I., Diekstra, R., & Wolters, W. (1991). The relationship between adolescent suicidal behavior and life events in childhood and adolescence. *American Journal of Psychiatry, 149,* 45–51.

Farmer, R. D., Preston, T. D., & O'Brien, S. E. (1977). Suicide mortality in Greater London: Changes during the past 25 years. *British Journal of Preventative Social Medicine, 31*(3), 171–177.

Fendrich, M., Kruesi, M. J. P., Freeman, K., & Grossman, J. A. (1998). Police collection of firearms to prevent suicide: Correlates of recent turn-in experience. *Policing: An International Journal of Police Strategies and Management, 21*(1), 8–21.

Fendrich, M., Kruesi, M. J. P., Wislar, J. S., Pokorny, S., Dontes, A., & Erickson, T. (1998). Implementing means restriction in urban EDs. *American Journal of Emergency Medicine, 16*(3), 257–261.

Garland, A. F., & Zigler, E. (1993). Adolescent suicide prevention: Current research and social policy implications. *American Psychologist, 48,* 169–182.

Garrison, C., Lewinsohn, P., Marsteller, F., Langhinrichsen, J., & Lann, I. (1991). The assessment of suicidal behavior in adolescents. *Suicide and Life-Threatening Behavior, 21,* 217–230.

Garrison, C., McKeown, R., Vallois, R., & Vinncent, M. (1993). Aggression, substance use, and suicidal behavior in high school students. *American Journal of Public Health, 83,* 179–184.

Gould, M. & Forman, J. (1994). *The psychological autopsy of cluster sucide in adolescents.* Presentation at the Sixth Scientific Meeting of the Society for Research in Child and Adolescent Psychopathology, London.

Gould, M., Wallenstein, S., & Kleinman, M. (1987). *A study of the space clustering of suicide, Final report.* Atlanta, GA: Centers for Disease Control and Prevention.

Grossman, J. A., & Cotes, C. (1996). Suicide morbidity and mortality in Latina youth: Prevention opportunities. In B. J. McElmurry & R. Spreen Parker (Eds.), *Annual review of women's health: Vol. III* (pp. 217–241). New York: National League for Nursing.

Grossman, J. A., Dontes, A., Kruesi, M. J. P., Pennington, J., & Fendrich, M. (1999). *Emergency nurses' responses to a survey about means restriction: An adolescent suicide prevention strategy.* Manuscript in revision.

Grossman, J. A., Hirsch, J., Goldenberg, D., Libby, S., Fendrich, M., Mackesy-Amiti, M., Mazur, C., & Hill-Chance, G. (1995). Strategies for school-based response to loss: Proactive training and postvention consultation. *Crisis, 16,* 18–26.

Grossman, J., Kruesi, M., & Hirsch, J. (1993). *Community Action for Youth Survival.* Unpublished proposal, University of Illinois at Chicago, Institute for Juvenile Research.

Handgun Epidemic Lowering Plan [HELP] Network. (1996). *The HELP handgun disposal handbook: A prescription for safety.* Chicago: Author.

Hennriksson, M., Hillvi, M., Martunnen, M., Isometsa, E., et al. (1993). Mental disorders and comorbidity in suicide. *American Journal of Psychiatry, 150,* 935–940.

Kachur, S., Potter, L., James, S., & Powell, K. (1995). *Suicide in the United States, 1980–1992.* Atlanta, GA: Centers for Disease Control and Prevention, National Center for Injury Prevention and Control.

Kellerman, A., Rivara, F., Somes, G., Reay, D., Francisco, J., et al. (1992). Suicide in the home in relation to gun ownership. *New England Journal of Medicine, 327*(7), 467–472.

Kruesi, M. J. P., Grossman, J. A., Pennington, J., Woodward, P., Duda, D., & Hirsch, J. (1999). Suicide and violence prevention: Parent education in the emergency department. *Journal of the American Academy of Child and Adolescent Psychiatry, 38*(3), 250–255.

Kruesi, M. J. P., Hirsch, J., & Grossman, J. A. (1995). *Three-step intervention for parents of suicidal adolescents* [brochure]. Chicago: University of Illinois at Chicago and Ronald McDonald House Charities.

Leenaars, A., & Lester, D. (1995). Assessment and prediction of sucide risk in adolescents. In K. Zimmerman & G. Asnis (Eds.), *Treatment approaches with suicidal adolescents* (pp. 47–70). New York: Wiley.

Loftin, C., McDowall, D., Wiersema, B., & Cottey, T. (1991). Effects of restrictive licensing of hanguns on homicide and suicide in the District of Columbia. *New England Journal of Medicine, 325*(23), 1615–1620.

Mackesy-Amiti, M. E., Fendrich, M., Libby, S., Goldenberg, D., & Grossman, J. A. (1996). Assessment of knowledge gains in proactive training for postvention. *Suicide and Life-Threatening Behavior, 26*(2), 161–174.

Maltzberger, J. (1986). *Suicide risk: The formulation of clinical judgement.* New York: New York University Press.

Martunnen, M. J., Aro, H. M., Henriksson, M. M., & Lönqvist, J. K. (1991). Mental disorders in adolescent suicides: DSM III-R axes I and II diagnoses in suicides among 13–19-year-olds in Finland. *Archives of General Psychiatry, 48,* 834–839.

Marzuk, P., Leon, A., Tardiff, K., Morgan, E., et al. (1992). The effect of lethal methods of injury on suicide rates. *Archives of General Psychiatry, 49*(6), 451–458.

McManus, B. L., Kruesi, M. J. P., Dontes, A. E., Defazio, C. R., Piotrowski, J. T., & Woodward, P. J. (1997). Child and adolescent suicide attempts: An opportunity for emergency departments to provide injury prevention education. *American Journal of Emergency Medicine, 15*(4), 357–360.

Moscicki, E. (1995). Epidemiology of suicide. *Suicide and Life-Threatening Behavior, 25*(1) 22–35.

National Center for Health Statistics. (1996). Advance report of final mortality statistics, 1994. *NCHS Monthly Vital Statistics Report, 45* (3, Suppl.).

Peters, K. D., Kochanek, K. D., & Murphy, S. L. (1998). Deaths: Final data for 1996. *National Vital Statistics Report, 47*(9). (DHHS Publication No. PHS 99-1120). Hyattville, MD: National Center for Health Statistics.

Phillips, D., & Cartensen, L. (1986). Clustering of teenage suicides after television news stories about suicide. *New England Journal of Medicine, 315,* 685–689.

Rotheram-Borus, M. J., Piacentini, J., Miller, S., Graae, F., & Castro-Blanco, D. (1994). Brief cognitive-behavioral treatment for adolescent suicide attempters and their families. *Journal of the American Academy of Child and Adolescent Psychiatry, 34*(1), 81–90.

Rotheram-Borus, M. J., Piacentini, J., Von Rossem, R., Graae, F., Cantwell, C., Castro-Blanco, D., Miller, S., & Feldman, J. (1996). Enhancing treatment adherence with a specialized emergency room program for adolescent suicide attempters. *Journal of the American Academy of Child and Adolescent Psychiatry, 35*(54), 564–663.

Ruiz, P. (1995). Assessing, diagnosing, and treating culturally diverse individuals: A Hispanic perspective. *Psychiatric Quarterly, 66*(4), 329–341.

Ryland, D., & Kruesi, M. J. P. (1992). Suicide among adolescents. *International Review of Psychiatry, 4,* 185–195.

Seidel, J. S. (1991). Emergency medical services and the adolescent patient. *Society for Adolescent Health, 12,* 95–100.

Shaffer, D., Garland, A., Gould, M., Fisher, P., & Trautman, P. (1988). Preventing teenage suicide: A critical review. *Journal of the American Academy of Child and Adolescent Psychiatry, 27,* 675–687.

Shaffer, D., Gould, M., & Hicks, R. (1994). Worsening suicide rates in black teenagers. *American Journal of Psychiatry, 151*(2), 1810–1812.

Shafii, M., Stelz-Lenarsky, J., Derrick, A., Beckner, C., & Whittinghill, J. (1988). Comorbidity of mental disorders in the postmortem diagnosis of completed suicide in children and adolescents. *Journal of Affective Disorders, 44,* 227–233.

Shneidman, E. (1985). *Definition of suicide.* New York: Wiley.

Silverman, M. M., Berman, A., Bongar, B., Litman, R., & Maris, R. W. (1994). Inpatient standards and the suicidal patient: Part II. An integration with clinical risk management. *Suicide and Life-threatening Behavior, 24*(2), 152–169.

Silverman, M. M., & Maris, R. W. (Eds.). (1995). *Suicide prevention: Toward the year 2000.* New York: Guilford Press.

Teutsch, S. M. (1992). A framework for assessing the effectiveness of disease and injury prevention. *Morbidity and Mortality Weekly Report, 41* (no. RR-3), 1–12.

Tierney, R. J. (1994). Suicide intervention training and evaluation: A preliminary report. *Crisis, 15,* 69–76.

Wislar, J., Grossman, J. A., Kruesi, M. J. P., Fendrich, M., Franke, C., & Ignatowicz, N. (1998). Youth suicide-related visits in an emergency department serving rural counties: Implications for means restriction. *Archives of Suicide Research, 4,* 75–87.

Zimmerman, J., & Asnis, G. (Eds.). (1995). *Treatment approaches with suicidal adolescents.* New York: Wiley.

Zimmerman, J., & La Sorsa, V. (1995). Being the family's therapist: An integrative approach. In J. Zimmerman & G. Asnis (Eds.), *Treatment approaches with suicidal adolescents* (pp. 174–188). New York: Wiley.

CHAPTER NINE

Suicidal Behavior in Later Life

Research Update

Jane L. Pearson, PhD

T wo of the most common demographic correlates of suicide are older age and male sex. Among industrialized countries that provide statistics on suicide, nearly all report that suicide rates rise progressively with age, with the highest rates occurring for men aged 75 and older (Pearson & Conwell, 1995). In the United States in 1997 (the most current national rates available), older white males had the highest suicide rates, far surpassing adolescent rates: white adolescents males aged 15–19 have a rate of 16 per 100,000, and older white adult males aged 85+ have a rate of 65 per 100,000. This latter rate is over six times the rate of all ages combined (Centers for Disease Control and Prevention, 1997). Despite these dramatically high rates and the fact that nearly all of these deaths are premature and preventable, research on later-life suicide still remains limited. The purpose of this review is to consider the available research evidence on risk factors and correlates in later-life suicidal behavior and to suggest opportunities for research. The identification and adequate treatment of depression is proposed as the most promising research avenue when preventive interventions in later-life suicide are considered.

AN UNDERRECOGNIZED PUBLIC HEALTH PROBLEM

Research and clinical treatment of suicidal persons in any age group present enormous challenges. Contributing to this challenge for geriatric suicide prevention are our attitudes about mental disorders, suicide, and aging. In multiple surveys, respondents perceive youth suicide to be a greater tragedy than later-life suicides (Marks, 1988/89). Ageism works against research and outreach efforts. For instance, many health providers (Duberstein et al., 1995), family members, and older adults themselves, report that depression and suicidal ideation are part of the aging process (Seidlitz, Duberstein, Cox, & Conwell, 1995).

Conwell (in press) has summarized the state of knowledge regarding the risk factors for later-life suicide. Although there are a number of correlates of completed suicide, there are no published studies of later-life suicide with adequate control samples where the potency of putative risk factors can be calculated. The correlates described here remain just that—"correlates"—until they can be distinguished from fixed markers of risk, or causal risk factors (Kraemer et al., 1997). Therefore the "risk factors" discussed here can only be considered, at best, possible leads. Moreover, there are multiple approaches to studying later-life suicidal behavior. Each has particular advantages and disadvantages for research approaches, depending on the research question and population (e.g., completed suicide as compared to suicide attempts), as has been reviewed by Pearson, Caine, Lindesay, Conwell, and Clark (1999). Some of the advantages and disadvantages to approaches are highlighted below.

SUICIDAL BEHAVIORS AND SOURCES OF EVIDENCE FOR CORRELATES AND POSSIBLE RISK FACTORS

Completed Suicide: Epidemiological Evidence

U.S. data on completed suicides by sex, age, race, marital status, and method of death are based on vital statistics information gathered by the Centers for Disease Control and Prevention's National Center for Health Statistics. From this data source we know that older age, male sex, white race, and unmarried status are associated with higher rates of suicide. These data have been obtained from state death certificates, and each state is responsible for its own vital registry system. In addition to the variation by state, the qualifications for the coroner, medical examiner, or others responsible for completing death certificates vary widely. In some states or jurisdictions the person may be an elected or appointed layman, lawyer, sheriff, mortician, general practitioner, or forensic pathologist. It is generally agreed that suicides are often under-reported on state certificates (O'Carroll, 1989). There are more "missed" suicides than deaths by other causes miscounted as suicides (see O'Carroll, 1989, for a review). While there is no clear consensus of the extent to which misclassification of the cause of death influences the conclusions from published research, medical examiners may be less likely to classify a death as a suicide if the victim had ingested alcohol prior to their death (Jarvis, Bolt, & Butt, 1991). However, since the vast majority of suicides for all age groups are by self-inflicted firearm in-juries (Kachur, Potter, James, & Powell, 1995), there is often little doubt about suicide intent. In fact, this may be even more evident for recent cohorts of older adults. That is, males aged 65 and older showed the greatest proportional increase in the use of firearms as a method of sui-cide between 1979 and 1992 (Kaplan, Adamek, & Johnson, 1994; Mee-han, Saltzman, & Sattin, 1991; Suicide among Older Persons, 1996).

Several studies that have reported on living arrangements among suicide victims have found living alone to be more common in older than younger suicide victims (Jarvis & Boldt, 1980; Rich, Young, & Fowler, 1986). However, older adults are also likely to be those members of the population who live alone (U.S. Bureau of the Census, 1996), so it is not clear whether living alone is a powerful risk factor for suicide or whether it interacts with other factors. A correlate associated with living arrangement is marital status. The suicide rate for unmarried older adults is higher than the suicide rate for married older adults. For older men, the suicide rate for those who are divorced or widowed is much higher when compared with older females or with their married coun-terparts (Buda & Tsuang, 1990). In a study of one Maryland county linking state death records, Li (1995) reported that the risk for suicide among older widowed men was three times that of married men. Older widowed women showed no increase in risk for suicide compared to married women.

Duberstein, Conwell, and Cox (1998) found that widowed older persons most at risk for suicide within four years of the death of a spouse were more likely to have had early loss or separation experiences, as well as a history of psychiatric treatment. Although the findings per-taining to gender differences and psychosocial histories in recent widow-hood strongly suggest an increased risk for suicide, there remains the need for studies that compare completed suicides with adequate control groups, as well as prospective studies that could help determine the risk factors for completed suicide in later life. In terms of malleable risk factors from this epidemiological evidence on demographic factors, it would appear that reducing access to firearms among older persons in psychological distress is a prudent step among the possible efforts to prevent later-life suicide.

Completed Suicide: Psychological Autopsy Method

In the absence of adequate prospective studies, the psychological autopsy (PA) method has been used to reconstruct a detailed picture of the victim's psychological state prior to death, including psychiatric symptomatology, behavior, and life circumstances during the weeks or months before death. This includes interviewing knowledgeable informants, reviewing available clinical records, and comprehensive case formulation by one or more mental health professionals with expertise in post-mortem studies (Beskow, Runeson, & Asgard, 1990; Clark & Horton-Deutsch, 1992).

The PA method has been used to provide an inclusive, well-defined sample of all persons who die by suicide within a defined catchment area, region, or population. This method assesses suicide completers' mental disorders, physical disorders, health service use, personality, and life events, without the bias of attempter samples (see the section entitled "Attempted Suicide," below). One of the most striking and consistent findings of the PA method is that psychiatric disorder and/or substance use is present in about 90% of all suicides, with affective disorder as the most common psychopathology, followed by substance use and schizophrenia (Conwell & Brent, 1995). This strong association between mental disorder and substance use among completed suicides has been reported in Finland (Henriksson et al., 1995) and the United States (Conwell et al., 1998; Dorpat & Ripley, 1960; Rich, Young, & Fowler, 1986).

The application of the PA method to suicides among older adults has been limited, partially due to early reports that older suicide victims were more likely to live alone compared to similarly aged people in the community (Barraclough, 1971). Researchers assumed that older suicide victims were socially isolated from both formal and informal contacts, leaving few knowledgeable informants from whom to obtain data. Younger, Clark, Oehmig-Lindroth, and Stein (1990) however, described ample numbers of informants available for later-life suicides. In their Cook County, Illinois, study, 70% of later-life suicides were married; 90% had one knowledgeable informant; and 50% had two informants. Similarly, other psychological autopsy studies have indicated few differences between older and younger suicide victims with respect to their frequency of social contacts prior to death (Carney, Rich, Burke, & Fowler, 1994; Heikkinen, & Lönnqvist, 1995).

The PA method in later-life suicide has yet to be applied with appropriate control groups. Therefore, PA studies to date allow for age-based comparisons between older and younger suicides. When compared to younger suicide victims, older victims are more likely to have had a physical illness and to have suffered from depression that is not comorbid with a substance disorder (Conwell, 1994; Conwell & Brent, 1995). The type of depression found in the majority of later-life suicides is usually a first episode of depression, uncomplicated by psychoses or other comorbid psychiatric disorders, and ironically is the most treatable type of late-life depression. Such age-related patterns have appeared in reports from a number of countries including the United States (Conwell et al., 1998; Conwell & Brent, 1995), Finland (Henriksson et al., 1995) and the United Kingdom (Lindesay & Murphy, 1987). Paradoxically, the pattern of depression being the most common disorder among completed suicides in later life, with a disproportionate number of suicides occurring among males, is not mirrored by rates of major depression in the population. Rates of major depression in later life are about half the rate (1%) of persons aged 45–64 (2.3%) (Weissman, Bruce, Leaf, Florio, & Holzer, 1991), with no sex differences in rates. Although the disorders of dementia and delirium increase substantially in later life, few studies have found these diagnoses to be risk factors for suicide (Conwell & Brent, 1995). Controlled PA studies are needed to determine what other factors in combination with mental and physical disorders are related to risk for later-life suicide.

Duberstein and his colleagues (Duberstein, 1995; Duberstein, Conwell, & Caine, 1994) used the PA method to explore possible personality traits that may increase risk for later life suicide. Duberstein (1995) used an informant-based measure of the NEO Personality Inventory (Costa & McCrae, 1985) to examine possible personality traits among older and younger suicides relative to age- and sex-matched controls. The NEO inventory measures five general personality traits: *n*euroticism, *e*xtroversion, *o*penness to experience, agreeableness, and conscientiousness. Suicides were found to have higher neuroticism scores than normal controls, and older suicide victims had lower openness to experience scores than both younger suicides and normal controls.

Clark (1993) has theorized that a "narcissistic" crisis, based on a personality predisposition, leaves the older adult with increasingly rigid, inflexible thoughts under stressful life events. Duberstein (1995) has theorized about the behavioral correlates of low openness to experience (OTE) with implications for clinical assessment, the possible sex differences in OTE and depression, biological correlates, and association between OTE and attempted suicide. Each of these offer important clinical implications and plausible research directions in suicidal behavior in late life. Some reports suggest that it may be the confluence of personality, poor coping skills, fear of illness, and hopelessness that influences the association between physical illness and suicide in older men in particular (see Canetto, 1992, for a discussion). Conwell, Caine, and Olsen (1990) presented a series of eight cases where the victims' fears that they had cancer played a major role in committing suicide. Among these eight cases, only one was reported to have cancer upon autopsy and five had diagnoses of major depression. Similarly, Horton-Deutsch, Clark, and Farran (1992), reporting on 14 older male suicide cases, described the co-occurrence of chronic dyspnea, increasing limitations in functional status, life events, and depression and anxiety. Common to both of these studies is the description that the personality characteristics of the majority of later-life male suicides were as follows: appearance of being overtly strong and self-sufficient; covertly or overtly having difficulty in being dependent and accepting help; and a rigid, inflexible coping style, similar to a lack of openness to new experience.

Although substance abuse is not a common disorder among later-life suicides, there is some evidence that for a subset of "young-old" suicide victims, alcohol may play a role. For men with early-onset alcoholism who have survived to their 50s and 60s, the combination of continued alcohol abuse and burnout among their social supports may be lethal. Murphy, Wetzel, Robins, and McEvoy (1992) described that, for older male alcoholics, loss of the last social support can be a pivotal event in suicide risk. Similarly, Duberstein, Conwell, and Caine (1993) reported that interpersonal stressors and recent alcohol use combined to increase risk for suicide. In a Finnish sample, Heikkinen et al. (1994) compared nonalcoholic depressives and alcoholics who had committed suicide. Unlike depressives, alcoholics were likely to have had recent interpersonal loss, unemployment, and financial trouble. Drinking patterns appeared to lead to these concurrent stressors. How current as well as past alcohol abuse lowers the threshold for suicidal behavior in later life requires further systematic examination. Consideration of veterans populations may be an excellent opportunity for this research area. For example, Lish and her colleagues (1996) found that in a Veterans Affairs (VA) hospital setting, substance abuse was related to suicidal ideation, even after controlling for the presence of depression. Although it is often assumed that medication misuse (e.g., benzodiazepine dependence, psychotropic medication with alcohol abuse) is a risk for later-life suicide, there is little or no published information on this topic.

Conwell and his colleagues (1998) reported on age differences in suicidal intent using the PA method. Older suicide victims had higher intent according to the Suicide Intent Scale (Beck, Schuyler, & Herman, 1974; Beck, Brown, & Steer, 1997). That is, older adults were more likely to have avoided intervention, taken precautions against discovery, and were less likely to have communicated their intent to others. Moreover, older men, in particular, were less likely to have had a history of previous attempts.

Research findings of increases in intent with age suggest that older persons who are at risk for suicide may be more difficult to identify as being at imminent risk than is the case for younger persons. Thus, clinical intervention strategies that target individuals who are at high risk for suicide, as indicated by a variety of demographic and psychiatric variables, may be more effective for preventing suicide than interventions that solely target individuals with suicide ideation or behavior.

Completed Suicide: Postmortem Neurobiological Evidence

A growing number of postmortem brain tissue studies of suicide victims have found that the sertonergic systems (presynaptic and nontransporter nerve terminal binding sites) had reduced activity (Mann, 1998). Although there is optimism about new refinements and applications of neurobiological, brain imaging, and candidate gene markers to identify high-risk individuals, there are currently no specific biological markers for suicidal behavior. With regard to older adults, it is conceivable that a "neurobiological vulnerability" to suicide might be modulated by age-related changes in neurobiological systems (Rifai, Reynolds, & Mann, 1992; Schneider, 1996).

The consistency of increased suicide risk with age and male sex across nations also suggests a possible neurobiological process (Conwell,

Raby, & Caine, 1995). Decreased brain concentrations of serotonin, dopamine, norepinephrine, and their metabolites (homovanillic acid, HVA; 5-hydroxyindoleacetic acid, 5-HIAA); increased brain monoamine oxidase (MAO-B) activity; increased hypothalamic–pituitary–adrenal (HPA) activity; and increased sympathetic nervous system activity are associated with both depression and normal aging (Schneider, 1996). Although it would seem that these correlates would have led to more neurobiological studies of later-life suicides, few have been conducted.

Several reviews have examined the evidence for neurobiological abnormalities among older suicide victims relative to controls and have found too few studies that had included sufficient "older" subjects (older than 60 years) to draw any conclusions (Conwell & Brent, 1995; Rifai, Reynolds, & Mann, 1992). This is particularly true of the subgroup of the older adults most at risk: those 85 and older. Conwell and Brent (1995) have also described the challenges to obtaining sufficient cases to test various neurobiological hypotheses and have outlined a protocol for standardization of data for postmortem research protocols. Until there are further data collected on the neurobiological correlates of later-life suicides and appropriate control groups, there is limited evidence for biological risk factors.

Attempted Suicide: Epidemiological Evidence

The PA approach, although providing a wealth of information, is most vulnerable to the retrospective reports of informants who may be biased by knowledge of the type of death of the subject of the inquiry. The PA method is also limited with regard to providing information on the decedent's private self-perceptions, coping, or cognitive distortions. By interviewing persons who have survived a suicide attempt, such data can be obtained.

There are currently no national surveillance data of suicide attempts in the United States. Using data from the National Institute of Mental Health Epidemiologic Catchment Area (ECA) study of five communities (Regier et al., 1984). Mościcki et al. (1988) found a much lower prevalence of lifetime suicide attempts for older adults than younger populations. For persons aged 65 and older, the lifetime prevalence for suicide attempts was 1.1%. By comparison, the rate was 4% for persons aged 25–44. A paucity of published ECA rates exist that examine older adults in smaller age groups or in combination with sex or race. Moreover, these data were limited to only one question—"have you ever attempted suicide?"—and dimensions of intent and lethality were not assessed.

Although interviews with suicide attempters can provide psychological insight into risk factors for completed suicide, attempters and completers are distinct but overlapping populations (Linehan, 1986). Among younger groups, there is great variability in attempters' intention to complete suicide and the ratio of attempts to completions is high (see also McIntosh, Chapter 1, this volume), indicating that many more persons attempt than complete suicide (Meehan, Lamb, Saltzman, & O'Carroll, 1992). In addition, women attempt suicide more often than men, but men more often complete suicide in the general population in both the United States and the United Kingdom (Barraclough, Bunch, Nelson, & Sainsbury, 1974; Mościcki et al., 1988).

The ratio of suicide attempts to subsequent suicide completions is lower for older adults than younger groups (Gardner, Bahn, & Mack, 1964; Kreitman, 1976; Nordentoft et al., 1993; O'Neal, Robins, & Schmidt, 1956). The ratio of attempts to suicide completion is estimated to be approximately 4:1 among older adults (Stenback, 1980), whereas for the population as a whole estimates for the ratio range between 8:1 and 20:1 (Shneidman, 1969; Wolff, 1970). These findings support Conwell and colleagues' (1998) report that older adults are more intent in their efforts to commit suicide. Thus older suicide attempters may be more similar to completers on a variety of risk factors compared to younger attempters (Frierson, 1991; Merrill & Owens, 1990).

Attempted Suicide: Clinical Follow-Up Studies

Follow-up studies presumably have the advantage of an efficient approach to obtaining data on potential risk factors for later-life suicide—they focus on the follow-up of persons who are believed to be most at risk: those with mood disorders, and in particular those who have already attempted suicide. In addition to the challenge of tracking persons in posttreatment time periods, however, this method also relies on medical records that are notoriously variable in accuracy and completeness. Although this approach has been used to examine both suicide attempts and completions among young adult and middle-aged persons, few studies have examined what characteristics, in addition to clinical treatment for depression, place the older adults at risk for suicidal behavior. One exception is a study by Zweig and Hinrichsen (1993). They reported that among older depressed (aged 60 and older) inpatients followed up after 1 year, 8.7% later attempted suicide. Incomplete remission of depression, history of suicide attempts, and familial interpersonal strain were more common among the older adults who later attempted suicide, compared to those who did not attempt suicide within the 1-year follow-up. Other follow-up studies that have considered persons 50 years and older have examined whether delusional depression is a risk factor for later completed suicide. One report indicated that delusional depression was a risk factor (Roose, Glassman, Walsh, Woodring, & Vital-Herre, 1983), whereas others have not found this type of depression to be related to increased risk for later suicide (Coryell & Tsuang, 1982; Robinson & Spiker, 1985).

There are a number of limitations of the follow-up approach to determining risk factors for suicide attempts and completion. There are still low base rates of attempted and completed suicide despite the high-risk samples, as well as sample selection biases. In terms of design problems, the following are typical: no control or random assignment to treatment; wide variation in age of illness onset, assessments, and treatments; variable follow-up periods; unequal sample sizes; and limited generalizability to other clinical and nonclinical populations. With regard to clinical sample bias, most older people who kill themselves have never received mental health services. Thus, follow-up studies have limited generalizability from samples of depressed older adults who have had mental health care to the majority of later-life suicide victims who do not receive mental health services. Since the older adults are unlikely to seek or obtain mental health services (German, Shapiro & Skinner, 1985), the biases of this approach are likely to select subgroups most likely to seek mental health services: women (Kessler, Brown, & Broman, 1981; Nathanson, 1977); those with more severe depression; those with comorbid personality disorders; and those who have used an overdose method (Lindesay, 1986; Vieta, Nieto, Gastó, & Cirera, 1992). Although studies of these biased samples may add to our understanding of what are safe and effective treatments in such service contexts, they minimally overlap with completed suicide community samples described by epidemiological and psychological autopsy methods. Common characteristics of later-life suicides in defined community samples include male sex, those with later ages of onset, unipolar depression, infrequent or no use of mental health care, and use of a firearm or other high lethality methods.

Attempted Suicide: Concurrent Studies

Attempted suicide in late life has been more frequently studied by examining the characteristics of older persons recently admitted to a hospital due to the attempt. Draper (1996) reviewed 12 studies of later-life suicide attempts published between 1985 and 1994. Despite variation in sampling contexts and approaches to measurement, and lack of adequate control groups, he reported several consistent factors associated with attempted suicide in later life: depression, social isolation, and being unmarried. The degree to which physical health was a risk factor was unclear. In some studies it appeared to play a major role (Draper, 1994; Frierson, 1991; Nowers, 1993); in another only about a third of the patients identified health as a salient factor (Pierce, 1987). Draper (1996) suggested that the interaction between psychosocial factors such as social isolation, loneliness, family conflict, and physical factors such as presence of pain and perceived limitations may be a more critical combination for risk of suicide attempts than physical illness alone. A pattern of sex differences by age was also noted across the studies. The proportion of males attempting suicide increased with age, particularly among those aged 75 and older. Without adequate control groups, however, these findings remain interesting hypotheses in need of further exploration rather than true advances in our understanding of risk factors for suicide attempts in later life.

Among the few studies with control groups, older adults with depression admitted for a suicide attempt have been more likely to have a later age of onset than patients with depression who were not suicidal (Lyness, Conwell, & Nelson, 1992). In a German study, an age–sex interaction in age of onset was noted, where men aged 50 and older were more likely to have had an affective illness of late onset, and women had a younger age of onset and were more likely to have had previous suicide attempts (Bron, Strack, & Rudolph, 1991).

Somatization has characterized the psychiatric symptoms of older adult suicide attempters. In a Japanese study of older urban attempters, Takahashi and his colleagues (1995) examined the rates of somatization (defined as a separate entity from depression) among attempters and controls. Consistent with earlier descriptive studies of high rates of hypochondriasis among later-life attempters (Barraclough et al., 1974; De Alarcon, 1964), they found higher rates of somatization among attempters relative to controls. The unique role of somatization and its co-occurrence with depression in later life needs further investigation to better understand its role as a possible risk factor for suicidal behavior.

Another risk factor that may be associated with suicidal behavior in later life is hopelessness. The construct of hopelessness refers to a set of negative beliefs about the future, accompanied by a lack of positive ones. There have been several studies linking hopelessness to completed suicide in adults (Beck, Brown, Berchick, Stewart, & Steer, 1990; Beck, Brown & Steer, 1989; Beck, Brown, Steer, Dahlsgaard, & Grisham, 1999; Beck, Steer, Kovacs, & Garrison, 1985; Fawcett et al., 1987, 1990). A prospective investigation of a retirement community found a single item asking about hopelessness was related to later completed suicides (Ross, Bernstein, Trent, Henderson, & Paganini-Hill, 1990). The relationship between hopelessness and suicide attempts in later life was examined by studying the course of hopelessness in depressed patients (Rifai, George, Stack, Mann & Reynolds, 1994). Patients who had attempted suicide in the past had significantly higher hopelessness scores than nonattempters during both the acute and continuation phases of psychiatric treatment. Moreover, a high degree of hopelessness persisting after the remission of depression in older patients appeared to be associated with a history of suicidal behavior. This study by Rifai and her associates also suggested that a high degree of hopelessness may increase the likelihood of premature discontinuation of treatment and lead to future attempts or suicide. Further research on the association between later-life suicidal behavior and hopelessness as trait- or state-dependent factors is needed.

Suicidal Ideation: Clinical Studies

There are limited published data on the epidemiology of suicidal ideation in later life. From the ECA study sites, Mościcki (1989) reported that similar to self-reported suicide attempts, rates of ideation were lower with increasing age and less frequent among males, blacks, and married persons generally.

Most studies of suicidal ideation in adults are typically gathered in clinic-based samples. Among younger adult populations, several studies have validated suicide ideation as a risk factor for completed suicide (Beck et al., 1999; Fawcett et al., 1990; Goldstein, Black, Nasrallah, & Winokur, 1991). Assessing and monitoring suicidal ideation is often justified as a research and clinical strategy because it is considered the best clue for predicting self-harming behavior. However, the variation in measurement approaches to suicidal ideation has made comparisons of rates and searches for risk factors or correlates difficult for all age groups, and in particular for older persons (Conwell, in press).

Several studies have examined the rates of suicidal ideation among older persons attending primary care clinics. Lish and her colleagues surveyed a VA primary care population where the average age of patients was 60 years (Lish et al., 1996). In this primarily male population, 7.3% of the patients reported thoughts of suicide. Patients with a history of mental health treatment were seven times more likely to have suicidal ideation compared to those without such histories. Racial differences in reporting were also apparent. Whites were twice as likely to have suicidal ideation (9.5%) compared to blacks (5%). Callahan, Hendrie, Nienaber, and Tierney (1996) evaluated suicidal ideation and depressive symptoms in older (aged 60 and greater) primary care patients. Among those with depression, approximately 5% of the patients reported suicidal ideation. Although depressed patients had more functional impairment than their nondepressed counterparts, the patients with suicidal ideation did not have a greater level of functional impairment than did depressed patients without suicidal ideation. Moreover, patients with moderate levels of depression reported ideation at similar rates to those with clinical depression. Assuming that suicidal ideation is a precursor to later suicide attempts or completions, this finding suggests that clinicians should not assume that suicide risk is necessarily related to severity of depression or functional impairment among older adults.

Investigations with younger adult psychiatric populations have indicated that hopelessness was more strongly associated with suicidal ideation than depression (Beck, Steer, Beck, & Newman, 1993; Silver, Bohnert, Beck, & Marcus, 1971; Wetzel, Marguiles, Davis, & Karam, 1980). In contrast, studies with older suicidal patients (Hill, Gallagher, Thompson, & Ishida, 1988; Trenteseau, Hyer, Verenes, & Warsaw, 1989) as well as institutionalized older males (Uncapher, Gallagher-Thompson, Osgood, & Bongar, 1998) did not find hopelessness more predictive of suicidal ideation than was depression. These studies suggest that screening for depression may be more effective for detecting suicidal ideation in older adults than screening for hopelessness. However, as noted above, hopelessness in later life should not be dismissed as insignificant, since hopelessness has been linked to suicide attempts in older patients with remitted depression (Rifai et al., 1994). Clearly, more research is needed to elucidate the role of hopelessness in contributing to the risk for later-life suicidal behavior across different settings and subgroups.

Indirect Life-Threatening Behaviors

Behaviors that appear to be a part of either high-risk or self-destructive patterns have been hypothesized to be "suicidal" and have been labeled "indirect" life-threatening behavior (ILTB, sometimes referred to also as indirect self-destructive behavior, ISDB). Nelson and Farberow (1976) were among the first researchers to document indirect suicidal behaviors among older adults. Observing hospitalized patients in a VA intermediate care unit, they developed an Inventory of Life-Threatening Behavior, including such behaviors as misuse of medications, self-injury, verbal abuse of other patients, and excessive intake or refusals of food or liquids. Rates of ILTB were related to hopelessness, low life satisfaction, and low religiosity.

Building on this work, Osgood and Brant (1990) conducted a pioneering study examining indirect life-threatening behaviors (ISTBs) in long-term care facilities. Through their survey of facilities, they found that most self-destructive behaviors in nursing homes were indeed indirect, including such behaviors as refusal of food or medications. ISDBs were also related to facility characteristics (Osgood & Brant, 1990; Osgood, 1992). Since this survey, there has been limited research attention to ISDBs. For example, an obvious question is whether older persons who exhibit indirect self-harming behaviors would also report suicidal ideation with these behaviors. Conwell, Pearson, and DeRenzo (1996) summarized a number of areas of self-destructive behaviors in nursing home patients requiring research attention. Included are patient-related factors (psychiatric illness, physical health, personality and coping styles, religious beliefs, and neurobiological status), setting influences (nature and size of facility, quality of care provided), and their interactions, as well as ethical issues involved. Given the high prevalence of mental disorders in nursing homes that go undetected and untreated (Rovner, Kafonek, Filipp, Lucas, & Folstein, 1986; Strahan, 1991), the need for further study of self-destructive behavior, both direct and indirect, is clearly needed in these settings.

RESEARCH OPPORTUNITIES IN THE PRIMARY CARE SETTING

Clark (1992) has noted that suicides in the United States are not higher for those with less access to health care. To the contrary, suicide rates are lower for blacks and Hispanics (groups who traditionally have less access to health care) relative to their white counterparts. Indeed, a phenomenon common among older suicide completers is that the majority *has* recently visited a health care provider. Several retrospective studies have indicated that more than 70% of older suicides have visited their primary care physician within the month of their suicide, and a third within the week of their suicide (Conwell, Olsen, Caine, & Flannery, 1991; Diekstra & van Egmond, 1989; Frierson, 1991; Miller, 1978; Murphy, 1975a, 1975b). Importantly, virtually none of these older patients had sought mental health services. This is in contrast to younger adults, where 25–30% were under the care of a mental health professional at the time of their death (Clark & Fawcett, 1992).

There are several reasons that may explain the failure to recognize and adequately treat older adults with depression and suicidal risk in the primary care setting. First, as noted above, older adults themselves and their family members may incorrectly attribute depressive symptoms and suicidal ideation to the aging process—indeed, see depression as a "normal" aspect of aging and as an expectable aspect of experiencing a physical illness. Second, there may be hesitancy or inability to report psychiatric symptoms even when specifically asked about them by their provider. Gallo, Anthony, and Muthén (1994) have found that older depressed adults are less likely to endorse dysphoric mood as part of their symptom clusters. Older men, in particular, are less likely to report depressive symptoms (Allen-Burge, Storandt, Kinscherf, & Rubin, 1994; Lutsky & Knight, 1994). Third, primary care physicians, who are the most sought-after health care providers among all persons with depression in the United States, typically do not recognize depression (e.g., Perez-Stable, Miranda, Muñoz, & Ying, 1990) nor adequately treat it among any age group (Sturm & Wells, 1995). Primary care physicians tend to spend less time with older patients and focus on physical problems to the exclusion of mental morbidity (German, Shapiro, & Skinner, 1985; Keeler, Solomon, Beck, Mendenhall, & Kane, 1982). Some physicians deliberately avoid diagnosing a mood disorder, even when recognized, to avoid stigmatizing the patient as well as reimbursement problems (Rost, Smith, Matthews, & Guise, 1994). Discussing depressive symptoms increases the length of physician–patient contact (Badger et al., 1994), and time-limited office visits are perceived to be a barrier to effective depression treatment (Banazak, 1996).

Even if psychiatric symptoms are recognized, there is a high probability that treatment by primary care providers will be inappropriate or inadequate. For example, anxiety symptoms are the most common kind of psychiatric comorbidity in older depressed patients (Blanchard, Waterreus, & Mann, 1994). Among depressed patients in general, recognition by primary care providers increases when they report being anxious as well (Coyne, Schwenk, & Fechner-Bates, 1995). All too often, primary care physicians are more likely to treat the anxiety symptoms with benzodiazepine medication, rather that treating the concurrent depressive symptoms directly with antidepressants (Ormel et al., 1990; Tollefson, Souetre, Thomander, & Potvin, 1993). This can lead to risk for benzodiazepine dependence and untreated lethal depression.

There is growing concern that the low rate of depression detection and treatment of later-life depression in primary care settings has significant implications for greater risk of morbidity and mortality, including suicide (Pearson, Conwell, & Lyness, 1997; Rihmer, 1996). This has led to requests by federal (NIH Guide, 1997) and private (e.g., *BlueLink*, 1998) agencies involved with health care services for increased depression screening, with the assumption that appropriate treatment will follow. Indeed, there is growing evidence that short, efficient, valid depression screening measures exist for older adults and that such screening measures may be better at detection than is clinical judgment by providers (Schade, Jones, & Wittlin, 1998).

However, it is becoming apparent that screening efforts do not automatically lead to improved treatment. Schade and his associates (1998), in their review of screening measures and their outcomes, concluded that screening alone offered little or no direct benefit. Many primary care providers lack knowledge and experience with depression and suicidal crisis assessment and treatment (Depression Guidelines Panel, 1993a, 1993b; Schulberg & McClelland, 1987). This has led to calls for research to test models purported to improve depression detection and treatment for older patients in the primary care setting (Substance Abuse and Mental Health Services Administration, 1998; NIH Guide, 1997). Several projects are now being fielded to test these models.

SUMMARY

Suicide among older white men is one of today's most critical and challenging public health problems. Yet there remains limited information on risk factors due to the small number of controlled studies that could help isolate and focus on the most potent risk factors, as well as protective factors present among lower-risk groups (i.e., older white women, and older black women and men). Because there are no proven, effective interventions showing reduced suicidal behaviors in older adults, the best approaches appear to be detecting and treating late-life depression. This approach may be especially needed in primary care settings, where the majority of our nation's older adults seek and receive their mental health care. There is a growing knowledge base of useful screening tools, assessments, and treatments for late-life depression, as well as a better understanding of the barriers to late-life recognition and treatment. Testing and determining effective treatment approaches and minimizing barriers to recognizing and treating depression should be immediate goals on the path to advancing the science and practice of later-life suicide prevention.

ACKNOWLEDGMENTS

This chapter was adapted from Pearson and Brown (2000) and Pearson et al. (1999). Copyright 2000 by Elsevier Science and copyright 1999 by the American Psychiatric Association. Adapted by permission.

REFERENCES

Allen-Burge, R., Storandt, M., Kinscherf, D. A., & Rubin, E. H. (1994). Sex differences in the sensitivity of two self-report depression scales in older depressed inpatients. *Psychology and Aging, 9*, 443–445.

Badger, L. W., deGruy, F. V., Hartman, J., Plant, M. A., Leeper, J., Ficken, R., Maxwell, A., Rand, E., Anderson, R., & Templeton, B. (1994). Psychosocial interest, medical interviews, and the recognition of depression. *Archives of Family Medicine, 3*, 899–907.

Banazak, D. A. (1996). Late-life depression in primary care: How well are we doing? *Journal of General Internal Medicine, 11*, 163–167.

Barraclough, B. M. (1971). Suicide in the elderly: Recent developments in psychogeriatrics. *British Journal of Psychiatry, 6*(Special suppl.), 87–97.

Barraclough, B. M., Bunch, J., Nelson, B. & Sainsbury, P. (1974). A hundred cases of suicide: Clinical aspects. *British Journal of Psychiatry, 125*, 355–373.

Beck, A. T., Brown, G., Berchick, R. J., Stewart, B. L., & Steer, R. A. (1990). Relationship between hopelessness and ultimate suicide: A replication with psychiatric outpatients. *American Journal of Psychiatry, 147*, 190–195.

Beck, A. T., Brown, G., & Steer, R. A. (1989). Prediction of eventual suicide in psychiatric inpatients by clinical rating of hopelessness. *Journal of Consulting and Clinical Psychology, 57*, 309–310.

Beck, A. T., Brown, G. K., & Steer, R. A. (1997). Psychometric characteristics of the Scale for Suicide Ideation with psychiatric outpatients. *Behaviour Research and Therapy, 35*, 1039–1046.

Beck, A. T., Brown, G. K., Steer, R. A., Dahlsgaard, K. K., & Grisham, J. R. (1999). Suicide ideation at its worst point: A predictor of eventual suicide in psychiatric outpatients. *Suicide and Life-Threatening Behavior, 29*, 1–9.

Beck, A. T., Schuyler, D., & Herman, I. (1974). Development of suicidal intent scales. In A. T. Beck, H. C. P. Resnick, & D. Lettieri (Eds.), *The prediction of suicide* (pp. 45–56). Bowie, MD: Charles Press.

Beck, A. T., Steer, R. A., Beck, J. S., & Newman, C. F. (1993). Hopelessness, depression, suicidal ideation, and clinical diagnosis of depression. *Suicide and Life-Threatening Behavior, 23,* 139–145.

Beck, A. T., Steer, R. A., Kovacs, M., & Garrison, B. (1985). Hopelessness, depression, and attempted suicide. *American Journal of Psychiatry, 142,* 559–563.

Beskow, J., Runeson, B., & Asgard, U. (1990). Psychological autopsies: Methods and ethics. *Suicide and Life-Threatening Behavior, 20,* 307–323.

Blanchard, M. R., Waterreus, A., & Mann, A. H. (1994). The nature of depression among older people in inner London, and the contact with primary care. *British Journal of Psychiatry, 164,* 396–402.

BlueLink. (1998, Fall). Theme of the quarter: Chronic illness and clinical depression. Newsletter of Blue Cross/Blue Shield of Maryland [available online: http://www.bcbsmd.com].

Bron, B., Strack, M., & Rudolph, G. (1991). Childhood experiences and loss and suicide attempts: Significance in depressive states of major depressed and dysthymic or adjustment disordered patients. *Journal of Affective Disorders, 23,* 165–172.

Buda, M., & Tsuang, M. T. (1990). The epidemiology of suicide: Implications for clinical practice. In S. J. Blumenthal & D. J. Kupfer (Eds.), *Suicide over the life cycle: Risk factors, assessment, and treatment of suicidal patients* (pp. 17–37). Washington, DC: American Psychiatric Press.

Callahan, C. M., Hendrie, H. C., Nienaber, N. A., & Tierney, W. M. (1996). Suicidal ideation among older primary care patients. *Journal of the American Geriatrics Society, 44,* 1205–1209.

Canetto, S. S. (1992). Gender and suicide in the elderly. *Suicide and Life-Threatening Behavior, 22,* 80–97.

Carney, S. S., Rich, C. L., Burke, P. A., & Fowler, R. C. (1994). Suicide over 60: The San Diego study. *Journal of the American Geriatrics Society, 42,* 174–180.

Centers for Disease Control and Prevention (1997). Available online: http://www.cdc.gov/ncipc/data/us9794/Suic.htm.

Clark, D. C. (1992). "Rational" suicide and people with terminal conditions or disabilities. *Issues in Law and Medicine, 8*(2), 147–166.

Clark, D. C. (1993). Narcissistic crises of aging and suicidal despair. *Suicide and Life-Threatening Behavior, 23,* 21–26.

Clark, D. C. & Fawcett, J. (1992). Review of empirical risk factors for evaluation of the suicidal patient. In B. Bongar (Ed.), *Suicide: Guidelines for assessment, management, and treatment* (pp. 16–50). New York: Oxford University Press.

Clark, D. C., & Horton-Deutsch, S. L. (1992). Assessment *in absentia:* The value of the psychological autopsy method for studying antecedents of suicide and predicting future suicides. In R. W. Maris, A. L. Berman, J. T. Maltzberger, & R. I. Yufit (Eds.), *Assessment and prediction of suicide* (pp. 144–182). New York: Guilford Press.

Conwell, Y. (1994). Suicide in elderly patients. In L. S. Schneider, C. F. Reynolds, B. D. Lebowitz, & A. J. Friedhoff (Eds.), *Diagnosis and treatment of depression in late life* (pp. 397–418). Washington, DC: American Psychiatric Association.

Conwell, Y. (in press). Suicide in late life. In *Suicide prevention now: Linking research and practice.* Atlanta, GA: Department of Health and Human Services, Centers for Disease Control and Prevention.

Conwell, Y., & Brent, D. (1995). Suicide and aging: I. Patterns of psychiatric diagnosis. *International Psychogeriatrics, 7,* 149–181.

Conwell, Y., Caine, E. D., & Olsen, K. (1990). Suicide and cancer in late life. *Hospital and Community Psychiatry, 41,* 1334–1339.

Conwell, Y., Duberstein, P. R., Cox, C., Herrmann, J. H., Forbes, N. T., & Caine, E. D. (1998). Age differences in behaviors leading to completed suicide. *American Journal of Geriatric Psychiatry, 6,* 122–126.

Conwell, Y., Olsen, K., Caine, E. D., & Flannery, D. (1991). Suicide in late life: Psychological autopsy findings. *International Psychogeriatrics, 3,* 59–66.

Conwell, Y., Pearson, J., & DeRenzo, E. G. (1996). Indirect self-destructive behavior among elderly patients in nursing homes. *American Journal of Geriatric Psychiatry, 4,* 152–163.

Conwell, Y., Raby, W. N., & Caine, E. D. (1995). Suicide and aging: II. The psychobiological interface. *International Psychogeriatrics, 7,* 165–181.

Coryell, W., & Tsuang, M. T. (1982). Primary unipolar depression and the prognostic importance of delusions. *Archives of General Psychiatry, 39,* 1181–1184.

Costa, P. T., & McCrae, R. R. (1985). *The NEO Personality Inventory: Manual.* Odessa, FL: Psychological Assessment Resources.

Coyne, J. C., Schwenk, T. L., & Fechner-Bates, S. (1995). Nondetection of depression by primary care physicians reconsidered. *General Hospital Psychiatry, 17,* 3–12.

De Alarcon, R. (1964). Hypochondriasis and depression in the aged. *Gerontology Clinics, 6,* 266–277.

Depression Guidelines Panel. (1993a). *Depression in primary care: Vol. 1. Clinical practice guidelines* (PHS, ACHPR Publication No. 93-0550). Rockville, MD: U.S. Department of Health and Human Services.

Depression Guidelines Panel. (1993b). *Depression in primary care: Vol. 2. Treatment of major depression in clinical practice guidelines* (PHS, ACHPR Publication No. 93-0551). Rockville, MD: U.S. Department of Health and Human Services.

Diekstra, R. F. W., & van Egmond, M. (1989). Suicide and attempted suicide in general practice, 1979–1985. *Acta Psychiatrica Scandinavica, 79,* 268–275.

Dorpat, T. L., & Ripley, H. S. (1960). A study of suicides in the Seattle area. *Comprehensive Psychiatry, 1,* 349–359

Draper, B. (1994). Suicidal behavior in the elderly. *International Journal of Geriatric Psychiatry, 9,* 655–661.

Draper, B. (1996). Attempted suicide in old age. *International Journal of Geriatric Psychiatry, 11,* 577–587.

Duberstein, P. R. (1995). Openness to experience and completed suicide across the second half of life. *International Psychogeriatrics, 7,* 183–198.

Duberstein, P. R., Conwell, Y., & Caine, E. D. (1993). Interpersonal stressors, substance abuse, and suicide. *Journal of Nervous and Mental Disease, 181,* 80–85.

Duberstein, P. R., Conwell, Y., & Caine, E. D. (1994). Age differences in the personality characteristics of suicide completers: Preliminary findings from a psychological autopsy study. *Psychiatry, 57,* 213–224.

Duberstein, P. R., Conwell, Y., & Cox, C. (1998). Suicide in widowed persons. A psychological autopsy comparison of recently and remotely bereaved older subjects. *American Journal of Geriatric Psychiatry, 6*, 328–334.

Duberstein, P. R., Conwell, Y., Cox, C., Podgorski, C. A., Glazer, R. S., & Caine, E. D. (1995). Attitudes toward self-determined death: A survey of primary care physicians. *Journal of the American Geriatrics Society, 43*, 395–400.

Fawcett, J., Scheftner, W., Clark, D. C., Hedeker, D., Gibbons, R., & Coryell, W. (1987). Clinical predictors of suicide in patients with major affective disorders: A controlled prospective study. *American Journal of Psychiatry, 144*, 35–40.

Fawcett, J., Scheftner, W., Fogg, L., Clark, D. C., Young, M. A., Hedeker, D., & Gibbons, R. (1990). Time-related predictors of suicide in major affective disorder. *American Journal of Psychiatry, 147*, 1189–1194.

Frierson, R. L. (1991). Suicide attempts by the old and the very old. *Archives of Internal Medicine, 151*, 141–144.

Gallo, J. J., Anthony, J. C., & Muthén, B. G. (1994). Age differences in the symptoms of depression: A latent trait analysis. *Journal of Gerontology: Psychological Sciences, 49*, P251-P264.

Gardner, E. A., Bahn, A. K., & Mack, M. (1964). Suicide and psychiatric care in the aging. *Archives of General Psychiatry, 10*, 547–553.

German, P. S., Shapiro, S., & Skinner, E. A. (1985). Mental health of the elderly: Use of health and mental health services. *Journal of the American Geriatrics Society, 33*, 246–252.

Goldstein, R. B., Black, D. W., Nasrallah, A., & Winokur, G. (1991). The prediction of suicide. *Archives of General Psychiatry, 48*, 418–422.

Heikkinen, M. E., Aro, H. M., Henriksson, M. M., Isometsä, E. T., Sarna, S. J., Kuoppasalmi, K. I., & Lönnqvist, J. K. (1994). Differences in recent life events between alcoholic and depressive nonalcoholic suicides. *Alcoholism: Clinical and Experimental Research, 18*, 1143–1149.

Heikkinen, M., & Lönnqvist, J. (1995). Recent life events in elderly suicide: A nationwide study in Finland. *International Psychogeriatrics, 7*, 287–300.

Henriksson, M. M., Marttunen, M. J., Isometsä, E. T., Heikkinen, M. E., Aro, H. M., Kuoppasalmi, K. I., & Lönnqvist, J. K. (1995). Mental disorders in elderly suicide. *International Psychogeriatrics, 7*, 275–286

Hill, R. D., Gallagher, D., Thompson, L. W., & Ishida, T. (1988). Hopelessness as a measure of suicidal intent in the depressed elderly. *Psychology and Aging, 3*, 230–232.

Horton-Deutsch, S. L., Clark, D. C., & Farran, C. J. (1992). Chronic dyspnea and suicide in elderly men. *Hospital and Community Psychiatry, 43*, 1198–1203.

Jarvis, G. K., & Boldt, T. M. (1980). Suicide in the later years. *Essence, 4*, 144–158.

Jarvis, G. K., Boldt, T. M., & Butt J. (1991). Medical examiners and manner of death. *Suicide and Life-Threatening Behavior, 21*, 115–133.

Kachur, S. P., Potter, L. B., James, S. P., & Powell, K. E. (1995). *Suicide in the United States, 1980–1992: Violence surveillance summary series, No. 1*. Atlanta, GA: Centers for Disease Control and Prevention, National Center for Injury Prevention and Control.

Kaplan, M. S., Adamek, M. E., & Johnson, S. (1994). Trends in firearm suicide among older American males: 1979–1988. *The Gerontologist, 34*, 59–65.

Keeler, E. B., Solomon, D. H., Beck, J. C., Mendenhall, R. C., & Kane, R. L. (1982). Effect of patient age on duration of medical encounters with physicians. *Medical Care, 20*, 1101–1108.

Kessler, R. C., Brown, R. L., & Broman, C. L. (1981). Sex differences in psychiatric help-seeking: Evidence from four large-scale surveys. *Journal of Health and Social Behavior, 22*, 49–64.

Kraemer, H. C., Kazdin, A. E., Offord, D. R., Kessler, R. C., Jensen, P. S., & Kupfer, D. J. (1997). Coming to terms with the terms of risk. *Archives of General Psychiatry, 54*, 337–343.

Kreitman, N. (1976). Age and parasuicide. *Psychological Medicine, 6*, 113–121.

Li, G. (1995). The interaction effect of bereavement and sex on the risk of suicide in the elderly: An historical cohort study. *Social Science and Medicine, 40*, 825–828.

Lindesay, J. (1986). Trends in self-poisoning in the elderly, 1974–1983. *International Journal of Geriatric Psychiatry, 1*, 37–43.

Lindesay, J., & Murphy, E. (1987). Suicide in old age. *International Journal of Geriatriatric Psychiatry, 2*, 71–72

Linehan, M. M. (1986). Suicidal people: One population or two? In J. J. Mann & M. Stanley (Eds.), *Psychobiology of suicidal behavior* (pp. 16–33). New York: Annals of the New York Academy of Sciences (No. 487).

Lish, J. D., Zimmerman, M., Farber, N. J., Lush, D. T., Kuzma, M. A., & Plescia, G. (1996). Suicide screening in a primary care setting in a Veterans Affairs Medical Center. *Psychosomatics, 37*, 413–424.

Lutzky, S. M., & Knight, B. G. (1994). Explaining gender differences in caregiver distress: The roles of emotional attentiveness and coping styles. *Psychology and Aging, 9*, 513–519.

Lyness, J. M., Conwell, Y., & Nelson, J. C. (1992). Suicide attempts in elderly psychiatric inpatients. *Journal of the American Geriatrics Society, 40*, 320–324.

Mann, J. J. (1998). The neurobiology of suicide. *Nature Medicine, 4*, 25–30.

Marks, A. (1988/89). Structural parameters of sex, race, age, and education and their influence on attitudes toward suicide. *Omega, 19*, 327–336.

Meehan, P. J., Lamb, J. A., Saltzman, L. E., & O'Carroll, P. W. (1992). Attempted suicide among young adults: Progress toward a meaningful estimate of prevalence. *American Journal of Psychiatry, 149*, 41–44.

Meehan, P. J., Saltzman, L. E., & Sattin, R. W. (1991). Suicides among older United States residents: Epidemiologic characteristics and trends. *American Journal of Public Health, 81*, 1198–1200.

Merrill, J., & Owens, J. (1990). Age and attempted suicide. *Acta Psychiatrica Scandinavica, 82*, 385–388.

Miller, M. (1978). Geriatric suicide: The Arizona study. *The Gerontologist, 18*, 488–495.

Mościcki, E. K. (1989). Epidemiologic surveys as tools for studying suicidal behavior: A review. *Suicide and Life-Threatening Behavior, 19*, 131–146.

Mościcki, E. K., O'Carroll, P., Rae, D. S., Locke, B. Z., Roy, A., & Regier, D. A. (1988). Suicide attempts in the Epidemiologic Catchment Area Study. *Yale Journal of Biology and Medicine, 61*, 259–268.

Murphy, G. E. (1975a). The physician's responsiblity for suicide: I. Errors of commission. *Annals of Internal Medicine, 82*, 301–304.

Murphy, G. E. (1975b). The physician's responsiblity for suicide: II. Errors of ommission. *Annals of Internal Medicine, 82*, 305–309.

Murphy, G. E., Wetzel, R. D., Robins, E., & McEvoy, L. (1992). Multiple risk factors predict suicide in alcoholism. *Archives of General Psychiatry, 49,* 459–463.

Nathanson, C. A. (1977). Sex, illness and medical care: A review of data, theory and methods. *Social Science and Statistics, 11,* 13–25.

Nelson, F. L., & Farberow, N. L. (1976). Indirect suicide in the elderly, chronically ill patient. *Psychiatria Fennica* (Suppl.), 125–139.

NIH Guide (1997). *Prevention of suicidal behavior in older primary care patients* (Vol. 26, No. 38). (RFA: MH-98-002.) Bethesda, MD: National Institutes of Health.

Nordentoft, M., Breum, L, Munck, L., Nordestgaard, A. G., Hunding, A., & Bjældager, P. A. L. (1993). High mortality by natural and unnatural causes: A 10-year follow-up study of patients admitted to a poisoning treatment centre after suicide attempts. *British Medical Journal, 306,* 1637–1641.

Nowers, M. (1993). Deliberate self-harm in the elderly: A survey of one London borough. *International Journal of Geriatric Psychiatry, 8,* 609–614.

O'Carroll, P. (1989). Validity and reliability of suicide mortality data. *Suicide and Life-Threatening Behavior, 19,* 1–16.

O'Neal, P., Robins, E., & Schmidt, E. H. (1956). A psychiatric study of attempted suicide in persons over sixty years of age. *Archives of Neurology and Psychiatry, 75,* 275–284.

Ormel, J., Van Den Brink, W., Koeter, M. W., Giel, R., Van Der Meer, K., Van De Willige, G., & Wilmink, F. W. (1990). Recognition, management and outcome of psychological disorders in primary care: A naturalistic follow-up study. *Psychological Medicine, 20,* 909–923.

Osgood, N. J. (1992). Environmental factors in suicide in long-term care facilities. *Suicide and Life-Threatening Behavior, 22,* 98–106.

Osgood, N. J. & Brant, B. A. (1990). Suicidal behavior in long-term care facilities. *Suicide and Life-Threatening Behavior, 20,* 113–122.

Pearson, J. L., & Brown, G. K. (2000). Suicide prevention in late-life: Directions for science and practice. *Clinical Psychology Review.*

Pearson, J. L., Caine, E. D., Lindesay, J., Conwell, Y., & Clark, D. C. (1999). Studies of suicide in later life: Methodologic considerations and research directions. *American Journal of Geriatric Psychiatry, 7,* 203–210.

Pearson, J. L., & Conwell, Y. (1995). Suicide in late-life: Challenges and opportunities for research. *International Psychogeriatrics, 7,* 131–136.

Pearson, J. L., Conwell, Y., & Lyness, J. M. (1997). Late-life suicide and depression in the primary care setting. In L. S. Schneider (Ed.), *Developments in geriatric psychiatry* (No. 76, pp. 13–38). San Francisco: Jossey-Bass.

Perez-Stable, E. J., Miranda, J., Muñoz, R., & Ying, Y. (1990). Depression in medical outpatients: Underrecognition and misdiagnosis. *Archives of Internal Medicine, 150,* 1083–1088.

Pierce, D. (1987). Deliberate self-harm in the elderly. *International Journal of Geriatric Psychiatry, 2,* 105–110.

Regier, D. A., Myers, J. K., Kramer, M., Robins, L. N., Blazer, D. G, Hough, R. L., Eaton, W. W., & Locke, B. Z. (1984). The NIMH Epidemiologic Catchment Area (ECA) Program: Historical context, major objectives, and study population characteristics. *Archives of General Psychiatry, 41*, 934–941.

Rich, C. L., Young, J. G., & Fowler, R. C. (1986). San Diego suicide study: I. Young vs. old subjects. *Archives of General Psychiatry, 43*, 577–582.

Rifai, A. H., George, C. J., Stack, J. A., Mann, J. J., & Reynolds, C. F. (1994). Hopelessness in suicide attempters after acute treatment of major depression in late life. *American Journal of Psychiatry, 151*, 1687–1690.

Rifai, A. H., Reynolds, C. F., & Mann, J. J. (1992). Biology of elderly suicide. In A. A. Leenaars, R. W. Maris, J. L. McIntosh, & J. Richman (Eds.), *Suicide and the older adult* (pp. 48–61). New York: Guilford Press.

Rihmer, Z. (1996). Strategies of suicide prevention: Focus on health care. *Journal of Affective Disorders, 39*, 83–91.

Robinson, D. G., & Spiker, D. G. (1985). Delusional depression: A one-year follow-up. *Journal of Affective Disorders, 9*, 79–83.

Roose, S. P., Glassman, A. H., Walsh, B. T., Woodring, S., & Vital-Herre, J. (1983). Depression, delusions, and suicide. *American Journal of Psychiatry, 140*, 1159–1162.

Ross, R. K., Bernstein, L., Trent, L., Henderson, B. E., & Paganini-Hill, A. (1990). A prospective study of risk factors for traumatic death in the retirement community. *Preventive Medicine, 19*, 323–334.

Rost, K., Smith, G., Matthews, D., & Guise, B. (1994). The deliberate misdiagnosis of major depression in primary care. *Archives of Family Medicine, 3*, 333–337.

Rovner, B. W., Kafonek, S., Filipp, L., Lucas, M. J., & Folstein, M. F. (1986). Prevalence of mental illness in a community nursing home. *American Journal of Psychiatry, 143*, 1446–1449.

Schade, C. P., Jones, E. R., & Wittlin, B. J. (1998). A ten-year review of the validity and clinical utility of depression screening. *Psychiatric Services, 49*, 55–61.

Schneider, L. S. (1996). Biological commonalities among aging, depression, and suicidal behavior. In G. J. Kennedy (Ed.), *Suicide and depression in late life: Critical issues in treatment, research and public policy* (pp. 39–50). New York: Wiley.

Schulberg, H. C., & McClelland, M. (1987). A conceptual model for educating primary care providers in the diagnosis and treatment of depression. *General Hospital Psychiatry, 9*, 1–10.

Seidlitz, L., Duberstein, P. R., Cox, C., & Conwell, Y. (1995). Attitudes of older people toward suicide and assisted suicide: An analysis of Gallup Poll findings. *Journal of the American Geriatrics Society, 43*, 993–998.

Shneidman, E. (1969). Prologue: Fifty-eight years. In E. S. Shneidman (Ed.), *On the nation of suicide* (pp. 1–30). San Francisco: Jossey-Bass.

Silver, M. A., Bohnert, M., Beck, A. T., & Marcus, D. (1971). Relation of depression of attempted suicide and seriousness of intent. *Archives of General Psychiatry, 25*, 573–576.

Stenback, A. (1980). Depression and suicidal behavior in old age. In J. E. Birren & R. B. Sloane (Eds.), *Handbook of mental health and aging* (pp. 616–652). Englewood Cliffs, NJ: Prentice-Hall.

Strahan, G. W. (1991). Mental illness in nursing homes: United States, 1985. *Vital Health Statistics, 13*(105). (DHHS Publication No. PHS 91–1766.) Hyattsville, MD: National Center for Health Statistics.

Sturm, R. & Wells, K. B. (1995). How can care for depression become more cost-effective. *Journal of the American Medical Association, 273*, 51–58.

Substance Abuse and Mental Health Services Administration. (1998). *Cooperative agreements to document and evaluate mental health/substance abuse services for older adults through primary health care* (Guidance for Applicants No. SM 98-009). Rockville, MD: Author.

Suicide among Older Persons—United States, 1980–1992. (1996, January 12). *Morbidity and Mortality Weekly Report, 45*(1), 3–6.

Takahashi, Y., Hirasawa, H., Koyama, K., Asakawa, O., Kido, M., Onse, H., Udagawa, M., Ishikawa, Y., & Uno, M. (1995). Suicide and aging in Japan: An examination of treated elderly attempters. *International Psychogeriatrics, 7*, 239–261.

Tollefson, G. D., Souetre, E., Thomander, L., & Potvin, J. H. (1993). Comorbid anxious signs and symptoms in major depression: Impact on functional work capacity and comparative treatment outcomes. *International Clinical Psychopharmacology, 8*, 281–293.

Trenteseau, J. A., Hyer, L., Verenes, D., & Warsaw, J. (1989). Hopelessness among later-life patients. *Journal of Applied Gerontology, 8*, 355–364.

Uncapher, H., Gallagher-Thompson, D., Osgood, N. J., & Bongar, B. (1998). Hopelessness and suicidal ideation in older adults. *The Gerontologist, 38*, 62–70.

U. S. Bureau of the Census. (1996). *65+ in the United States* (Current Population Reports, Special Studies, P23-190). Washington, DC: U.S. Government Printing Office.

Vieta, E., Nieto, E., Gastó, C., & Cirera, E. (1992). Serious suicide attempts in affective patients. *Journal of Affective Disorders, 24*, 147–152.

Weissman, M. M., Bruce, M. L., Leaf, P. J., Florio, L. P., & Holzer, C. E. (1991). Affective disorders. In L. N. Robbins & D. A. Regier (Eds.), *Psychiatric disorders in America* (pp. 53–80). New York: Free Press.

Wetzel, R. D., Marguiles, T., Davis, R., & Karam, E. (1980). Hopelessness, depression, and suicide intent. *Journal of Consulting and Clinical Psychology, 41*, 159–160.

Wolff, K. (1970). Observations on depression and suicide in the geriatric patient. In K. Wolff (Ed.), *Patterns of self-destruction: Depression and suicide* (pp. 33–42). Springfield, IL: Thomas.

Younger, S. C., Clark, D. C., Oehmig-Lindroth, R., & Stein, R. J. (1990). Availability of knowledgeable informants for a psychological autopsy study of suicides committed by elderly people. *Journal of the American Geriatrics Society, 38*, 1169–1175.

Zweig, R. A., & Hinrichsen, G. A. (1993). Factors associated with suicide attempts by depressed older adults: A prospective study. *American Journal of Psychiatry, 150*, 1687–1692.

CHAPTER TEN

Considering Cultural Beliefs and Behaviors in the Study of Suicide

Julia Shiang, EdD, PhD

I am often asked this question by clinicians and researchers alike: So what difference does culture make anyway? Aren't similarities and differences among people really due to biology, the basic temperament, the personality, psychological motivation, and environmental forces? What we know is that there are clear similarities among people everywhere in the world. People generally need to interact with others, need food, need shelter, have emotional experiences, procreate. Yet there are obvious differences among people in how they interact, what types of food and shelter they prefer, as well as how they exhibit emotional and procreative behaviors. Thus, it is not surprising that we should find in the study of suicide and death that, although all societies assign meaning to death and suicide, these particular meanings and consequences for living are varied.

While the study of suicide may well be largely academic, we, as mental health scholars, are also concerned with promoting meaningful and sustainable ways of life. Thus, one of our basic concerns is with creating conditions (in the environment and within individuals) that lead people to think of other ways of coping with problems than the use of suicide. Further, we are involved in developing prevention programs that can address individuals' problems more effectively.

But still, what difference can the study of culture make, you ask? Let me start with a case from our study of suicide in San Francisco, California. "Mei-ling" was a 23-year-old Chinese woman who killed herself at the time of Chinese New Year by overdosing on sleeping pills. She had no previous psychiatric hospitalizations but had many physical complaints: a persistent stomachache, headache, and back problems. A checkup with the medical doctor a week prior to her suicide did not reveal any organic problems. She had just broken up with her boyfriend after her parents insisted that he was "not from a good family." A week ago her father caught them drunk in her bedroom. She was told never to see him again. Her parents were distraught and shamed; when they talked to the community worker they also mentioned the "bad luck" this act brought on the family at the time of the New Year.

Issues we might have considered had we been the health worker who saw Mei-ling a week before her death included the following:

1. Diagnosis: Was she exhibiting physical problems that could be diagnosed as depression or neurasthenia (a diagnosis more commonly used in China, which includes some but not all of the symptoms we associate with depression)? Were her symptoms manifestations of psychological problems? Did the patient have a belief system based on a view of the mind and body as a unit (the Chinese belief) or a belief system based on viewing the mind–body as split (the U.S. belief)?
2. She and her parents disagreed on her choice of boyfriend. Whose view was more important? Was a generational difference or a cultural difference a major concern? Did the patient understand the potential "bad luck" that her family would feel by completing suicide at the time of the New Year?

Mei-ling was one of the young adults included in the database of suicides that we studied in San Francisco from 1987 to 1996. I will present the broad findings of this study to illustrate some of the similarities and differences among racial/cultural/ethnic groups. I will then illustrate the variation in the underlying meanings of completing suicide by discussing the beliefs and behaviors of many (not all) Chinese people. I will conclude with some observations that may be helpful to the clinician.

SUICIDE IN SAN FRANCISCO, 1987–1996[1]

In our study of competed suicide in San Francisco one of the questions we asked was whether, given the racial/cultural/ethnic diversity of the city, there would be identifiable similarities and differences when the issue of racial designation was taken into account. Suicides were studied for 10 years in the city of San Francisco. Data for 1,519 cases were collected from January 1, 1987 through December 31, 1996 (see Shiang, 1998).

The data were obtained in cooperation with the Medical Examiner's Office of San Francisco County, which routinely documents cases of mortality, including the completed suicides in the city of San Francisco. Official records include information on age, gender, race, and method of suicide. Data were extracted for 10 years on age, gender, method, racial/ethnic designation, and use of alcohol at the time of death. The decisions of that office related to these variables were used as documented.

The racial designations of the individuals used in this study were accepted as determined by the Medical Examiner's Office in San Francisco. Possible designations of race were as follows: unknown, Asian, black, Hispanic, Oriental, Pacific Islander, Native American, and white. When information from the deceased's family or friends was not available, the personnel from the Medical Examiner's Office made the determination of race. For the purposes of this study, we relabeled the designations as follows: (1) the Oriental, Asian, and Pacific Islander categories were collapsed and designated as "Asian"; (2) designations of the category of "whites" were uniformly relabeled as "Caucasians" (the term "Caucasian" here signifies a European American heritage); (3) Hispanic included people of Latino heritages from Central and South America, Mexico, Puerto Rico, etc.; (4) designations of the category of "blacks" were relabeled as "African Americans." Further discussion of the limitations and decision-making process for racial/ethnic designations can be found in Shiang et al. (1997).

---

[1]My collaborators on suicide projects are Drs. D. Allison, R. Blinn, B. Bongar, D. Clark, M. Kalehzan, A. Schatzberg, B. Stephens, C. Tam, and S. Y. Xiao.

RESULTS: STATISTICAL ANALYSES

1. *Men:* The absolute numbers of completed suicides among African Americans, Hispanics, and Native Americans was very low; the proportion of the population of these groups in San Francisco was relatively low as well. However, the rates (per 100,000 population) calculated were age adjusted so that they are comparable (see Figures 10.1 and 10.2 for a comparison of San Francisco and U.S. national data). The men's rates among the racial groups in San Francisco shows that Asians, Hispanics, and Native Americans (10/100,000) are completing suicide at approximately the same rate, whereas African Americans are next higher and Caucasians are the highest (45/100,000), far beyond the national average.

2. *Women:* The women's rates in San Francisco of completed suicide range from the lowest for Hispanic women (2/100,000) to the highest for Caucasian women (12/100,000).

3. *Gender ratios:* Significant differences were found for gender across the racial/cultural/ethnic groups; a higher ratio of men completed sui-

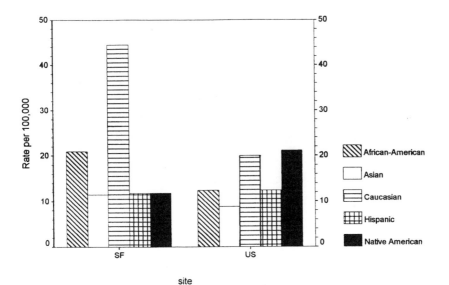

FIGURE 10.1. Comparison of men's rate of completed suicides in San Francisco (1987–1996) and the United States (1990). From Shiang (1998). Copyright 1998 by the American Association of Suicidology. Reprinted by permission of The Guilford Press.

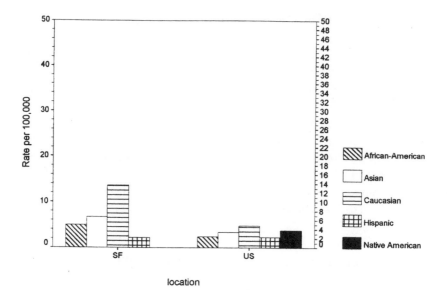

FIGURE 10.2. Comparison of women's rates of completed suicides in San Francisco (1987–1996) and the United States (1990). From Shiang (1998). Copyright 1998 by the American Association of Suicidology. Reprinted by permission of The Guilford Press.

cide than women, but these ratios varied (Hispanic, 5.45 men:1 woman; Asian, 1.58 men:1 woman).

4. *Methods:* There was no significant difference found for the use of guns as a method for completing suicide; death by gunshot wounds ranged between 20% and 30% across all racial groups. The predominant methods used were as follows: gunshot wounds, by 30% of African Americans and 26% of Caucasians; hanging, by 31% of Hispanics and 27% of Asians; overdose, by 28% of Caucasians.

Having found some evidence that racial groups complete suicide according to different patterns, we next sought to determine how aspects of cultural beliefs and behaviors might have an impact on completed suicide.

UNDERSTANDING SUICIDE: HOW CULTURE MAKES A DIFFERENCE

In the United States, suicide has begun to be studied within a contextual framework. The search for psychological "universals" has been tempered by an understanding that alleviating pain and suffering must be targeted to the needs of the individual in cultural context. This has largely been due to the recognition that people of diverse cultural backgrounds now constitute a larger proportion of U.S. society and that the needs of non-Caucasians must be addressed as well as those of Caucasians.

In the past it was possible to use mainly Western models of health and well-being to develop treatments because most therapists and clients generally operated according to Western concepts. Thus, the specific cultural context of the individual was ignored. There have been several driving forces for the lack of importance that has historically been placed by U.S. researchers on the study of culture. First, cultural beliefs and behaviors are difficult to study because so many aspects of culture are ingrained into our daily functioning and thinking, reinforced through ritual. They are difficult to identify, much less talk about—we just "do it." In my teaching and supervision, I have found that many people find it difficult to clearly articulate aspects of their own culture; it is something taken for granted and therefore less defined. Some people do not even think they have a culture. As one student said to me, "I'm American, I don't have a culture. I just do the same as everyone else around me." This person is unaware of her culture—she just lives it. This is especially true for people who identify strongly with "mainstream" U.S. culture; the dominant group thinks of itself "without" culture. It is often only when someone identifies with a nondominant aspect of the society that the person says he or she has a culture. However, when people visit a culture very different from their own, suddenly the culture (and their relationship to the culture) becomes apparent. Suddenly they are labeled as "American" regardless of whether they identify themselves as being American.

Moreover, as Markus, Kitayama, and Heiman (1996) suggest, a basic assumption in the Northern European–United States orientation of science is to see the "ideal" person as an individual standing alone—unfettered by the constraints of particular situations or other people. Thus, much of scientific study of human behavior has been based on the belief that we can predict individual actions (through "universal" laws) across most situations; the focus of interest is the single person and the context is generally considered secondary, if at all. Thus, Western psychologists ask questions and expect types of answers that are based largely on Western premises and assumptions. In a seminal review of the core principles of motivation, cognition, and interpersonal behavior,

Markus et al. (1996) state that "psychologists may be prematurely settling on *one* psychology, that is, on *one* set of assumptions about what are the relevant or most important psychological states and processes, and on one set of generalizations about their nature and function" (p. 858). These assumptions have formed the bedrock upon which most psychological study in the United States has been based. Markus et al. suggest that it has become increasingly clear over time that this is not the only viable foundation upon which psychological study should be based. In the last 10 years mainstream psychology has begun to endorse the viability of many varied definitions of the healthy, good, moral person.

If we turn to other disciplines, we see that greater emphasis has been placed on studying people in their cultural contexts. Research in the areas of anthropology (Geertz, 1983), cross-cultural psychology (Bond & Hwang, 1986), psychiatric anthropology (Kleinman, 1988), and ethnic minority studies (Padilla & Lindholm, 1995; Sue & Zane, 1994) as well as recent research in the area of cultural psychology (Markus et al., 1996; Shweder & LeVine, 1984) suggest that cultural practices determine, to a large degree, the person's day-to-day behaviors as well as life transitions. Figure 10.3 shows the conceptualization of those aspects that influence the development of emotional states, including the immigration process (adapted from Markus & Kitayama, 1994). The collective reality provides core cultural ideas (left side of the figure), which then influence the sociopsychological processes that are reinforced through customs, norms, practices, and institutions. When migration occurs, the individual is faced with the stimulus of the old cultural reality as well as the new cultural reality in adapting to the new environment. The individual reality acts to personalize the core ideas, which are, in turn, reinforced by habitual emotional tendencies. All of these aspects lead to instrumental action or outward behavior. Markus and Kitayama (1994) provide evidence to show that emotions are expressed in different forms depending upon the cultural setting. With the use of this framework, we can begin to see how the seemingly endless diversity displayed in cultures is maintained.

In addition, cross-cultural psychology provides a framework to help organize and order such diversity. Triandis, Kashima, Shimada, and Villareal (1987) have conceptualized societies along a spectrum that ranges from groups that have an orientation toward individualistic premises (Northern Europe, United States) to those that have an orientation toward collectivistic premises (e.g., Asia, Africa). More recently, cultural psychologists have built upon these ideas at the individual level.

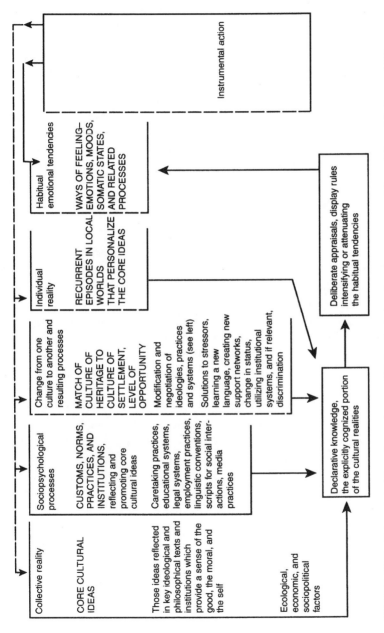

FIGURE 10.3. Cultural shaping of emotion, modified to include migration processes. Adapted from Markus and Kitayama (1994). Copyright 1994 by the American Psychological Association. Adapted by permission.

Markus and Kitayama (1994) suggest that the individual's self-construal (definition of self) can also be oriented more toward independence (i.e., Northern European, North American/U.S.) or toward connectedness–interdependence (i.e., Asian, African). In the United States, the orientation is toward development of the good, moral self, seen as a person who is highly individualistic and autonomous—and who seeks to conquer new frontiers; in the People's Republic of China, where traditional Confucian beliefs still are important, the orientation is toward the development of the good, moral self, seen as a person who puts the good of the group before individual needs (Shiang, Kjellander, Huang, & Bogumill, 1998). The accurate application of these frameworks to predict actual behaviors of people will require empirical testing in specific contexts.

MENTAL HEALTH CONSIDERATIONS

The culture is the "stuff" and "way" of everyday living. It also provides the meanings and "solutions" to problems in life's trajectories. These solutions can be thought of as culture specific; solutions are promoted through transmission from parent to child and are considered successful adaptations to environmental pressures. However, only certain kinds of solutions are acceptable in the culture, and these are often gender related. Canetto and Lester (1998) suggest that narratives of suicidal behavior can be examined through the lens of gender-specific cultural "scripts." Analyzing U.S. beliefs about suicide, they suggest that researchers' assumptions of suicidal men and women, while based on fact, are also based on specific cultural "scripts" that are associated with life goals of men and women in the given society. In addition, they provide examples of non-Western cultures (e.g., Micronesia or Sri Lanka) that provide evidence that the gender-specific scripts vary across cultures. This type of analysis helps us to understand how it is essential to consider specific life goals, as influenced by cultural beliefs and behaviors, when determining the meaning of suicide within a given population.

     Every individual in a particular cultural milieu learns to use culturally specific coping strategies to promote health and development. Cross-cultural studies have shown that responses to stress are culturally relevant (Tanaka-Matsumi & Draguns, 1997). The strategies and behaviors used by people to reduce stress can often be understood as "logical" within the specific cultural system. The decision to attempt suicide has an understandable culture-specific meaning, especially when psychopathology is absent. By using the spectrum of orientations mentioned above, we can consider how the act of suicide expresses the main focus along the spectrum of individualism–collectivism. In the societies where the individual is of primary focus, suicide is viewed as an individual's decision; we exhibit concern when we know that someone has suicidal ideation, but it is only when he or she tells us they have a plan to act that we have obligations to confine them in order to prevent the act. Within societies that view the self as an interdependent self, there are generally societal interventions that are woven into the fabric of daily interactions (the auntie who drops by or the neighbor who keeps an eye on the person) and yet, when unusual behavior is exhibited (severe mental health, suicide due to mental health problems), the person is generally stigmatized and even shunned. This behavior appears to contradict the inclusiveness of the collective good. One way to understand this is that "not fitting in" would have greater negative consequences in societies that value the cohesiveness of the larger group; the person is therefore shunned. This can help explain why public opinion in these societies rarely links suicide with mental abnormality (Hsieh & Spence, 1980).

The cultural script in collectivistic societies, as it is exhibited in a suicidal act, depends therefore on the specific cultural scripts of the small group, the degree of social influence of the act, the social position held by the suicidal individuals and their family members, and how the act can be interpreted in light of the predominant gender script. The public reaction is mainly concerned with the social cause, not the personal one. In fact, a personal reason for suicide is often deliberately neglected because that would place too much emphasis on the individual.

CLINICAL CONSIDERATIONS: PSYCHOPATHOLOGY IN CONTEXT

Now let us return to the situation of Mei-ling. As an 18-year-old, she might have talked about being misunderstood, which could be partially understood in terms of her developmental stage (i.e., a young adult separating from her parents). She also might sit at the intersection of two cultures: her parents retain the cultural beliefs and behaviors of their country of origin (they believe they have more wisdom in choosing a mate), whereas she believes more fully in Western values and behaviors concerning her behavior with peers (she should be able to freely choose her peers and boyfriend). At the same time, Mei-ling's belief system concerning health and physical problems may well be understood within the context of a belief system where mind and body are not separated. Thus, while her symptoms must be taken seriously and can be addressed in order to provide immediate relief, the clinician must also consider them as signals of internal psychological or systemic problems. In this context, shame or stigma are also generally associated with expressing mental health problems. The question is one of relative degree. Shame and stigma may contribute to the lack of finding a good match between a specific setting (institution, rural setting, etc.) and Mei-ling's behaviors. For the Chinese families, a suicide at the time of Chinese New Year can be symbolic of "bad debt"; the family may or may not accept this symbol.

Mei-ling's presenting behaviors raise several issues. One is the assignment of a diagnosis. One of the major issues in determining treatment goals is deciding on the nature of the problem. What diagnosis is to be assigned? Do the diagnostic categories capture the illness presentation? Does the initial presentation of the problem provide the clinician with a comprehensive overview of the client's situation? What specific focal goals are to be addressed? How is the diagnosis to be assigned?

One aspect of traditional Western psychology which needs to be reexamined is the application of the fourth edition of the *Diagnostic and Statistical Manual of Mental Disorders* (DSM-IV; American Psychiatric Association, 1994) to cultures not based on U.S. and Western civilizations. For instance, as researchers and clinicians, we know that depression does not look the same across all cultures (Kleinman & Goode, 1985).

The recent inclusion of culture-bound syndromes in an appendix in DSM-IV acknowledges this fact. The acknowledgment of the presence and power of these syndromes has been an important step in working toward greater understanding of the importance of culture and its impact on mental health. There is substantial evidence that some cultures based on the connected–interdependent model express sad feelings in ways that emphasize the unity between mind and body (Kleinman & Goode, 1985). Thus, psychological problems are normally expressed in the physical realm. For example, in the societal context of the People's Republic of China, the diagnosis of neurasthenia (worries, sadness, lethargy, body pain) is a common way to express sadness, troubles, and problems with other people. The symptom constellation associated with neurasthenia has considerable overlap with the Western constellation of mood disorder, but the client often emphasizes somatic concerns in a societal climate where expressing emotional problems receives disapproval (Kleinman, 1986). Chinese populations in Asia have been found to prefer "externalizing idioms of distress" (Hsu, 1985; Kleinman & Kleinman, 1985; Kleinman, 1986, 1987; Lum, 1982). Kleinman notes that the expression of somatic symptoms have been adaptive in specific cultural and social contexts, particularly in the People's Republic of China, which emphasizes group cohesion over individual expression. Expressing problems in somatic form allows for the elicitation of caretaking from others, the maintenance of valued social harmony, the reintegration of the individual into his or her social network, the avoidance of shame and stigma, and reductions in the experience of painful emotional intensity (Kleinman & Kleinman, 1985). Recent Chinese immigrants to the United States who have more traditional cultural beliefs are likely to manifest distress as health concerns (Kleinman, 1977, 1980, 1987; Sue & Sue, 1974; Sue & Sue, 1987; Tseng, 1975).

In collectivistic societies the emphasis on presenting distress through the body rather than through expressing emotions is part of a system that has evaluated the presence of a mental illness (rather than somatic illness) as a societal stigma. The mentally ill person is considered somehow "bad" rather than "good," and the close association of individual acts with family worth thus creates a situation of serious social consequences for individual Chinese patients (Katon, Kleinman, & Rosen, 1982; Kleinman, 1980, 1988; Lin, 1981; Lin & Lin, 1981). The general stigma associated with mental illness often pushes families to "hide" such illness. Families generally wait until the patient becomes so severely mentally ill that the family is unable to cope; hence the patients who finally come into the mental health system often are gravely impaired.

These belief systems are carried to the culture of settlement and can even endure for many years after migration. In a study of Chinese families in Canada it was found that if a family member had a chronic or intractable mental health problem such as psychosis, the family often ended up completely abandoning the patient in anticipation of rejection by the wider community (Lin & Lin, 1981). In fact, it was also found that even among third- and fourth-generation Chinese in the United States, where we would expect greater adherence to U.S. norms, shame and stigma were still found to be associated with emotional difficulties (Yamamoto & Acosta, 1982).

The presentation of somatic symptoms by Chinese people in the United States therefore cannot be viewed primarily as "conversion symptoms" that mask cognitive or psychodynamic issues, but rather stem from a different conceptualization of "health." The presentation of somatic problems among Chinese people in the United States might well also be multidetermined. The perception of general prejudice against Asians, the general community stigma associated with exhibiting mental health problems, and an overriding concern about family welfare may all contribute to the use of the more indirect ways of expressing "worries."

The clinician trained in a Western model of health may be tempted to view somatization as a defensive reaction that must be dismantled in order to make progress in therapy. However, conceptualizing somatic symptoms as disguised intrapsychic conflicts can cause differences in problem conceptualization between the therapist and client (Sue, 1988; Sue & Zane, 1987), potentially leaving the client feeling misunderstood. As noted above, such a conceptualization would fail to recognize the integration of mind and body espoused by traditional Chinese culture (Lin, 1981; Lum, 1982). The emphasis placed on intraindividual mental processes by Western psychotherapists may understandably perplex more traditionally inclined Chinese American clients. Symptoms that are conceptualized as conversion disorders are not necessarily a guise for "deeper" psychological problems; rather, they should be treated with concern for healing the body–mind conjointly—as a unit.

Another issue that arises in Mei-Ling's history is generational conflict. If we had her sitting in our office, we might determine that her feelings of being misunderstood are based on differences in beliefs between Mei-Ling and her parents—now highly charged in emotional terms. However, the therapist might intervene through providing education for both parents and Mei-Ling about each party's perspective (e.g., she will be seen by her peers as a "loser" if she does not continue her friendships, and her parents see this as a betrayal of the effort and sacrifice they have made to give her a "better" life). A defusing of the emotional charge from both sides is also necessary. It would be essential to treat this aspect of the problem in a systemic manner by addressing the concerns of both generations. The goal for each party would be to come to a solution such that each might hold intact his or her self-image (e.g., "face").

CONCLUSION

Our attempts to study and prevent suicide will meet with greater success once we move to using a general framework that best characterizes the individual and contextual influences of a specific suicidal act. My attempt in this chapter has been to provide some beginning tools to help us along this path.

ACKNOWLEDGMENT

Dr. Shiang's work was supported by the American Foundation for Suicide Prevention and The Pritzker Foundation.

REFERENCES

American Psychiatric Association. (1994). *Diagnostic and statistical manual of mental disorders* (4th ed.). Washington, DC: Author.

Bond, M. H., & Hwang, K. (1986). The social psychology of the Chinese people. In M. H. Bond (Ed.), *The psychology of the Chinese people* (pp. 213–266). New York: Oxford University Press.

Canetto, S., & Lester, D. (1998). Gender, culture, and suicidal behavior. *Transcultural Psychiatry. 35*, 163–190.

Geertz, C. (1983). *Local knowledge: Further essays in interpretive anthropology*. New York: Basic Books.

Hsieh, A. C., & Spence, J. (1980). Suicide and the family in pre-modern Chinese society. In A. Kleinman & T. Y. Lin (Eds.), *Normal and abnormal behavior in Chinese culture* (pp. 29–47). Boston: Reidel.

Hsu, J. (1985). The Chinese family: Relations, problems, and therapy. In W. Tseng & D. Wu (Eds.), *Chinese culture and mental health* (pp. 95–112). New York: Academic Press.

Katon, W., Kleinman, A., & Rosen, G. (1982). Depression and somatization: A review. *American Journal of Medicine, 72*, Pt. I, 127–135; Pt. II, 241–247.

Kleinman, A. (1977). Depression, somatization and the new cross-cultural psychiatry. *Social Science and Medicine, 11*, 3–10.

Kleinman, A. (1980). *Patients and healers in the context of culture: An exploration of the borderland between anthropology, medicine, and psychiatry.* Berkeley: University of California Press.

Kleinman, A. (1986). *Social origins of distress and disease: Depression, neurasthenia, and pain in modern China.* New Haven, CT: Yale University Press.

Kleinman, A. (1987). Culture and clinical reality: Commentary on culture-bound syndromes and international disease classifications. *Culture, Medicine and Psychiatry, 11,* 49–52.

Kleinman, A. (1988). *Rethinking psychiatry: From cultural category to personal experience.* New York: Free Press.

Kleinman, A., & Goode, B. (Eds.). (1985). *Culture and depression.* Berkeley: University of California Press.

Kleinman, A., & Kleinman, J. (1985). Somatization: The interconnections in Chinese society among culture, depressive experiences, and the meanings of pain. In A. Kleinman & B. Good (Eds.), *Culture and depression* (pp. 429–490). Berkeley: University of California Press.

Lin, K. (1981). Traditional Chinese medical beliefs and their relevance for mental illness and psychiatry. In A. Kleinman & T. Y. Lin (Eds.), *Normal and abnormal behavior in Chinese culture* (pp. 95–111). Boston: Reidel.

Lin, T., & Lin, M. (1981). Love, denial and rejection: Responses of Chinese families to mental illness. In A. Kleinman & T. Y. Lin (Eds.), *Normal and abnormal behavior in Chinese culture* (pp. 387–401). Boston: Reidel.

Lum, R. G. (1982). Mental health attitudes and opinions of Chinese. In E. E. Jones & S. J. Korchin (Eds.), *Minority mental health* (pp. 165–189). New York: Praeger.

Markus, H., & Kitayama, S. (1994). *Emotion and culture.* Washington, DC: American Psychological Association Books.

Markus, H. R., Kitayama, S., & Heiman, R. J. (1996). Culture and "basic" psychological principles. In E. T. Higgins & A. W. Kruglanski (Eds.), *Social psychology: Handbook of basic principals* (pp. 857–913). New York: Guilford Press.

Padilla, A. M., & Lindholm, K. J. (1995). Quantitative educational research with ethnic minorities. In J. A. Banks & C. A. McGee Banks (Eds.), *Handbook of research on multicultural education* (pp. 97–113). New York: Macmillan.

Shiang, J. (1998). Does culture make a difference?: Racial/ethnic patterns of completed suicide in San Francisco, 1987–1996, and clinical applications. *Suicide and Life-Threatening Behavior, 28*(4), 338–354.

Shiang, J., Blinn, R., Bongar, B., Stephens, B., Allison, D., & Schatzberg, A. (1997). Suicide in San Francisco, CA: A comparison of Caucasians and Asian groups, 1987–1994. *Suicide and Life-Threatening Behavior, 27*(1), 80–91.

Shiang, J., Kjellander, C., Huang, K., & Bogumill, S. (1998). Developing cultural competency in clinical practice: Treatment considerations for Chinese cultural groups in the U.S. *Clinical Psychology: Science and Practice, 5,* 182–209.

Shweder, R. A., & LeVine, R. A. (1984). *Culture theory: Essays on mind, self, and emotion.* New York: Cambridge University Press.

Sue, D., & Sue, S. (1987). Cultural factors in the clinical assessment of Asian Americans. *Journal of Consulting and Clinical Psychology, 55,* 479–487.

Sue, S. (1988). Psychotherapeutic services for ethnic minorities: Two decades of research findings. *American Psychologist, 43*, 301–308.

Sue, S., & Sue, D. (1974). MMPI comparisons between Asian-American and non-Asian students utilizing a student health psychiatric clinic. *Journal of Counseling Psychology, 21*, 423–427.

Sue, S., & Zane, N. (1987). The role of culture and cultural techniques in psychotherapy: A critique and reformulation. *American Psychologist, 42*, 37–45.

Sue, S., & Zane, N. (1994). Research with culturally diverse populations. In A. E. Bergin & S. L. Garfield (Eds.), *Handbook of psychotherapy and behavior change* (pp. 783–817). New York: Wiley.

Tanaka-Matsumi, J., & Draguns, J. G. (1997). In J. W. Berry, M. H. Segall, & C. Kagitcibasi (Eds.), *Handbook of cross-cultural psychology* (pp. 149–492). Boston: Allyn & Bacon.

Triandis, H., Kashima, Y., Shimada, E., & Villareal, M. (1986). Acculturation indices as a means of confirming cultural differences. *International Journal of Psychology, 21*, 43–70.

Tseng, W. S. (1975). The nature of somatic complaints among psychiatric patients: The Chinese case. *Comprehensive Psychiatry, 16*, 237–245.

Yamamoto, J., & Acosta, F. (1982). Treatment of Asian Americans and Hispanic Americans: Similarities and differences. *Journal of the American Academy of Psychoanalysis, 10*, 585–607.

CHAPTER ELEVEN

The Relationship between Occupation and Suicide among African American Males
Ohio, 1989–1991

Ira M. Wasserman, PhD
Steven Stack, PhD

M ost of the research on suicide has concentrated on the white population, ignoring black suicide. The reason for this neglect of black suicide has been their historically low rate compared to whites (Stack, 1982; Lester, 1992). The study of racial variations in suicide is rare. Works on black suicide consider the impact of black religious and/or kinship systems on suicide (e.g., Davis, 1980a; Davis & Short, 1979; Early, 1992; Griffith & Bell, 1989; McIntosh, 1989). The analysis of black suicide assumes that their religious and kinship institutions protect African Americans against racism, and also give them protection against suicide (e.g., Davis, 1980a; Hendin, 1969; Manton, Blazer & Woodbury, 1987; Swanson & Breed, 1976). A number of studies (Breault, 1986; Breault & Barkey, 1982; Maris, 1981; Trovato, 1986, 1987; Wasserman, 1990) have shown the importance of these two institutions for reducing suicide risks for whites and the general population. Since there has been a recent disintegration of the black family (e.g., increased divorce and births out of wedlock), one might expect increased black suicide, especially among the younger generation.

One factor that may significantly influence black and white suicide is socioeconomic status. McCarthy and Yancey (1971) show that the variation in black and white suicide is highest among lower-status groups while it is similar for blacks and whites among higher-status groups. They explain the racial variation in relation to socioeconomic status by arguing that lower-status blacks can blame their economic and personal failures on racism whereas lower-status whites are unable to do this; by contrast, upper-status blacks lack this social justification for their individual failures. Given this explanation, one would expect white and black suicide to narrow with increases in African American socioeconomic status. This chapter further explores the issue by examining mortality data from Ohio between 1989 and 1991 that use individual-level data to avoid problems associated with ecological inference (Robinson, 1950).

Whites have a suicide rate double that of African Americans (Stack, 1982, 1996). For example, in 1996 the white rate was 12.7 and the black rate was 6.5 (Peters, Kochanek, & Murphy, 1998). A common explanation for this variation is the impact of overt racism. Racism produces stress, a legitimation of individual failures, and a kind of "survival solidarity" among African Americans (Davis, 1980a; Woodford, 1965). Familial and communal organizations within black society maintain and support these beliefs. For investigators of black suicide behavior, the social bonds of marriage and family life, the church, and other communal and social groups are crucial in preventing suicide among blacks (e.g., Bush, 1976; Comer, 1973; Davis, 1980a, 1980b; Davis & Short, 1979). When these social support networks are weakened, African Americans are likely to accept individual blame for failure, while losing the social support of their community and becoming at higher risk of committing suicide. The increase in the suicide of young black males illustrates this process (Davis, 1980a).

Associated with the survival strategy is the finding that blacks have a lower level of suicide acceptability. An analysis of national opinion poll data determined that African Americans were less accepting of suicide as a legitimate response to such circumstances as terminal illness, dishonoring one's family, and just being tired of living (Stack 1998a). The lower cultural approval of suicide may also lower black suicide rates overall. Davis (1980a) hypothesizes that upwardly mobile blacks break many of their social ties to familial, religious, and social organizations, thereby increasing their risk of suicide. Research on suicide by race supports this hypothesis. For example, Maris (1969) found in Cook County, Illinois, that between 1959 and 1963 the higher the socioeconomic status of blacks and whites, the smaller the variation in black and white suicide.

Frazier (1957), in his classic study, found that the black middle class exhibited considerable identity crisis. The "black bourgeosie" was ambivalent regarding the masses of black society, preferring to identify with the white elites, which socially excluded them. An illustration of this identity crisis is seen in the black press (Myrdal, 1944, pp. 908–924), which tended to parrot the views of the white middle class on nonracial matters (e.g., expounding an almost religious faith in economic and social progress). On racial matters that affected all African Americans (e.g., lynching), the black press took a more militant stand than the white press, but it usually blamed lynching on morally sick individuals within the white community. The "black bourgeosie" attempted to escape the constraints of their socially defined race (e.g., viewing blacks as similar to whites with different skin color), and at the same time were trapped by their given racial identity.

The previous research relating occupation and race to suicide was conducted prior to the increased growth of the black middle class in the 1970s and 1980s. It is possible that the increased size of this class may have altered their identity crisis and influenced their individual attitudes toward stress and social failure. The newly emerging black middle class may have either reestablished traditional ties to black family, church, and social institutions, or they may have adopted white middle class norms regarding the internalization of aggression (Henry & Short, 1954). This chapter reexamines the relationship between race, occupation, and suicide by employing more recent Ohio mortality data.

METHODOLOGY

Suicide and other mortality data were extracted from mortality tape records from the state of Ohio between 1989 and 1991, which included 305,005 cases. This data set listed the demographic characteristics of all individuals who died in the previous time period, including their age, gender, marital status, formal education, race, and occupation. This study is concerned with the impact of occupation on suicide among whites and blacks who are in the labor force (Burnett, Boxer, & Swanson, 1992; Wasserman, 1992). Since females have a more erratic occupational career pattern, with higher levels of exit and reentry into the workforce due to childbearing and family obligations, they were excluded from the study. Also, since the study is concerned with individuals most likely to be in the labor force, it was restricted to males 16–65 years of age. Finally, since the work is concerned with comparing white and black suicide patterns, other nonwhites (e.g., Asians, Native Americans) were excluded from the study. The racial variable was coded 0 = black and 1 = white.

Using the occupational codes in the 1989–1991 Ohio mortality data, the following broad occupational categories were differentiated: (1) executive, administrative, and managerial occupations; (2) professional specialty occupations; (3) sales occupations; (4) service occupations; (5) protective service occupations; (6) food preparation and service occupations; (7) precision production, craft, and repair occupations; and (8) handlers, equipment workers, and laborers. The previous differentiation of occupational categories was dictated by the availability of information on these categories in the 1990 census for Ohio. Categories 5 and 6 above further subdivided the service occupations to make it compatible with the 1990 Ohio census categories. For each of the previous eight occupational categories this study compared the suicide rates of whites and blacks in the state in the time period 1989–1991.

Part of the racial and occupational variation in suicide may be related to the different socioeconomic characteristics of the two groups (i.e., age, marital status, and formal education; see Durkheim, 1897/1966; Lester, 1989; Neighbors, 1986; Peck & Litman, 1973; Pescosolido & Wright, 1990; Seiden, 1972). The age of the individual was coded as the actual age of the decedent at death. Formal education was coded into six categories: 1 = 8 years of schooling or less; 2 = 9–11 years; 3 = 12 years (high school graduate); 4 = 1–3 years of college; 5 = college graduate; and 6 = 5 years of college or more. Marital status was coded as a dummy variable, where 0 = not married and 1 = married.

In order to control for the previous demographic characteristics, the study determined whether an individual died of suicide or natural causes, excluding all individuals who died of homicide or accidents. A dummy variable was then created that had a score of 0 if the decedent died of natural causes and a score of 1 if the individual died of suicide.

In order to determine the impact of race on the probability of suicide for the eight different occupational categories, the dummy variable related to mortality was correlated with age, race, marital status, and formal education for each of the eight categories, using logistic regression to estimate the coefficients in the model. Logistic regression (Hosmer & Lemeshow, 1989; Morgan & Teachman, 1988) estimates the probability of whether an individual is more likely to die of natural causes or suicide for each of the independent variables within each occupational category. The exponential of the slope [exp(b)] for each variable determines the relative probability of an individual dying of natural causes or suicide. A value of 1.0 indicates that an individual in the category is equally likely to die of natural causes or suicide; a value of less than 1.0 indicates that an individual with certain characteristics is more likely to die of natural causes; a value of greater than 1.0 indicates that an individual in a certain category is more likely to die of suicide. For example, since whites were coded as 1 in the study, if the exponential of the slope was 2.0 for the racial variable, this result would indicate that with controls whites were twice as likely to die of suicide than blacks in relation to all natural causes. The previous type of analysis allows us to determine how suicide varies by race and occupation after proper controls are introduced into the model.

We must be cautious in interpreting the results of the present study, given that it employs official suicide data. However, in most cases the measurement errors involved with these suicide data are not large enough to cause systematic errors in the estimates of the variables in the model (Pescosolido & Mendelsohn, 1986).

ANALYSIS

As a first step in the analysis, the relative suicide rates of whites and blacks were computed. Using the Ohio mortality data from 1989 to 1991, the number of suicides of whites and blacks between 16 and 65 in each occupational category was determined. Using the 1990 census data for Ohio (Bureau of the Census, 1993, p. 128), the number of whites and blacks in each occupational category in 1990 was also ascertained. The number of suicides in each occupational category was averaged over the 3-year period, divided by the number of individuals in each occupational category, and multiplied by 100,000 to determine the suicide rate of whites and blacks in each occupational category. The racial suicide ratio (SR), defined as SR = (white suicide rate/black suicide rate) × 100, was also computed. If SR is 100, this indicates equal suicide rates for whites and blacks; if the value is greater than 100, it indicates greater white suicide rates; if its value is less than 100, it shows greater black suicide rates.

For higher-status occupations, such as executive, administrative, and managerial occupations, the ratio was 64.69, indicating that for these higher-status occupations blacks have a higher suicide rate than whites. By contrast, for the lower-status food preparation and service occupations the ratio was 142.88, indicating that whites have approximately 1.43 greater propensity to commit suicide than blacks for this occupational category. The descriptive findings suggest that occupational status is an important variable for explaining white–black differences in suicide rates: for higher-status occupations blacks have a higher suicide rate than whites, whereas for lower-status occupations blacks have the expected lower suicide rate.

It is necessary to employ logistic regression analysis on the data in order to control for racial variations in age, marital status, and formal education among the two populations. Table 11.1 specifies the logistic regression estimates relating mortality from natural causes (0) and suicide (1) to a set of independent variables for individuals in executive, administrative, and managerial occupations. For these occupational categories whites are more likely (1.588) to die of suicide compared to natural causes than are blacks, but the results are not significant at the .05 level. Age is the only control variable that is significant, and the findings indicate that, with increased age, individuals of both races are more likely to die of natural causes than suicide.

Table 11.2 shows the size of slope b and exp(b) for the racial variable for the other seven occupational categories. For these lower-status occupations the probability of whites committing suicide is higher than for the high-status executive, administrative, and managerial occupations, and in five of the seven cases the result is significant at the .05 lev-

TABLE 11.1. Logistic Regression Estimates of Slope b and exp(b) Relating Death from Suicide and All Natural Causes to a Set of Independent Variables for Executive, Administrative, and Managerial Occupations for Ohio Male Mortality Data, 1989–1991

Variable	Slope b	exp(b)
Age	−.090	.914[a]
Marital status	−.143	.867
Race	.463	1.588
Formal education	.133	1.143
Constant	.477	

Note. $N = 3,594$.
[a]Significant at .05 level.

TABLE 11.2. Logistic Regression Estimates of Slope *b* and exp(*b*) Relating Deaths from Suicide to All Natural Causes for the Race Variable for Different Occupations for Ohio Male Mortality Data, 1989–1991

Occupational category	Slope *b*	exp(*b*)	N
Professional specialty occupations	1.214	3.368[a]	2,524
Sales occupations	0.631	1.880	2,715
Service occupations	0.970	2.639[a]	3,197
Protective service occupations	0.616	1.852	854
Food preparation and service occupations	1.181	3.257[a]	455
Precision production, craft, repair occupations	1.071	2.917[a]	7,813
Handlers, equipment workers, and laborers	0.873	2.393[a]	4,789

[a]Significant at .05 level.

el. The results do not show a linear decrease in suicide probability with a fall in occupational status, as illustrated by the fact that professional specialty occupations have the highest exp(*b*) value (3.368). By contrast, handler, equipment workers, and laborers have a value of 2.393. However, in relation to the first high-status occupation, the value of exp(*b*) is more likely to be significant for lower-status occupations; the results imply that for lower-status occupations whites are more likely to die of suicide compared to natural causes than are blacks.

DISCUSSION

Our present study replicated the findings of previous research (e.g., Maris, 1969; Rushing, 1969) that showed that white–black variation in suicide rates decreased as socioeconomic status increased. Initial descriptive findings demonstrated, unlike earlier findings, that the suicide rate for higher-occupational-status blacks was greater than for whites in the same occupational category. However, the two racial groups differed in other demographic characteristics (e.g., age, marital status, formal education) that may have influenced their suicide rates independent of their occupational status. In order to control for these variations, the study created a dummy variable linked to whether an individual died of natural causes or suicide, and correlated this variable with race, marital status, formal education, and age for the eight occupational categories. With these controls in the model, it was found that for all occupational categories whites were more likely to die of suicide than were blacks. However, with a drop in occupational status, the propensity to die of suicide decreased among blacks—a result consistent with previous research findings.

It is not possible to use the mortality tape data to determine the underlying causes for the racial variation in suicide by occupational category. One would expect that suicide is related to the economically unstable position of upwardly mobile blacks in the larger economic order, as well as to their social isolation from the larger black society. Many of these upwardly mobile blacks have achieved their higher-status positions as a result of government policies (e.g., removal of discriminatory economic barriers, affirmative action), but they are newcomers in the higher economic order and are thus more likely to be unemployed than whites. It has been shown that unemployment is statistically linked to suicide and social stress (Platt, 1984; Wilson & Aponte, 1985), and if these upwardly mobile blacks have higher unemployment rates than whites, one would expect this situation to influence their suicidal behavior.

In addition to being more susceptible to economic downturns, these middle and upper class blacks are more likely to have a higher degree of isolation from the social support institutions in the black community, such as the church and the family (e.g., Davis, 1980a). This isolation, in conjunction with economic factors and racial discrimination, is likely to cause a relatively higher rate of suicide among this group.

In a related study of national data, Stack (1998b) determined that for every year of education among black males, the risk of suicide increases 8%. By contrast, each year of education among white males is associated with a decrease in risk of suicide of 2%. These results also indicate relatively high suicide risk among blacks of higher socioeconomic status, although the measure of socioeconomic status (education) is different than the one employed in the present study.

Unfortunately, the mortality data have no information on employment patterns, or social behavior such as religious participation, or involvement in extended family relations. Further research is required, perhaps from a population with mental disorders and/or survey data from a general population, to obtain such information and more precisely test the previous hypotheses.

ACKNOWLEDGMENT

We would like to thank Dr. Edward Stockwell of the Population and Society Research Center at Bowling Green State University for kindly supplying us with these mortality data.

REFERENCES

Breault, K. (1986). Suicide in America: A test of Durkheim's theory of religious and family integration. *American Journal of Sociology, 92*, 626–656.

Breault, K., & Barkey, K. (1982). A comparative analysis of Durkheim's theory of egoistic suicide. *Sociological Quarterly, 23*, 321–331.

Bureau of the Census. (1993). *1990 Census of population: Social and economic characteristics. Ohio. Section 1*. Washington, DC: U.S. Government Printing Office.

Burnett, C. A., Boxer, P., & Swanson, N. (1992*). Suicide and occupations: Is there a relationship?* Cincinnati, OH: National Institute for Occupational Safety and Health.

Bush, J. A. (1976). Suicide among blacks: A conceptual framework. *Suicide and Life-Threatening Behavior, 6*, 216–222.

Comer, J. P. (1973). Black suicide: A hidden crisis. *Urban Health, 2*, 41–44.

Davis, R. (1980a). Black suicide and the relational system: Theoretical and empirical implications of communal and family ties. *Research in Race and Ethnic Relations, 2*, 43–71.

Davis, R. (1980b). Suicide among young blacks: Trends and perspectives. *Phylon, 41*, 223–229.

Davis, R., & Short, J. (1979). Dimensions of black suicide: A theoretical model. *Suicide and Life-Threatening Behavior, 8*, 161–173.

Durkheim, E. (1966). *Suicide* (J. A. Spaulding & G. Simpson, Trans.) New York: Free Press. (Original work published 1897)

Early, K. E. (1992). *It's a white thing: Religion and suicide in the African American community*. Unpublished doctoral dissertation, University of Florida. (University Microfilms No. AAG9209004).

Frazier, E. F. (1957). *Black bourgeoisie*. Glencoe, IL: Free Press of Glencoe.

Griffith, E. E. H., & Bell, C. C. (1989). Recent trends in suicide and homicide among blacks. *Journal of the American Medical Association, 262*, 2265–2269.

Hendin, H. (1969). *Black suicide*. New York: Harper Colophon Books.

Henry, A. F., & Short, J. (1954). *Suicide and homicide*. Glencoe, IL: Free Press of Glencoe.

Hosmer, D. W., & Lemeshow, S. (1989). *Applied logistic regression*. New York: Wiley.

Lester, D. (1989). *Suicide from a sociological perspective*. Springfield, IL: Thomas.

Lester, D. (1992). *Why people kill themselves*. Springfield, IL: Thomas.

Manton, K., Blazer, D., & Woodbury, M. (1987). Suicide in middle age and later life: Sex and race specific tables and cohort analysis. *Journal of Gerontology, 42*, 219–227.

Maris, R. W. (1969). *Social forces in urban suicide*. Homewood, IL: Dorsey Press.

Maris, R. W. (1981). *Pathways to suicide*. Baltimore: John Hopkins University Press.

McCarthy, J. D., & Yancey, W. L. (1971). Uncle Tom and Mr. Charlie: Metaphysical pathos in the study of racism and personal disorganization. *American Journal of Sociology, 76*, 648–672.

McIntosh, J. L. (1989). Trends in racial differences in U.S. suicide statistics. *Death Studies, 13*, 275–286.

Morgan, S. P., & Teachman, J. D. (1988). Logistic regression: Description, examples, and comparisons. *Journal of Marriage and the Family, 50*, 929–936.

Myrdal, G. (1944). *An American dilemma: The Negro problem and modern democracy.* New York: Harper & Row.

Neighbors, H. W. (1986). Socioeconomic status and psychological stress in adult blacks. *American Journal of Epidemiology, 124,* 779–793.

Peck, M. L., & Litman, R. E. (1973). Current trends in youthful suicides. *Medical Tribune, 14,* 11.

Pescosolido, B. A., & Mendelsohn, R. (1986). Social causation of social construction of suicide?: An investigation into the social organization of official rates. *American Sociological Review, 51,* 80–100.

Pescosolido, B., & Wright, E. R. (1990). Suicide and the role of the family over the life course. *Family Perspective, 24,* 41–60.

Peters, K. D., Kochanek, K. D., & Murphy, S. L. (1998). Deaths: Final data for 1996. *National Vital Statistics Report, 47,* 9. (DHHS Publication No. PHS 99-1120.) Hyattsville, MD: National Center for Health Statistics.

Platt, S. (1984). Unemployment and suicidal behavior: A review of the literature. *Social Science & Medicine, 19,* 93–115.

Robinson, W. S. (1950). Ecological correlations and the behavior of individuals. *American Sociological Review, 15,* 351–357.

Rushing, W. A. (1969). Two factors in the relationship between social class and mental hospitalization. *American Sociological Review, 3,* 533–541.

Seiden, R. H. (1972). Why are suicides of young blacks increasing? *Health Services and Mental Health Administration, 87,* 3–8.

Stack, S. (1982). Suicide: A decade review of the sociological research. *Deviant Behavior, 4,* 41–66.

Stack, S. (1996). The effect of marital integration on African American suicide. *Suicide and Life-Threatening Behavior, 26,* 405–414.

Stack, S. (1998a). The relationship between culture and suicide: An analysis of African Americans. *Transcultural Psychiatry, 35,* 253–269.

Stack, S. (1998b). Education and risk of suicide: An analysis of African Americans. *Sociological Focus, 31,* 295–302.

Swanson, W., & Breed, W. (1976). Black suicide in New Orleans. In E. Shneidman (Ed.), *Suicidology: Contemporary development* (pp. 103–128). New York: Grune & Stratton.

Trovato, F. (1986). The relationship between marital dissolution and suicide: The Canadian case. *Journal of Marriage and the Family, 48,* 341–348.

Trovato, F. (1987). A longitudinal analysis of divorce and suicide in Canada. *Journal of Marriage and the Family, 49,* 193–203.

Wasserman, I. M. (1990). The impact of divorce on suicide in the United States, 1970–1987. *Family Perspective, 24,* 61–67.

Wasserman, I. M. (1992). Economy, work, occupation, and suicide. In R. W. Maris, A. L. Berman, J. T. Maltsberger, & R. I. Yufit (Eds.), *Assessment and prediction of suicide* (pp. 520–539). New York: Guilford Press.

Wilson, W. J., & Aponte, R. (1985). Urban poverty. *Annual Review of Sociology, 11,* 231–258.

Woodford, J. (1965). Why Negro suicides are increasing. *Ebony, 20,* 89–100.

PART FOUR

ETHICAL ISSUES
IN SUICIDOLOGY

CHAPTER TWELVE

Recent Developments in the Debate over Physician-Assisted Death

James L. Werth, Jr., PhD

During the past 5 years, end-of-life issues have generated a tremendous amount of activity in the press, the courts, scholarly journals, state legislatures, the U.S. Congress, and professional organizations. Much of the attention has focused on the way people die, especially the problems of pain and suffering, and on the options that should be available to people as they approach death, primarily "physician-assisted suicide."

This chapter will provide an overview of the most significant developments over the past 5 years in the United States related to the dying process. Because of the significant controversy associated with this issue, the emphasis will be placed on situations involving the possibility of physician-assisted death (this term, defined as a procedure whereby the physician provides medication and information that he or she knows will be used to hasten a person's death but does not administer the death-causing agent, is used in this chapter instead of "physician-assisted suicide" because of the clinical and lay public association of "suicide" with impulsivity and mental illness impairing judgment, both of which are explicitly ruled out in the context being discussed herein). In order to best convey the trends, the chapter is divided into several major sections. The first is on the Oregon Death with Dignity Act, followed by material on legislative activity, court decisions, and the activities of professional organizations. The chapter concludes with projections for the future.

THE OREGON DEATH WITH DIGNITY ACT

History and Specifics

In late 1994 the citizens of Oregon passed a public initiative called the Oregon Death with Dignity Act (1995) by a slim 51%–49% majority (Lee & Tolle, 1996). The Act specifies that, in order for an individual to be able to request assisted death, the person must be an Oregon resident who is at least 18 years old; must have a terminal illness that, in the reasonable medical opinions of both an attending and consulting physician, will lead to death within 6 months; and must not be incapable of making the decision to end his or her life.

The law requires one written and two oral requests by the patient. At least 15 days must pass from the time of the initial oral request, and at least 48 hours must pass from the time of the written request, before the physician can write the prescription for lethal medication. Further, at the time of the second oral request the person must decline a required physician offer to rescind the request. The attending physician is supposed to suggest that significant others be notified, but actually informing them is at the discretion of the dying person.

The role of the attending physician is to determine whether the person (1) has a terminal illness, (2) will die within 6 months, (3) is mentally capable, and (4) has made the request for assisted death voluntarily. The physician must make sure the person has made an informed decision and then must refer the individual to another physician for confirmation. If either the attending or consulting physician is concerned that the person is "suffering from a psychiatric or psychological disorder, or depression causing impaired judgment," then the dying person must be referred to a licensed psychiatrist or psychologist for assessment and possible counseling. If this referral is made, then a lethal prescription is not to be written until the evaluator determines that the person's judgment is not impaired.

Although proponents of the Death with Dignity Act claim that the safeguards protect vulnerable parties and restrict access to physician-assisted death, many commentators have been critical of the language and limitations imposed, such as the lack of specification of how long a person must live in Oregon before being eligible to use the Act (e.g., Callahan & White, 1996; Emanuel & Daniels, 1996; Grant & Linton, 1995). In addition, a district judge held that the Act did not provide adequate protection for terminally ill adults who were depressed and thus permanently enjoined the Act (see below).

Developments between the Initial Vote and Implementation

In an attempt to provide some assistance to health care providers who might be approached with requests for assisted death, in January 1995 the Center for Ethics in Health Care at Oregon Health Sciences University convened a group representing 25 health care organizations to develop a manual outlining professional standards related to the Act (Task Force to Improve the Care of Terminally Ill Oregonians, 1998). The guidebook is only 91 pages long, with 15 chapters and 8 appendices that cover topics such as "family needs and concerns," "mental health consultation and referral," and "liability and negligence." Each chapter has a short introduction, a set of guidelines, and references. The guidelines do not have the force of law, but—to the extent that they are implemented in practice—they might be used to define the standard of care for the different professionals involved. In addition, several commentators have summarized issues for physicians (e.g., Drickamer, Lee, & Ganzini, 1997; Lee, 1997) and for psychiatrists or psychologists (Werth, Benjamin, & Farrenkopf, in press).

Although the Act was passed in 1994, it did not officially go into effect for almost 3 years, due to legal and legislative challenges described in the following sections. As a result of a legislative order, the same measure was placed on the ballot again in 1997; this time the public voted 60%–40% to reject the attempt to repeal the Act (Murphy, 1997).

Between the time the Act was initially passed by the voters and actually implemented 3 years later, there were tremendous changes in the way the Oregon medical systems worked with persons who were dying. An early summary (Lee & Tolle, 1996) indicated that in the months following the vote some hospices reported 20% increases in referrals, several hospitals developed comfort care consultation teams based on the hospice model, Oregon Health Sciences University expanded its curriculum to provide more education about end-of-life issues for students, and a series of education programs on pain control was developed for

professionals. A subsequent report (Tolle, 1998) indicated that the referrals to hospice continued to increase, raising the state from fifth to third
nationally in terms of the rate of hospice admissions. Thus, each year
almost 30% of Oregonians who die do so with hospice support, compared with 17% nationally. Nearly all terminally ill residents have been
covered through the Oregon Health Plan, so that since 1994 the number of uninsured individuals enrolled in hospice programs dropped
from 15% to 2%. Further, Oregon had the lowest rate of in-hospital
deaths in the country, 31% in 1996. In terms of pain control, between
1994 and 1996 Oregon increased its medical use of morphine by 70%
and the state is one of the country's leaders in terms of milligrams per
100,000 persons (Tolle, 1998).

A new study, however, may point to a distressing trend. In the last 2
months of 1997, following the revote on the Act, family members of
people who died in the hospital reported their loved ones had moderate-
to-severe pain significantly more than had been the case in the preceding 10 months (E. H. Barnett, 1998; see also Barnett, 1999a). The reasons for the increase in pain are not clear, but some in the medical
community believe that increased U.S. Drug Enforcement Agency
(DEA) scrutiny (see the section on *Legislative Activity*, below) and the increase in pain were related.

Use of the Act

There is a provision in the Act which states that, in order to protect confidentiality, no information would be released on the numbers or circumstances of people requesting and receiving prescriptions to hasten
death until there were at least 10 such individuals on record. It took
more than 9 months for this to happen, and on August 18, 1998, the
Oregon Health Division reported that 10 people had received prescriptions and 8 of them had used the medications to hasten death (Frazier,
1998).

The report indicated that the physicians prescribing the medications followed the Act's requirements in screening and reporting (Frazier, 1998). The average age of the five men and five women, all of
whom were Caucasian, who received the medication was 71 years, and
cancer was the precipitating condition in nine of the cases (heart disease
was the other). The people who took the medication did so over a span
of time that ranged from the day the pills were received to 16 days later,
with an average of 2 days; the two who died of their illnesses lived an

average of 10.5 days after receiving the medication. The eight taking the medication died an average of 40 minutes later, but the range was up to 7 hours, with no complications reported in any of the deaths.

In February 1999 the Oregon Health Division released its long-awaited report on the implementation of the Act during 1998 (Chin, Hedberg, Higginson, & Fleming, 1999; see also Coombs Lee & Werth, in press). The investigators also compared the individuals who used the Act with those who died from similar illnesses but who did not receive prescriptions under the Act.

Twenty-three people were provided prescriptions, 15 of whom used them and died, 6 died of underlying illnesses, and 2 others remained alive at the time of the report. The median age of the 8 men and 7 women who used medication was 69 years, all were Caucasian, and 13 had cancer. The case and control patients were similar on many demographic characteristics, except that those who died under the Act were significantly more likely to have never married and were significantly less likely to be completely disabled at the time of death. No case or control patients indicated that financial issues were of concern, and very few individuals in both groups stated that their pain was inadequately controlled. The people who used medication, however, were significantly more likely to have concerns about loss of autonomy and loss of control of bodily functions. For those who used medication, the median time from ingestion to death was 26 minutes, with a range of 15 minutes to 11.5 hours, but no complications such as vomiting were reported. These results led Chin et al. (1999) to conclude that

> many people feared that if physician-assisted suicide was legalized, it would be disproportionately chosen by or forced on terminally ill patients who were poor, uneducated, uninsured, or fearful of the financial consequences of their illness. In our study of physician-assisted suicide in Oregon in 1998, we found no evidence to support these fears. (p. 581)

Other commentators, however, have not shared these optimistic conclusions (e.g., Callahan & White, in press; Edwards & Connor, 1999; Fins & Bancroft, 1999; Foley & Hendin, 1999; Hendin, Foley, & White, 1998). These reviewers have criticized the report as being inadequate, incomplete, and biased. Even supporters of the Act have acknowledged the shortcomings in the research (Coombs Lee & Werth, in press; Orentlicher, in press), but until controlled research can be conducted, the report is the best official data collected to date in the United States.

Other States

Following the initial passage and the subsequent repassage of the Act in Oregon, several other states began considering efforts to use the public initiative process to place similar measures on their ballots. At the time of this writing, Michigan is the only state in which an initiative has gone before the public. However, individuals in Maine have stated that they will attempt a public initiative, modeled after Oregon's Act, in 1999 or 2000 (Harkavy, 1998).

The ballot initiative in Michigan was begun by a group called "Merian's Friends." The organization was named for the mother of one of the founders, who had been assisted in her death by Dr. Jack Kevorkian. However, the group argued that it was not aligned with Dr. Kevorkian and that many of the people he had assisted would not qualify for assistance under their proposal. In addition, Kevorkian publicly stated that he opposed the initiative because it was too bureaucratic (Herman, 1998). Incidentally, Kevorkian made a personal attempt to place an initiative on the ballot in 1994 but could not collect the required number of signatures (Hoffman, 1994).

The Michigan proposal was basically modeled after Oregon's; however, there were some notable differences ("Two States Share Approach," 1998). First, in Michigan there was a mandatory mental health evaluation by a psychiatrist, in addition to the physical evaluations by two physicians—one of whom was required to be a specialist in the individual's disease. There was only a 1-week waiting period. Also, significantly, parents, siblings, adult children, and spouses of state residents could come to Michigan and qualify under the law. Finally, there was a 17-member oversight committee that would have reviewed 25% of the assisted deaths every year to assess compliance with the safeguards and make annual reports.

The Michigan initiative, called Proposal B, appeared on the 1998 ballot. Prior to the vote, opponents of the initiative spent almost $5.5 million compared to approximately $75,000 for proponents. The proposal was defeated by about a 2–1 margin (Cain & Kiska, 1998).

LEGISLATIVE ACTIVITY

The greatest amount of legislative activity has occurred in Michigan, Oregon, and the U.S. Congress. However, many other states have seen bills introduced to either allow (e.g., Maine—Higgins, 1998) or more forcefully criminalize (e.g., Oklahoma—"Governor Signs Anti-Suicide Bill," 1998; South Carolina—"Bill to Make Assisted Suicide Illegal Heads to Governor's Desk," 1998) physician-assisted death.

In addition, the Hawaiian Blue-Ribbon Panel on Living and Dying urged the governor to support legislation allowing physician-assisted death (Omandam, 1998), and the issue was placed before the legislature in early 1999; however, the state Senate Health and Human Services Committee held the bills so they died in committee (Omandam, 1999). A different conclusion was reached by the New York State Task Force on Life and the Law (1994), which unanimously decided that neither physician-assisted death nor voluntary euthanasia should be legalized.

Michigan

Over the past 9 years, Dr. Kevorkian has been involved in the deaths of more than 100 people in Michigan (Durbin, 1998), with 20 of the deaths occurring prior to 1994 ("Kevorkian Aids Suicide," 1994; for an analysis of the first 75 people Kevorkian assisted, with an emphasis on gender issues, see Canetto & Hollenshead, in press). In response to Kevorkian's actions, the state legislature attempted to enact a ban, making assisting a suicide a felony ("Kevorkian Aids Suicide," 1994). In a series of challenges that saw the ban declared alternately invalid and then valid, the Michigan Supreme Court eventually declared that the statute was valid and that common law would also allow for prosecution (*People v. Kevorkian*, 1994), but by then the ban had lapsed after the legislature failed to act within the time frame established by the initial bill and then could not agree on a subsequent bill ("Kevorkian Aids Suicide," 1994; "Mich. Lawmakers Give Up," 1994).

In a more recent attempt to restrict physician-assisted death, the Michigan legislature passed another law, the Assisted Suicide Ban Bill, which went into effect on September 1, 1998 (Woolston, 1998). The Bill makes it a felony to provide the means to someone who is planning on killing him- or herself or to participate in any way in the act.

The statute was to receive its first court test in late March 1999 because prosecutors initially charged Kevorkian with assisting a suicide, first-degree murder, and delivering a controlled substance (Murphy, 1998). The charges stemmed from the death of Thomas Youk, which occurred on September 17, 1998, but apparently was not being investigated until Kevorkian delivered a videotape that was shown on the CBS television show *60 Minutes* on November 22, 1998. The tape seemed to show Kevorkian injecting Youk with substances that killed him. During the TV program, Kevorkian stated that he had performed euthanasia and then dared the prosecutors to charge him in order to force a final showdown with the law: either they prosecute him and he is found guilty, in which case he dies in jail, or they prosecute him and he is acquitted, indicating that future prosecutions would be fruitless.

Before the trial, the judge ruled that Kevorkian could use Youk's suffering as a defense for assisted suicide but not for the first-degree murder charge; this lead the prosecution to drop the assisted suicide charge (Hyde, 1999). After a brief trial, where Kevorkian served as his own attorney and did not call a single defense witness, the jury found him guilty of second-degree murder and delivery of a controlled substance, and later the judge sentenced him to 10–25 years in prison (Belluck, 1999). The same judge also denied Kevorkian's first appeal—that he had inadequate representation—saying that he had every opportunity to allow an attorney to take over the case; his new lawyer has indicated the appeal will be taken to the Michigan Court of Appeals ("Kevorkian to Appeal Conviction," 1999).

Dr. Kevorkian had been brought to trial four previous times for the role he played in the deaths of six of the people he assisted. Three times he was found not guilty by a jury (Durbin, 1998). Another case ended in a mistrial, and after that development the prosecutor said he was dropping the case against Kevorkian ("After Mistrial," 1997).

Oregon

In Oregon, the other state where assisted death has been an almost daily news item, the state legislature became involved when the U.S. Ninth Circuit Court of Appeals removed the injunction that had prevented implementation of the Death with Dignity Act (see the next subsection). At first the legislators considered voiding the Act or passing some legislation that would essentially make the Act impossible to be implemented; however, based on negative feedback from the voters, the legislature took the unprecedented step of sending the same measure back for a revote, this time on an initiative that would repeal the Act ("Oregon to Vote Again," 1997). As mentioned above, this attempt failed 40%–60%, and many commentators attributed the larger margin of support for the Act as a negative reaction to the legislature second-guessing the will of the voters (Claiborne & Edsall, 1997). Although some legislators talked about adding regulations or refining the wording of the Act, ultimately they decided that such actions would not be in their political interest and they let the Act go into effect as it was passed in 1994.

However, in early 1999 the possibility of making changes to the Act arose again (Barnett & Lednicer, 1999). Although several bills were proposed, the one that was approved by the Oregon legislature and signed by the governor made minor clarifications to the law in areas such as residency requirements and health care center rights to prohibit assistance on-site (Barnett, 1999b; Oregon Senate Bill 491 [www.leg.state. or.us—bill and amendments]).

The U.S. Congress

Although the Oregon state legislature declined to take further action, the day after the Oregon voters rejected the repeal effort Congress and the federal government became involved. The Chairs of the House of Representatives and Senate Judiciary Committees (Henry J. Hyde and Orrin G. Hatch, respectively) wrote to the administrator of the DEA to ask for clarification of whether the Controlled Substances Act, which regulates the use of narcotics, applied to the use of such medication to end life. Without conferring with his superiors, the DEA chief stated that the use of narcotics for such acts would violate federal guidelines and that physicians prescribing medications for this purpose could lose their licenses to prescribe these drugs (Lewis, 1998). This assertion was immediately taken up for consideration by the U.S. Attorney General's office. While Janet Reno's staff was reviewing the issue, more than 190 U.S. Representatives and Senators wrote to her office telling her that she should rule that the use of medications for physician-assisted death was indeed against regulations ("Reno to Announce," 1998). However, after 7 months of consideration, she declared that the federal regulations in question did not apply to the use of narcotics for the purposes of hastening death (Lewis, 1998).

The Attorney General's ruling was met with an immediate outcry in both houses of Congress, and bills designed to make the prescription of medications intended to hasten death illegal were quickly submitted. Initially, there was widespread support for both bills within Congress and it appeared as if they were headed for swift passage ("Assisted Suicide Bill Introduced," 1998). Soon, however, major medical and palliative care organizations as well as highly visible specialists in end-of-life care criticized the bills and predicted that if they passed they would have a "chilling" effect on the way pain is managed for dying people. The opposition from organizations and individuals who were adamantly opposed to physician-assisted death, such as the American Medical Association and the National Hospice Organization, appeared to have an impact on the amount of enthusiasm for the bills ("Congress Unlikely to Act," 1998). In addition, President Bill Clinton (who is also on record as opposing physician-assisted death) announced that he would veto either of the bills because they were flawed; instead, he proposed establishing a national commission on care at the end-of-life (J. Barnett, 1998). Between the opposition to the bills and the preoccupation with improprieties in the White House, the bills made it out of the House and Senate Judiciary Committees but never came to floor votes ("Congress Unlikely to Act," 1998; Hughes, 1998).

In an effort to shift the focus away from preventing assisted death and onto the broader issues of pain management and improved end-of-life care, Oregon Senator Wyden introduced the Conquering Pain Act; however, Senator Nickles and Representative Hyde introduced a revised version of their bill and renamed it the Pain Relief Promotion Act of 1999. This version secured the approval of the AMA, but others, such as the Oregon Hospice Association and the Task Force to Improve Care of Terminally Ill Oregonians, opposed the new Nickles/Hyde bill too (Hogan, 1999). At the time of this writing, neither the Wyden nor the Nickles/Hyde bills have advanced to the floor of either the House or Senate.

COURT DECISIONS

Oregon

As alluded to in the first section, soon after the Oregon Death with Dignity Act was passed, a suit was filed that led to the Act being put on hold until after the court could rule. The plaintiffs contended that the Act threatened the lives of terminally ill individuals and did not afford them equal protection (see Cohen, 1995, for a review of the cases). In 1995 the judge granted first a temporary injunction (*Lee v. State of Oregon*, 1995a) and then a permanent injunction (*Lee v. State of Oregon*, 1995b), on the Act because he deemed that it put people at risk. However, in 1997 the U.S. Ninth Circuit Court of Appeals lifted the injunctions: holding that the ill person who remained eligible to continue the case was not actually at risk at the time the case was heard, it therefore dismissed the case (*Lee v. State of Oregon*, 1997). The Act finally went into effect in late October 1997 (just before the public rejected the attempt to repeal the Act) after the U.S. Supreme Court declined to hear an appeal of the case (*Lee v. Harcleroad*, 1997).

Opponents of the Act tried another route, arguing that terminally ill people are stigmatized by the law because they are treated differently from non-terminally ill people and there is the presumption that their lives are less worth living than those of the latter group. However, before they could argue this in court, their plaintiff died. Therefore, they tried to make it a class action suit (Beggs, 1998). Ultimately, and apparently reluctantly, the judge said that the U.S. Ninth Circuit Court of Appeals ruling that overturned his earlier injunction did not permit him to hear the case. Thus, although opponents have vowed to continue efforts to overturn the law, there appear to be few, if any, court-related options available to them (Green & Barnett, 1998).

Washington and New York States

At the same time that the Oregon voters were considering the Death with Dignity Act the first time (i.e., 1994), lawsuits were brought in the states of Washington and New York challenging statutes that prohibited assisting a suicide. In both states plaintiffs were terminally ill individuals and physicians who provide care for dying people (an organization, Compassion in Dying, was also a plaintiff in the Washington case). The Washington decision came first, and the judge there found that laws that prohibited physicians from assisting mentally competent, terminally ill persons from hastening death were unconstitutional (*Compassion in Dying v. Washington*, 1994). She ruled that such laws placed an undue burden on the liberty interest protected by the 14th Amendment and that they also violated the Equal Protection clause of that amendment. The New York court, however, ruled that the contested law was not unconstitutional (*Quill v. Vacco*, 1994). Both cases were appealed to their respective U.S. Circuit Courts.

The Washington case went before a three-judge panel of the Ninth Circuit Court of Appeals. This court eventually ruled, 2–1, that the laws were not unconstitutional, thereby reversing the decision of the original judge (*Compassion in Dying v. Washington*, 1995). This decision was appealed, and the case was retried before an 11-judge panel of the Ninth Circuit. This group held, by an 8–3 margin, that the law was unconstitutional on both equal protection and due process grounds. Thus, this judgment reversed the three-judge panel and reinstituted the first judge's decision (*Compassion in Dying v. State of Washington*, 1996). The New York case was appealed before a three judge panel of the Second Circuit. In a 3–0 decision this court ruled that the law violated the Equal Protection clause of the 14th Amendment and therefore was unconstitutional, but it declined to find that there was a constitutionally protected liberty interest at stake (*Quill v. Vacco*, 1996). Both rulings were appealed to the U.S. Supreme Court and were heard in January 1997.

In late June 1997 the Supreme Court announced that, by 9–0 margins in both the Washington (*Washington v. Glucksberg*, 1997) and New York (*Vacco v. Quill*, 1997) cases, there was no constitutional right to physician-assisted death. Instead the Court left it to each state to decide whether it wanted to legalize physician-assisted death. In an unexpected development, a majority of the Court appeared to endorse the concept of the double effect (where a dying person could be given sufficient medication to control pain and other symptoms, even if such a dose might lead to death) as well as terminal sedation (where a person is purposefully sedated and then the tubes providing artificial nutrition and hydration are withdrawn, leading to the person's death days later). There also appeared to be a mandate that states not interfere with appropriate palliative care, and the language employed implied that if any state did so, the Court would rule against the state (see especially Justice Sandra Day O'Connor's concurring opinion).

Florida

While the U.S. Supreme Court was preparing to hear the Washington and New York cases and then was deliberating upon them, the Florida Supreme Court was hearing its own case on physician-assisted death. A man with AIDS (two other plaintiffs died of cancer before the case went to trial) and his physician challenged the state's law prohibiting physician-assisted death under the Florida Constitution's privacy clause as well as the Equal Protection and Due Process clauses of the 14th Amendment to the U.S. Constitution. A lower court ruled that the plaintiff, and the plaintiff alone, could receive assistance in dying from his identified physician (*McIver v. Krischer*, 1997). The judge based his decision on Florida's privacy clause and the Equal Protection clause but did not find a due process right. Because part of the ruling was based on the state constitution, the Florida Supreme Court and not the U.S. Supreme Court was the final arbiter of the case. However, upon appeal, the Florida Supreme Court, which held off ruling until after the U.S. Supreme Court made its decision, in a 5–1 vote reversed the lower court and ruled the plaintiff could not have his physician help to hasten his death (*Krischer v. McIver*, 1997).

PROFESSIONAL ORGANIZATION ACTIVITY

Health Care Associations

The recent activities of a few organizations were mentioned above. This subsection will provide a more comprehensive discussion of actions taken by various professional associations regarding physician-assisted death and other end-of-life decisions.

Associations of health care workers have been involved in discussions about hastened death for many years (see the collection of such statements in Lipman, 1996; see also Brief of the American Medical Association et al., 1996). Both the American Medical Association and American Nurses Association, for example, have consistently taken strong stands against physician-assisted death and voluntary euthanasia, but they fully support the double effect, withholding/withdrawing treatment, terminal sedation, and voluntarily stopping eating and drinking. The organizations submitted an *amicus curiae* (friend of the court) brief to the U.S. Supreme Court, urging it to overturn the Second Circuit Court of Appeals decision. They argued that there is a legitimate distinction between withholding or withdrawing treatment and physician-assisted death (Brief of the American Medical Association et al., 1996).

However, following several developments, the medical establishment admitted that the dying process could be improved. One of these events, a study by the SUPPORT Principal Investigators (1995), documented that physicians did not know the end-of-life desires of patients and that a substantial number of patients die in significant pain. Relatedly, the Institute of Medicine reported (Field & Cassel, 1997) on the poor quality of care at the end of life. The medical organizations stated that once care reached the appropriate level, the desire for physician-assisted death would disappear ("AMA Initiatives Address Death," 1997). Therefore, the AMA developed a "bill of rights" for dying people ("AMA Initiatives Address Death," 1997; "AMA's Guidelines," 1997).

Further, with the help of a grant from the Robert Wood Johnson Foundation, the AMA began an initiative designed to improve the knowledge of currently practicing physicians about dealing with people who are dying and to improve physicians' abilities to effectively manage pain and suffering ("AMA Begins Nationwide Initiative," 1998). Some medical schools have also made curricular changes to provide greater exposure to end-of-life matters (Drell, 1998; Griego, 1998; but see Fink, 1998, for a different perspective).

Mental Health Organizations

The American Psychiatric Association is closely aligned with the AMA and signed onto the aforementioned Supreme Court *amicus curiae* brief with the AMA and American Nurses Association (ANA; Brief of the American Medical Association et al., 1996). Basically, the association stated that psychiatrists, as physicians, should not be involved in activities that actively hasten a client's death.

Of the major mental health organizations, the National Association of Social Workers (NASW) was the first to address the roles that its members could play with clients who were considering hastened death. A document entitled "Client Self-determination in End-of-Life Decisions" was passed by the delegate assembly in 1993 and published in 1994. In this paper the NASW described how social workers could be of assistance to people who were dying and their significant others. In a radical move, the organization stated that social workers were not obligated to prevent a client from hastening death and, in fact, could be present at an assisted death as long as it was not illegal and the social worker did not actually administer the death-causing agent.

More recently, the NASW has published a document that outlines how social workers can be involved in situations where clients are considering or have implemented advance directives (Rosen & O'Neill, 1998). This material, though less detailed than the earlier publication on end-of-life decisions (National Association of Social Workers, 1994), provides some examples of how social workers can and should be involved when advance directives are appropriate options for people.

The American Counseling Association (ACA) position on hastened death can be inferred from the fact that it signed onto an *amicus curiae* brief for the U.S. Supreme Court with the Washington Psychological Association, the Association for Gay, Lesbian, and Bisexual Individuals in Counseling, and an ad hoc coalition of mental health professionals (Brief of the Washington State Psychological Association et al., 1996). The organization stated that its joining on the brief was consistent with the counseling profession's long history of promoting autonomy and self-determination. The document focused on the mental health issues associated with assisted death. In addition, it suggested that the involvement of mental health professionals in the end-of-life decision-making process could decrease the possibility that persons wanting to hasten death would make decisions as a result of impaired judgment.

The American Psychological Association (APA) was the last of the major mental health groups to formally address hastened death. In anticipation of the U.S. Supreme Court's ruling on physician-assisted death, the APA convened a small working group of members to prepare an educational statement for the general public about the roles mental health professionals can play when someone is considering hastening death (American Psychological Association, 1997). The statement did not indicate that the organization had an official policy position on assisted death:

> The American Psychological Association does not advocate for or against assisted suicide. What psychologists do support is high quality end-of-life care and informed end-of-life decisions based on the correct assessment of the patient's mental capacity, social support systems, and degree of self-determination. (p. 1)

The document, however, did provide some basic suggestions for mental health professionals who provide clinical services to dying individuals.

In an effort to continue the work started by this first group, the following year the APA formed a second working group that was charged with helping to provide some direction to the field and to address the lack of psychology's presence in the national debate over hastened death. This group is producing a report to the Board of Directors that includes specific recommendations for how the APA can support psychologists in a variety of roles. In addition, it is creating an extensive document that outlines the mental health issues involved, so that psychologists can begin to become better educated about end-of-life matters (Working Group on Assisted Suicide and End of Life Decisions, 1999). However, the group's existence is not guaranteed past the beginning of 2000, so the extent of the APA's continued involvement in these matters is unclear.

The American Association of Suicidology

In 1996, after a year and a half of study, the American Association of Suicidology (AAS) Committee on Physician-Assisted Suicide and Euthanasia published its report on these matters. In summary, the report stated:

> At this time, the committee recommends that the American Associa-
> tion of Suicidology take no positions on physician-assisted suicide or
> euthanasia. Further, we do not recommend the support of legislation,
> for or against, any of these matters. Quite apart from the diverging,
> deeply held moral and ethical positions on these issues that divide our
> organization and our society, much research is needed to answer
> many important questions before this association might properly take
> positions on these problems. Research can never answer all the
> wrenching questions associated with physician-assisted death, but it
> can certainly inform the debate. (1996, p. 2)

Discussions about hastened death have been common at the AAS annual conventions for many years, and the organization's journal has published a few articles on the subject. In addition, recently, the group has
discussed a "physician-prevented suicide" initiative to respond to the research which documents that a large percentage of people who suicide,
especially elderly individuals, have seen their physicians fairly close to
the time they died. The physicians, however, did not detect either the
suicidality or any clinical depression.

CONCLUSIONS AND PROJECTIONS FOR THE FUTURE

Clearly the discussion about the way people die in the United States and
the acceptable methods of hastening death will not disappear quickly or
easily. As the U.S. Supreme Court indicated, in ruling on the Washington case (*Washington v. Glucksberg*, 1997, p. 2275), "Throughout the nation, Americans are engaged in an earnest and profound debate about
the morality, legality, and practicality of physician-assisted suicide. Our
holding permits this debate to continue, as it should in a democratic society."

The aforementioned AAS Task Force report stated that it is likely
that the only areas about which nearly everyone can agree are that in-
voluntary euthanasia is completely unacceptable and that no one should
have to suffer intolerably in order to preserve life at all costs. However,
there will likely never be consensus about areas that have been settled
legally, such as the withdrawal of treatment from persons in persistent
vegetative states who made their wishes clear before becoming uncon-
scious. For example, the decision to discontinue artificial nutrition from

Hugh Finn, a former news anchor in Virginia, led to a protracted family battle all the way to the state Supreme Court, as well as public protests and the involvement of the governor (Masters, 1998; "'Right-to-Die' Subject Dies," 1998).

Yet, a respectful dialogue must continue, for these are issues about which many people have fundamental differences based on their individual and community (broadly defined to include neighborhood, spiritual group, profession, friendship circle, family, and so forth) value systems. Perhaps it is exactly these inevitable differences that will help advance the discussion and action for proper care of dying and of suicidal people. The goals of both sides of the discussion about whether a desire to hasten death can be reasonable are the same: Decrease individuals' suffering and reduce the incidence of irrational suicide.

With these overall goals in mind, it is my prediction that over time assisted death will become accepted as another point on the continuum of care. However, I also believe that efforts to improve the care of the dying will take place so that fewer people will believe they have to resort to death to receive relief from their suffering. I expect that as aid-in-dying becomes a more legitimate alternative, mental health workers will be more involved in the process as physicians realize the limitations of their skills and training as well as their vulnerability to legal action if there are any questions about the appropriateness of a particular person's request for aid-in-dying.

The implications for mental health workers, in general, and suicidologists, in particular, revolve around competence and the state of the art in assessment and treatment. Currently, there is little or no training regarding how to assess the reasonableness of a decision to hasten death (see Farrenkopf & Bryan, 1999; Werth et al., in press). Thus, what would psychologists or psychiatrists in Oregon do when called in by a physician to evaluate a terminally ill person's request for assisted death? With whom could these clinicians consult? What instruments, if any, could be used? How much of an evaluation is necessary? How much depression is acceptable, and how much precludes accepting the decision at face value? What impact should nonphysical pain concerns have on the decision-making process and the professional's assessment?

Each counselor, and especially each suicidologist, has the professional obligation to be prepared to deal with clients who approach them with questions about hastened death. We must do the research, or at least start it; we need guidelines for these circumstances; we have to know how our own values will impact treatment with these types of

clients. Ignoring the problem, waiting for the research to appear, or trying to hide from the issues will not make these matters disappear. We
cannot afford to continue to be reactive about this issue. We must instead be proactive and prepare ourselves so that we can give clients and
professionals needing help with these issues the competent care and
consultations they deserve and need.

REFERENCES

After mistrial, Kevorkian won't be tried again in woman's death. (1997, August
   2). *Pittsburgh Post-Gazette*, p. A5.
AMA begins nationwide initiative to educate nation's physicians on caring for
   dying patients. (1998, May 12). *U.S. Newswire.* [1998 WestLaw 5685713]
AMA initiatives address death. (1997, June 23) *Pantagraph* (Bloomington, IL), p.
   A1.
AMA's guidelines for care of the dying. (1997, September 13). *Patriot Ledger*
   (Quincy, MA), p. 6.
American Association of Suicidology (1996). Report of the Committee on
   Physician-Assisted Suicide and Euthanasia. *Suicide and Life-Threatening Be-
   havior, 26*(Suppl.).
American Psychological Association. (1997, July). *Terminal Illness and Hastened
   Death Requests: The Important Role of the Mental Health Professional.* Washington,
   DC: Author. [Reprinted in *Professional Psychology: Research and Practice, 28,*
   544–547 (1997).]
Assisted suicide bill introduced. (1998, June 26). *Associated Press Report.* [1998
   WestLaw 6687502]
Barnett, E. H. (1999a, June 30). Many die in pain, survey finds. *Portland Oregon-
   ian*, p. A01.
Barnett, E. H. (1999b, April 2). Revision of suicide law draws less heat. *Portland
   Oregonian*, p. C01.
Barnett, E. H. (1998, October 7). Oregon study finds increase in pain among
   the dying. *Portland Oregonian*, p. C4.
Barnett, E. H., & Lednicer, L. G. (1999, Feb. 7). Assisted suicide remains a hot
   issue in legislature. *Portland Oregonian*, p. C08.
Barnett, J. (1998, September 17). Study could stall attack on assisted suicide law.
   Portland Oregonian, p. A1.
Beggs, C. E. (1998, July 14). Oregon's suicide law foes look to revive suit.
   Columbian. [1998 West Law 11744730]
Belluck, P. (1999, March 27). Kevorkian convicted of 2nd degree murder. *New
   York Times*, p. A1.
Bill to make assisted suicide illegal heads to governor's desk. (1998, May 28). *As-
   sociated Press Political Service.* [1998 WestLaw 7418103]
*Brief of the American Medical Association, American Nurses Association, and the American
   Psychiatric Association, et al.* (1996, November). Filed with the Supreme Court

of the United States, October 1996 term for *Washington v. Glucksberg* and *Vacco v. Quill*.

Brief of the Washington State Psychological Association; the American Counseling Association; the Association of Gay, Lesbian and Bisexual Issues in Counseling; and the Coalition of Mental Health Professionals Supporting Individual Self-Determination in Decisions to Hasten Death. (1996, December). Filed with the Supreme Court of the United States, October 1996 term for *Washington v. Glucksberg* and *Vacco v. Quill*.

Cain, C., & Kiska, T. (1998, November 4). Proposal B: Assisted suicide: Religion key factor in defeat. *Detroit News*, p. A6.

Callahan, D., & White, M. (1996). The legalization of physician-assisted suicide: Creating a regulatory Potemkin Village. *University of Richmond Law Review, 30,* 1–83.

Callahan, D., & White, M. (in press). Oregon's first year: The medicalization of control. *Psychology, Public Policy, and Law.*

Canetto, S. S., & Hollenshead, J. D. (in press). Gender and physician-assisted suicide: An analysis of the Kevorkian cases, 1990–1997. *Omega.*

Chin, A. E., Hedberg, K., Higginson, G. K., & Fleming, D. W. (1999). Legalized physician-assisted suicide in Oregon—The first year's experience. *New England Journal of Medicine, 340,* 577–583.

Claiborne, W., & Edsall, T. B. (1997, Nov. 6). Affirmation of Oregon suicide law may spur movement. *Washington Post*, p. A19.

Cohen, M. A. (1995). Plaintiffs' standing in *Lee v. Oregon*: The judicially-assisted demise of the Oregon Death with Dignity Act. *Oregon Law Review, 74,* 741–780.

Compassion in Dying v. Washington, 850 F.Supp. 1454 (W.D. Wash. 1994).

Compassion in Dying v. Washington, 49 F.3d 586 (9th Cir. 1995).

Compassion in Dying v. State of Washington, 79 F.3d 790 (9th Cir.(Wash.), 1996).

Congress unlikely to act on Oregon's assisted-suicide law. (1998, September 25). *Salt Lake Tribune*, p. A24.

Coombs Lee, B., & Werth, J. L., Jr. (in press). Observations on the first year of Oregon's Death with Dignity Act. *Psychology, Public Policy, and Law.*

Drell, A. (1998, October 18). Doctors of the future deal squarely with death. *Chicago Sun-Times*, p. 27.

Drickamer, M. A., Lee, M. A., & Ganzini, L. (1997). Practical issues in physician-assisted suicide. *Annals of Internal Medicine, 126,* 146–151.

Durbin, D. A. (1998, September 1). Kevorkian "doesn't care" about Michigan's ban on assisted suicide. *State Journal-Register* (Springfield, IL), p. 12.

Edwards, M. J., & Connor, W. E. (1999). Legalized physician-assisted suicide in Oregon [Letter to the Editor]. *New England Journal of Medicine, 341,* 212.

Emanuel, E. J., & Daniels, E. (1996). Oregon's physician-assisted suicide law: Provisions and problems. *Archives of Internal Medicine, 156,* 825–829.

Farrenkopf, T., & Bryan, J. (1999). Psychological consultation under Oregon's 1994 Death with Dignity Act: Ethics and procedures. *Professional Psychology: Research and Practice, 30,* 245–249.

Field, M. J., & Cassel, C. K. (Eds.). (1997). *Approaching death: Improving care at the end of life.* Washington, DC: National Academy Press.

Fink, S. (1998, August 12). Suicide topic rare in OHSU classrooms. *Portland Oregonian*, p. A1.

Fins, J. J., & Bancroft, E. A. (1999). Legalized physician-assisted suicide in Oregon [Letter to the Editor]. *New England Journal of Medicine, 341*, 212.

Foley, K., & Hendin, H. (1999). The Oregon Report: Don't ask, don't tell. *Hastings Center Report, 29*(3), 37–42.

Frazier, J. B. (1998, August 19). 8 in Oregon have used suicide law. *Rocky Mountain News*, p. 31A.

Governor signs anti-suicide bill. (1998, May 5). *Daily Oklahoman*, p. 3.

Grant, E. R., & Linton, P. B. (1995). Relief or reproach?: Euthanasia rights in the wake of Measure 16. *Oregon Law Review, 74*, 449–537

Green, A. S., & Barnett, E. H. (1998, September 23). Challenge to suicide law is dismissed. *Portland Oregonian*, p. A1.

Griego, T. (1998, September 22). Opening death's door. *Rocky Mountain News*, p. 5A.

Harkavy, J. (1998, July 23). Advocates eye suicide bill referendum. *Bangor Daily News*. [1998 WestLaw 13313260]

Hendin, H., Foley, K., & White, M. (1998). Physician-assisted suicide: Reflections on Oregon's first case. *Issues in Law and Medicine, 14*, 243–270.

Herman, B. (1998, October 29). Mich. may not pass assisted suicide. *Associated Press Report*. [1998 WestLaw 21781272]

Higgins, A. J. (1998, February 12). Maine House rejects assisted suicide, backer vows to bring issue back. *Bangor Daily News*. [1998 WestLaw 3119006]

Hoffman, K. B. (1994, July 11). 52% in survey favor doctor-aided suicide: Support higher in tricounty area, but Kevorkian fails to get issue on Nov. 8 ballot. *Detroit News*, p. 7.

Hogan, D. (1999, June 25). AMA endorses legislation to block assisted-suicide law. *Portland Oregonian*, p. B01.

Hughes, J. (1998, Oct. 15). A bill that would have overridden Oregon's . . . . *Associated Press Political Service*. [1998 WestLaw 7455264]

Hyde, J. (1999, March 12). Kevorkian charge to be dropped. *Associated Press On-Line*. [1999 WestLaw 13837843]

Kevorkian aids suicide as Michigan law expires: Controversial pathologist says ailing woman's health isn't linked to end of oft-challenged ban. (1994, November 27). *Indianapolis Star*, p. A1.

Kevorkian to appeal conviction. (1999, July 17). *Newsday*, p. A08.

Krischer v. McIver, 697 So.2d 97 (Fl. 1997).

Lee, M. A. (1997). The Oregon Death with Dignity Act: Implementation issues. *Western Journal of Medicine, 166*, 398–401.

Lee, M. A., & Tolle, S. W. (1996). Oregon's assisted suicide vote: The silver lining. *Annals of Internal Medicine, 124*, 267–269.

Lee v. Harcleroad, 118 S.Ct. 328 (U.S. 1997).

Lee v. State of Oregon, 891 F.Supp. 1429 (D.Or. 1995a).

Lee v. State of Oregon, 891 F.Supp. 1439 (D.Or. 1995b).

Lee v. State of Oregon, 107 F.3d 1382(9th Cir.(Or.) 1997).

Lewis, N. A. (1998, June 6). U.S. won't prosecute doctors who aid suicide via Oregon law. *New York Times*, p. 1.

Lipman, A. G. (1996). Position statements on euthanasia and assisted suicide. In M. P. Battin & A. G. Lipman (Eds.), *Drug use in assisted suicide and euthanasia* (pp. 245–289). New York: Haworth Press.

Masters, B. A. (1998, October 10). The battle outlives Hugh Finn. *Washington Post*, p. A01.

McIver v. Krischer, 65 USLW 2544, WL 225878 (Fla.Cir.Ct., 1997).

Mich. lawmakers give up on suicide ban: Stalemate comes in wake of state high court ruling against Dr. Kevorkian. (1994, December 15). *Rocky Mountain News*, p. 58A.

Murphy, B. (1998, December 10). Kevorkian ordered to face trial for murder, intent to kill "based on 60 Minutes" tape. *Pittsburgh Post-Gazette*, p. A11.

Murphy, K. (1997, November 5). Voters in Oregon soundly endorse assisted suicide. *Los Angeles Times*, p. A–1.

National Association of Social Workers (NASW). (1994). Client self-determination in end-of-life decisions. *Social Work Speaks* (3rd ed., pp. 58–61). Washington, DC: NASW Press.

New York State Task Force on Life and the Law. (1994). *When death is sought: Assisted suicide and euthanasia in the medical context.* Albany, NY: Health Education Services.

Omandam, P. (1998, May 28). Legalize euthanasia, Hawaii panel urges. *Honolulu Star-Bulletin.* [Available at http://starbulletin.com/98/05/28/news/story4.html].

Omandam, P. (1999, February 20). Legislators take assisted death off slate, seek more discussion. *Honolulu Star-Bulletin.* [Available at http://starbulletin.com/1999/02/20/news/story5.html].

Oregon Death with Dignity Act. (1995). Or. Rev. Stat. § 127.800–127.995.

Oregon to vote again on assisted suicide. (1997, June 10). *Morning News Tribune* (Tacoma, WA), p. B8.

Orentlicher, D. (in press). The implementation of Oregon's Death with Dignity Act: Reassuring, but more data are needed. *Psychology, Public Policy, and Law.*

People v. Kevorkian, 447 Mich. 436, 527 N.W.2d 714 (Mich. 1994).

Quill v. Vacco, 870 F.Supp. 78 (S.D.N.Y. 1994).

Quill v. Vacco, 80 F.3d 716 (2d Cir.(N.Y.), 1996).

Reno to announce federal law does not bar assisted suicide, Oregonian says. (1998, June 5). *Associated Press Report.*

"Right-to-die" subject dies. (1998, October 9). *Associated Press Report.* [1998 WestLaw 21170348]

Rosen, A., & O'Neill, J. (1998, March). Social work roles and opportunities in advanced directive and health care decision making. *NASW Social Work Practice Update.*

SUPPORT Principal Investigators (1995). A controlled trial to improve care for seriously ill hospitalized patients. *Journal of the American Medical Association, 274,* 1591–1598.

Task Force to Improve the Care of Terminally Ill Oregonians. (Ed.). (1998). *The Oregon Death with Dignity Act: A guidebook for health care providers.* Portland, OR: Center for Ethics in Health Care, Oregon Health Sciences University.

Tolle, S. W. (1998). Care of the dying: Clinical and financial lessons from the Oregon experience. *Annals of Internal Medicine, 128,* 567–568.

Two states share approach. (1998, October 12). *Detroit News,* p. A4.

Vacco v. Quill, 117 S.Ct. 2293 (1997).

Washington v. Glucksberg, 117 S.Ct. 2258 (1997).

Werth, J. L., Jr., Benjamin, G. A. H., & Farrenkopf, T. (in press). Requests for physician assisted death: Guidelines for assessing mental capacity and impaired judgment. *Psychology, Public Policy, and Law.*

Woolston, D. (1998, September 21). States consider rights of the terminally ill to put an end to life. *Memphis Commercial Appeal,* p. C4.

Working Group on Assisted Suicide and End-of-Life Decisions. (1999). *Resource guide on end of life issues.* Manuscript in preparation.

Index

Abuse, history of, 165
Additive components to treatment, 54, 94, 104
Adolescent suicidal behavior. *See also* Approaches to youth suicide
   alcohol and, 174, 182
   assessment of, 188–189
   as cause of death, 5–7, 170
   cluster phenomena in, 160, 192–193, 195
   explanations of, 20–22
   family and, 174, 189, 190
   firearms and, 7, 17, 20, 171–172, 174
   frequency of, 4–5
   overview of, 3
   risk factors for, 163, 173–174
   suicide rates: levels, 9–11, 13, 171, 202
   suicide rates: trends, 13–17, 20
   survivors of, 27–28
   years of potential life lost, 7–9
Adolescents
   attempted suicide in, 23–26, 172–173
   attributional style of, 121–122
   avoidance and social withdrawal in, 123
   depression in, 166, 174
   hopelessness and, 118
   prevention and, 160–161, 176–177, 183, 184, 185
   somatic therapy for, 190
   suicidal ideation in, 26–27, 172
   treatment strategies for, 189–192
African Americans. *See also* Racial differences
   occupation and suicide in, 244, 247–249
   survival solidarity among, 242–244
Age and suicide rates, 10–11, 202
Alcohol and suicide
   in adolescents, 174, 182
   in adults, 115, 131, 140–141, 148, 205
   in older adults, 207–208
American Association of Suicidology, 181–182, 183, 269–270

American Counseling Association (ACA), 268–269
American Foundation for Suicide Prevention, 183
American Medical Association (AMA), 264, 267
American Nurses Association, 267
American Psychiatric Association, 268
American Psychological Association (APA), 269
Amitriptyline, 151
Anafranil (clomipramine), 144
Anticonvulsants, 151
Antidepressants. *See* Selective serotonin reuptake inhibitors; Somatic therapy; *specific medications, such as Prozac*
Anxiety in older adults, 216–217
Approaches to youth suicide
   Community Action for Youth Survival, 184–186
   grassroots, 177
   health communication, 182–183
   hospital safety practices, 179–182
   means restriction, 178–179
   mental health, 174–175
   prevention, 187–188
   public health, 175–177
   school gatekeeper training, 183–184
Assessment
   of adolescent suicidality, 188–189
   of cognitive risk factors, 113–116
   of risk, 131–132, 141
Associated symptoms, 61
Attempted suicide. *See* Suicide attempts
Attributional style, 121–122
Avoidance, 123, 124

"Baby boom" cohort, 22
Beck, Aaron T., 112, 125
Beck Depression Inventory (BDI), 114

Beck Hopelessness Scale (BHS), 115–116
Beck Self-Concept Test (BST), 116
Befriending contacts, 52–53
Behavioral approaches to treatment, 91
Bereavement process, 27
Biological approaches to treatment, 91–92
Birth and Fortune (Easterlin), 22
Borderline personality disorder (BPD), 85, 89–90, 104, 105, 150–151
Broken promises, 42–43

Carbamazepine (Tegretol), 146, 151
Causes of death, 5–7, 43, 162, 170
CAYS (Community Action for Youth Survival), 184–186
CBT (cognitive-behavioral therapy), 54, 57, 191
CD-ROM prevention information dissemination, 185–186
Ceiling effect, 58, 61
Centers for Disease Control and Prevention (CDC) guidelines for youth suicide prevention, 176–177, 183, 184, 185
Child suicidal behavior. *See* Prepubertal child suicidal behavior
Chinese beliefs and behaviors, 227, 234, 236, 237, 238
Clinical presentation of suicidal clients, 131–132
Clinician's Hopelessness Scale, 115–116
Clomipramine (Anafranil), 144
Clozapine (Clozaril), 147
Cluster phenomena, 160, 192–193, 195
Cobb County, Georgia, 173
Cocaine-related disorders, 148–149
Cognitive-behavioral therapy (CBT), 54, 57, 191
Cognitive distortions, 112, 119
Cognitive rigidity, 119–120, 122, 132, 207
Cognitive risk factors
    assessment of, 113–116
    attributional style, 121–122
    clinical presentation and, 131–132
    cognitive distortions, 112, 119
    cognitive rigidity, 119–120, 122, 132
    dysfunctional assumptions, 120–121
    hopelessness, 116–119
    models of, 112–113, 129–131
    problem-solving deficits, 122–125
    reasons for living, 126–129
    self-concept, 119
    suicide seen as solution, 125–126
    treatment of, 132
Cognitive Therapy of Depression (Beck et al., 1979), 125
Cognitive triad (Beck), 112–113, 119, 121
Cognitive vulnerability to depression model, 112–113, 129–131
Cohort size, 22
Community Action for Youth Survival (CAYS), 184–186
Coping style, 123–124, 131–132

Cultural differences
    cross-cultural studies, 232, 234
    difficulty in studying, 231
    focus on individual, 231–232, 234
    generational conflict, 238–239
    life goals and responses to stress, 234–235
    overview of, 226–227
    view of mental health problems, 235–239
Cytomel (liothyronine), 144

Date and suicide levels, 34–38, 40
Death dates, 41
Demographic factors
    attempted suicide and, 25–26, 209–210
    occupation and suicide, 243–244, 247–249
    suicide and, 17, 20, 162, 202, 203–205
Depot preparations, 147
Depression
    in adolescent suicide survivors, 194–195
    in adolescents, 166, 174
    alcohol-related disorders and, 148
    in children, 163–164, 166
    cognitive vulnerability model, 112–113, 129–131
    cultural differences in, 227, 236–237
    delusional type, 145, 211
    in later-life suicide, 206
    major depression, 84
    in older adults, 214, 216–217
    schizophrenia and, 146
    somatic treatment of, 142–145
    suicidal behaviors and, 92, 140–141, 174
    undertreatment of, 142–143, 216–217
Diagnosis and funding of research, 91
Dichotomous thinking, 119–120, 131
Direct markers of treatment outcome, 61
Direct treatment success, 63
District of Columbia, 178
Double effect, 266, 267
Drug abusers, 117, 148–149
Dysfunctional assumptions, 120–121
Dysfunctional Attitude Scale, 114

Easterlin's hypothesis, 22
Electroconvulsive therapy (ECT), 144, 145
Elements of suicide-related behavior, 60
Empirical foundation to practice, 47–49
End-of-life issues. *See* Physician-assisted death
Ethical issues. *See* Physician-assisted death
Evaluation of prevention strategies, 177
Exclusion of high-risk cases from clinical trials, 50, 55, 90, 105, 106–107
Explanations of youth suicide, 20–22

Family and suicidal behavior
    in adolescents, 174, 189, 190
    in children, 161, 164–165
    generational conflict and, 238–239
Finn, Hugh, 270–271
Firearm deaths
    adolescents and, 7, 17, 20, 171–172, 174
    cocaine and, 149

means restriction strategy and, 178–179, 180–182
    month boundary and, 36–37
    older adults and, 204, 205
Florida, 266–267
Fluoxetine (Prozac), 92, 143, 166
Flupenthixol, 150–151
Follow-up letters and phone calls, 52, 53

Gatekeeper training, 182–184
Gender differences
    attempted suicide and, 25, 210, 212
    culture and, 234
    explanations of youth suicide trends and, 21
    hopelessness and, 118
    month boundary and, 37–38
    in suicidal ideation, 27
    in suicide rates, 11, 13, 162, 171, 229–230
    in trends of suicide rates, 15–17
Geographical distribution of suicide rates, 17, 20
Geriatric suicide. See Later-life suicide
Grassroots approach to youth suicide, 177
Great Britain, 178
Group psychotherapy for adolescents, 191–192

Haloperidol, 151
Hastening death. See Physician-assisted death
Hawaii, 261
Health care, access to, and suicide, 215–217, 270
Health communication campaigns, 182–183
Healthy People 2000, 175–176
High-risk cases
    exclusion from clinical trials, 50, 55, 90, 105, 106–107
    intensive outpatient treatment and, 55, 56, 57
Holding on to life, 42
Home visits, 51–52, 53, 54–55, 105
Hopelessness
    definition of, 116
    dysfunctional assumptions and, 120
    intent and, 117, 118–119
    as key psychological variable in suicide, 113, 116–117
    in older adults, 212–213, 214
    problem-solving deficits and, 129–130
    social desirability and, 128–129
    as stable schema, 117–118
Hopelessness Scale for Children, 115
Hospice support, 257–258
Hospital safety practices, 179–180
Hospitalization for parasuicide, 105, 106
Hypothesis of relative cohort size, 22

Imitative suicidal behavior, 192–193, 194
Improved ease of access to crisis services, 52, 53, 54–55
Impulsivity and suicidal behavior, 178–179

Indirect life-threatening behavior, 214–215
Indirect markers of treatment outcome, 61
Indirect treatment success, 63
Individualized action plan, 188–189
Injury Control, National Plan for, 176
Instrumental behavior, 59
Intensive case management, 50–51, 53
Intensive follow-up as additive component, 55, 57
Intent
    age differences in, 208, 210
    assessing, 60
    hopelessness and, 117, 118–119
    lethality of attempt and, 113
    measuring, 87, 88–89
    parasuicide and, 87–88
    suicide attempt, use of term, and, 86–87
    Suicide Intent Scale, 115
International Classification of Disease (ICD) Codes for suicide, 39
Interpersonal relation problems
    child suicide and, 164
    problem-solving deficits and, 122–125
    youth suicide and, 20–22
Intervention studies, 49–53

Kevorkian, Jack, 260, 261–262

Later life
    attempted suicide in, 209–213
    indirect life-threatening behaviors in, 214–215
    suicidal ideation in, 213–214
Later-life suicide
    epidemiological evidence on, 203–205
    postmortem neurobiological evidence and, 208–209
    psychological autopsy method and, 205–208
    rates of, 202
    as underrecognized problem, 203
Lethality of attempt, 113
Lifetime prevalence for suicide attempts, 209–210
Liothyronine (Cytomel), 144
Lithium carbonate, 144, 146
Living arrangement, 204
Logistic regression, 245–246
Long-term care facilities, 215
Long-term treatment studies, 53–54, 55–56
Long-term trends in youth suicide, 14–15

Major depression, 84. See also Depression
Mania, 145–146
MAOIs (monoamine oxidase inhibitors), 144, 151
Marital status, 204–205
Means restriction, 178–179, 180–182
Media coverage of suicide, 193–194
Medical care and day of month, 41
Medical hospitalization, 53, 189
Mellaril (thioridazine), 147

Mental disorder
  correlation with suicide, 140–141, 205
  firearms and, 172
  treatment of underlying, 91, 92–93, 106
Mental health approach
  to physician-assisted death, 268–269,
      271–272
  to youth suicide, 174–175
Methods of suicide
  adolescents, 7, 17, 20, 171–172, 174
  demographic factors and, 25–26, 230
  lethality of and intent, 113
  means restriction strategy and, 178–179,
      180–182
  month boundary and, 36–37
  substitution of, 179
Michigan, 260, 261–262
Monoamine oxidase inhibitors (MAOIs), 144,
  151
Month boundary, 36–38, 40, 41–43

National Association of Social Workers
  (NASW), 268
National Center for Health Statistics (NCHS),
  3–4
National Institute of Mental Health (NIMH),
  113
National Plan for Injury Control, 176
Neurasthenia, 227, 236–237
Neurobiological risk factors, 165–166,
  208–209
Neuroleptics and parasuicidal behavior, 104,
  107, 152
New York, 261, 265–266
Nomenclature. See Terminology
Nonfatal self-injury. See Parasuicide

Objective markers of intent, 60
Occupation, race, and suicide, 243–244, 245,
  247–248, 249
Ohio. See Occupation, race, and suicide
Older adults. See Later life
Openness to experience, 207
Oregon, 173
Oregon Death with Dignity Act (1995)
  court decisions regarding, 264–265
  developments between initial vote and
      implementation, 257–258
  history and overview of, 256–257
  legislative activity regarding, 262–263
  use of, 258–259
Overgeneralization, 119, 131

Pain control at end of life, 257–258, 263–264,
  267–268
Panic disorder, 149–150
Parasuicide. See also Suicide attempts
  definition of, 87–88
  direct treatment of, 91, 93–94, 104–105,
      106
  indirect treatment of, 91, 92–93, 106
  neuroleptics and, 104, 107, 152

  rates of, 84–86
  repetitive nature of, 89–90, 122
Pattern of suicide over time, 10–11
Perceived problem-solving ability, 124–125
Perfectionism, 120–121
Personality characteristics, 61, 206–207
Personality disorder, 85
Physician-assisted death
  American Association of Suicidology and,
      269–270
  definition of, 255
  in Florida, 266–267
  future of, 270–272
  in Hawaii, 261
  health care associations and, 267–268
  mental health organizations and, 268–269
  in Michigan, 260, 261–262
  in New York, 261, 265–266
  in Oregon, 256–259, 262–263, 264–265
  U.S. Congress and, 263–264
  in Washington (State), 265–266, 270
Poisoning, 25, 36
Population growth, 41
Postmortem brain tissue studies, 208–209
Postvention, 28
Prepubertal child suicidal behavior
  emergence of, 159–160
  epidemiology of, 162
  family and, 161, 164–165
  natural history of, 163–164
  neurobiology of, 165–166
  psychopathology and, 161
  rates of, 160–161
  treatment of, 165–166
Prevention efforts. See also Approaches to
      youth suicide
  adolescents, 160, 161
  CDC and, 176–177, 183, 184, 185
  older adults, 208
  survivors of suicide, 165
Primary care setting and depression, 215–217
Primary prevention, 187
Problem solving
  as core intervention, 54, 55–56, 57
  deficits in, 122–125, 129–130
  state- compared to trait-like aspects of,
      130–131
  suicide seen as solution, 125–126
Prozac (fluoxetine), 92, 143, 166
Psychoeducation, 190–191
Psychological autopsy, 205–208
Psychological study and culture,
  231–232
Psychopharmacological treatment. See Somatic
      therapy
Psychotherapeutic intervention. See Treatment
      strategies
Public health approach to youth suicide,
  175–177

Racial differences
  in mental health utilization, 174–175

in occupation and suicide, 243–244,
247–249
in suicidal ideation, 214
in suicide rates, 9, 11, 13, 17, 162, 171,
229–230, 242–244
Random assignment, importance of, 85–86
Rate of attempted suicide, 23–25, 84–86
Rate of suicide
among adolescents, 9–11, 13–17, 20
month boundary and, 36–38, 40
occupation and, 247–248
in prepubertal children, 160–161
San Francisco, 229–230
Reasons for living, 126–129
Reasons for Living Inventory (RFLI), 126
Repetitive nature of suicide attempts, 89–90,
122
Replacement, 124
Research
agenda for, 58, 63–64, 106–107
impediments to, 90–91
priorities for, 177
prospective studies (Beck), 113
Risk. *See also* Cognitive risk factors
assessment of, 131–132, 141
of attempters, 26
diagnosis and, 84–85
firearm in house and, 172, 174
follow-up approach to determining,
210–211
neurobiological factors, 165–166
of older adults, 212–213
suicide rates and, 13
of youth, 23–24, 163, 173–174
Risperdone (Risperdal), 147

San Francisco, 228–230
Scale for Suicide Ideation (SSI), 115–116
Schema concept, 112
Schizophrenia, 146–148
School gatekeeper training, 183–184
Secondary prevention, 187–188
Secretary's Task Force on Youth Suicide
(1989), 161
Selective abstraction, 119, 131
Selective serotonin reuptake inhibitors
(SSRIs), 143–144, 145, 148, 152, 166
Self-concept, 119
Self-cutting, 25
Self-destructive behaviors in long-term care
facilities, 215
Self-poisoning, 25, 36
Sensitivity to social criticism, 120
Serotonin-related measures, 165–166
Sex differences. *See* Gender differences
Short-term treatment studies, 53, 54–55
Skill deficits, 61
Social desirability, 128–129
Social withdrawal, 123
Somatic approaches to treatment, 91–92
Somatic therapy
for adolescents, 190

alcohol-related disorders and, 148
antidepressants and suicidal behavior, 92,
94
assessment and, 141–142
benzodiazepines, 217
borderline personality disorder and,
150–151
cocaine-related disorders and, 148–149
delusional depression and, 145
depression and, 142–145, 152, 166
mania and, 145–146
panic disorder and, 149–150
schizophrenia and, 146–148
Somatization and suicide attempt, 212
SSRIs. *See* Selective serotonin reuptake
inhibitors
Standards of care, 90, 93, 106, 192
Stress–vulnerability model, 112–113, 129–131
Subjective markers of intent, 60
Substance abuse. *See* Alcohol and suicide;
Drug abusers
Suicidal acts, 59
Suicidal behavior. *See also* Adolescent suicidal
behavior; Later-life suicide; Prepubertal
child suicidal behavior
classification of, 113
imitation and clusters, 160, 192–193, 194,
195
impulsivity and, 178–179
targeting directly, 91, 93–94, 104–105, 106
Suicidal ideation
in adolescents, 26–27, 172
characteristics of persons with, 130–131
in children, 163
definition of, 60
in later life, 213–214
Suicide, definition of, 59
Suicide attempts
by adolescents, 23–26, 172–173
characteristics of persons who make, 131
by children, 163
definition of, 88
in later life, 209–213
use of term, 86
with and without injuries, 59
Suicide gestures, 87
Suicide Intent Scale (SIS), 115, 117
Suicide precautions, 179–180
Suicide Prevention Advocacy Network
(SPAN), 177
Suicide threat, 59–60
Suppression, 124
Survivors of suicide, 27–28, 164–165, 193,
194–195

Tardive dyskinesia, 147
Tegretol (carbamazepine), 146, 151
Terminal sedation, 266, 267
Terminology, importance of standard, 58–59,
60–61, 86–88
Tertiary prevention, 187–188
Thioridazine (Mellaril), 147

Thiothixene, 151
Trazadone, 144
Treatment alliance, 141–142
Treatment outcome, conceptualizing, 61–63
Treatment strategies. *See also* Somatic
    therapy
  for adolescents, 189–190
  cognitive-behavioral therapy, 191
  cognitive risk factors, 132
  family intervention, 190
  group psychotherapy for adolescents,
      191–192
  for prepubertal children, 166
  psychoeducation, 190–191
  target suicidal behaviors directly, 91, 93–94,
      104–105, 106
  treat underlying mental disorder, 91, 92–93,
      106
Treatment studies, 50, 53–56
Treatment success, defining, 63
Tricyclic antidepressant (TCA), 143, 144
Tryptophan, 166

Undertreatment of depression, 142–143
United States
  Congress, 263–264
  Drug Enforcement Administration (DEA),
      258, 263
  Supreme Court, 266

Violent Injury Prevention Center, 182
Vital Statistics of the United States, 4

Washington (State), 265–266, 270
Weyrauch, Gerald and Elsie, 177
WHO/Euro parasuicide epidemiological
    studies, 87, 88, 89
Widowhood, 204–205
Withdrawal of treatment, 266, 267, 270–271

Years of potential life lost (YPLL), 7–9
Youk, Thomas, 261–262
Youth Risk Behavior Surveillance System, 172

Zimelidine (Zelmid), 148